MOUDUD AHMED

BANGLADESH:
ERA OF SHEIKH MUJIBUR RAHMAN

BEITRÄGE ZUR SÜDASIENFORSCHUNG
SÜDASIEN-INSTITUT
UNIVERSITÄT HEIDELBERG

BAND 93

FRANZ STEINER VERLAG WIESBADEN GMBH
1984

BANGLADESH:
ERA OF SHEIKH MUJIBUR RAHMAN

by

MOUDUD AHMED

FRANZ STEINER VERLAG WIESBADEN GMBH
1984

First published by The University Press Limited, Red Cross Building, 114 Motijheel Commercial Area, P. O. Box 88, Dhaka 2, Bangladesh, 1983

CIP-Kurztitelaufnahme der Deutschen Bibliothek

Ahmed, Moudud:
Bangladesh: era of Sheikh Mujibur Rahman / Moudud Ahmed. - Wiesbaden : Steiner, 1984. —
(Beiträge zur Südasienforschung ; Bd. 93)
ISBN 3-515-04266-0

NE: GT

BANGLADESH :
ERA OF
SHEIKH MUJIBUR RAHMAN

BANGLADESH:
Era of Sheikh Mujibur Rahman

Moudud Ahmed

FRANZ STEINER VERLAG · WIESBADEN
1983

First published by The University Press Limited, Red Cross Building, 114 Motijheel Commercial Area, P. O. Box 88, Dhaka 2, Bangladesh, 1983

Printed in Dhaka, Bangladesh

INTRODUCTION

Bangladesh today stands as a challenge to development particularly in the third world context and therefore, a study of the politico-economic conditions of this country should be of significant interest to the readers. If Bangladesh can make its economy and politics viable, it would be setting an example and would also be a source of inspiration for the other least developed countries.

Unlike many countries which freed themselves from colonial rule through negotiation, Bangladesh had to achieve her independence through a bloody war. This itself makes the case of Bangladesh different from others and any development study on this country needs to be looked at from this particular angle. When the country achieved independence, there was no foreign exchange reserve, no central policy planning agency in respect of foreign relations, defence and economic planning. Excepting an old colonial administrative infrastructure, the country received nothing substantive from the war-torn victory. The road and rail communications were almost destroyed by the war and the industrial and commercial life was thoroughly disrupted. Above all, the country faced the gigantic task of rehabilitation of about 10 million people who crossed into India for shelter during the war. It would not have been easy for any government to handle these problems of great magnitude : particularly the two challenging tasks of rehabilitation and restoration of normal life at the end of the war and the reconstruction and development for a future Bangladesh.

In the present work I have attempted to study and analyse the problems faced by the Awami League government and the methods it adopted to approach the problems. Series of laws were made by the government of the day to handle the situation and it would be interesting to see the effects of these laws and how they were implemented in the socio-economic and political context. This study also attempts to provide an insight to the general problems faced by a newly established independent country.

It is not an unknown scenario that the democratic regimes in developing countries tend to become authoritarian and such governments arrogate to themselves more and more power to perpetuate their rule. Related to this would be the question whether democracy in the western sense can at all work in a poor country ? How far and to what extent stability can be achieved in a poverty-stricken society through democratic institutions ?

In what circumstances the army's rise to power in the third world countries become inevitable? From this angle too the study of Bangladesh would be an interesting one. The ruling party which rose to power by democratic means, moved from one extreme of political framework to another, from democracy to one party system. What were the socio-economic needs and the political compulsion or contradictions which led them to go for a one-party rule? If, in the course of my assessment the readers find answers to some of these leading questions I shall feel amply rewarded.

The politics pursued in Bangladesh during this period had far-reaching consequences on the life of the people of the country. The socio-economic and political measures taken by the Awami League government in the initial years will have its bearing on the events of subsequent years and years to follow. The ruling party's treatment of the freedom fighters, the so-called collaborators and the army as an institution are examples which had bleeding effects on the body politic of this newly achieved country and these effects will continue to be on the political scene for a long time to come. It will be seen that the rise of the army to power in Bangladesh originates from the assassination, if not the rule of Sheikh Mujibur Rahman.

The period under discussion in this book is the era of Sheikh Mujibur Rahman, a man who might be considered as the greatest phenomenon of our history. Not only he was the central figure of Bangladesh since before the independence, he became an omnipotent personality and ruled Bangladesh single handedly with his charisma and unparalleled popularity. The whole political history of Bangladesh centered round him till his death and after. A separate chapter has been devoted to provide an appreciation of his personality.

The publication of this work has been delayed primarily for two reasons. Firstly, I planned to write on this period in 1976 when I went to Heidelberg on a Fellowship. In the course of making preparation to write on this period I discovered that many issues and events of our history still remained untold. I could not find any satifactory account dealing with the factors that actually lead to the creation of Bangladesh. So I changed my plan and wrote instead *Bangladesh : Constitutional Quest for Autonomy* covering the period from 1950 to 1971. The second reason of the delay is that although I completed the present work soon after I left Government, political preoccupations did not allow me to make the manuscript ready for publication. It is only since the imposition of the Martial Law on March 24, 1982 that I could go back to work on the manuscript.

October 1983

Moudud Ahmed

ACKNOWLEDGEMENT

I wrote the first 3 chapters of this book at Heidelberg and the rest at Harvard between July, 1980 and January, 1981. I thank the Federick Ebert Stiftung of the Federal Republic of Germany for extending a research scholarship for me to work for 2 months at the Heidelberg University and the Centre for International Affairs of the Harvard University for granting me a Fellowship which enabled me to spend 4 months working on this book at the Centre. My sincere thanks to Professor Dieter Rothermund, Director South Asia Institute, Heidelberg University who was always kind to assist me in my discussion with him and for his valuable comments on the manuscript. I am grateful to Dr. Benjamin Brown, Programme Director of the Center for International Affairs for his encouragement and assistance and Dr. Grant Hammond for the kind facilities he provided for me.

I am immensely grateful to Dr. Dieter Conrad of the Department of Law of the South Asia Institute for going through the manuscript and making detail comments on different aspect of the book. Without Dr. Conrad's encouragement and guidance it would not have been possible to write this book and finalise the manuscript within such a short period. I thank Mr. Mohiuddin Ahmed, Managing Director of the University Press Limited for his care and assistance in the publication of this book. Finally I thank my Secretary, Mr. M.A. Wadud for typing the manuscript several times.

The views expressed in this book are exclusively mine and if there are mistakes in facts or otherwise, I shall appreciate if readers come forward to have it corrected by me so that the second edition can be a better volume.

October 1983 **Moudud Ahmed**

CONTENTS

CHAPTER I	BEGINNING OF A NEW STATE		1
	Return of Sheikh Mujibur Rahman		3
	The Proclamation of Independence		4
	The Laws Continuance Enforcement Order	..	6
	The Provisional Constitution of Bangladesh Order, 1972	..	7
CHAPTER II	AWAMI LEAGUE GOVERNMENT : ECONOMIC AND SOCIAL MEASURES	..	12
	Taking over of Abandoned Properties : Laws and Decisions	..	13
	Nationalisation of Banks, Insurance Companies and Major Industries	..	19
	Banks and Insurance Companies	..	27
	Relief and Rehabilitation Programme	..	27
	Relief Committees	..	28
CHAPTER III	LAW AND ORDER SITUATION		39
	Politics of Arms: National Militia and the Freedom Fighters	..	39
	The Collaborators	..	43
	The Rakkhi Bahini and the Law Enforcing Agencies	..	52
	Court's Decisions		56
	Smuggling and other Economic Offences	..	63
	Court's Decisions	..	68
	The Civil Administration	..	70
	The Bangladesh Public Servants' (Retirement) Order, 1972	..	76
	Exemption of Taxes and Land Ceiling	..	80
	Industrial Workers	..	81
CHAPTER IV	THE CONSTITUTION-MAKING PROCESS	..	90
	Demand for a New Constituent Assembly	..	90
	The 1972 Constitution : Basic Principles	..	92
	The Fundamental Rights	..	98
	Provision relating to Preventive Detention and Emergency	..	100
	Westminister-type Parliamentary System	..	104
	The Defence Services	..	106
	Local Government	..	107
	Legislature	..	107
	Ombudsman	..	110
	Law-Making Procedure : Supremacy of Parliament	..	110
	Judiciary	..	113
	The Writ Jurisdiction	..	115
	Administrative Tribunals	..	115
	Election	..	118

	The Services	..	119
	The Amendment of the Constitution	..	122
	Bengali Text of the Constitution		125
	Summary and Conclusion	..	127
CHAPTER V	MOVE FOR POLITICAL CONSOLIDATION : THE GENERAL ELECTIONS, 1973	..	136
	Manifestos	..	138
	The Elections	..	141
	The Lal Bahini	..	146
	Amendment of the Constitution and Enactment of Certain Laws	..	148
	Press and Publication Ordinance		150
	The Special Powers Act, 1974	..	152
	Court Decisions	..	154
CHAPTER VI	ECONOMIC PLANNING AND REORGANISATION		160
	The First Five Year Plan : A Move for a Socialist Transformation	..	160
	Philosophical Base of the Plan	..	161
	Preconditions for a Socialist Development	..	162
	The Objective Conditions Prevailing in Bangladesh	..	163
	Socio-Political Assumptions of the Plan	..	165
	External and Domestic Resource Target	..	167
	GDP and Per Capita Income	..	167
	The Plan	..	168
	Performance of the Plan	..	172
	Dependence on Foreign Aid	..	175
	Private Sector	..	176
	Reorganisation of Salary Structure	..	177
CHAPTER VII	THE BANGLADESH-INDIA RELATIONSHIP	..	181
	The Friendship Treaty	..	185
	The Indo-Soviet and Afghan-Soviet Treaty	..	188
	The Conflicting Interests between Bangladesh and India	..	190
CHAPTER VIII	THE PRISONERS OF WAR	..	195
	A Central Issue in Foreign Relations		195
	Simla Agreement	..	196
	Joint Settlement offer by Bangladesh and India	..	199
	Reply of Pakistan	..	200
	Delhi Agreement between India and Pakistan		202
CHAPTER IX	FOOD, FLOOD AND FAMINE	..	207
CHAPTER X	ROLE OF THE POLITICAL PARTIES AND THE THREE-PARTY ALLIANCE	..	215
	Role of JSD : The *Gherao* Movement	..	219
	Role of the NAP (B) and Opposition Unity		220
	The Committee for Civil Liberties and Legal Aid		222
	Three-Party Alliance	..	223
CHAPTER XI	THE PROCLAMATION OF EMERGENCY AND SWITCHING TO ONE-PARTY SYSTEM	..	231
	The Fourth Amendment of the Constitution	..	235
	The President becomes the Chief Executive	..	235

	The Vice President	..	236
	The Council of Ministers	..	236
	Local Administration	..	236
	Parliament and Legislation	..	237
	Judiciary	..	238
	One National Party	..	240
	Other Features	..	240
	Justifications for the Change in the System	..	242
	Formation of the Bangladesh Krishak Sramik Awami League (BAKSAL) : Its Philosophy and Programme	..	245
	Annulment and Taking over of Newspapers	..	247
	National Unity	..	247
	Summary and Evaluation	..	250
	Domestic Situation	..	254
	Perpetuation of Power	..	254
	Socialist Economic Order	..	254
	Towards Some Improvement : Mujib Seeks Moulana's Support	..	256
	Law and Order	..	256
	Economic Recovery	..	257
	End of the BAKSAL Regime : Brutal Killing of Sheikh Mujib	..	258
CHAPTER XII	SHEIKH MUJIBUR RAHMAN	..	263
Appendix A	The Proclamation of Independence	..	269
Appendix B	Laws Continuance Enforcement Order	..	270
Appendix C	Provisional Constitution of Bangladesh Order, 1972	..	271
Appendix D	Position Paper Prepared by the Research Cell, External Publicity Division of the Bangladesh Government in Exile, June, 1971	..	272
Appendix E	Treaty of Friendship, Co-operation and Peace between the People's Republic of Bangladesh and the Republic of India	..	274
	Index	..	277

CHAPTER ONE

BEGINNING OF A NEW STATE

On the 16th day of December, 1971 Lt. General Amir Abdullah Khan Niazi, the Commander of the Eastern Command of Pakistan received Lt. Gen. Jagjit Singh Aurora, the Commander of the Eastern Command of India and the GOC-in-Chief of the Indian and Bangladesh Forces at the Dhaka Airport with smart military salute[1]. They then drove together to the Ramna Race Course where a small contingent of the Pakistan Army presented a guard of honour to the Indian Commander and at 4.00 in the afternoon both the Generals signed the Instrument of Surrender. With this ended the war in 1971 and came the formal birth of Bangladesh.

Once the Pakistan Army surrendered, the victors took the charge of the vanquished but Bangladesh continued to exist without any government within its own territory. Although Aurora was commanding the allied forces, Bangladesh remained unrepresented in the surrendering ceremony except the last minute inclusion of Group Captain Khondker who was despatched from Calcutta to accompany the Indian Commander. The Acting President, the Prime Minister[2] the Commander-in-Chief[3] and the Defence Secretary of the Mukti Bahini were all sitting at Calcutta on that day. Once the Instrument of Surrender was signed, Aurora left, so did Khondker and Bangladesh was left in the hands of the Indian Army Officers.

It was a delicate situation. The men who were the formal leaders in the struggle from Bangladesh side did not take part in the actual war nor had they any clear idea about the situation inside the country. The hundreds and thousands of young men who took active part in the war both from within and outside the country had already established their political influence in their respective areas in the absence of any Government. Kader Siddiqui, one of the valiant freedom fighters had already reached Dhaka and started the process of reprisals by slaying a few 'Beharis' ceremoniously at the Outer Stadium field[4]. Soon after the surrender of the Pakistan Army a new band of fake freedom fighters appeared on the streets who just switched their labels in order to keep themselves on the winning side[5]. No one actually knew what was happening including the Cabinet Ministers at Calcutta.

But nevertheless the entire country, particularly Dhaka wore an extremely festive look. At least a million people, men, women and children were on the streets to greet the Indian Army and the members of the Mukti Bahini. The people were relieved of the agony and torture inflicted on them by the Pakistan Army for 9 long months. The reception accorded was therefore a spontaneous one.

With a contingent of Indian "advisers" comprising civil servants and technical experts, a handful of Bengali civil servants arrived in Dhaka the same week and under the guidance of the Indian bureaucracy the civil administration was gradually set in motion[6]. At Calcutta from the Bangladesh side a continued pressure was put on the leaders and Cabinet Ministers even prior to the surrender to immediately go to Dhaka to take over the charge of the new Government. But due to their timid character and non-involvement in the actual war, the leaders were scared and reluctant to face the situation[7]. None took the initiative to take the responsibility of the new government[8]. At last, after about seven days of the surrender some of the leaders left Calcutta to proceed in their homeway journey to Dhaka to manage an independent country.

In this confusing state, although the Indian Army and the civil personnel were received well but the men who actually fought for the country did not like their dominating role. They did not like the installation of men in the government, who were sitting in Calcutta and did not take any part in actual war. This difference between the freedom fighters and the political leaders was already evident during the 9 month struggle. Although the Independence War of Bangladesh was not an armed struggle in the classical sense and had no strong ideological or philosophical foundation yet it is only natural that a war of that nature generate new thoughts and ideals amongst the millions who took part in it with or without the gun[9]. They had dreams and hopes about their new country ; they knew what they wanted but did not know how to get it. Within the Awami League itself, the separately created and specially trained Mujib Bahini[10] hoped to take control of the government. Leaders like Sheikh Moni and others were openly opposed to Tajuddin's leadership. In a way Bangladesh was plunged into a counter-revolution the day it was born in the sense that power went into the hands of those who did not fight. This had a far-reaching consequence in the Bangladesh body politic.

In the absence of an effective political government and without Sheikh Mujibur Rahman, the freedom fighters, the 16th Division notwithstanding, took position in their respective areas and started running the administration. Except in the city of Dhaka there was practically no government in the country for several weeks. During those days the Tajuddin Government could have been easily overthrown had there been no Indian Army to protect it. However, after their arrival in the capital, the Dhaka-based government started issuing directives primarily in an attempt to bring the monetary and fiscal institutions under control.

But once in Dhaka, Tajuddin quickly tried to consolidate his own position and one of the first steps he took was to remove Khondker Moshtaque Ahmed from the important post of the Ministry of Foreign Affairs and put Abdus Samad Azad there. Moshtaque was asked to retain his other porfolio of Law and Parliamentary Affairs. Tajuddin also tried to come to an understanding with the freedom fighters and drew up an elaborate plan to rehabilitate and utilise them in the national reconstruction programmes. He was also successful in restraining a sizeable section of Mukti Bahini from resorting to reprisals against the collaborators, particularly the Beharis. But being the Prime Minister of a divided government and in the absence of Sheikh Mujibur Rahman the new government continued to be weak and was under the influence of the Indian authorities[11].

In the meantime, Bhutto on his assumption of office as the President of Pakistan and having fulfilled the ambition of his life, with the intention of releasing Mujib, his arch Political rival from jail kept him in a house in Rawalpindi in an attempt to negotiate a compromise[12]. Whatever might have been the consideration or pressures, national or international, Bhutto at last had obtained a political mandate at a public meeting at Karachi and announced on January 3, 1972 that Mujib would be freed. The news of the possible release of Mujib brought a deep sense of relief to all the people in Bangladesh who were living in the midst of most dangerous uncertainties.

Return of Sheikh Mujibur Rahman

On January 8, 1972 Mujib was put on a P.I.A. jet aircraft to leave Pakistan for a destination of his own choice. Mujib arrived in London as the President of Bangladesh, not yet recognised by the British Government but he addressed a large press conference and the British leaders including the Prime Minister met him and extended to him all courtesies. It is not yet known why Mujib chose not to use the Red Cross plane hired by the Indian Government or why he decided to go to London first[13]. Nevertheless, on his way back Mujib stopped at Delhi where he was given a grand reception. Mujib paid his personal tributes to the people of India and met Mrs. Indira Gandhi and other Indian leaders.

Then the triumphant moment came and with that Mujib brought with him the heaviest responsibility to straighten a country ravaged by war and to meet the hopes, dreams, expectations of seventy-five million people built up through a struggle of long 24 years. It was a mammoth reception, warm and spontaneous for an undisputed leader. Known to be a moderate politician and a liberal democrat, Mujib struggled and suffered for many years for the restoration of human rights and a democratic system. He was in prison again and again on countless occasions, and passed most of his creative age in prison cells. As a genuine leader of the people, he travelled from village to village. He never forgot a face he once saw and having a sharp memory, Mujib could remember names of hundreds and thousands of his workers. So long an agitator, a demagouge, a spitfire orator belonging to the opposition for almost his entire life, he now arrived in the midst of his own people as the President and father of the nation[14].

The same day, to keep in line with his earlier commitment, Mujib ordered to change the law. He did not want to act as the President but chose to be the Prime Minister of the country in line with a Westminister-type Parliamentary system. So long the country was being run under a Proclamation of Independence which named Sheikh Mujib as the President. Following the Pakistan Army crackdown on March 25, 1971 the Awami League leaders who could escape and assemble in India had to adopt a legal instrument in order to enable them to form a government-in-exile and receive assistance from India. Accordingly, the Proclamation was drafted and adopted on the 10th April, 1971[15] with retrospective effect from March 26, 1971 in order to legalise the government and the Independence war[16].

The Proclamation of Independence

The Proclamation of Independence laid down the fundamental law for the country in war. So it continued to provide the legal cover for all the acts done by the government not only during the war period but also thereafter. The Proclamation became the fountain of law and the source of authority ; it was the constitution of the country till the new constitution was made effective on and from December 16, 1972. The Proclamation was made to handle a special situation. The main feature of the Proclamation was that the governmental system was made Presidential and for strategic and popular reasons Sheikh Mujib was named as the President in the instrument itself[17] and he was to continue as the President till such time a constitution was framed. War is always met by special laws to eanble a government to handle the affairs of the state effectively. So it was nothing unusual that in the special circumstances power was concentrated in one hand, giving the President both the executive and the legislative powers. Besides this, the President was made the supreme Commander of the armed forces with power to grant pardon, appoint a Prime Minister and other Ministers, levy taxes and expend monies, summon and adjourn the Constituent Assembly and do all things necessary to give to the people of Bangladesh "an orderly and just" government.

Since everyone knew that Mujib was not present to function as the President, the Proclamation provided that in the event of there being no President or where the President was unable to enter upon his office or was unable to exercise his powers and duties for any reason, the Vice-President would have all the powers, duties and responsibilities of the President[18]. The Proclamation further declared that Bangladesh would observe and give effect to all the duties and obligations developed upon it as a member of the family of nations under the charter of the United Nations.

According to the Proclamation the elected representatives (MNAs and MPAs) constituted themselves into a Constituent Assembly and having held mutual consultations declared and constituted Bangladesh as a sovereign people's republic. They thereby confirmed the declaration of independence already made by Sheikh Mujibur Rahman on March 26, 1971[19]. The reasons for justifying the Proclamation were stated to be that after the free election held in the country for the purpose of framing a constitution Yahya Khan summoned the elected representatives of the people to meet on March 3, 1971 for the said purpose but the Assembly so summoned was arbitrarily and illegally postponed for an indefinite period and instead of fulfilling their promise, the Pakistan authorities declared an unjust and treacherous war. So the representatives from Bangladesh met and constituted themselves into a Constituent Assembly and declared independence.

In other words, the Awami League having won the majority both in the National and Provincial Assemblies and having been deprived by the Pakistan authorities from fulfilling their commitment acquired a legal right to assemble and exercise the right of self-determination for and on behalf of their people. Having won 167 seats out of 169 the Awami League could claim to represent the entire people of East Pakistan and also the majority population of the entire Pakistan.

The Proclamation stated that as the elected representatives were honour bound by the "mandate" given to them by the people of Bangladesh, they constituted themselves into a Constituent Assembly and declared independence, though the "mandate" was impliedly given for achieving an autonomous status within the framework of Pakistan and not for independence[20]. The authenticity of Sheikh Mujib's declaration of independence at Dhaka on March 26, 1971 has also not been established the way it is claimed[21]. Nevertheless in the context of the overall politics the Proclamation as a whole served the purpose extremely well.

The question of legality of such a Proclamation drawn by a group of people belonging to one single political party attempting to divide the country of a sovereign state has also to be judged from the actual circumstances. It is true that no national election of any sovereign state can give an instant right to such elected representatives of a particular area to declare independence of that part of its territory but each of such cases of right of self-determination has to be examined on its own merit in the light of the charter of the United Nations.

One can also look at the struggle of the American people to achieve their independence in the eighteenth century from the British colonial rule. Throughout the entire movement for independence, suppression and exploitation of the Americans by the British Empire was the underlying factor. Jesus Otiss' great argument in opposing the use of the odious "units of assistance" as a means of repressing struggle in Massachussetts and "an act of Parliament contrary to natural right" was one of the first issues which aroused public opinion against England and ultimately led the American people to adopt the Declaration of Independence. Thomas Jefferson, John Adams, Benjamin Franklin, Roger Thomson and Robert R. Livingston were the heroes of the independence war. At every stage of the oppression, peaceful and constitutional means were first adopted by making petitions to the rulers for redress in the most humble terms but all were in vain. The British despatched new troops to suppress their agitations and the Americans were determined to meet them with resistance and reprisal. So finally the representatives of the United States of America assembled in a general convention on July 4, 1776 and by the authority of the good people of the "colonies (America)" they absolved themselves from all the allegiance to the British government and established free and independent states[22]. In support of this declaration the representatives pledged to each other, "their lives, fortunes and the sacred honour".

It was basically the same story—a struggle to achieve equality, honour and human dignity. Independence has been achieved in many countries since the American Declaration in the same manner to free themselves from oppression, economic exploitation and political suppression. This is an universally accepted right of every such area where people struggle to acquire their self-determination. The United Nations Charter guarantees this right.

However, once the Pakistan Army surrendered, the Proclamation gained significant importance both from a historical and constitutional point of view. After December 16, 1971 the Proclamation continued to remain fully effective as the fundamental instrument of law for the country and the laws made thereunder were obeyed by the entire population. The Proclamation became a reality—it created a new nation on the map of the world.

The Laws Continuance Enforcement Order

In the exercise of powers conferred by the Proclamation another important law was made by the Acting President in order to ensure continuity in all spheres. This was the Laws Continuance Enforcement Order dated April 10, 1971 which was made effective from March 26, 1971. For legal, constitutional and international reasons both the Proclamation of Independence and the Laws Continuance Enforcement Order were made effective from March 26, 1971[23]. The Continuance Order legalised and made effective all the existing laws inherited from Pakistan subject to the Proclamation. The existing laws would also not be effective if they were inconsistent with the consequential changes as would be necessary on account of the creation of Bangladesh as a sovereign state. It provided that all the government officials civil, military, judicial and diplomatic, who would take an oath of allegiance to Bangladesh would continue in their office on terms and conditions of service so long enjoyed by them. The administration of such oath of allegiance was to be arranged by all District Judges, Magistrates and the Diplomatic representatives within their respective jurisdiction.

The Continuance Order was issued to maintain process of continuity in the given circumstances. Although it had put the government at great disadvantages in many respects, it had to be made primarily to gain support of the government officials who had served the Pakistan government. The Government of Bangladesh, although in exile built up a huge bureaucratic machine at Calcutta. The Continuance order was passed not so much for the continuity of laws but more to satisfy the government officials who had joined the government and to encourage those who yet did not. In other words, it meant that all the government officials were guaranteed that despite all dislocations due to war, their service conditions would not be changed and they would continue to enjoy the same rights and privileges as those under the Pakistan authority[24].

The Provisional Constitution of Bangladesh Order, 1972

However, Mujib wanted to change the system by exercising the legislative power he had as the President under the Proclamation of Independence. Accordingly, on January 11, 1972 by a Presidential Order the entire character of the government was changed. The Presidential form was substituted by a form aiming at a Westminister type Parliamentary system through a decree called the Provisional Constitution of Bangladesh Order, 1972[25]. The reason stated for changing the system was that it was the "manifest aspiration of the people of Bangladesh to establish a parlimentary democracy" and so in order to achieve this objective the new order was proclaimed.

By this order under section 5, a Cabinet of Ministers was created with the Prime Minister at its head and the all powerful position of the President under the Proclamation was reduced to a mere titular head as section 6 laid down that the President "shall in exercise of all his functions act in accordance with the advice of the Prime Minister". To keep in line with the system section 7 provided that the President would commission as Prime Minister a member of the Constituent Assembly who commanded the confidence of the majority of members of the Constituent Assembly. All other Ministers would be appointed by the President on the advice of the Prime Minister.

The Order also provided a device to enable Sheikh Mujib to become the Prime Minister and justice Abu Sayeed Chowdhury to become the President of Bangladesh. Section 8 provided that in the event of a vacancy occuring in the office of the President the Cabinet would appoint as President a citizen of Bangladesh who would hold the office of President until another President enters the office in accordance with the Constitution to be framed by the Constituent Assembly. The interesting point of this provision was that the office of the President was left open for anyone and was not limited to a member of Parliament or the Constituent Assembly[26] facilitating the appointment of Justice Abu Sayeed Chowdhury as the President of the country. The Provisional Order, by section 9, created a high Court for Bangladesh and provided by section 10 that the Chief Justice of the High Court would administer an oath of office to the Prime

Minister and other Ministers and the form of oath would be prescribed by the Cabinet.

Besides the introduction of a sort of Parliamentary system the Provisional Constitution Order dealt with some other areas where constitutional vacuum continued to exist. On the functions of the Constituent Assembly the Proclamation was silent but the Provisional Order not only defined the Constituent Assembly but clearly envisaged that the Constituent Assembly would frame the Constitution of the country. In other words, it meant that those MNAs and MPAs who were elected in the elections held in December 1970, January 1971 and March 1971 were to comprise the Constituent Assembly[27]. The Proclamation provided a provision for oath only to the President and the oath to the Vice-President was to be administered by a duly constituted potentiary. In the Proclamation a kind of a Presidential administration was envisaged to meet a special situation with no concept of cabinet as such, but the Provisional Order created a 'cabinet of Ministers'.

However, in order to accomplish this process of changing the Presidential form into a Parliamentary one Mujib as the President first appointed Justice A. S. M. Sayem as the Chief Justice under the Provisional Constitution Order and administered oath to him in the morning of January 12, 1972 and then he himself resigned. On his resignation under section 8 of the Provisional Order the cabinet appointed Justice Abu Sayeed Chowdhury as the President who in turn was administered oath by the newly appointed Chief Justice[28]. Thereafter, Sayed Nazrul Islam, Tajuddin Ahmed and others of the government resigned and the President commissioned Mujib under section 7 of the Provisional Order as the Prime Minister. Mujib then formed his new cabinet consisting of eleven Ministers[29]. The President then under section 10 administered oath of office to the Prime Minister and other Ministers.

Why did Mujib rush to change the governmental system? The first reason was a historical one. The people of Bangladesh were used to have elective local bodies for a long time and it was introduced in Bengal before any other part of British India and the elective legislatures functioned in Bengal for over 50 years[30]. Secondly, from the inception of the Awami League in 1949 the Party was committed to introduce a parliamentary system in the country. Through all the major political movements from the 21-point programme in 1954 to the 6 and 11 point programmes in 1968-69 and finally the election in 1970-71 firm pledge was made to the people by Sheikh Mujib that he believed in a democratic system and parliamentary form of government would be established in the country[31]. By promulgating the Provisional Constitution Order, Mujib felt proud of himself in the sense that he could keep his commitment to the people. The long cherished dream of people for having a Parliamentary system was now fulfilled. Thirdly Tajuddin having led the war-government became too much identified with India and for strategic and international reasons it was better to change the old government and bring a new one.

In reality however there was another side of the Provisional Constitution Order. Although the Order was made "to establish a Parliamentary democracy" the actual effect was that the power remained concentrated in one hand. It was a change in form and it enabled Mujib to redesignate his position as the Prime Minister in place of the President. The legislative powers continued to remain vested in the executive. Although it visualised a parliamentary system there was no Parliament in existence ; there was a cabinet of Ministers which was not accountable to the people and a Prime Minister could not be removed from his office. The fundamental rights remained suspended and the High Court's jurisdiction to issue any writ, order or directive in the nature of habeas corpus, mandamus, prohibition, quo warranto or certiorari was closed down[32].

FOOTNOTES

1. Siddiq Salik, *Witness to Surrender*, Karachi : Oxford University Press, p. 211.
2. On delegation from the Acting President, the Prime Minister was exercising all the executive powers. Sayed Nazrul Islam was the Vice President-cum-Acting President and Tajuddin Ahmed was the Prime Minister.
3. Abdus Samad, a member of the Pakistan Civil Service was the Defence Secretary and General M.A.G. Osmani was the C-in-C of the Mukti Bahini.
4. See *Newsweek*, January 3, 1972. "Beharis" were those who migrated primarily from the Indian State of Bihar on the partition of the sub-continent but the term became widely known to identify all non-Bengali speaking immigrants irrespective of their origin.
5. They became popularly known as "16th Division" meaning those who became freedom fighters after 16th of December. A huge number of Peace Committee members and Razakars got into this bandwagon. Peace Committees were formed by Pakistan authorities to assist them in apprehending the freedom fighters in different localities. The Razakars were the members of the para-military force raised by Pakistan Government in assisting them to combat the freedom fighters.
6. The Bengali civil servants were led by Ruhul Quddus as the Secretary-General of the Bangladesh Government.
7. See detail as to how the Government in exile was formed and their character and behaviour. Author's book, *Bangladesh : Constitutional Quest for Autonomy*, Dacca : University Press Limited, 1980. pp. 264-277. This book was originally published by Franz Steiner Verlag, Wiesbaden, West Germany, 1978 under the auspices of South Asia Institute, University of Heidelberg. The book was subsequently published with due permission by the University Press Limited, Dhaka.
8. A section of people alleged that the Indian Government advised the Bangladesh leaders to wait till the situation improved. The author who was present in Calcutta took an active part in pressing the leaders to go to Dhaka. The author helped in establishing the External Publicity Division of the Government in exile at Calcutta and was deeply associated with it till the end of the war.
9. See author's observations about the character of the independence war in his book, *Bangladesh : Constitutional Quest for Autonomy*, pp. 272-77.
10. Under the leadership of Serajul Alam Khan and Sheikh Fazlul Huq Moni a special corps of trained boys were raised in India, 'Mujib Bahini' by name, who claimed to represent Mujib and his leadership as opposed to Tajuddin and others.

11. From the very inception the Government-in-exile was divided. Although officially there was only one government, it was not difficult to see that there was no cohesion or coordination between the different leaders in the government. There were in fact 6 parallel government, one led by Tajuddin, second led by Khandker Moshtaque, third by Qamruzzaman, fourth by Mansur Ali, fifth by the Mukti Bahini and sixth by the Mujib Bahini. No account was ever made public as to how the 82 crores taka of allegedly taken away from various East Pakistan banks and deposited with the Government-in-exile were spent.
12. The full text of the negotiation between Bhutto and Mujib is not yet known. Mujib however, mentioned in his 10th January speech that Bhutto requested him to maintain some kind of link, presumably at least in the form of a confederation with Pakistan. Mujib, however, assured Bhutto that Bangladesh would function as a sovereign state and he would not allow the Indian Army to remain on the soil of Bangladesh for long.
13. Mujib's associates claimed that he wanted to maintain a neutral position vis-a-vis India till he could receive a full-scale briefing. See his Delhi airport statement of January 10, 1972.
14. I met Mujib the same day at his residence—he looked the same, warm and optimistic, as ever.
15. The Proclamation was made back-dated after the government was formed. For more about the government see the author's *Bangladesh ; Constitutional Quest for Autonomy*. pp. 264-69.
16. Indian lawyers and bureaucrats assisted in drafting the Proclamation. Amirul Islam, an eminent lawyer of Bangladesh and an MNA played an important role. When the Proclamation was issued in Calcutta the Government-in-exile was in contact with only about 35 MNAs and MPAs. For the text of the Proclamation, see Appendix A. MNA—Members of National Assembly ; MPA—Members of Provincial Assembly.
17. Without naming Sheikh Mujib as the President of Independent Banglaeesh it would have been impossible to rally round the people.
18. In order to resolve the internal fight for portfolios, Syed Nazrul Islam, a softer personality was named as the Vice-President in the instrument itself. The author's *Bangladesh : Constitutional Quest for Autonomy*, pp. 265-66.
19. On the declaration of independence on March 26, 1971 See author's *Bangladesh ; Constitutional Quest for Autonomy*, pp. 256-57 and 269-70.
20. On this issue and on the controversy arising from it, more will be said in Chapter IV.
21. See author's book, *Bangladesh : Constitutional Quest for Autonomy*, pp. 269-270.
22. Edward Dembauld, The Declaration of Independence and what it means to them, Norman, University of Oklahoma Press, 1950.
23. For the text see Appendix 'B'.
24. The condition of the Mukti Bahini members and other fighters were miserable. They were receiving only Rs. 1.25 per day per person for their food, etc. This created a deep resentment amongst the freedom fighters.
25. This provisional Constitution was drafted at the Law Consultants, a law firm of which the author is a partner. Justice Abu Sayeed Chowdhury, Dr. Kamal Hossain and Amirul Islam prepared the draft. See for the text of the Order, Appendix 'C'.
26. Under the Proclamation Mujib was made the President although he was a member of the Constituent Assembly.
27. The female members were elected indirectly in March, 1971.
28. Here the cabinet under section 8 must have meant the old one created under the Proclamation. Otherwise, Mujib could not have summoned himself as the new Prime Minister. On the other hand, the cabinet was to come into existence only under the Provisional Order.

29. The first cabinet under Sheikh Mujib consisted of Sayed Nazrul Islam, Tajuddin Ahmed, Mansur Ali, Khandker Moshtaque Ahmed, Abdus Samad, A.H.M. Qamruzzaman, Sheikh Abdul Aziz, Yusuf Ali, Zahur Hossain Chowdhury, Phani Bhushan Majumder and Dr. Kamal Hossain.
30. Dr. Kamal Hossain, *Bangabandhu and Bangladesh, Sheikh Mujib*, London Radical Asia Books, January, 1977, p. 18.
31. Almost all political parties of Bangladesh including the rightist parties were committed to a parliamentary system.
32. The High Court of Bangladesh Order, 1972 (C.P.O. No. 5 of 1972). Article 4. See also 25 DLR 1973, p. 390 Jadu Nath Majumder vs. Hasina Begum.

CHAPTER TWO

AWAMI LEAGUE GOVERNMENT : ECONOMIC AND SOCIAL MEASURES

The immediate problems faced by Sheikh Mujib and the Awami League Government were as follows : (1) straightening the administration ; (2) rehabilitation of about 10 million refugees who were to return from India ; (3) restoration of the law and order situation and handling of the freedom fighters and others possessing arms ; (4) restoration of roads, bridges and railway lines destroyed or damaged during the war ; (5) putting the economy back on the rails, particularly industries and the financial institutions. Besides these, there were some urgent social and political problems and issues relating to and arising out of (a) the presence of the Indian Army in Bangladesh ; (b) smuggling across the border ; (c) presence of the collaborators who assisted the Pakistan Army during the war ; (d) the issue of the prisoners of war ; (6) the presence of the non-locals or 'Beharis' and the stranded Pakistanis in Bangladesh and the Bengalis in Pakistan. Then there was of course the question of meeting the expectations and aspirations of the people which were raised to a great height through all the struggling years. So it was now Mujib's turn to recreate his dreamland "Sonar Bangla" and have smile in every face of his people.

It would be interesting to see how and what laws were made and actions taken to meet these problems and their effects and consequences. The purpose of the laws and their actual use are very relevant for the socio-economic and political study of the initial years of this new born country. With these issues the background of the constitution-making process is also linked and a careful study of this becomes essential in order to understand the real import of the constitution itself.

Other than the manifesto prepared during 1970-71 elections the Awami League had no defined social or economic programmes. Even during the 9-month war period when most of their leaders resided in Calcutta they did not draw any concrete plan as to how the situation would be tackled once the country became independent and they did not think about the measures they would draw for the reconstruction and economic development[1]. So with no national policy-planning experience and knowledgeable expertise and without any definite political or economic plan, the Awami League embarked on building a new nation.

During the period between December 16, 1971 to December 15, 1972 series of laws were made, about 150 in number and some of them were of fundamental nature. 26 of these laws and one law dating from the Pakistan period were saved by the constitution itself and made effective notwithstanding any inconsistency with any other provision of the constitution[2]. The fundamental nature of these laws, their background and their socio-political consequences deserve careful examination. Other laws were made mostly for straightening the administration and other agencies of the government or for handling a particular situation on a routine basis without having much socio-economic or political consequence.

Taking over of Abandoned Properties: Laws and Decisions

One of the first laws affecting the status of property and subsequently given constitutional protection was made on 3rd January, 1972. It was the law relating to the taking over of control and management of industrial and commercial concerns. With the emergence of Bangladesh large number of business units were left by Pakistanis[3] worth billions of takas, and laws were made for taking them over in order to protect them. The object was to keep them running so that the production continued and the economy did not suffer.

The law known as the Acting President's Order No. 1 of 1972 provided that the Government could take over the control and management of the industrial and commercial concerns whose owners, directors and managers or majority of them had left Bangladesh or were not available to control and manage the concerns. The government could also take over such units whose owners or directors were present but could not be allowed to run them in the public interest. It provided that the government would appoint management boards or administrators to run such units.

It further provided that all the powers and duties including the power to operate bank accounts of the owners, directors and managers of the concerns would now vest in the government or Management Boards or Administrators or any other authority which took over the control and management of the concern. The law also provided that the government would determine the terms and conditions of those who would control and manage such concerns and that they would submit to the government such information as they would be directed to.

In the original order an official gazette notification was required before taking over any concern, but by a subsequent amendment made by P.O. 151 of 1972 the provision for a notification was deleted giving the government more power to take over any concern. In the case of Messrs. Speedbird

Navigation Co.[4] the Court held that even though the notification was no more required under the amendment contained in P.O. 151 of 1972 still any action of taking over under A.P.O. No. 1 of 1972 would have to be preceded by a decision of the government. The Court further held that the Government could not delegate such a power to any other authority for taking any decision on its behalf. The Court also restricted the scope of Article 2(1) by contemplating certain situations for taking over any concern[5].

However, by the time the Court's pronouncement came the law itself for all practical purposes had lost its effectiveness and as mentioned earlier, was integrated into another law called the Bangladesh Abandoned Property (Control, Management and Disposal) Order, 1972[6]. While the A.P.O. 1 was made only to take over for the purpose of control and management, the effect of the P.O. 16 was far-reaching. The APO 1 only vested the right of control and mangement, whereas the P.O. 16 vested in the government the property itself and enabled the government to dispose of the properties.

The promulgation of the P.O. 16 of 1972 was necessitated by the same logic which existed for APO 1 of 1972 but it was made more comprehensive and brought under its power the whole spectrum of the properties abandoned mainly by the Pakistanis. The law provided wide and almost unlimited powers to the public functioneries to take over properties of its own bonafide citizens. The object of the law was to make provisions for the control, management and disposal of the properties abandoned by persons who were not present in Bangladesh or whose whereabouts were not known or who had ceased to occupy or supervise or manage 'in person' their property, or who were enemy aliens.

The essential and interesting features of this law were :

(1) The government could indirectly take over the property of any person who was not occupying or supervising or managing his property in person. In other words, a citizen who was temporarily outside the country or who was living in another town within the country could have lost his property.

(2) The property owned by any citizen of Pakistan would be treated as abandoned property.

(3) Any property taken over by the A.P.O, 1 of 1972 would be treated as abandoned property. This was interesting in the sense that under APO 1 industrial and commercial concerns were taken over only for control and management but now under P.O. 16 the same properties were taken over including their ownership and the right of disposal.

(4) On the commencement of the Order all abandoned properties would vest in the government and those properties would be administered,

controlled and managed and disposed of through transfer or lease or otherwise. This involved a fundamental point of acquiring ownership of property by the government by mere operation of law. It meant that the government would not only control or manage such property but could sell them off to another person.

(5) With regard to the liabilities of such abandoned properties the government would determine them in a prescribed manner meaning that the creditors however much entitled they were, would have to rely on or wait for the government to decide the liabilities of such properties. (Article 9).

(6) The Government also could cancel any allotment or lease or agreement or annull the terms of such instruments which were granted or entered into after the 25th March, 1971[7]. By reason of any such action of the government, any person who had ceased to be entitled to possession of any abandoned property had to surrender the property on demand or the government could eject such person without going through the process of established laws. In this Article also the government was allowed to have such powers which even the original owners did not enjoy (Article 10).

(7) The law further provided under Article 14 that any property so vested in the government would be exempt from all legal process including seizure, distress, ejectment, etc. and no court would grant any injunction or admit any process and the government could not be divested or disposed of such property. Any such legal process subsisting immediately before the commencement of the Order would cease to have any effect[8].

(8) The Law however provided some provision for getting relief by affected people if the property was wrongly treated as abandoned by the Government. Any such person could submit an application to the "prescribed authority" within 3 months from the date of the commencement of the Order. It provided for a summary enquiry in a prescribed manner and thereby, a summary proceeding would dispose of such application. Any person not satisfied with an order of the prescribed authority under Article 7 could file an appeal within one month before another "prescribed authority". The government however retained the power to revise any of its order passed under Article 7 and 15 either of its own motion or on an application[9].

(9) Lastly, no court could question anything done or any action taken or any order passed under this Order and thereby the court's jurisdiction was excluded with regard to abandoned property.

Under the P.O. 16 the government therefore, assumed extra-ordinary powers with regard to properties not only of Pakistanis but also of its own citizens. The definition of abandoned property appeared to be harsh. At least two Attorney Generals argued in cases where I was conducting them to defend the rights of citizens where they tried to justify the action of the government saying that the government could take over the property of a citizen under this law and the action of the government would be legal in that respect.

The provisions relating to the taking over of shares in companies where government was not in majority and where it was in majority, the provisions relating to appointment of Board and Administrators, dispossessing person from otherwise lawfully occupying premises and finally, the power of transferring and selling of properties — all called for valid questions whether so much power given to the executive branch were justifiable or not.

Although under Article 7, 15 and 16 provisions for summary proceedings to show-cause etc. were provided in effect they were of no consequence and granted no relief to the members of the public. The "prescribed authority" in a "prescribed manner" did not come into force till July and August, 1972 after nearly 6 months of making the laws by which time the wrath of the law had already affected the socio-economic life of a very important section of society[10]. The provision of submitting applications under Article 15 became meaningless and infructuous and in almost all the Articles where actions were to be taken in the "prescribed manner" by the "prescribed authority" became superficial. As the rules relating to the carrying on the provision of the Order were framed much later, the immediate rigours of law went without any remedy. With Article 15 saying application of grievances to be submitted within 3 months from the date of "commencement of the Order", the right of the citizens to even complain was taken away as the Rules came much later than three months of the date of the commencement of the order. So the little respect that appeared to have been shown to protect the rights of citizens in Article 7, 15 and 16 had no substance and the entire law may be said to have been kept outside the provision of the established principle of natural justice. Although relief under Article 7 could be availed of once the Rules were framed, in the meantime in most cases dispossession had taken place.

The Article 8 with regard to the companies having abandoned shares and Article 10 with regard to dispossessing persons on terminating agreement etc. provided no scope to even lodge a complaint. The law did not only make the government the owners of properties but gave more powers and authority than the original owners had as would be evident from Articles 5, 7, 8, 10 and 14 — in all the vital Articles of the law. Then finally, the jurisdiction of the court was also taken away by Article 24 as a result of which the district and subordinate courts could not entertain or adjudicate any petition with regard to any property once touched by the government under the P.O. 16 of 1972.

The High Court has played its due role in this regard. The definition clause has been thoroughly examined by the judges and the wild argument that under P.O. 16 even a property of a citizen of Bangladesh not present in person to occupy the property could vest in the government has been nullified. The court even went to the extent of saying that mere absence would not be enough to acquire a property ;—in such cases the government would have to form a clear opinion that such absence of a particular person had been prejudicial to the interest of Bangladesh and in not a single case which came before the court, the government could show any such opinion. In the case of Speedbird Navigation versus Government, of Bangladesh,[11] Justice Bhattacharya held that "a literal interpretation of the definition clause will lead to absurd consequences" and so the court tried to gather the true meaning from a consideration of the whole statute as the law makers could not have intended to declare every absentee's property as abandoned. In another case Justice Munim went to the extent of saying that in the absence of the owner of the property, if any member of the family was present, the property could not be treated as abandoned property[12]. Justice Kemaluddin Hossain went to the extent of saying that a mere non-occupation of a property by any owner resident should not make the property abandoned[13]. With regard to the companies registered in Bangladesh Justice Hossain held in the same case that the assets and properties of such a company were outside the ambit of the definition of abandoned property and they were immune from the operation of the provision of the Abandoned Property Order. As a company is a juristic person and would only hold and manage properties through a Board of Directors etc. such properties would not come within the purview of the abandoned property. A decision on a similar point was awarded by Justice S.M. Hossain in Messrs. Helal Jute Press Ltd. versus Government of Bangladesh[14]. In this case the court held that a company incorporated in the territory of Bangladesh could not be said to be availabe simply because the majority shareholders and the "Managing" Director were away from Bangladesh for a temporary period. Justice Munim in Messrs. A.T.J. Industries versus Government of Bangladesh[15] went further to say that the "logic of the circumstances is such that no property can be treated as abandoned property unless the Government has formed an opinion about the nature of absence of its owner and unless the formation of such opinion is established, the consequential result would be that the property cannot be viewed as having vested in the Government as an abandoned property".

The appellate Division of the Supreme Court, the highest court in the country in the first abandoned property case before it also upheld the views expressed by the Judges of the High Court or High Court Division in limiting the wideness and ambiguity of the definition of abandoned property. The court hermonised the meaning of all the clauses of the difinition in order to remove the complexity and asserted that opinion of the government was essential about the nature of absence of any person and whether such absence was prejudicial to the interest of Bangladesh[16]. The Court further held that a property taken over as an abandoned property would not *ipso facto* vest in the government unless it was really so, otherwise the government would be bound to restore the possession to the owner[17].

In this manner in a series of decisions the Court limited the scope of arbitrariness of the government machinery and gave relief to the public. But because writs from the High Court were only available from 1973, and also because of the delays and the long procedure built in the judicial system itself justice could not be availed of by all[18]. By the time the courts made their pronouncements the harshness of the law had already touched its ground and the damage was done. A large section of those who were affected could not come before the court due to fear of those who were enjoying the properties under the Awami Leage patronage or due to financial and security reasons.

Whenever a war breaks out or for that matter a new country emerges, migration and economic dislocation disturb social tranquility and economic equilibrium and in all such cases laws are made to handle special situation. Every law is claimed to have been enacted for the good of the society and so the P.O. 16 also had a meaningful purpose to serve. How good a law is depends on how it is implemented. There is always a danger that any such laws like the P. O. 16 with so much discretionary power in the hands of the executive will have a serious corroding effect in the socio-economic life of a country and more so in Bangladesh.

While the necessity of the law could not be questioned its implementation immediately provided a scope for loot and plunder mainly by the ruling class proteges. The law also provided a wide scope for exercising discretion and as a result, not only the properties of those who had left the country or who were not available but of those who were present were also taken over under the law. It was a wealth which was squandered at the very inception of Bangladesh.

In the implementation of P.O. 16 it was noticed that due to the weak and disorganised bureaucratic machine operating immediately after the independence, the political elite and the Awami League as a party in power virtually dictated the terms. The law provided a scope to loot the property of others under a legal cover. The leaders and workers of the ruling party through the terrified government officials took all the advantage of the situation and under their patronage in turn, some government functionaries, also managed to share the booty. There were cases where due to social or political petty rivalry, properties were taken over as abandoned knowing that the owners were present. Almost every property of every non-local or Bihari who migrated originally from India years ago and settled and had not opted for Pakistan was taken over as abandoned property or was under the threat of being taken over. The politicos took the advantage of the miserable state of these people[19].

As no Rule was forthcoming at the beginning, every Manager, Administrator or Board appointed under the law for any abandoned property from the largest to the smallest went to the party workers or to those who enjoyed the patronage of the Ministers or party leaders. The Management Boards created for control and administration of different classes of properties in different areas were mostly handled by the local leaders of the party or officers enjoying their patronage[20]. In various industrial and commercial units, either party workers or junior employees having no experience or technical know-how were employed as Managers. The Jute Mills, Textile Mills and hundreds of other large industries which were managed by West Pakistani businessmen or their experienced trusted Managers now fell into the hands of some unknown incompetents. The result was chaos, corruption, loot and plunder. The machineries and raw materials were sent out of the country through organised smuggling, production plummetted, properties were sold or exchanged at any price of convenience. The cash money in the office or bank belonging to such units went into private hands unaccounted. Soon most of the industries and other units either went into the red or closed down or sold out. It was perhaps a singular field where patriotism did not touch the soul of any person whether he was a Minister or a freedom fighter or a govt. employee or a member of the 16th Division—not to speak of their relatives, supporters and proteges.

Nationalisation of Banks, Insurance Companies and Major Industries

The Awami League claimed to have been committed to establish 'socialist' economic order. So it did not stop there. In order to establish 'socialism' and remove 'exploitation of man by man'[21] in less than a month from the promulgation of the Abandoned Property Order, a 'bold' step was taken on 25th March, 1972, the first anniversary of the country's independence. The Laws for nationalisation of Jute, Textile and Sugar Industries and the Banks and Insurance companies were passed and by doing so about 80 to 85 percent of the nation's entire industrial, banking and insurance business were placed under "government control". Most of these businesses, however, having belonged to the Pakistanis, were already under control of the Government under the Abandoned Property Order and the status of the Jute, Sugar and Textile Mills, the Banks and Insurance Companies left by the Pakistanis did not therefore change much as far as the control and ownership was concerned excepting that they now stood 'nationalised' instead of being abandoned.

In the Abandoned Property Order there was some scope to make representation to the Government for the release of the property and there was also scope to invoke the right of natural justice. Also the superior courts under their inherent writ jurisdiction could adjudicate an action of the Government in respect of an abandoned property. But under the Nationalisation Order there was neither any scope to make any representation nor had the government any authority to release such property. Any property once vested in the government could not be divested. According to Sheikh Mujib "measures taken were revolutionary in nature" and the new policy adopted would go "a long way towards eliminating the perennial conflict that has divided labour and capital". Mujib asserted on that day that his government believed in internal social revolution and government and party were pledged to establish an "scientific socialistic economy". In order to build a society free from exploitation and inujstice and to lay the foundation for a new society Mujib declared that his government had decided to move forward to implement the phased programme of nationalisation of key sectors of the economy[23].

Along with the Banks (excluding branches of foreign banks) Insurance Companies (excluding branches of foreign insurance companies), Jute, Textile and Sugar Industries the government also nationalised the major portion of inland and coastal shipping, all abandoned and absentee owners property with fixed assets valued at Tk. 1.5 million and the major portion of foreign trade "in pursuance of the comprehensive programme for nationalisation of foreign trade". The national airline and the national shipping organisation which were owned by the state already were now formally brought under the nationalised sector.

This nationalisation programme had a long history, and the transformation of the Awami League itself from a right-wing communal political party to a progressive nationalist party was closely linked with it. Although primarily a petty bourgeois political party, the Awami League worked gradually through different phases towards adopting a more radical programme in its public commitment. Whether the minimum economic and political base needed to sustain a socialist economy was prevailing in the country or not, from a long time even prior to the independence of Bangladesh almost all the major political parties of the country were committed to establish some form of a socialist economy[24]. Whether the parties understood the actual ramifications of nationalisation of such magnitude in an extremely weak socio-economic infra-structural framework and whether they had the political machinery to implement such programmes need to by examined. Further, as some argued, whether they were just influenced by radical thoughts and beliefs has to be studied in its correct perspective. Even if the National Awami Party (Bhashani) or the National Awami Party (Muzaffar) or the Jatio Samajtrantik Dal had been in the place of the Awami League in the same given socio-economic conditions and under the prevailing administrative framework, it would have had to be seen how much they could be successful in this regard.

The Awami League and all the major political parties made a commitment for nationalisation of jute as far back as 1954 when they staged a crushing defeat on the ruling Muslim League[25] on the basis of their historic 21-point programme[26]. Beside the nationalisation of jute, the United Front also pledged to ensure fair prices for the jute growers and to minimise the income disparity between the high and low salaried employees[27]. The latter two demands, though they did not directly feature as a socialist programme, were indicative of the cause of the have-nots of the society. They were included in the 21-point Programme at the instance of the leftists in the United front and were considered as progressive demands.

From then on at various stages of political movements and developments, the political parties adopted more and more radical programmes. Although the Awami League suffered a political set back due to its role in 1956-57[28] when it joined the central government of Pakistan and supported the one unit programme for West Pakistan, the party did not change its pledge on these issues. On the contrary, when it exposed itself as a rightist political party and lost its face in public in the context of the inner-struggle led by the Moulana,[29] the Awami League in order to recover its lost popularity tried to compete with the newly formed National Awami Party in respect of economic programme.

In the 1960s when the left led by the Moulana lent support to Ayub Khan because of the latter's China policy the Awami League fully recovered its position as a mass-based political party and emerged as a nationalist force in the political vacuum created by the Moulana. In the 1965 Presidential election under the Basic Democracy system the Awami League's position further improved due to the National Awami Party's indirect support for Ayub Khan. Finally after the Indo-Pak War in 1965 and with the announcement of the 6-point Programme for a 'real and meaningful' autonomy for East Pakistan, the popular movement of the Bengalis came to the fold of the Awami League[30].

In 1968-69, during the great mass-upsurge, the popular movement led by the students, was based on the 11-point Programme. The Programme was an extension of the Awami League's 6-point scheme while it included the demand of autonomy as envisaged in the 6-point Programme ; it also incorporated certain economic demands which included nationalisation of banks, insurance companies and all big industries. It also demanded reduction of taxes and revenues for peasants and fair wages and bonuses for workers. This 11-point programme, although not a well-drafted document, became the rallying point of a historical nationalist convulsion backed by sponteneous mass support[31]. The success of this movement, which led to the unconditional withdrawal of the Agartala Conspiracy Case and established

Mujib as the undisputed leader of the Bengalis, had a deeper impact and it ultimately resulted in the independence movement in 1971. The Awami League accepted the 11-point programme in full and so did many other political parties ; the programme dominated the political scene right through the 1970-71 general elections[32].

In the manifestos of the 1970-71 elections of all the major political parties, the economic programmes reflected the earlier movements and demands. Although in this election the demand for autonomy and its quantum was the principal issue, yet the economic programme was not unimportant. The Awami League pledged to establish a socialist economic order in order to remove economic injustice between man and man and in the process nationalisation of all key industries in the following priority—banking, insurance, heavy industries, foreign trade, jute trade, cotton trade, inter-wing and international transport including shipping and other key industries to be determined by planning agency. It also pledged for the industrial workers participation in equity capital and management of industrial enterprise, abolition of Zamindari, Jaigirdari and Sardari system and exemption of land revenue upto the holding of 25 bighas (8.2 acres).

The National Awami Party (Bhashani) also through its manifesto pledged nationalisation of all basic industries including banking, insurance and vested capital of bureaucrats and imperialists by which they meant to take some more drastic measures than the Awami League had pledged. The National Awami Party of Wali Khan (pro-Moscow) had in its programme included nationalisation of basic industries, banks, insurance etc. and setting up of socio-economic order free from all types of exploitation. The Pakistan People's Party of Zulfikar Ali Bhutto aimed at achieving "equality among all classes of people through Islamic socialism." The party pledged for nationalisation of all financial institutions and all the basic industries.

The right-wing parties generally kept silent on the issue of nationalisation and gave more importance to the preservation of Islamic values. Almost all of them were in favour of establishing a society re-oriented in true Islamic spirit and Islamic values (PDP) and "preservation of ideology of Pakistan guided by equality as enunciated by the Holy Quran and Sunnah" (ML Convention). "Social environment to be moulded in accordance with the tenets of Islam (Jamat-i-Islam) and "integrity and solidarity of Pakistan based on Islam" was to be maintained (ML Council). But interestingly enough, although they did not directly argue for nationalisation none of these political parties took up any stand against nationalisation of key sectors.

So the demand for nationalisation of the key industries in Pakistan developed through a socio-political process. Mass starvation, poverty, unemployment and other social conditions demanded radical changes and adoption of progressive programmes by the political parties. Further, the idea of nationalisation gained support rapidly because the bulk of wealth had concentrated in the hands of a few families in Pakistan and all the major political parties of both the wings of Pakistan were led to demand nationalisation of assets enjoyed by a few business houses. For the Bengalis however the programme received strength from the fact that all these families belonged to West Pakistan. The overall effect of exploitation by the West Pakistani merchant class widened the disparities between the two wings more and more and this laid the foundation of their struggle for achieving economic justice through nationalisation[33]. Moreover in East Pakistan, as politics continued to stimulate radical concepts, major political forces committed themselves to introduce socialism. Unlike in West Pakistan, the major political forces in East Pakistan were subjected to an inherent compulsion to change the socio-economic structure of the society quickly on an ideological basis. The question is whether these compulsions were matched with capacity and preparedness require a seperate study.

Nevertheless, the fact is that although the demand for nationalisation of key sectors primarily developed in the context of the economic structure of Pakistan, it was also a political commitment made to the people for about 2 decades. With the emergence of Bangladesh, the over-all context might have changed but the Awami League continued to proceed with the same manifesto. In the changed circumstances, the industries and business belonging to Pakistanis had already come under the control of the government, there were no 22-families any more to amass national wealth and the exploitation of East Pakistan had ended. It is not known whether the leaders of the Awami League looked into this aspect in the new context and yet felt the necessity of going ahead with their programme. Was the party guided by ideological commitments?

But the tragedy is that the Awami League as a political party had no ideological foundation and it had no socialist orientation. It had no cadre who could bring the fruits of a socialist economic order to the common man through their dedication and hard work. The socio-economic background, and class character of the Awami League did not suggest that they could have a cadre of that kind[34]. What happened was that the Awami League made public commitments which they were unable to accomplish. Every modern political party suffers from such kind of contradictions but this contradiction was much too serious in nature and the Awami League could not over come it. With all the sincere intention Mujib might have had to establish a socialist order he was in effect cought between public morality and private life and between public commitment and private beliefs and habits.

Interestingly enough, although Mujib in his address to the nation outlined that as a step to build "a society free from exploitation and injustice" a phased programme of nationalisation was necessary, the Nationalisation Order itself did not mention anything to that effect. The preamble of the Order only said that "it was expedient to provide for the nationalisation of certain industrial enterprises". The interesting feature is that unlike the nationalisation of all assets as was done when steel was nationlised by the British government, only the shares of the industrial enterprises were vested in and allotted to the government free of any trust, mortgage, charge, lien, interest or other encumbrances whatsoever and the government was made the sole shareholder of such industrial enterprise (Article 4). The immediate legal effect of it was that the industries which were either private or public companies was to continue to retain their legal entity along with their respective assets and liabilities.

The other salient points were : (1) the industrial enterprises of the basic sectors such as jute, textile and sugar were identified separately and put into 3 schedules. The first schedule included 67 jute mills, the second schedule included 64 cotton mills and the third schedule included 15 sugar mills. Three distinct corporations, namely Bangladesh Jute Mills Corporation, Bangladesh Cotton Mills Corporation and Bangladesh Sugar Mills Corporation were created to manage these 3 sectors (Article 10). Besides these 3 corporations, seven more corporations were also created to manage the industries vested in the government under the Abandoned Property Order or any other property owned by the government which could be placed under them[35]. The corporations were Steel, Paper and Board, Fertilizer, Chemical and Pharmaceutical, Engineering and Shipbuilding, Mineral, Oil and Gas, Food and Allied Products and Forest (Article 10(d)).

With regard to the payment of compensation the order provided that the government would pay such compensation as would be determined in respect of the shares vested in the government under article 4 but the compensation would not exceed the paid up value of such shares (Article 9).

Although many amendments were made subsequently to this Order, they are not relevant for this discussion with one vital exception. The Nationalisation Order envisaged two categories of properties, one directly falling in the Nationalised sectors—Jute, Cotton and Sugar and the other were the Abandoned Properties brought under the purview of the Order. This distinction was introduced by naming the industries in the nationalised sector as "scheduled industrial enterprises". It was to be noticed that almost all the operative provisions were related to only the nationalised or scheduled industrial enterprises. However, by a subsequent amendment excepting Article 9 relating to the payment of compensation difference between the scheduled enterprises (nationalised) and the abandoned properties was removed and both kinds of properties were treated as the same with all legal consequences. The effect was that once an industrial enterprise was placed under any of the 7 corporations other than those corporations set up for the industries originally nationalised the same industries also stood automatically nationalised and could not be divested. Once vested under this Order even the government had no authority to divest it[37]. If some shares in a company were not abandoned under the Abandoned Property Order, all the shares of the company including those not abandoned could vest in the government under Article 4[38]. So under the garb of this amendment of the Order not only were a large number of abandoned industrial units nationalised but the abandoned units in which all shares did not vest in the government or were disputed or could be released under the Abandoned Property Order, could also be nationalised.

Nevertheless, the Supreme Court in The Chairman, Bangladesh Steel Mills Corporation vs. Md. Masood Reza and others held that property of a citizen could not be acquired by the government so easily[39]. The Court went on to argue that if a property was not abandoned at the first instance its taking over by the government was illegal ; such action could not be legalised under the garb of another statute. If a property was not an abandoned property, mere placement of it with a corporation under Article 10(1)(d) would not *ipso facto* vest it in the government under Article 4 of the Nationalisation Order. The Court held that since the government could place a property mentioned in Article 10 (1) (d) of the Nationalisation Order under a corporation it could as well withdraw the same[40]. But following the decision of the Supreme Court and despite the fact that the government was given the power under Ordinance 1 of 1976 to transfer such properties back to its owner,[41] the government went for a despotic law by promulgating a Martial Law Regulation VII[42] to nullify even the decisions of the Supreme Court with respect to abandoned properties and assumed absolute control over the abandoned properties whether taken over by the government with or without the sanction of Law.

As indicated earlier a vast majorty of the properties had already come under the absolute control of the government under the Abandoned Property Order. About 90% of the bank and insurance business and about 80% of the industries belonged to the Pakistanis were already being treated as abandoned and managed by the management Boards, Administrators, Managers and persons appointed by the Government. So the Nationalisation Order immediately affected the Bengali entrepreneurs who owned a sizeable number of Jute and Textile Mills and were engaged in foreign trade particularly relating to jute. Had there been no nationalisation, the few industries owned by the Bengali entrepreneurs would have remained in the private sector and yet the government could still control the vast majority of industries, banks and insurance companies i.e. the overall economy. But nationalisation was a political act pursued to control the economy of the country leaving no scope to the Bengali capitalist class to dominate or influence the politics of the country.

Further, it is evident that no detail plan to handle the nationalisation scheme was drawn up. The vast majority of the industries were already under government control and were by this time largely managed by the Awami League leaders, workers and their favourites. No principles or criterion were fixed and no minimum qualifications were prescribed for them who were appointed to run the business and above all, no inventory was in the hand of the government of any industry whether taken over earlier or now. The measures taken by the government now were limited to the creation of some corporation to supervise and co-ordinate the affairs of the business and as far as the industries owned by the Bengali entrepreneurs were concerned the government for the time being allowed the existing owners to continue with the management of those industries (Article 8 of the Nationalisation Order).

It took a long time for the Corporations to establish their offices, appoint staff and other facilities to start functioning effectively and bring the industries under their control. The Government also took time in appointing the Boards and other higher Executives for such Corporations. Besides, nepotism and favouritism in constituting and manning these corporations vitiated any nation-building mission the Government might have attempted to set in motion. The properties both abandoned and nationalised remained in the meantime virtually without any account. The properties of the industries were plundered and machineries and raw materials were smuggled out,[44] corruption rose to its height and a huge flight of capital during this trasition made the country only poorer. The Bengali owners who were asked to manage the industries also had no more interest in developing them in this interim period. Although they had the experience and know-how of running their Mills, they employed this expertise more for their own benefit than for the industries which they grudged to have been taken away from them. For a while, nationalisation took the form of expropriation by the gunboots of the ruling party. The result was that the production went down, the volume of black money not only increased but multiplied and a soaring inflation affected every sphere of the economic life.

If the nationalisation was necessary so soon in the context of a free Bangladesh the utter carelessness shown in management of the properties vitiated all the justification it could have. It is true that the magnitude of dislocation occured due to the war and the consequent migration of a large number of expertise to Pakistan was beyond any comprehension and the industries suffered a great set-back for these reasons too, the fact remained that the performance of the Government was poor and the behaviour of the ruling party members did not match the ideology they preached.

So it is not so much the act of nationalisation but its management that disappointed the people, brought failure for the Awami League and miseries to the nation. Compared to 1969-70, the export earning went down by 36. 38% in 1972-73, The production of sugar declined by 79%, newsprints by 25%, matches by 44%, cigarettes by 65%, paper by 51% jute manufacturing by 24% and the earning from raw jute was less than 2/3 of the estimate. The jute mills alone lost 250 million taka in 1972-73. The money supply increased from Tk. 387 crores as on 16.12.1971 to Tk. 696 crores in 1972-73,[45] without having much relation with production,

Banks and Insurance Companies

On the same day, 26th March, 1972 the Bangladesh Banks (Nationalisation) Order was promulgated[46]. Altogether 12 banks, including all their branches were taken over by the government under this Order and they were reconstituted and integrated into six newly created banks with new names. The Order provided the mechanism by which these banks would be managed and specified the kinds of business the banks would transact. All the existing banks were dissolved and unlike the provisions made in the Nationalisation Order, in the Banking sector no interim arrangement was made for the management of the banks in the sense that all the existing Board of Directors particularly those owned by the Bengalis were also dissolved and on the commencement of the Order the Chairman and other Directors of such Boards ceased to function (Article 32). Unlike the nationalisation of industries the undertaking of the banks as a whole including all their assets were nationalised and not the shares as in the case of the former.

As in the case of the industrial enterprises the government through the nationalisation order though created separate bodies to run the businesses retained adequate scope for political control over these institutions. As a result, on the Board of Directors in respect of the bank, the government appointed members or supporters of the Awami League many of whom had otherwise no qualification to be on such Board. Like the Corporations, it also took a considerable time to organise the administrative machinery of these banks, and hence anarchy prevailed in the financial institutions too. Because of the general chaos, the banking industry suffered considerably. The Banking rules and lending procedures were violated frequently to meet political economic pressure. Allegedly, it was difficult for genuine businessmen to take the advantage of banking in those days, as banks were largely used as sources of political patronage. Nepotism and favouritism in manning the banks made it difficult to restore any discipline. At one stage bank-loot became almost a daily affair[47]. Organised groups in connivance with the bank employees would break open the safe and take the cash away without any resistance. Because of the weak administration and frequent political interference a large number of these bank robberies used to go either undetected or unpunished.

Relief and Rehabilitation Programme

On achieving independence the Awami League government faced two broad challenges, one was of rehabilitation and restoration, the other was of reconstruction and development. The gigantic task of rehabilitation included the return of 10 million refugees who took shelter in India, repair and construction of 4.3 million houses which were burned or destroyed during the war, restoration of homeless destitutes created by the war situation within the country and arrangement of land, food and other supplies to those who required rehabilitation[48]. The entire exercise was taken up mainly through administrative orders and by creating new political agencies down to the grass-root level.

A massive relief and rehabilitation programme was therefore undertaken by the government financed and assisted by the United Nations agencies and innumerable foreign charitable organisations Assistance also came from a large number of countries all over the world. The government reconstituted the Red Cross Society at the national level and down below and created agencies of its own dominated by the party leaders and workers. While the operation was a difficult and complicated one, steps taken and men employed for the purpose and the implementation progress of the operation itself produced far-reaching social, economic and political consequences.

In this national operation the Awami League did not want to involve any other political party, More so, they were suspicious of others including the officials and an overall sense of distrust prevailed at that time. They suspected everyone who was not directly involved in the independence struggle. The extent of genuineness of this feeling was difficult to assess but in the process it was found that they wanted to keep everything under their control and thereby enjoy the benefits of independence. The government or the party could not entrust this task with the existing local councils and municipal committees who traditionally carried out these functions. It was alleged that many of them were members of peace committee created for the collaboration with the Pakistan Army. So the government created a new agency called the Relief Committees.

Relief Committees

On January 9, 1972 Kamaruzzaman the Relief Minister outlined the constitution of the Relief Committees from village to District levels for the purpose of organising and implementing the programme of relief and rehabilitation[49]. Under administrative order, the government sought the co-operation of the people of all walks of life in resettling and rehabilitating the returnees of Bangladesh evacuees from India as well as displaced and affected persons inside the country. Dedicated efforts of every citizen was thought to be essential "to handle the greatest programme of relief and rehabilitation that the world had ever seen." A committee, according to the government statement, was to be constituted at every village, union, thana, sub-division and District level with elected representatives, members of the public and officials of the concerned departments.

The Village Relief and Rehabilitation Committee, popularly became known as Relief Committee, was constituted with 5 to 10 members, depending on area and population of the village. They were selected by the MNAs and MPAs[50] of the area from amongst local leaders, teachers, freedom fighters and local workers.

In the same manner, following almost the same line, instructions were issued to form committees at the Union, Thana and Sub-divisional level. The District Relief committe consisted of 5 MNAs and MPAs as members to be selected by all the MNAs and MPAs of the District. The Chairman of the Sub-divisional Relief Committee was also a member of this Committee. Five other non-official members were nominated by the government from amongst the members of the public. The MNAs and MPAs of the District also selected one to be the Chairman of the District Committee.

A few words may be said about these Committees :

(1) The powers., and functions of the committees were vague and undefined.

(2) The formation of these committees had no legal backing[51] ; the rights and obligations of the members and chairmen of the committees were neither defined nor enforceable.

(3) These Committees were dominated by the Awami League members at all levels.

(4) Since there was hardly any MNA or MPA belonging to the opposition (only one belonged to opposition and one was independent in the Constitutent Assembly) all committees from the District down to the village level were either consisted of the Awami League MNAs or MPAs or of people selected by them including the chairmen of such committees.

(5) The Committees were merely an extension of the ruling party.

(6) There was no legal way to make the committees accountable in terms of accounting and inventory.

Bangladesh received more than a billion dollar in aid and grant for relief, and rehabilitation purposes, and reliefs were distributed through these committees all over the country. The decisions to handle a situation of this magnitude through a political machinery might not have been bad provided dedication and patriotic zeal were the guiding spirit. The constitution of these committees to go into the first major national rebuilding programme over the head of the bureaucratic machine established the superiority of the political elite in the execution of the work.

In the actual implementation of the rehabilitation programme what happened was something different. The Awami League leaders immediately got into the business of appointing committees in their respective areas and in the process entered into serious fights between themselves. Every one wanted to have his own man in the committee and as a result. right from the grass-root level, bitter factionalism developed and their organisational unity was destroyed. As these committees became the principal instrument to share power and authority, attempts to get included in the committees amongst the workers became fierce. As a result, the main purpose of having a political missionery zeal was lost and a large portion of the relief goods was squandered with no system of maintaining and checking the inventories. Without any accountability. corruption now trickled down to the grass-root level of the society. The social impact was that whoever could get involved in such committees made something for himself, destroying the moral fibre on some very petty gains. The Relief Committees at large earned a bad name all over the country. the stigma of which the Awami League had to bear for a long time[52]. One of the reasons why the people dislike the Awami League even today was because of their handling and mismanagement of the relief goods.

On the other hand once the Relief Committees were constituted, the existing local councils and Municipal Committees were found to create rivalry or friction. Provisions were made to dissolve and reconstitute all the existing local councils and municipal committees[53] by a Presidential order on 1st January 1972.

The reasons put forward for the dissolution of these committees were said to have been that they did not represent the people and that there had been persistent demand from the party workers for their dissolution. The law also made provisions for the performance of functions of such committees by alternative means. Accordingly, all the local councils and municipal committees were dissolved at once and all the chairmen of the union councils, administrators and members of such committees ceased to hold office. A union council was now to be called a Union Panchayat, a Thana Committee as Shahar Committee, a District Council as Zilla Board and a Municipal Committee as Pourashava (Article 3). Provisions were made to constitute new adhoc committees for the exercise of powers and functions of the dissolved local councils and municipal committees. The Sub-Divisional Officer was to appoint a committee in the case of a Union Panchayat or Shahar Committee and the Government would appoint a committee in the case of Zilla Board or Pourashava. The Union Panchayat and Shahar Committees were to have one Chairman and such number of members to be decided by the Government and in the Zilla Board there would be a Chairman, a Vice-Chairman and such number of members as the Government would determine. In the interim period till such committees were constituted the powers and functions of the Union Panchayat or Shahar Committee was to be exercised and performed by a Chairman to be appointed by the Sub-Divisional Officers and the powers and function of a Zilla Board or Pourashava were to be exercised and performed by an administrator to be appointed by the Government (Article 4). According to this Order, the Divisional Councils, Thana Councils and the Union Committees were not to be reconstituted.

So the local councils and municipal committees, the important local institutions were now dissolved and the government did not take any action in this regard for a long time. Though the law provided that the Sub-divisional Officer would appoint union and shahar committees and the government would appoint zilla and pourashava committees, none of them could be done in the absence of rules or instructions from the government.

On February 11, the Minister for Local Government announced that the government had decided to introduce a "Panchayat System" as an interim arrangement with immediate effect at the union level till a fresh election was held by the local bodies after a new law was made. The government had decided that the members of the local union panchayats would be selected from each ward (the lowest block comprising one or more villages) by the local members of the Constituent Assembly in consultation with other local "political leaders". The Chairman of the Panchayat would be appointed from among the members selected by the Sub-divisional Officer in consultation with the local members of the Constituent Assembly and other political leaders. The Minister also announced that the Thana Councils would be reconstituted into Thana Development Committees by the representatives of the people and there would be no official nominee. In Zilla Boards every Thana would be represented. Nothing more was elaborated excepting that the Minister announced that the government had adopted a programme of Gram Karmi Bahini—Village Workers Force consisting of 1,00,000 young men largely drawn from among the freedom fighters and unemployed youths with a minimum ten members from each union. The proposal relating to the Gram Karmi Bahini did not come within the purview of the law and so need not be discussed here.

Following the statement made by the Minister on 28th February an amendment was made to the original Order in which Article 3 was substituted dissolving all the local councils and municipal committees : the union committee and Thana council which were omitted earlier were renamed as Nagar Panchayat and Thana Development Committee respectively[54]. The amendment also provided that till such committees were constituted the power and function of the Nagar Panchayat would be exercised and performed by a Chairman to be appointed by the Sub-divisional Officer and the Thana Development Committee by the Circle Officer (Dev.) concerned.

It therefore now appeared that almost identical principles were applied for the constitution of committees at the union level as in the case of Relief committees. The intention was clearly a political one i. e. to take over the local bodies under the control of the ruling party. However, undemocratic the previous bodies were, the new committees could not be called democratic either. So all the local committees were to go into the hands of the Awami League. When it was said that the committee was to be formed in consultation with the local leaders meant consultation with the local Awami League leaders. This created further factionalism among the Constituent Assembly members and the Awami League leaders. While efforts were made in constituting the Committees, the party central leadership faced the same experience of increased feud among its own party workers as they noticed earlier when the Relief Committees were formed. Consequently, the fear of having parallel or rival committees to the already formed Relief Committees also discouraged the government at the end from going ahead with constituting committees at the Union and Thana level. On 10th September a second amendment was introduced giving retrospective effect from 26th April, 1972[55]. Article 4 relating to the appointment of committees was again substituted to provide running of these institutions other than the Divisional Council and Union Committee, simply by an administrator. For the Union Panchayat, the Union Agricultural Assistant and if no such assistant was available, then the Tahsilder was made the Administrator : For the Thana Agricultural Council, Circle Officer (Dev). and Shahar Committee, Circle Officer (Revenue) or if there was no such officer, any officer appointed by the Sub-divisional Officer. It did not say who would run the Union Committee i.e. Nagar Panchayat and the Divisional Council.

In the course of the massive rehabilitation programme for refugees and the destitutes, the government faced another serious problem for which a new special law had to be made. When the refugees who had left Bangladesh during the war had returned to their houses besides the damage and destruction of property, a large number of them particularly the Hindus discovered that some other people were occupying and enjoying their properties. In many cases the Pakistan government had auctioned the properties of the political leaders and workers who took part in the war and transferred their properties to other people during that period and the persons whose properties were auctioned mainly belonged to the Awami League. So in order to provide law for the restoration of possession of evacuee property in Bangladesh and for matters incidental thereto on February 17, 1972 the Bangladesh (Restoration of Evacuee Property) Order, 1972[56] promulgated. That was meant to remain in force upto 25th March, 1974.

To give effect to the provision of this law for the restoration of possession of properties to their original owner three forums were created. One was an Arbitration Court at the Union level, a Court of Thana Magistrate at the Thana level and a Tribunal at the Sub-division level.

The law provided that any person who was in an unauthorised occupation of any property which was in actual possession of an evacuee on March 25, 1971 must deliver possession of that property to the evacuee within 7 days of the demand made by the evacuee for such possession (Article 6). But if such person refused or failed to deliver possession of such property within the time allowed the evacuee could file an application to the Arbitration court of the relevant union asking for restoration of such property by evicting the unauthorised occupant.

On receipt of such an application, the Arbitration court first had to ascertain from both the parties whether they agreed to arbitration and if so then it was to hold a local enquiry, examine evidence, oral and documentary adduced by both sides and on the basis of its findings pass the necessary order either allowing or rejecting the application. Such order would be final and binding upon the parties. If the parties however did not agree to the arbitration even then the Arbitration Council would hold local enquiry etc. and send its findings along with the record of the case to the Thana Magistrate. The Thana Magistrate then would consider the findings of Arbitration Court and other evidence on record and on further enquiry and hearing both the parties pass an order in writing either allowing or rejecting the application, making such order final and binding on both the parties unless the aggrieved party filed an appeal (Article 7 (b)). The Tribunal was made an appellate forum where any person aggrieved by an order of a Thana Magistrate could within fourteen (14) days file an appeal and the order of the Tribunal on such appeal was to be final and binding on both the parties. Moreover, on an application for the restoration of possession once allowed by the Arbitration Court or Thana Magistrate or the Tribunal would cause the possession of the property to be delivered to the applicant by evicting the unauthorised occupant byusing necessary force if required [Article 7(5)].

With regard to the movable property of an evacuee it was provided that anyone who had misappropriated such property or caused loss or damage to the property unlawfully would be liable to pay compensation to be assessed by the Arbitration Court or the Magistrate. If however, the property could be restored without causing much loss, in such case no compensation would be payable. The provision for appeal in this regard was also made.

In order to ensure smooth and quick operation of these forums, provisions were made in the Act so that (1) the Arbitration Court or the Tribunal could hold their sittings within their jurisdiction as the Chairman of the Court or Tribunal would fix. (2) If any member of the Court or Tribunal was unable to attend for any reason during the course of hearing in a case, the hearing would continue before other members. (3) If there was any difference of opinion, amongst its member whether Court or Tribunal, the opinion of the majority would prevail (4) Administrative arrangements would be made by the Chairman of the Court or Tribunal.

Under Article 10, the Court, Magistrate and the Tribunal could issue summons to any person to appear within 3 days and give evidence or to produce or cause the production of any document and if any person wilfully disobeyed such summons, the Court or the Magistrate or the Tribunal could take cognizance of such disobedience and after giving such person an opportunity to explain, could sentence him to fine not exceeding 20 takas and provision made for recovery of such fine. It was provided by Article 13 that every police officer of his respective area would assist the Arbitration Court or Thana Magistrate or any person authorised by them seeking aid in the lawful exercise of any power conferred upon them under this Order. All settlements of evacuee property granted by the government between March 26, 1971 and December 16, 1971 were made null and void by Article 12.

Despite this law however any person could move any competent court to establish his right to title to any evacuee property or to execute any decree or order for possession and in a case where a suit was filed in a civil court, the period of limitation was relaxed to the extent of the period between the specified date and the commencement of the Order. The law however at the same time took away the jurisdiction of all the courts including the High Court to call in question any order passed or any action taken under the law except as expressly provided in the Order.

Unlike the instructions or provisions made relating to the formation of Relief Committees and local bodies this law was an instrument of superior quality and contained a more professional approach, although the procedure adopted was summary in nature the legal process delayed the remedy. The scope for nomination by the Sub-divisional Magistrate was though subject to interference by the political leaders but on the whole the mechanism to some extent ensured a system outside political influence.

Although Article 11(4) provided that the law would not affect the right of any person to go to any competent court to establish his right or title but it appeared to be somewhat contradictory to the entire spirit of the law including Article 14 which excluded the Court. But nevertheless this exception was meant to relate only to the title and not to the possession of the property.

FOOTNOTES

1. During the war the government in exile under pressure from people like the author himself and many others created certain cells like planning cell, research cell, etc. but no substantial result was produced by any one of them. The cells could have contributed a lot if the leaders had shown interest. A position paper prepared by the Research Cell where the author was also working pointed out some problems the Government was going to face once the independence was achieved. The paper is produced in appendix 'D'. The paper is in possession of the author in its original form.
2. Article 47 of the Constitution of 1972 first, schedule, The law of the Pakistan period was the State Acquisition and Tenancy Act, 1950.
3. They left 725 industrial enterprises with assets worth Tk. 2886 million. These companies controlled 47% of the Bangladesh's modern industrial assets and 71% of its private industry. They relinquished six of the leading commercial banks which controlled 70% of the deposits of the entire banking system in the region and in the insurance sector Bengali firms only held 10% of life assets.
   See Rahman Sobhan, " The Crisis of the Bourgeois Order and the Growth of Authoritarian Political Trends in Bangladesh", *South Asian Studies* 2 Delhi, Oxford University Press. 1982.

4. 27 DLR 1975 p. 171. Para 21, See also p. 35 infra and footnote.
5. See also 27 DLR 1975 p. 51 paragraph 26 on the same point.
6. Known as the P.O. 16 of 1972 promulgated on 28th February, 1972.
7. From the day the Pakistan Army cracked down the effective control was still with the Pakistan Government till the Pakistan Army surrendered on 16th December, 1971.
8. This ouster clause in the P.O. 16 however did not take away the writ jurisdiction of the High Court Division which was later reintroduced by Article 102 of the Constitution. This clause therefore, ousted only the jurisdiction of the District Courts and below known as subordinate courts.
9. But these remedial provisions could not be availed by the public.
10. The Bangladesh Abandoned Property (Taking Over Possesion) Rules, 1972.
The Bangladesh Abandoned Property (Buildings in Urban Areas) Rules, 1972.
The Bangladesh Abandoned Property (Commercial Concerns) Rules, 1972.
The Bangladesh Abandoned Property (Industries) Rules, 1972.
11. This was the first substantive judgement by the High Court Division on abandoned property matter delivered on June 18, 1974.
Speedbird Navigation Company vs. Government of Bangladesh, 27 DLR 1975 p. 170.
12. Abdur Rashid vs. Government of Bangladesh
27 DLR 1975 p. 615.
13. M/s. Khan Brothers vs. Government of Bangladesh
27 DLR 1975 p. 423.
14. 27 DLR 1975 p. 551.
15. 28 DLR 1976 p. 27.
16. 28 DLR 1976 p. 120.
17. 30 DLR 1978 p. 101.
18. The earliest case in the High Court Division was decided only in 1974 and in the Appellate Division in 1976.
19. Messrs. Standard Manufacturing Co. Ltd. Speedbird Navigation Co. Ltd. and ATJ
20. The most important one was headed by Gazi Golam Mostafa as Chairman. It was named the Central Board for supervision, control and management of all commericial and industrial establishments of Dacca, Tejgaon and Tongi industrial area including firms, shops, abandoned houses, petrol pumps, cottage industries, hotels and cinema halls.—*The Morning News*, Dacca, January 4, 1972.
21. The Awami League leaders and workers suffered humiliation. imprisonment and death for about 20 years and now they behaved in such a manner as if it was their turn to compensate themselves and enjoy their life. The Awami League members thus claimed to have acquired a right to improve their economic condition.
22. The Bangladesh Banks (Nationalisation) Order, 1972 P.O. No. 26 of 1972.
The Bangladesh Industrial Enterprises (Nationalisation) Order, 1972 (P.O. 27 of 1972).
23. *Bangabandhu Speaks*: *A collection of speeches and statements* published by the External Publicity Division, Ministry of Foreign Affairs, Government of Bangladesh, BGP-71. 72-2787 F-3M
24. The Muslim League was no more considered as a major political party. It lost its hold over the people and alienated itself from the mainstream of political current in the country. Other than the Muslim League and some other minor right-wing parties, all major political parties particularly of East Pakistan, were committed for some kind of a socialist economy. See the author's book, *Bangladesh*: *Constitutional Quest for Autonomy*. *op. cit.*
25. The Muslim League never regained their strength and continued to be considered as a political party without any mass support.
26. Point 12 of the 21-point Programme.

27. By restructuring the Government Employees Pay Scales both the governments of Mujib and Ziaur Rahman have maintained this commitment. See the National Pay Scales implemented in 1973-1974 and 1978-1979.
28. During this period Suhrawardy claimed that 98% autonomy was guaranteed for East Pakistan in the 1956 constitution and he became the Prime Minister of Pakistan.
29. In July, 1957 Moulana, the founder of the Awami League formed a new political party, consisting of all porgressive forces. For more on this see author's book, *Bangladesh : Constitutional Quest for Autonomy*, pp. 56-60.
30. For the role of the opposition in 1962-69 see author's book, *Bangladesh ; Constitutional Quest for Autonomy*, pp. 77-81.
31. On the great mass upsurge, 1968-69 including movement of the 11-point programme. See author's book, *Bangladesh* : *Constitutional Quest for Autonomy*, pp. 132-160.
32. After winning a massive victory in the elections, the Awami League on January 3, 1971 held an oath-taking ceremony at the Dacca Race Course before a mamoth gathering administered by Sheikh Mujib himself to the effect that the elected representatives would never betray the cause of the people as envisaged in the 6 and 11 point programmes.
33. On economic dispartities and concentration of wealth in West Pakistan see the Tables in author's book, *Bangladesh* : *Constitutional Quest for Autonomy*, p. 12-15.
34. On the class character of the Awami League, and the socio-economic background of Awami League leaders, See Talukder Muniruzzaman, *Radical Politics and the Emergence of Bangladesh*, pp. 29-36 ; Raunaq Jahan, *Bangladesh Politics* : *Problems and Issues*. Dacca, University Press Limited, Table 3, 4 and 5, pp. 148-150.
35. 237 industries were nationalised and 526 manufacturing units were brought under the control of the government as abandoned property. 12 banks and 44 insurance companies were nationalised. The Awami League supplement published in Dacca newspapers on 4th March, 1973.
36 President's Order No. 145 of 1972.
37. Article 47(2) of the Constitution of the People's Republic of Bangladesh. See the proviso.
38. Case of Esastern Refinery Ltd. —27 DLR 1975, p. 468.
39. 30 DLR 1980, p. 169.
40. *Ibid.*
41. By Ordinance No. 1 of 1976 the Government was however, empowered to transfer such properties or interests which were owned by Bengalis if prior to the placing under a Corporation such properties or shares or interests were vested in the Government under the Abandoned Property Order. The Ordinance was issued under the Martial Law authority. This aspect of the Ordinance superseded Article 47 (2) of the Constitution where divesting of any such property could not be done by the Government. See Article 47(2) of the Constitution. Only the Parliament with not less than two-thirds of the total number of members could pass a bill for divesting such property.
42. Masood Reza case was decided on 30th June, 1977 and the Martial Law Regulation No. VII of 1977 was promulgated on 7th October, 1977. By this regulation any property which was taken over as an abandoned property by the government despite any defect in the right or authority to take it over would vest and be deemed always to have vested in the government. Furthermore, any such action of the government could not be questioned by any court. The Regulation also abated all pending proceedings before any court and annulled all the judgements of the courts relating to abandoned property excepting where property was already restored in pursuance of the judgement declared earlier. The Regulation defeated the Supreme Court judgement. See the effect of this Regulation in Halima Khatoon v. Government of Bangladesh, 30 DLR 1980, SC, p. 208.

43. During the era of Ayub Khan, privileges to set up industries meant almost 85 to 90% government subsidy in the form of loan, tax holiday etc. Very few entrepreneurs could be said to have suffered much of personal financial loss although they were deprived of the facilities enjoyed as Chairman, Directors, etc. and lost their entrepreneurship. All the industries owed a huge sum of money to the Government and the financial institutions. The total liability of the nationalised sector stood at Tk. 5375.8 million, *Daily Ittefaq* July, 17, 1973.

44. Statement of Mr. A. N. Hamidullah, Governor, Bangladesh Bank, *The Daily Ittefaq*, September 2, 1973.

45. Collected from different newspapers, Planning Commission's Reports and the Parliamentary Proceedings. 1973-74.

    The 12 corportions in the nationalised sector incurred a loss of Tk. 930 million in less than 18 months.—The *Daily Ittefaq*, June 3, 1973.

    The Industry Minister admitted it to be Tk. 320 million.—The *Daily Ittefaq*, June 23, 1973.

    The total liability of the nationalised sector stood at Tk. 5375.8 million.—The *Daily Ittefaq*, July 23, 1973.

    Since the nationalisation the Jute Mills Corporation lost Tk. 250 million, Sugar Corporation 70 million, Paper Mills 35 million, Steel Mills 15 million and Mineral Corporation 11 million,—*Sonar Bangla*, October 7, 1973.

    By June, 1974 in the Jute Sector alone the loss rose to Tk. 421.8 million-The *Daily Ittefaque*, June 29, 1974.

46. The Bangladesh Banks (Nationalisation) Order, 1972 (President's Order No. 26 of 1972).

47. The *Daily Ittefaq*, September 17, 1972 ; January 11, 1973 ; The *Daily Ganakantha* January 29, 1973 ; The *Daily Ittaefaq* April 5, 1973 ; June 20, 1973 ; July 22, 1973 ; July 28, 1973 ; August 15, 1973 ; January 3, 1974 ; March 10, 1974 ; March 16, 1974 ; April 21, 1974,

    See also Statement of the Home Minister in the Parliament,—The *Daily Ittefaq*, June 20, 1973.

48. According to the Awami League supplement published on March 4, 1973 in Dacca Newspapers just before the elections, it claimed that within that period the government had rebuilt 9,00,000 houses which were damaged or destroyed. In the preliminary rehabilitation work 256.3 million taka for the relief and for rehabilitation of homeless and dstitutes 190.8 million taka were spent. About 14.1 million maunds of foodgrains were distributed and for the supply of food 2 million taka was spent. For the total rehabili tation work the government spent 727.5 million taka and the government agreed to allot 9000 plots of land to the landless and destitutes.

    Also see Dr. Mazharul Islam, *Bangabandhu Sheikh Mujib*, Bangla Academy, Dacca, 1974.

49. The *Morning News*, Dacca, January 10, 1972.

50. i.e. by the Members of the Constituent Assembly as constituted under the Provisional Constitution Order : See Ch. 1 *supra.*

51. That these committees were formed under administrative orders and not under any law or act of parliament.

52. The Chairman of these Committees at the end used to be called as "Kambal Chor" meaning 'blanket thief'. Reference to blankets came because millions of blankets were sent to Bangladesh from abroad as relief goods but a large number of people did not receive them physically. A large quantity of relief goods was smuggled out of the country and many of these items used to be found in open markets on the other side of the border including Calcutta. The value of estimated relief goods which were smuggled to India was assessed at Tk. 15000 million.—*Janatar Mukhapatra*, November 1, 1975.

53. P.O. No. 7 of 1972. The Bangladesh Local Councils and Municipal Committee (Dissolution and Administration) Order, 1972, 20th January, 1972.
54. The Bangladesh Local Councils and Municipal Committee (Dissolution and Administration) (Amendment) Order, 1972, P.O. 17 of 1972.
55. The Bangladesh Local Councils and Municipal Committee (Dissolution and Administration) (Second Amendment) Order, 1972 (President's Order No. 110 of 1972).
56. The Bangladesh (Restoration of Evacuee Property) Order, 1972 (President's Order No. 13 of 1972.)

CHAPTER THREE

LAW AND ORDER SITUATION

The foremost of all the issues was the law and order situation. After having gone through a war, what the people demanded was peace, security of life, liberty and property and in short a normal life. But this was not easy to achieve. The police force was in disarray, the Bangladesh Rifles who guard the borders were yet to regroup and other minor para military forces were virtually not in existence. On the other hand, all sorts of firearms were in the hand of all sorts of people—hundreds and thousands of people unlisted, unregistered, unknown and unaccountable had sophisticated automatic arms in their possession. The collaborators, the freedom fighters, Mujib Bahini, Mukti Bahini and hundreds of small groups and individuals, the professional miscreants and the members of the '16th division' all had arms, each enjoying power and influence in areas scattered all over the country.

Politics of Arms : National Militia and the Freedom Fighters

The political leaders comprising the government were not armed fighters who took an active part in the war. Although they provided support and logistics in collaboration with India, they did so from a distance residing in the city of Calcutta. This alienated them from the main stream of freedom fighters who in the process of war had now developed a dream to establish a new social order in the country[1]. They returned home with great hopes that they would now be engaged in the national reconstruction. The Government-in-exile was warned about this problem of handling the freedom fighters and they were advised to chalk out a plan for implementation immediately after the independence but nothing meaningful was prepared[2]. As a matter of fact, none of the leaders except Tajuddin, gave much of a serious thought to it. Tajuddin's plan was to have a national militia where all freedom fighters whether enrolled or not would report. There would be camps all over the country for their food and lodging at the initial stage and they would be asked to surrender their arms at the initial stage for redistribution according to assigned work. They would be given training in the respective field of their own and would be absorbed in various national reconstruction programmes. According to qualifications and aptitude they would be absorbed in various agencies of the Government. As the Awami League was committed within the context of Pakistan not to have a large army, the idea was to integrate also the regular forces into the Militia, thus making the members of the National Militia drawn from all walks of life, the vanguard for the defence of the country in case of any external aggression[3]. Accordingly, on 2nd January, 1971 an 11-member Central Board of National Militia was constituted with Tajuddin as the Chairman[4]. Interestingly enough, Moulana Bhashani was named as a member of this Board for National Militia[5].

However, once Mujib arrived, he assumed the leadership of the country. Contrary to Tajuddin's earlier strategy of allowing the armed guerillas to hold on to their arms, Mujib gave much emphasis in the firsti nstance on disarming them and the idea of an 'integrated' National Militia on Tajuddin's line received less attention. Mujib did not reject the idea of National Militia but he looked at it from a different angle and laid maximum importance on the surrender of arms. Mujib in a statement made on January 17 directed all members of the "Gonobahini"[6] to surrender their weapons to the sub-divisional officers of the country within 10 days. While paying tributes to them he expressed his confidence that they would respond to his call in the greater interest of the country. He also warned that possession of arms by any person after 10 days would be considered as unauthorised and illegal. He reiterated the government scheme of establishing National Militia through which they would be provided with jobs for national reconstruction, development, defence and law and order agency according to their ability, aptitude and skill. The idea behind the scheme was to bring the members of the Gonobahini under an organisational discipline. According to Mujib the 'Gonobahini' was the best reservoir of talents which could provide a new kind of motivated leadership for the reconstruction of the country. He expected the 'heroes of the war of liberation'[7] to provide leadership of the new Army. Air Force and Navy of Bangladesh and said that the government had decided to select officers and policemen from the members of the Gonobahini. The scheme therefore was to organise all members of Gonobahini both enrolled and unenrolled, into a productive force so that the unprecedented zeal and enthusiasm displayed by the youth of the country during the war could be properly utilized for national reconstruction provided that they had submitted their arms and ammunition to their respective Sub-divisional National Militia camps[8].

The statement of Mujib and the scheme outlined for the National Militia disappointed the vast majority of the freedom fighters including some of those who belonged to the Mujib Bahini. A large section of them resented the scheme which was, according to them, nothing but an eye-wash. They suspected that allurement for training and job was only offered to take away the arms—their only possession which provided them status and authority. Once the arms were surrendered their *locus standi* would go and they would be thrown into the backyard. They claimed that Mujib not having been present with them in the war could not understand their sentiments. In the series of discussions Mujib held with the Mukti Bahini and Mujib Bahini members and other group leaders and individuals, the freedom fighters openly contradicted his statement and emphasised the need for establishing their authority in the government. Having not taken part in the war they argued that the present leaders were not eligible to run the country. The freedom fighters also continued to expose the role of the Awami League leaders during the war and after.

This was not an unexpected phenomenon. With arms in the hands of so many people, the Government could not establish its political control and authority over the people and the freedom fighters continued to be a threat to the existence of the Government. Some of the Awami League leaders were terrified by the freedom fighters because of the latter's role during the war and so also were the collaborators, Biharis and people who accumulated ill-gotten money. As a result, the Ministers and the Awami League leaders tended to patronise the freedom fighters for their safety and political position.

On a psychological plane, what the freedom fighters wanted was not the job of a policeman but some status and authority to have something to do more than just doing jobs ; something creative and productive. They wanted to enjoy the status of those who took the risk of their life to fight for the independence of their country as opposed to those who surrendered to Pakistan or sat in Calcutta to claim leadership of the war. As a result the vast majority of them refused to respond to the call excepting those who surrendered through a ceremony at Dacca on January 30, 1972[9]. Some other arms were also recovered but they were of smaller quantity[10]. Having failed to convince and control the freedom fighters Mujib in a desperate move banned the Mukti Fouz on February 24, 1972 and the Mujib Bahini and all other such Bahinis on February 27, 1972[11]. The fact that they were running almost parallel governments would be evident from the press note released by the government on these dates.

No law as such was made especially to define the role of the freedom fighters or their status or to guarantee their jobs, training, food and shelter as outlined in the statement of Mujib—excepting that some administrative orders were made to give them certain facilities. At the end what the freedom fighters got was a quota in the jobs in the government and semi-government offices, promotions, military honours and a Foundation. Those freedom fighters who out of desperate situation of unemployment accepted the offers now mostly became only clerks, or policemen or ranks in the Army amongst thousand others, sinking not only their identity but their spirit and enthusiasm with which they fought the war and returned home to build a nation[12].

In the final analysis, there was no philosophical concept or approach in engaging the freedom fighters for national reconstruction. The zeal with which they fought could be employed to build the nation also but for that perhaps a different kind of vision and political leadership was required. Rehabilitation of disabled freedom fighters and their dependants was necessary but an able-bodied true freedom fighter wanted to be involved in creative work where he would get some job satisfaction and which would ensure more participation in the national development programmes.

Finally the only law which was passed relating to the freedom fighters—the Bangladesh (Freedom Fighters) Welfare Foundation promulgated as late as on August 7, 1972[13]. The law provided for the creation of a Foundation for the welfare of the disabled freedom fighters and the dependants of the disabled freedom fighters and the dependents of Shaheeds (those who died in war). Under the law a corporation was created in the name of the Foundation, laying down the functions and powers of the Board of Directors who would run the Foundation. It was provided with cash fund and also some abandoned industries from the income of which the Foundation was to carry out the purpose of the Order. Under the law the beneficiaries were only those who were disabled freedom fighters and the dependants of the shaheeds (martyrs).

Later in December 1972 the law was amended in order to enable the Foundation to provide assistance to the members of the Mukti Fouz who were in distress and who required such assistance. By the amendment the word 'Foundation' was substituted by the word 'Trust' and the 'Board of Directors' by a 'Board of Trustees'. The law provided for a charitable institution and not what the freedom fighters demanded.

So the conflict and contradictions between the freedom fighters and the government were deep rooted and Mujib's appeal to surrender arms went almost in vain. Even many of Mujib's own partymen did not surrender arms, they argued that they would be defenceless without arms unless all their adversaries had surrendered their arms[14].

This led to another area of conflict between the freedom fighters and the 'collaborators' which was much sharper in nature since the day the war began and it had to be handled in almost parallel form. So the areas of conflict arising out of the armed struggle for independence could be identified as (1) between the freedom fighters and the government, (2) between the freedom fighters and the collaborators and (3) between the freedom fighters themselves.

The freedom fighters were not a cohesive group either and as indicated earlier they had contradictions within themselves. There were different groups and Bahinis having different loyalties to different parties and leaders. This state of affairs complicated the issue further particularly where the question arose as how to hold them together politically. In the process, which was devoid of any political philosophy, guidance and leadership, the freedom fighters took refuge to different means of livelihood. Some got inspired to establish scientific socialism, some for a class struggle and a considerable number turned bandits. They opted for robbery, extortion, intimidation and looting, grabbing properties and shooting adversaries, hijacking, sabotage and kidnapping. Along with such elements, a large number of unknown non-political people having arms and the new freedom fighters known as '16th division' in which many Razakars and Al-Badars[15] had mingled—now started to stampede the whole country[16]. Looting of Police Station, banks and bazars, hijacking of cars and kidnapping young women became a daily phenomenon[17]. The law and order situation thus continued to deteriorate.

The Collaborators

Simultaneously the situation with regard to the collaborators was taking a new turn. Besides the sporadic reprisals on plain political account some freedom fighters started to settle their personal scores. From petty self-interest down to family quarrels motivated their action against those people who were called 'collaborators'. In the name of punishing the collaborators, old enmity and vengeance came to the surface and a huge number of innocent people were continuously harrassed, their property taken away and a large number of them was put behind bars. Many of the collaborators who actually were active members of the organisations which were formed by the Pakistan Government in the name of Razakars, Al-Shams and Al-Badars also had considerable arms in their possession. Some of them managed to become 'freedom fighters' after the 16th of December through relatives and friends belonging to the other camp but a large number of them were frightened and went into hiding. Some turned miscreants and joined groups mentioned in the last paragraph[18]. Every war of the kind Bangladesh had, produces collaborators. Some collaborate from political conviction some for personal safety and survival and some out of socio-economic compulsion. Laws are therefore made to deal with collaborators depending on how a government would like to handle them. Immediately after the independence, when the memory of the atrocities of the Pakistan Army was still fresh and the role of some of the collaborators who killed, burnt, raped and looted a large number of people inside the country was not to be forgotten, emotion rose to its peak and the sense of vengeance demonstrated during that time was not unnatural[19]. The intensity of such a feeling was beyond any comprehension and the pressure for a wide-spread reprisal from the Awami League's own rank and file was gaining momentum. So, soon after Mujib's order to surrender the arms was issued and the scheme for the national militia was announced, the Bangladesh Collaborators (Special Tribunals) Order, 1972 was promulgated on January 24[20]. The objects and reasons for the promulgation of the law, as stated in the preamble were that there were certain persons who individually or as members of some organisations were directly or indirectly collaborators of the Pakistan Armed Forces or had aided or abetted them in committing genocide and atrocities against men, women and children and the person, property and honour of the civilian population of Bangladesh. These people contributed towards the perpetuation of a reign of terror and committed crimes against humanity on a scale which had horrified the moral consciousness of the people of Bangladesh and of the right-thinking people of the world. It therefore, became imperative to deal with such persons effectively and to punish them adequately in accordance with the due process of law.

The law defined 'collaborator' as a person who had (i) participated with or aided or abetted the occupation army in maintaining, sustaining, strengthening, supporting or furthering the illegal occupation of Bangladesh by such army ; (ii) rendered material assistance in any way whatsoever to the occupation army by any act whether by words, signs or conduct ; (iii) waged war or abetted in waging war against the People's Republic of Bangladesh ; (iv) actively resisted or sabotaged the efforts of the people and the liberation forces of Bangladesh in their struggle against the occupation army ; (v) attempted to aid or aided the occupation army in furthering its design of perpetuating its forcible occuption of Bangladesh by making a public statement or by voluntary participation in propagandas within or outside Bangladesh or by associating in any delegation or committee or by participating in purported by-elections.

The law was a comprehensive one covering almost all areas of co-operation of any kind extended towards the Pakistan Army excepting however only those who had performed in good faith functions which they were required to do by any purported law in force at the material time[21]. The law defined the 'liberation forces' to include all forces of the Government in exile which were engaged in the liberation of Bangladesh' and the 'occupation army' meant the Pakistan Armed Forces.

The main features of the law were :

(1) it provided trial and punishment of collaborators for categories of offences as mentioned in the Schedule in 4 parts reconciling them with the existing provisions of Penal Code and keeping in line with the crimes against humanity and person, property and honour of the civilian population as mentioned in the preamble of the Order[22]. Even if not covered by these sections mentioned in the Schedule an act which was mentioned in the definition clause would also be tried. As a result, the content of the schedules did not remain static. By an amendment in June, 1972 Section 140 was added to Part III[23] and Section 143 and 147 were added to Part IV. But finally the whole schedule was reviewed as the cases were tested before the Court and the first parts of the Schedule were regrouped and the number of offences mentioned in the Schedule was increased from 60 to 69.

(2) Any police officer or any person empowered by the government could arrest any person who could reasonably be suspected of having been a collaborator without warrant. On making such an arrest a report would be submitted to the government with a precis of information and materials on

the basis of which the arrest was made and pending receipt of any order the government, could commit such person to custody. On receipt of such a report the government could by an order in writing detain such person for an initial period of six months for the purpose of enquiry or investigation into the case and if more time was required for further enquiry, the government could extend the period of detention. The persons who were arrested before the commencement of the order as alleged collaborators were brought under the purview of this law by deeming to have been arrested under the Order. In order to make the the law more functional and for speedy implementation this provision was soon amended to give the power of the government to the Sub-divisional Magistrate. In other words, any arrest was now to be reported to the Sub-divisional Magistrate who in turn would pass the order of detention (Section 3).

But the responsibility given to the Police for arresting the collaborators were alleged not to have been effective enough. In some case it was pointed out that they were reluctant in arresting the collaborators or were not arresting those demanded by the 'people'. Article 3 was therefore further amended to enable 'any person' to make a written complaint to the Sub-divisional Magistrate[24]. On receipt of such report or on his own motion the Sub-divisional Magistrate would hold an enquiry and if he was satisfied he would direct a police officer not below the rank of the Sub-Inspector to cause the arrest to be made and send him to the Tribunal for trial.

(3) One-member Special Tribunals were created to try the collaborators who were charged with having committed offences specified in the schedule and no other court was to have any jurisdiction to take cognizance of any such offence (Article 4). At the first instance special tribunals were to be constituted only by a Sessions Judge or Additional Sessions Judge or Assistant Sessions Judge (Article 5) and special tribunal consisting of Sessions and Additional Sessions Judges was to try offences enumerated in Parts I and II and the special tribunal consisting of Assistant Sessions Judges was to try offences enumerated in Parts III and IV. But as time passed and the volume of cases increased the machinery for trial of offences had to be reorganised[25]. The Tribunal consisting of the Sessions Judges or Additional Sessions Judges could try and punish any offence of the entire schedule but the Tribunal consisting of Assistant Sessions Judges would continue to try and punish any offence under Part III and Part IV as before. But the special tribunal consisting of only the Sessions Judges could transfer any case for trial to and withdraw from any other special tribunal within his jurisdiction.

(4) This arrangement could not cope with the situation and by a further amendment tribunals of special magistrates were created and the schedule was also rearranged[26]. Any First Class Magistrate could be appointed as a Special Magistrate who would try and punish any of the offences in Part IV of the Schedule. The Sub-divisional Magistrate could also transfer to or withdraw

any case from any Special Magistrate within his jurisdiction. In the trial in Special Tribunal the provisions of the Criminal Procedure Code would apply to all matters excepting those inconsistent with the Order. (See President's Order No. 11 of 1972, Section 8), but the trial by the Special Magistrate would be done summarily following the procedure of summary trial of summons cases under the Criminal Procedure Code (Article 8).

As a large number of alleged collaborators were absconding, by an amendment made later, provision for trial in absentia was made[27], and persons accused of more than one offence could be tried in one trial anywhere in Bangladesh. The law however made provision for providing legal aid by the state. Where a trial took place in absentia or any accused was not defended by a legal practitioner of his choice, the Tribunal or the Magistrate could appoint a legal practitioner to defend such accused persons.

(5) On matters of evidence which would otherwise have been of utmost importance, provisions had to be made to cope with a special situation. The country was in a war and one of the main difficulties faced both by the government and the courts was to collect evidence. By an amendment made later, provisions were made by Article 10A that no fact would be deemed to be disproved and not proved merely on the ground that there was no post-mortem report, medical report or report of any chemical examiner or delay in giving information to the police or in making a complaint or that the dead body was not found. With respect to official documents produced by any officer having the custody of such document in the ordinary course of official duty concerning members of any force raised to assist the occupation army, unless the contrary was shown, such documents were made admissible evidence. This related mainly to persons accused as members of Al-Badar, Al-Shams and Razakar.

The above new provision caused serious variations from the established principles of law of evidence and provided a wide scope for misuse of power and ultimately led to furstrate the administration of justice.

On the question of making an exception in the amended Article 10A that delay in giving information to the police or in making a complaint would not be called in question while disproving or not proving a fact, the court however intervened and limited the scope of this unlimited time to submit complaints. Justice K.M. Sobhan in Lutfur Mridha v. The State[28] held that delay in giving information to the police referred to in Article 10A must be due to the abnormal situation in 1971 but one and a half year delay after the independence could not be condoned without sufficient explanation. Although a large number of complaints continued to be submitted to the police even after a long time since independence for which a good section of such accused persons had already suffered, the decision of the court limited the scope of such action and brought some relief to the accused persons. In the case mentioned above, the court ordered the release of the accused person.

In another case it was held that although Article 10A exempted the submission of the post mortem reports from being required for disproving or not proving a fact, once a post mortem examination took place, the defence side could not be prevented from raising relevant questions relating to the post mortem examination[29].

(6) The punishment for the offences was made more severe compared to the established law varying from death sentence to a sentence for not less than 3 years (Article II). It also included punishment of persons who harboured a proclaimed absconder (Art. 11A) but in order to reduce frivolous cases which were already filed in large numbers only to harass individuals, the Special Tribunal or the Magistrate was empowered to punish any person for instituting false charges by imprisonment for a period of three years or rigorous imprisonment and fine or both (Article 11C[30]).

(7) On conviction, the properties of a collaborator was to be forfeited to the government (Article 12). By a subsequent amendment provision was made for attachment of property of any person who was arrested under the Order and unless sooner released would remain under attachment till he was released from custody. The government however, retained the power to release the attachment. If a person who was required for the purpose of any investigation, enquiry or other proceedings connected with an offence was absconding or remaining abroad to avoid appearance, the government in a written proclamation published in the official gazette could direct that person to appear at a specified place and time and/or direct attachment of all his properties and the 'property' included all the properties not only of the proclaimed person but those standing in the name of his wife, children, parents, minor brothers, sisters or dependents or any *benamdar*[31]. The government could appoint administrators to look after these properties and could sell them if they were of perishable nature (Article 17). If the proclaimed person did not appear within time, the government could forefeit his properties under attachment and could dispose of them[32].

(8) The law provided an opportunity for appeal with the same right given to the government to file an appeal against an order of acquittal (Article 16). It further provided that if an appeal was filed against an order of acquittal, the person concerned would continue to remain in custody (Article 21). The period of limitation for an appeal was fixed for 60 days from the date of either acquittal or conviction (Article 16 (3)). Apart from the provision of an appeal under article 16, no action or proceeding taken under the Order could be called in question by any court. This did, however, not bar the extra-ordinary writ jurisdiction of the Supreme Court later introduced by Article 102 of the Constitution (see below).

(9) No person who was in custody, accused or convicted of an offence punishable under the Order could be released on bail.

As the provision of the law was clear, the superior courts in a series of cases refused to grant bail to a person arrested and detained under the Collaborators Order. The Appellate Division of the Supreme Court held that no bail could be granted to a person convicted under Article 14 by the High Court Division as the words used were clear and unambiguous[33]. However, the court in a case where the accused person was acquitted, held that the discretion of enlarging such person on bail lay with the High Court. In the State vs. Mohammed Hossain[34] the High Court Division held that although where appeal may be admitted against an order of acquittal and on such admission of appeal a person could be treated as an accused yet no one could be detained more than 60 days after his acquittal.

The Appellate Division went further in the Superintendent of Remembrancer of Legal Affairs vs. Jobed Ali[35] that denial of bail referred to Article 14 had no reference to a person who had been acquitted of an offence under the Order as it solely related to one who had been convicted or one who was facing a trial under the Order. The Court held that after an acquittal an accused gets back his liberty. But with regard to Article 16(2) which provided that if an appeal was filed from an order of acquittal the person concerned would continue in custody. The Appellate Division held in the same case that the Collaborators Order being silent in the matter the High Courts' discretionary power to release a person who had been acquitted of an offence under the Order remained unaffected. If an appeal was filed under Article 16(2) the limit of the period of custody after acquittal would extend upto the time when the High Court Division was to be in session of the appeal against acquittal or for a period of 60 days allowed to file an appeal counted from the day of acquittal.

The court in certain cases granted relief by awarding bail or releasing the accused person on some other grounds, such as, delay in making complaints or in completing investigation as mentioned in the earlier precedents. During the entire year of 1972 and to some extent in 1973 hundreds and thousands of complaints were lodged and cases were initiated either by police or Subdivisional Magistrate or members of the public bringing all sorts of allegation of collaboration against individuals. The special nature of the law and its provisions limited the scope of the ordinary courts to interfere in the proceedings. A large section, either because of financial reasons or because of the time factor could not avail of the limited opportunity for appeal provided in the law. Nevertheless, the courts even then interpreted the law liberally and granted relief wherever it could, keeping themselves within the framework of the law.

It started with an outstanding pronouncement made by the High Court Division in the case of A.T. Mridha vs. the State in May, 1973[36]. Although the case, which we will discuss later challenged the provisions of President's Order 50 and the order of the High Court was subsequently set aside by the Appellate Division on a technical ground, it related to the similar provisions of the Collaborators Order particularly with regard to the fundamental issues of arrest and bail. Justice Badrul Haider Chowdhury in his judgement held that "arrest without warrant by a police officer must be made on reasonable grounds and if after investigation lasting for 5 months no sufficient materials could be produced, the accused was entitled to be released on bail". In such cases continuance of arrest would amount "to abuse of the process of court" and so the proceedings were quashed for ends of justice and the accused was set at liberty.

In a similar case Maimunnessa v. the State[37] under the Collaborators Order, Justice Ruhul Islam in November, 1974 held that an arrest without warrant would not be justified without sufficient materials to raise reasonable suspicion that the person was a collaborator. Article 3(1) of the Collaborators Order authorised a police officer to arrest without warrant any person who "may reasonably be suspected of having been a collaborator." The Court held that the expression "reasonably be suspected" ought to be based on definite facts and there must exist sufficient materials on the basis of which the police officer could reasonably suspect a person to be a collaborator. The Court also held in this case that the authority to detain for the initial period of 6 months was exclusively given to the Sub-divisional Magistrate and it would not be delegated to someone who was doing the Sub-divisional Magistrate's routine work.

Justice Kemaluddin Hossain in Mashiur Rahman alias Jadu Mia vs. the State[38] in August, 1973 held that "wherever power was conferred and its exercise was qualified by the word 'reasonable' it was held that such exercise of power must be performed on proper materials and exercise of such power would be subject to judicial review". In such case of arrest "there will have to be some grounds on which a reasonable man and a reasonable court would come to the conclusion that there were materials sufficient for the officer to exercise his power and they were related to the offence committed and they manifestly connected the suspect with the offence". The court in this case also held that under Article 3(4) of the Order that the Government after the initial detention of 6 months by the Sub-divisional Magistrate could only extend the undertrial detention for once—for another period of 6 months and not more and accordingly ordered the release of the accused.

There were a large number of cases alleging collaboration on the ground that the alleged persons participated in the purported by-elections to aid the occupation army in furthering its perpetuation of the occupation. During the war period a large number of the elected representatives elected in 1970 fled the country and the Pakistan Government decided to hold by-elections to fill those seats. This had been referred to specifically in Article 2(v), the definition clause of a 'collaborator'. Consequently, a number of initial cases were directed to apprehend those person who took part in the by-election as it was easy to identify such persons. Since some of the Special Tribunals did not take cognizance of offences in cases where nomination was withdrawn by such candidates, Article 2(6)(v) was amended in August, 1972 in order to apprehend even those who had withdrawn their nomination. By this amendment it was provided that a person would be deemed to have participated in any purported by-election even if he withdrew his candidature afterwards[39].

Justice Kemaluddin Hossain however held in Abdur Rahman Bakaul vs. the State[40] in August, 1973 that this provision as contained in sub-clause (v) of Article 2(6) would not apply to someone who filed nomination paper under duress and coercion. The court argued that the ordinary grammatical meaning of the word 'participation' was that "a man participates when he acts on his own motion i.e voluntarily and not at the behest of some one or under intimidation, duress or coercion". On this ground the Court set aside the order and sentence of the Special Tribunal and acquitted the person of the charge of collaboration.

Justice Ruhul Islam in A.K.M. Nazmul Huda vs. the State[41] in interpreting Article 2(b)(v) on the question of participating in the by-election went to determine 'mens rea' or guilty mind of a person charged with the offence of participation in the purported by-elections. The Court held that unless 'mens rea' or 'guilty knowledge' was established, the burden of which lay with the prosecution—there could not be any conviction for collaboration under the law. He went further to say that the act alone did not amount to guilt it had to be accompanied by a guilty mind. The 'participation' included the element 'volition' in the participation. In the same case the Court held that the action of the proposers and seconders for a candidate in the by-election could not be treated as participation in the election. As a result the Court had set accused person at liberty.

Although the Appellate Division in Hafez Moulana Md. Nooruddin vs. the State[42] in August, 1973 held that filing of a nomination paper showed that 'participation' in the by-election had taken place in that particular case. The Appellate Division held that filing of nomination paper could not be disputed as to be a step taken with a view to contesting an election. Besides, due to the subsequent amendment appended as explanation II to Article 2(b)(v) as mentioned earlier the Appellate Division held that "it could not therefore, be disputed that the mere filing of a nomination paper amounted to participation in such by-election". In this case however like in other cases before the High Court, it was not contended that filing of nomination paper was not wilful or voluntary and the act was done under duress and coercion.

As mentioned earlier the Collaboration Order was promulgated at a time when the country was in an euphoric state. The law was welcomed by the vast majority of the population as the people generally wanted the collaborators to be punished. For the collaborators or the people who were alleged to be collaborators, such as, the Biharis, the promulgation of the Collaborators Order was also taken as a great blessing. It saved them from the imminent danger of a wrath of reprisals which could occur in a large scale at any time. Already in the absence of any law, sporadic reprisals in different forms including killing were taking place and a large number of people were taken to jail without cover of law. In a situation where a cause for reprisal was existing without any law to redeem, reactions were bound to be violent. A law, however, harsh or rigid it might have been, which provided redemption of some kind through due process for justice was better than not to have any. In the context of the situation that prevailed at that time, the lives of hundreds and thousands of people were therefore saved on the introduction of the Collaborators Order. What social impact it had in implementing the law is however a different matter.

At the time when this law was introduced there were not very many people to criticise the law although the serious and highly implicating provisions of the law which varied from the established law of the land could lead to denial of justice in many cases. The excessive power given to the police officer to arrest anyone without any warrant, the wide definition of 'collaborator' which could include almost everyone in the country who did not cross the border, the power to Sub-divisional Magistrate to detain anyone for the first six months, trial of a person in absentia, attachment of property as soon as someone was merely arrested or someone was absconding, the high degree of punishment, the denial of the right to bail—all or any of them could easily produce a miscarriage of justice and could be said to have all the elements of a repressive law. But even then in its own prevailing context it was not considered so at the beginning. The people hailed the decision of the government when 15 eminent personalities alleged to have been collaborated with the Pakistan Army were declared as to be 'proclaimed persons' and directed them to appear before the Magistrates[43].

But as soon as the whole spectrum of law was put into operation it started receiving adverse reaction not so much for the intent of the law itself but for the way in which it was implemented. The police force by itself being weak and disorganised and the Awami League's complete political control over the country provided a unique scope to go for motivated action under the cover of the law. While the law provided a due process for justice it also provided by its boundless powers to a large section of the Awami League workers for revenge, extortion, torture, harrassment, humiliation and blackmail. As a result, a large number of people were arrested or victimised on personal consideration. On the other hand, because of this role played by the Awami League in interfering with the process of law, some actual collaborators who could procure the party blessing either by bribery or personal relationship or patronage could get away from the wrath of the law. This created a further credibility gap in the social reaction to its implementation.

One of the first persons who came forward to criticise the law as early as in March, 1972 was Mr. Ataur Rahman Khan, the Founder Vice-President of the Awami League and the former Chief Minister of East Pakistan. Mr. Khan contended that "instead of going for national reconstruction, the government considered to take action against collaborators and imaginary enemies all over the country as its first and foremost duty"[44]. He said, serious punishment for those who held different political views and did not commit crime like murder, arson, rape or looting could not be beneficial to the country. He pleaded for amnesty for all opposition political persons and trial for those who committed criminal offences—according to him it was necessary to forge a national unity at that juncture. He alleged that many people who before 16th December 1971 deliberately opposed the Bangladesh movement were now holding high positions in the government but those who were genuine patriots and supporters of the freedom struggle but had to pretend to co-operate with the Pakistan Army were now under arrest or turned refugees. He castigated the Awami League saying that "at different levels their workers took full advantage of the Collaborators Order to put political, social, family and economic rivals into prison. The nation was being divided by implementing this law." He alleged that the trial under the law was a sham[45].

It is not known how many were arrested nor it is known how many were actually convicted. The estimate of the persons arrested varied between 50 to 60 thousand, with another equal number believed to be in hiding. The social reaction to the implementation of the Collaborators Order was bad. The handling of the situation by the Awami League divided the nation immediately after independence. On the one hand, they gave protection to a large number of collaborators who enjoyed their favour but on the other hand, their attitude was that other than those who fled the country or took part in the actual war, all were collaborators. It diverted the attention of the government from a far more important matter to a very tricky and sentimental subject not connected with any productive purpose. In tended to increase bribery, corruption and favouritism and lastly, as the entire force of its implementation was applied mainly to those people who were pro-islamic and known as devout Muslims, the reaction went deep down to the grass root level having a corroding effect. The propaganda that it was all done against the 'believers' at the instigation of Hindu India was taken to be true by a large section of the rural population. This also led to the thought of establishing a Muslim Bengal from then on, consciously or unconsciously. Although the law helped to avoid a catastrophe of one kind it had sown the seeds of another, perhaps a much deeper one with far-reaching consequences.

The Rakkhi Bahini and the Law Enforcing Agencies

With all this going on, there was no effective law enforcing agency in existence. Mujib's dream to establish a new 'Peoples' Police Force' which was not going to be "an instrument for coercion and repression as in the past" was never fulfilled. He wanted his 'Peoples' Police Force' only to be manned by people drawn from the heroic "gonobahini"[46]. The existing Police force was in disarray due to the war. The Police that offered the touch of resistance to the Pakistan Army at the Rajarbagh on 25th March, 1971 and earned respect of the nation was no more there for the consolidation of indepedence for which they fought. They got scattered during the course of the year and those who joined the war as a freedom fighter considered themselves as heroes and had developed new hopes. With arms in their hand when they returned home after achieving independence, they were reluctant to become half-fed poor salaried policemen again. The trust and inspiration required to motivate them to devote themselves to police work with a new sense of purpose was lacking and so they did not respond to the call of the Father of the Nation.

Moreover, the war produced a new social dimension with arms in the hands of thousands of people scattered all over the country. The members of the Mukti Bahini went on exerting political influence in every sphere of administration. The police, equipped and trained in the colonial style was no more an agency to meet the situation. The kind of weapons the miscreants or the collaborators or the freedom fighters or the underground revolutionaries had were of far superior quality than those of the police.

The condition of Bangladesh Rifles formerly known as East Pakistan Rifles was the same. With the surrender of the Pakistan Army to the Indian Commander of the Allied Forces, the border between Bangladesh and India became a free zone and smuggling became a broad-daylight affair. With the presence of the Indian Army in Bangladesh it became even more difficult to impose any meaningful restrictions. Yet the Bangladesh Rifles had to be organised. The new Bangladesh Rifles was not equipped sufficiently to do its defined job in those circumstances, not to speak of assisting the Government in enforcing law for internal peace.

The Army was still not organised. The Army also could not be called in so easily to assist the civilian authority. Apart from the financial involvement in assigning the army to do any civil work a more fundamental point involved was a political one. The Awami League believed that the country would do better without an institutional Army[47]. It could live with only a ceremonial unit. Having seen the Pakistan Army eating up almost half the nation's wealth and being inspired by the thought that a poor and small country like Bangladesh did not need a large regimental Army, the Awami League wanted to keep the existing Army at a low profile. Moreover, calling the Army to solve a civilian problem so soon after the independence would have undermined the political authority of the Awami League and its government who claimed to have the entire population behind them. Above all, an organised institutional army was considered to be a threat to the ruling government as in many Third World countries they constituted a separate force to strike a political balance. For defending the country the concept of having a National Militia initiated by Tajuddin was in their mind. This suited India also as those Divisions of troops which would otherwise be deployed for Bangladesh would not be necessary. From India's point of view also Bangladesh did not require a regimental army as she would always be available to stand by Bangladesh in case of aggression. It was argued that Bangladesh therefore ought to divert all her wealth for national reconstruction.

All these led to one conclusion : the necessity to form a new para military crack-force to remain under complete political control. That the country would face a serious peace keeping problem following the independence was not unexpected and with the thoughts in mind as mentioned above, under the guidance of the Indian Advisers, the idea of having the Rakkhi Bahini was conceived originally by the Government in exile at Calcutta[48]. The force had to be well-trained and well-equipped in order to fill the vacuum ; as an effective law enforcing agency it would do the job of the police on the one hand and that of the army on the other and yet remain under complete control of the political authority. It was argued that the situation prevailing in the country demanded a strong force equipped with modern weapons and from that point of view formation of a new para military force could not be said to have been unjustified. It was also true that the idea of having a new force was politically motivated for the purpose of creating a counter-balance to the Army.

Thoughts on the formation of the Rakkhi Bahini crystalised prior to making a law for the purpose. Preparations were going on for weeks for the training and recruitment of the men to be inducted into the Force and it started its actual operations before it was formally constituted. Once all arrangements in close collaboration with the Indian Advisers and military consultants were complete, the Jatiya Rakkhi Bahini Order[49] was promulgated on March 7, 1972 giving a retrospective effect from the 1st day of February.

Unlike the Army or the Police Act, the Rakkhi Bahini Order lacked the basic framework of law within which a law enforcing agency could develop into an institution. The law provided for the constitution of a Jatiya Rakkhi Bahini and matters ancillary thereto but no other object or reason was stated in the preamble of the Order. It defined "Rakkhi" as a member of the Bahini other than an officer and stated that there would be raised and maintained, a Bahini to be called Jatiya Rakkhi Bahini and it would consist of such members and classes of officers and Rakkhi and in such manner as would be determined by the Government (Article 4). With regard to the purpose and function of the Bahini the law provided that it would be employed to assist the civil authority in the maintenance of internal security when required by a prescribed authority ; it would also assist the Armed Forces when called upon by the Government to do so and the Bahini would prefer such other function as the Government would direct (Article 18). With regard to the running and managing the Bahini the law provided that the superintendence of the Bahini would vest in the Government and the Bahini would be administered, commanded and controlled by the Director in accordance with the provisions of the Order and the rules made thereunder and such orders and instructions as would be made or issued by the Government from time to time (Article 7). The Government would appoint a Director and such officers under certain terms and conditions as would be prescribed (Article 5). Article 11 to 15 related to the punishment or disciplinary action that could be inflicted or taken against the Rakkhi and the subordinate officers under the rules to be framed. Article 10 provided that any person subject to the Order would get discharge on the expiry of his term of appointment but also could be discharged earlier subject to conditions as would be prescribed.

Article 16 provided that the Director and authority to delegate his power and Article 17 provided that the Government would by notification in the official gazette make rules for carrying out the purposes of the Order and for any matter mecessary for the constitution, maintenance, administration, command, control and discipline of the Bahini for carrying the provisions of this Order.

This is what the whole law contained. The Police Act of 1861 in its preamble stated that the law was made "for the prevention and detection of crime." Here the law was silent with regard to its object and the purpose described in Article 8 was an omnibus provision saying that it would be employed for the purpose of assisting the civil authority in the maintenance of internal security when required and it would perform such function as the government would direct. The law as it appeared was sketchy and it did not provide any insight into the organisation of the Bahini itself—how it would operate in public, its powers and authorities, and its accountability as a law enforcing agency. The provision made in Article 17 only envisaged that the Government would make rules and regulations for its functioning, conduct of its members and their powers and functions.

But the operations of the Bahini did not wait for any regulations to come out or for the creation of any prescribed authority. The Government required its assistance immediately and as mentioned earlier, the Rakkhi Bahini started functioning even without any law being in existence and subsequently the order was made to provide some legal cover only. The major task the Rakkhi Bahini assumed was to recover unauthorised arms, checking smuggling at the border, hoarding, black marketing and finally to eliminate the political dissidents. It acted like a storm trooper, a crack-force for a lightening strike. It would surround a whole village combing for arms, miscreants and political opponents and at times to recover 'fake ration cards'. In the process they would kill, loot and even rape—there was no regulation to control their conduct or make them accountable. Soon it assumed the name of a private Bahini working outside legal norms. They could enter any house, arrest anyone, detain any number of people including women and children in their camps all over the rural areas. With almost every operation conducted by the Rakkhi Bahini, the Force continued to allienate itself from the people as in most of the operations a large number of innocent people were victimised. The people were frightened of them and started hating them and within a few months the Bahini started losing public credibility.

It was difficult to challenge any action of the Rakkhi Bahini before any court. The main reason was that they were not working under any regulation as the Army, Police or any other force whose action was subject to strict regulations. They did not have to follow any procedure in arresting a person or detaining him or in searching or seizing property or in keeping an account of the arms and ammunition they had or were using. They had no code of conduct or structural discipline in dealing with life and property of the members of the public.

When the public criticism of the role and activities of the Rakkhi Bahini reached its height and the newspapers were full of questions on their role, power and functions, the government after allowing it to operate unfettered for more than 20 months introduced an ordinance to confer retrospective legality on some of the actions of the Rakkhi Bahini[50]. The Ordinance was the first amendment to the original order which added a new Article 8A with retrospective effect from lst February, 1972 and provided that notwithstanding anything contained in the Criminal Procedure Code or any other law, any officer while performing any function under Article 8 could without a warrant (1) arrest any person whom he reasonably suspected of having committed a coganizable offence under any law, (2) search any person, place, vehicle or vessel and seize anything found in the possession thereof in respect ef which or by means of which he had reason to believe an offence punishable under any law had been committed. Any person arrested or anything seized were to be forwarded with a report to the officer in charge of the nearest police station for taking necessary action according to law.

The amending ordinance further legalised all the acts committed by the Rakkhi Bahini in the past or in future by adding a new Article 16A which provided that no suit, prosecution or other legal proceedings would lie against any member of the Bahini for anything which was done in good faith or intended to have been done so.

Court's Decisions

The first and one of the very few cases in which the Jatiyo Rakkhi Bahini was directly made a party along with both the Secretary, Ministry of Home and the Secretary, Ministry of Defence was the case of Shahjahan, a young boy of eighteen of Naria, Faridpur District. It may be treated in some detail here as it illustrates the conditions then prevailing[51]. This boy was arrested at Dacca on 28.12.1973 by three personnel of the Defence Field Intelligence unit of the Army and was handed over to Ramna Police Station and a General Diary entry of the same date was made stating his arrest under section 54 of the Criminal Procedure Code[52]. Soon thereafter, the officer-in-charge of the Ramna Police Station was asked by the Rakkhi Bahini authority to hand over Shahjahan to a Subedar of the Jatiya Rakkhi Bahini at the Rakkhi Bahini headquarters at the Sher-e-Bangla Nagar, Dacca. It was alleged in this case by the brother of Shahjahan that he was tortured by the Rakkhi Bahini and he was last seen by his brother at the Head Quarters of the Rakkhi Bahini on 2.1.74. Since then there was no trace of Shahjahan, who was barely 18 years old. In an application of Habeas Corpus the petitioner prayed for the production of his brother before the Court and challenged his unlawful detention. The Government through the Secretary of Home made appearance and in their affidavit-in-Opposition the Rakkhi Bahini maintained that Shahjahan was an accused in a case with the Naria Police Station and as he was in possession of some hidden arms the Rakkhi Bahini was asked to take him over from the police custody for interrogation and recovery of arms. According to the Rakkhi Bahini, Shahjahan had made a confession and led a Rakkhi Bahini party to a spot near Rayer Bazar, Dacca the day after he was arrested and on the same night at 3 in the morning Shahjahan entered into a by-lane and suddenly ran away and escaped. The Rakkhi Bahini thereafter lodged a First Information Report[53] with the Mohammadpur Police Station on 31st December. So Shahjahan was not in detention and therefore, it was not possible for the Rakkhi Bahini to produce him before the court. Then Shahjahan's brother produced a certified copy from the concerned lower court stating that his brother was never an accused in the Naria Police Station case mentioned by the Rakkhi Bahini and charged that the story of Shahjahan's alleged escape on 29.12.73 was a concocted one and he apprehended that Shahjahan was killed by the Rakkhi Bahini since he met his brother only on 2.1.1974 at the Headquarters of the Rakkhi Bahini.

For the court it was the first opportunity to examine the role of the Rakkhi Bahini under the law and because of the seriousness of the matter the court went deeper into the subject so much so that the Director-in Charge and other relevant officers were called to the court for examination. The Court was also not inclined to believe the story of the Rakkhi Bahini about the alleged escape by Shahjahan and their suspicion was further raised by seeing that the First Information Report was lodged by the Rakkhi Bahini 3 days after the escape, on 31st December at midnight being the last entry in the book of that year. The Court held that "the introduction of Naria Police case in the General Diary entry of the Ramna Police was a pure concoction and the story of the discovery of the arms on the showing of Shahjahan hardly impress any belief in the said story and 3 days delay in lodging First Information Report about the discovery of arms is inexplicable and throws grave suspicion on the whole story of the arms discovery as well as Shahjahan's alleged escape. What they (Rakkhi Bahini) purported to have done demonstrates complete disregard of the law of the country."

This is exactly what was happening. With modern weapons in their hands and full backing of the government and without any accountability whatsoever it was not unnatural that the Rakkhi Bahini would be dominating the law enforcing arena. In the process, the age old Police became a subservient and secondary agency and reports started arriving from all over the country about the Rakkhi Bahini's excesses[54]. Soon after the Rakkhi Bahini went into operation in one of the first cases, they involved themselves with the Rickshaw pullers at Maijdi Court, Noakhali, as a result of which there was a total strike in the district town. In Rajshahi, Kushtia, Jessore, Pabna and Faridpur, the excesses of the Rakkhi Bahini were to be reported first. When the Jatiya Rakkhi Bahini went for searching arms they would not touch the members of the Awami League or its frontal organisations and this partisan role of the Rakkhi Bahini was resented by the people. In order to demonstrate their authority disregarding other agencies including the Deputy Commissioner in different districts, they used to establish their own camps and not being accountable or under any obligation to report to anybody in the district, subdivision or thana headquarters, they posed to be the masters of the area. They used to be in constant clash with other government authorities particularly the police and the district administration. Due to lack of coordination between the Rakkhi Bahini and other organisations of the government including the Army, it created deeper (resentment) and jealousy as to whose authority was superior. As the Jatiya Rakkhi Bahini had no rules or procedure or code of conduct to follow for their activities[55] they could easily flex their muscle over other organisations in dealing with the people.

Justice D.C. Bhattacharya in his illustrious judgement in this case in May, 1974 said, "the Rakkhi Bahini's activities being such which affect the rights and liberties of the people at large, it discloses a serious state of affairs to allow them to function in any manner they like and as such what they do may not have the proper legal protection for the function they have been discharging[56]." A large section of the people including the newspapers since long had been raising the question of the legal authority of the Rakkhi Bahini to perform any function. The lawyers at different Bars of the country raised protests and made several attempts to have such a serious matter resolved both in the court room and outside but they were frustrated. Justice Bhattacharya wrote :

> "the tragedy of the whole matter is that though a law called the Jatiya Rakkhi Bahini Order, 1972 has been enacted under which the Bahini has been constituted, no rules as required by Article 17 has been framed to serve as guideline to the Bahini without which it is impossible for them to carry on their functions which are similar to those of the police force

who are guided and controlled by a very elaborate set of regulations and whose activities are subject to meticulous rules of the law[57]."

During the cross-examination, officers of the Rakkhi Bahini admitted that the Bahini had no rules or procedure or code of conduct. They did not have to maintain any paper or document or record of their activities or conduct in the operations they used to undertake. There was no record of any arrest or search or seizure they made. When asked how then did they work ? The Senior Deputy leader, Hafizuddin answered "we work the way we decide."

The Court was surprised to see how the officers of the Rakkhi Bahini behaved. It observed :

"we must say that we have been greatly surprised to notice the fashion in which the officers of the Rakkhi Bahini have conducted themselves. It is in evidence that absolutely no records of the activities of the members of the Bahini have been maintained in connection with this case and no report thereof. Nothing in writing could be found to check up the activities of the Bahini while dealing with the person in their custody[58]."

Senior Deputy Leader, Hafizuddin stated in course of his deposition that no register or diary was maintained in respect of the operation undertaken by them and no register of the arms and ammunition carried by the members of the Party conducting the operation kept. The Court reflected the sentiments of the people about the Rakkhi Bahini by saying :

"the misgivings and the apprehensions which may arise in the mind of people in this background do not seem to be unnatural[59]."

So the constitution of the Rakkhi Bahini might have been legal because there was a law saying how they would be constituted but functioning of the Rakkhi Bahini in the absence of the Rules was illegal and yet they continued to function in full vigour backed by the support of the government. The court also went to confirm the same by stating that :

"on an examination of the various provisions of the aforesaid Order it appears to us that the functioning of the Jatiya Rakkhi Bahini without any rules framed under the said Order has the necessary legal foundation[60]."

It was evident that Shahjahan, like so many others was killed by the Rakkhi Bahini, because he allegedly belonged to an opposition student organisation of Jatiyo Samajtantrik Dal in Naria, but there was no evidence as such that could be produced at that stage to prove anything more with their limited jurisdiction. Nevertheless the court in view of the seriousness of the matter suggested that the Government hold an enquiry to determine the whereabout of Shahjahan. The Court observed that

"however on the basis of the materials before us, we are not in a position to hold that the grave allegation made by the petitioner has been substantiated. But the irregular and very unsatistactory manner of the handling of the matter by the Rakkhi Bahini has created a situation which urgently calls for an effective action on the part of the authorities to clear the cloud and create a sense of assurance in the mind of the people."

Although the Court directed that a copy of its order be sent to the Secretary, Home Affairs and the Secretary, Ministry of Defence the order of the Court was sent along with a letter from the lawyers of Shahjahan urging upon the Government to hold and enquiry but no such enquiry was ever held.

In some places the excess committed by the Rakkhi Bahini went beyond comprehension. They behaved like an alien force. They would be sent to remote rural areas to recover arms, smuggled goods and apprehend hoarders and 'miscreants'[61] for which purpose they would set up a camp at the Thana headquarters. In the course of their search they would arrest the 'suspects' and bring them back to the camp and torture them in all sorts of ways for getting confessions. In such operations they would seize things without preparing a list or giving any receipt. It was usual for them to take away a transistor or a radio or a watch from any well-to-do village home and none would protest for fear of life and honour. They would collect money from Bazars, and animals and poultry from the homesteads for their meals. If there was any confrontation or a possibility of that with suspected armed people, they would shoot indiscriminately and throw the dead bodies in the rivers.

A case of such torture was brought before the High Court around the same time in a Habeas Corpus petition challenging the unlawful detention of three women of Rambhadrapur of Bederganj Sub-division[62]. In January, 1974 the Rakkhi Bahini in one of its operations at the village Rambhadrapur went to search for Shanti Sen, a Marxist underground political leader but not having found him, arrested his wife, Aruna Sen, 60 along with his son's wife, Rina Sinha, 19 and Hanufa Begum, 16 who came to visit the old woman from the nearby place. The Rakkhi Bahini took them to their local camp, kept them there for about 2 weeks and then they were shifted to another place. It created an alarm in the mind of the villagers and for weeks no one knew what had happened to them. Ultimately the news came to the capital and a section of the press published the news with allegation that the Rakkhi Bahini had seriously tortured these women. At first, the government remained silent, but when the public pressure increased it came out with a press note admitting that these women were in the custody of the police. The government in the press note alleged that a section of press and some political leaders were propagating motivatedly and mischievously against the activities of the Rakkhi Bahini from the time the Rakkhi Bahini was created. The press note maintained that such allegations that Aruna Sen and others were humiliated or killed were baselsss and they were very much alive in as much as they were in the custody of the police at Dacca. The press note alleged that a large quantity of arms were recovered from the accused persons by the Rakkhi Bahini and also some printing materials implying their involvement in anti-state activities and they were kept in custody with regard to the above allegations. According to the press note the arms recovered from them were : 1 LMG, 2 LMG magazine, 1 SMG, 2 SMG magazine, 4 Rifles, 303 2 Mark 4 Rifles, 1 SLR, 2 hand granade, 2 hand bowls, 1200 round of 9S 500 round 303 ammunitions and one gun. The press note however did not disclose clearly whether there was any criminal case against them[63].

Almost simultaneously, a writ petition was moved before the High Court Division challenging the detention of these 3 persons for issue of a Writ of Habeas Corpus. In the petition it was alleged that they were all severely tortured by the Rakkhi Bahini in the camp. Aruna Sen used to be thrown in the cold water of a nearby river with a long rope tied round her waist and then pulled up again every morning. The two young girls went through every kind of torture including physical assault. The petitioner prayed for production of these women in the court to ensure their safety and freedom.

The Court issued a Rule directing the Government to produce Aruna Sen, Rina Sinha and Hanufa Begum before the Court within 7 days. The Government was on its heel as these women were held in custody for about 2 months without any lawful authority and there was no case against them. The highest authority in the country had intervened and the Attorney-General appeared out of the way before the Court thrice during that week to urge upon the Court to modify its order so that the women did not have to be produced before the Court. The Attorney General argued that it would embarrass the Government as well as the Court and as it involved national security, the court would be surrounded by armed guards which would not look good. The Court did not give in but modified their order to the extent that the women would be produced before them in their chamber instead of court room. On the fixed date they were brought to the court in a prison van not by Rakkhi Bahini but by police. All the allegations contained in the petition were placed before the court and a final date of hearing was fixed on the expiry of 2 days. In the face of the sensation created in the crowded court room and the already built-up publicity in newspapers about the case, the Government decided not to proceed further. The night before the date of final hearing I received a telephone call from the Jail Superintendend that the government had decided to release all these women unconditionally[64]. Myself, Badruddin Umar who had initiated the filing of the case and Enayetullah Khan went to Dacca Central Jail to receive Aruna Sen and the other two girls. The Government Press Note was a lie and the next day the court was informed about the release of the detenus[65].

The Rakkhi Bahini was not under the control of any particular Ministry. It used to be under the direct authority of Sheikh Mujib as the Prime Minister, later as the President. It used to function in a mysterious way. Despite repeated demands from various section of people including the newspapers, the Government never disclosed its budget and composition.

A large section of public alleged that Rakkhi Bahini was an extension of Indian authority in Bangladesh. Not only the training but all its materials and equipments were supplied by India. Their uniform was identical with the uniform of the BSF[66] and people generally identified Rakkhi Bahini with India as its creator. Its pro-Awami League role only strengthened this belief. The *modus operandi*, purpose and composition of the Rakkhi Bahini was the same as the Central Reserve Police in India. It is true that the Bahini started with Indian instructors training both in India and Bangladesh but it is unlikely that some of the Rakkhis were actually from India.

It is however, not true that the Jatiya Rakkhi Bahini did not do anything good. They recovered a large quantity of arms and smuggled goods and the hoarders and black marketeers were frightened of them but the Rakkhi Bahini ultimately failed to hold its image because it was used for political purposes[67]. The vast majority of the smugglers, black marketeers, hoarders, miscreants and possessors of arms who either enjoyed the support of the Awami League workers or enjoyed patronage of their leaders remained outside the ambit of the Rakkhi Bahini operation. The Rakkhi Bahini also failed to recover arms from a large number of those who belonged to the Awami League. So it immediately lost its credibility as a genuine law enforcing ageney. They committed excesses which affected a large number of common and innocent people. They treated the opposition particularly the youths opposed to the Government ruthlessly and killed a large number of them. In the absence of rules or code of conduct, the unaccountability of the Rakkhi Bahini led it to go beyond their limit and in the process it earned the reputation of being a fascist and repressive agency of the government.

In the absence of any code of conduct or any sound administrative structure, the Bahini did not have any discipline within itself. Because of the organisational weakness in the hierarchical authority there used to be continuous squables and fights between themselves—starting from deciding on the rank and status of the officers down to the quantum of food ration of the Rakkhis. With public image fast deteriorating, the desertion from the Bahini only increased. In order to restore discipline and hierarchical authority within the Bahini which had in the meantime grown bigger with men, materials and equipments, the Government made a further amendment to the order. It is interesting to note that the Government did not go for making rules or code of conduct and instead chose to amend the law itself.

The amendment was mainly made to define and strengthen its hierarchy, and discipline within the 'Bahini'[68]. The entire Article 2 or definition clause was substituted to include the definition of 'Battalion', 'Company', 'Platoon', 'Regiment', and 'Zone' which were not there before. In order to discipline the members of the Bahini the definition of 'miscreant', 'Special Court' and 'Special Summary Court' were introduced and to determine the hierarchy the words 'Superior Officers' and 'Subordinate Officers' were defined. A new clause in Article 4 was added saying that the Bahini would be a disciplined force within the meaning of the definition of "disciplined force" as given in Article 152(1) of the Constitution. Article 5 was substituted wholly in order to establish a large hierarchy of superior officers and new class of subordinate officers. By this amendment post of Joint, Deputy and Asstt. Directors and post of Leader, Senior Deputy Leader, Deputy Assistant Leaders were created.

Two special units were created for the officers and the Rakkhis to bring discipline among them and for this purpose two new Articles, 10A and 10B were incorporated. Article 10A meant for all officers and Rakkhis other than the Director. Offences for which trial and disciplinary action could be held and taken included among others mutiny and sedition, criminal force to or assault on superior officers, directly or indirectly protecting any enemy or person in arms against the state, leaving the commanding officer without authority and going in search of plunder, quitting his guard without leave or without authority breaking into any house or any other place for plunder of property of any kind or intentionally causing a false alarm[69]. The punishment could be upto 7 years and the offence would be tried in Special Courts.

Similarly under Article 10B officers and Rakkhis other than the Director were to be tried and punished by Summary Special Court for 25 categories of offences which included among others, intoxication, striking or forcing any sentry, permitting gambling or other prejudicial behaviour while on duty, insubordination, misbehaviour with subordinates, plundering, desertion, etc. Trial for these offences was to be held at Special Summary Court and punishment could go upto 2 years imprisonment and a fine upto 2000 Takas. The Article 17 was amended to provide that any rules made under this Article could be made retrospective from the date of the commencement of the Order.

It is again to be noted that the amendment came much later when the expansion of the Bahini had already taken place and the tendency persisted to give retrospective effect in order to legalise the actions already taken. Judging from the new definition of Regiment, Platoon, etc. it became clear that the Rakkhi Bahini was made into a special force in military form. Although by this amendment effort was made to improve discipline within the Bahini even then in the absence of Rules of Procedure and code of conduct for the functioning of the Rakkhi Bahini the operational side remained the same as far as the public was concerned. The necessity of the amendment also reflected the weaknesses that prevailed within the Rakkhi Bahini and confirmed the public allegation about the offences and the excesses committed by the Rakkhi Bahini.

Smuggling and other Economic Offences

Taking the advantage of an overall scarcity following a devastating nine-month long war and its consequent dislocations and weak administration of political patronage the traders, smugglers and political touts lost no time in making their fortune. The country was sunk in blackmarketeering, hoarding and smuggling. With bank notes printed in India[70] and a considerable increase in the money supply having no relation with production, a high degree of inflation occurred and a sudden rise in the prices of essential commodities took place. The blankets, medicines and even biscuits which came from abroad for relief and rehabilitation of the 10 million refugees who were returning from India were found in abundance on sale at the Calcutta markets. The Jute, life line of Bangladesh's foreign exchange, was found more readily at Calcutta's jute mills. While Indias export of jute went up and all on a sudden their mills started operating 3 shifts a day, the industries at home were in a crippling state and the country got 35% less jute in the first year of independence. Bangladesh was born with a food deficit but still the price of rice and other vital food stuff were cheaper than in India and so the deficit only multiplied due to large scale smuggling. Hides and skins, industrial raw materials, machineries, spare parts, and every possible item that came from abroad including motor cars made their way to India causing a serious shortage within the country and an irreparable damage to its economy.

To check these, another law had to come into force with a more severe punishment clause, covering every possible aspect of black marketing, hoarding, smuggling, misappropriation of relief properties and possessing arms or explosives etc. and these offences were to be tried by specially created tribunals only. The Bangladesh Scheduled Offences (Special Tribunals) Order,[71] was promulgated on 22nd May, 1972 in order to make special provisions for the suppression of certain offences of grave nature.

The operational mechanism of the law was made in the same line as that of the Collaborators Order,—as a matter of fact both were almost identical. The constitution of the Special Tribunal and Special Magistrate, persons to be employed for such courts and their duties, functions and powers were similar in nature. On the question of arrest, detention, bail, forfeiture of properties on conviction and appeal, identical provisions were made. On the question of attachment of properties on mere arrest, unlike the Collaborators Order, the President's Order 50 did not make any such provision but the rest remained the same including proclaiming persons and attaching and disposing their properties. The trial procedures were also identical – the trial was without jury and as summons cases held by Magistrates. The main variation was that under the Collaborators Order sentence could go upto death for murder etc. but under the President's Order No. 50 it could go upto 14 years, the minimum sentence of 3 years remaining the same in both laws.

The law defined "dealing in the black markets" in the most elaborate form and attempted to seal every loophole in black marketeering including the use or dealing with any licence, permit or ration document issued by or under any law. Amongst many other restrictions it prohibited storing, taking, causing, permitting or suffering delivery of anything upon any premises or withholding anything from sale (Article 2(2). It included certain offences as "grave offences" to bring within the purview of this law although there were other laws to deal with most of them (Article 2(2). The offences defined in detail related to arms and explosives, theft or misappropriation of government property or nationalised industries or causing destruction to the functioning of such industries, interfering with the means of transport of any work necessary for the supply or distribution of any essential commodity or its maintenance and services required for that ; interfering with the administration of law and the maintenance of law and order ; causing, carrying out or aiding the import or export of any goods across customs frontiers of Bangladesh.

The "grave offence" under the law also included the offences punishable under section 121, 121A, 122, 123A, 124A, 125 or section 131 of the Penal Code ; robbery or dacoity including hijacking armed with any weapon, firearms or explosives ; offences punishable under Article 19 and 20 of the Abandoned Property Order ; kidnapping or abduction ; rape, adulteration of drugs, medicine, foodstuffs or manufacturing of or dealing in or possession of such things, offence punishable under section 435 or 436 of the Penal Code under the Foreign Exchange Regulation Act ; attempt or making preparation to commit or abetment or the commission of any of the offences mentioned above or any offence committed while armed with firearms or explosive substance. The offences defined in Article 2 were all consolidated in a Schedule of the Order and were named "Scheduled offences."

In the original order like the Collaborators Order only Special Tribunals were created making the Court of Sessions Judge the Special Tribunal but subsequently, due to the pressure of cases it was decided as in the other case to have Special Magistrates. The Sub-divisional Magistrates were made the Special Magistrates with power to transfer cases to any First Class Magistrate within his jurisdiction[72]. But unlike the Collaborators Order, in President's Order No. 50 both the Special Tribunal and Special Magistrate could sentence upto 10 years of rigorous imprisonment or with fine or with both although offences which were to be tried by the Special Magistrate were specified. But subsequently, when by an amendment in 1973 the maximum punishment was raised from 10 to 14 years of rigorous imprisonment for an offence committed under the President's Order No. 50, the Special Magistrates were not authorised to award sentence beyond 10 years and accordingly, their jurisdiction to try the offences was modified.

Under the original Order all cases which were to be tried by the Special Tribunal pending before any other court were transferred to Special Tribunal and there was no need to recall or rehear any witness for the disposal of the case. This provision was widely criticised for various reasons and was soon withdrawn by an Amendment[73]. As in the Collaborators order, under Article 8 of President's Order No. 50 the Government could forfeit the properties of an accused convicted by the Special Tribunal or Special Magistrate and similarly no person who was in custody accused or convicted could be released on bail (Article 10 of President's Order No. 50 and Article 14 of President's Order No. 8). The time for filing an appeal to the High Court both from conviction and acquittal was raised from 30 to 60 days in this case also (Article 12 of the President's Order No. 105 of 1972).

Under the Scheduled Offences Order also Asstt. Inspector or any Police officer or any person empowered by the Government could, without any warrant arrest any person (Article 13, same as Article of P.O.38). Subsequently, under this Order another agency was given power to arrest without warrant and that was the Bureau of Anti-Corruption and by this amendment made in September, 1972 any Police Officer or any person empowered by the government could on suspicion arrest any person without warrant. As in the Collaborators Order this law also provided that any person arrested and detained on or from 1.2.72 alleged to have committed a Scheduled offence would be deemed to be arrested under this Order. Originally it was to be from the date of commencement (May 22, 1972) but later, it was amended on October 24, 1972 to give retrospective effect from 1.2.72.

For the persons absconding or concealing similar provisions for proclamation and attachment were made. Anyone having any claim over the property could make a representation and the Government could release the attachment if the proclaimed person reported before the authority but if he failed to appear could pass an order forfeiting the property. Excepting an appeal as provided in Article 12 no court could call in question any action or proceeding taken or purported to have been taken under the Order.

As will be evident from the offences described in the Schedule and defined in the law, widest possible powers were given to the government and the law enforcing agencies including the Rakkhi Bahini to bring the situation under control. Offences were defined elaborately and broadly and almost anyone could be implicated under one or the other provision—from a political worker to a thief, from a bonafide businessman to an unscrupulous and fake trader. Words continued in Article 2 of the Order such as, "withholding anything from sale" or "causing, permitting or suffering the delivery of anything upon any premises or issuing or dealing with any licence, permit or ration document" issued by or under any such law or "interfering with or encouraging or inciting interference with the administration of law or the maintenance of law and order" could mean anything and be interpreted in any manner and consequently, they provided the law enforcing agencies with a long arm to use their power either way.

As mentioned earlier, there were already established laws to deal with most of the offences including the ones under this Order but even then such a situation required urgently a special way of handling it. If the law was implemented effectively and with prudence the situation could perhaps improve and save the country from economic collapse. In the absence of an institutionalised system, power is either used in excess or misused and this tendency is predominant, particularly in developing societies. The fact that the power to arrest without warrant with no provision for bail was given to any police office or an officer of the Bureau of Anti-corruption was good enough to frustrate the main purpose of the law. At the beginning it was applied to people who were involved in smuggling, black marketeering and hoarding etc. but within a very short time that fear had disappeared as it was found that not a single renowned smuggler or black marketeer was arrested or punished. Either through political patronage or bribery they were able to keep themselves safe and found it easy to go ahead with their activities. So the impact of the law lost its weight within 6 months or so.

On the contrary it was found that the law was being used for political and personal purposes. As a result, a large number of political opponents were put in jail and a large section of innocent people were harrassed and victimised. The law placed the genuine traders and businessmen on the same footing as the dishonest and spurious ones. Most affected in its implementation were those who were bonafide entrepreneurs having proper licence etc. However good the intention might have been on the part of the Government the President's Order No. 50 at the end was condemned as an extremely repressive law and before the year ended a strong demand was raised from all opposition quarters for its repeal. But on the contrary the law was included in the schedule of protected laws under the Constitution then adopted. It would be interesting to note that not many smugglers, hoarders or black marketeers worthy of name were tried and convicted. The implementation of this law only confirmed the view that "in poorer countries laws always benefit the rich and punish the poor". True, there were hundreds of cases tried but they mostly related to poorer people many of whom even could not come to the High Court for any redress. Most of these victims were those who lived near the border, carrying seer of rice or half pound of sugar or a lungi or a couple of sarees and yet they were deprived of bail. The Rakkhi Bahini or the police would stop buses plying within the country, search the passengers on mere suspicion and take into custody men and women carrying small things.

So at the end, the President's Order No. 50 also could not contribute much in restoring normalcy in the country and the perilous cancer that had gone deep in the fibre of the society could not be checked. Organised smuggling across the border continued on a massive scale as before, perhaps with more vigour. The number of secret killings increased and the prices of commodities continued to go up. When all the law.enforcing agencies failed, the Army was called in four times during the rule of the Awami League to assist the Civil administration but each time Mujib had to call them back due to pressure from his own partymen.

Court's Decisions

One of the first and the most elaborate judgements with regard to the provisions of the President's Order No. 50 was delivered in A. T. Mridha vs. The State in May, 1973 by the High Court Division[74]. In this illustrious and lengthy judgement delivered by Justice Badrul Haider Chowdhury the court touched almost all the basic issues of law arising out of the Constitution and the President's Order No. 50, from the concept of human dignity down to the interpretation of an 'accused' person. Altogether 36 decisions were discussed and the court held that it had the power to intervene and more so when subordinate courts or Tribunals were created by special enactment with special powers ousting the jurisdiction of other courts.

The case involved several people and arose out of a fire that broke out at a jute godown in Khulna. The complainant suspected that Mridha who owned the stock and his people had done it in order to make wrongful gain and caused damage to others deliberately. Mridha moved the Court under its revisional jurisdiction and the court issued a Rule and also granted bail which meant at once that the court assumed its jurisdiction over the action of the Sub-divisional Magistrate notwithstanding what was contained in Article 10 with regard to bail and Article 15 with regard to jurisdiction of the Court. The Court assumed this jurisdiction under Article 109 of the Constitution which provided that the High Court Division "shall have superintendence and control over all courts and Tribunals subordinate to it". The Court did not accept the contention of the Attorney General that in view of Article 15 of the President's Order No. 50 read with article 47(2) of the Constitution the High Court Division had lost its jurisdiction of superintendence and control over any action or proceeding taken under this Order. The provision of appeal in Article 12 was allowed only after if any person was convicted or acquitted.

The Court discussed and analysed every relevant aspect of the constitution and its background and philosophical foundation, the corresponding provisions of the Indian constitution and also compared the provisions made in similar special laws as the President's Order No. 50. The Court analysed the fundamental rights enshrined and guaranteed in the Constitution and concluded that the "constitution established rule of law as the guiding principle for the governance of the country". It discussed Article 47(2)[75] with Article 26 of the Constitution and then Article 15 of the President's Order No. 50 and Article 109 of the Constitution in the context of the decided cases cited or referred to by the Attorney General. The Court held that there was no inconsistency between what the Constitution in Article 109 contained and the President's Order No. 50 because the scope of President's Order No. 50 was only for trial of certain grave criminal offences whereas the field of activity of the High Court Division under Article 109 was the superintendence of the entire subordinate judiciary. It was held that wherever an appellate jurisdiction was created the power of interference became necessary for the purpose of doing complete justice. The Court held that Article 15 of the President's Order No. 50 was not inconsistent with Article 109 of the Constitution to bring the same within the mischief of Article 47(2) of the Constitution.

The order of Sub-divisional Magistrate under section 13 of the President's Order No. 50 was an administrative order or judicial order? The court held that the Sub-divisional Magistrate in Article 13 (2) of the Order was the Magistrate within the meaning of section 13 of the Criminal Procedure Code and therefore, was an inferior criminal court within the meaning of section 435 of the Criminal Procedure Code. The Court held that "the Sub-divisional Magistrate under President's Order No. 50 on information or materials placed before him has to come to hold the opinion that the arrested person has committed a scheduled offence and then he may commit the person to custody". So the Court held that as the Sub-divisional Magistrate was committing a person to custody with a stigma he was performing a judicial function.

On the question of bail, the Court held that if no offence against the person was disclosed under the President's Order No. 50 when the arrest of such person was made outside the purview of President's Order No. 50 Article 10 of the Order would not be applicable. Justice Badrul Haider Chowdhury argued that "refusal of bail or withholding of bail tantamounts to punishment without trial and since no time limit had been given in President's Order No. 50 for completion of the investigation or enquiry, it cannot be the intention of the legislature that the moment the information is lodged against a person he has to be detained for an indefinite period." In this case as no materials sufficient enough could be collected after investigating for 5 months and no connection could be established between the person arrested and the offences alleged, the Court therefore held that the petitioner was not an accused and was entitled to be released on bail and the proceeding were to be quashed in such circumstances.

On appeal the Appellate Division had however set aside the order of the High Court Division in March, 1974,[76] but the court did not go into all the points of law raised by the High Court Division. On a technical point the validity of which can yet be questioned the Court held that the Sub-divisional Magistrate was functioning in his administrative capacity and was not performing a judicial function and therefore, the order was not open to the revisional jurisdiction of the High Court under Section 435 or 439 of the Criminal Procedure Code. The Court held that "the Sub-divisional Magistrate when only after completion of the enquiry starts functioning as a special Magistrate commences his judicial function". The Appellate Division however, did not touch the point that whether an order committing a person to custody with a social stigma could be done at all through an administrative Order nor did the Court distinguish between an order of preventive detention and an order of committing a person to custody.

However, since the decision was based on a very narrow and technical point, the main issues on the revisional jurisdiction of the High Court Division and their power to grant bail and quash proceedings in such cases were not disputed by the Appellate Division and the case in the High Court Division helped in establishing certain principles of law in this regard.

As a result, Justice Fazle Munim in Abu Tayeb Md. Masood and Tipu vs. the State[77] upholding the principle laid down by the Appellate Division allowed the petitioner to remain on bail and observed further that the High Court Division had the authority to quash the proceedings if no cognizable offence of any kind was disclosed. In Mashiur Rahman alias Jadu Mia vs. The State[78] Justice Kemaluddin Hossain, with regard to the arrest by a police officer without warrant held that whenever any grant of power was qualified by the word 'reasonable' the said power would be subject to judicial review. There must be "some grounds on which a reasonable man and a reasonable court might come to the conclusion that there were materials sufficient for the officer to exercise his power and they were relatable to the offence committed and they manifestly connect the suspect with the offence."

Nevertheless, it could not be denied that the President Order No. 50 provided itself with the widest possible power to deal with the menaces which were eating up the economic strenght of the new country. Although the powers given were unusual and excessive as a result of which the Police and the Rakkhi Bahini victimised a large number of innocent people in controlling smuggling and other anti-social offences.

The Civil Administration

The Awami League had earlier committed themselves, even in the context of Pakistan that a total structural change would be necessary to discard the colonial type of administration and they would introduce a pro-people administrative machinery[79]. This approach was further strengthened during the Pakistan regime when bureaucracy was allowed to play a major political role in the country. Gholam Mohammad, Chowdhury Mohammad Ali and Iskander Mirza, all bureaucrats played the most unconstitutional role during the formative period of Pakistan. The elitism created in the Civil Service of Pakistan (CSP) alienated it from the political forces of the country. In the years of struggle for democratic rights and against political and economic repression, the civil service was considered a legacy of the British rule and the ruling class[80]. It not only created a social and political contradiction between the highest cadre of service and the political forces, it also created a great amount of tension and imbalance between them and the rest of the lower cadres of servicemen who constituted the vast majority of the government employees. In relation to the social and economic condition of the people as a whole, the service developed as an alien class and despite whatever good the individual members of the service did to Pakistan or his service, the system was constantly under attack by almost all sections of people including the major political parties.

The Awami League was therefore in favour of restructuring the administrative machinery to serve the needs of a dynamic democratic society. It pledged to abolish the existing all-Pakistan and Central Superior Services and entrust the district administration to elected councils assisted by specialised staff[81]. One of the steps the Awami League would take was to reduce the gap in income between the higher income employees and the lower income employees. Now with the achievement of independence through a war, the demand to rationalise the administration only consolidated further. All through these years the Awami League enjoyed a vast support from the low-income-group employees and lower civil officers of the government who contributed in constituting the vanguard for the nationalist movement. As long back as in 1954 the Awami League committed itself through the historical 21-point programme that it would minimise the gap of income disparities between the high and low salaried employees[82]. Since then, the Awami League moved a long way and moved further at the last phase of the nationalist movement when they pledged to establish a socialist economic order in the country.

To summarise, the Awami League's policy towards the civil administration and bureaucracy was as follows : (1) They proposed a radical restructuring of the administrative machinery to serve the needs of a dynamic democratic society and to abolish the elite cadres of the service. (2) It would entrust the district administration to elected councils assisted by specialised staff. (3) The party advocated for strengthening local government institutions, including widening the size of the basic administrative unit by converting sub-divisions into districts. (4) It proposed to create specialised professional cadres subject to a new framework of service rules. This was suggested to replace the existing superior service created in the context of running a federal government in Pakistan. (5) It would adopt effective measures for supervision and control of administrative action in order to eliminate corruption, nepotism and arbitrariness in the discharge of the administrative functions[83].

In the manifesto of 1973 election too the Awami League made pledges in the same line. It was committed to establish progressive administrative system, free of corruption, suitable for a socialist economic order. It pledged to hand over local administration to elective representatives and reorganisation of administration by turning the sub-division into districts[84].

What it all implied was that the Awami League intended to establish complete political authority over the bureaucracy. Like its attitude towards the Pakistan Army, the Awami League developed a sense of negation towards the bureaucratic elite of Pakistan. Both acted as political forces in Pakistan and both were threats to the political leadership in the country. So according to the Awami League these were not to be allowed in Bangladesh—the elitism in these forces was to be destroyed. Whether to keep in line with their 'socialistic programme' or to establish their political control over the existing bureaucracy, the Awami League continued to pursue their programme of reorganising the administration including the pay structure and services. The Sheikh told the officials on the first February address in 1972 to change their bureaucratic outlook of the past and consider themselves as servants of the people. He told them that the country was freed through a revolution and therefore, revolutionary steps would have to be taken on a basis of urgency to build up the country. Notwithstanding the immediate bad effect of the application of the Collaborator's Order and President's Order No. 9 the independence through a war gave the Awami League an opportunity to rebuild the bureaucracy to suit, according to them "the need of the people".

Whether it was because of his socialist thinking or a public commitment made as far back as in 1954 or by the United Front or due to the sheer economic necessity arising out of the war which led Tajuddin to cut the salary of the higher government employees in one of his first decisions after Bangladesh was formally established, is not known. In Calcutta, by promulgating the Laws Continuance Enforcement Order, the government in exile assured all employees the same terms and conditions of service they so long enjoyed. Nevertheless, within 7 days after their arrival from Calcutta the Cabinet decided as an "austerity measure" to cut the salary for the time being till the entire pay structure was looked into[85]. This was made applicable to all government, autonomous, local bodies and university. The balance amount due to an employee was to be disbursed in the form of national savings certificate. The government further decided not to allow any increment to an employee drawing above Tk. 500/- per month.

In the prevailing circumstances the decision was not opposed and the people at large accepted the decision. Soon pressure was mounting to introduce austerity measures for the private employees also. Accordingly on 31st December, 1971 the Acting President's Order No. 5 was promulgated to regulate the payment of remuneration of employees of private organisations, companies, firms or any other institution or body not created by the government. The pay structure prescribed was in line with the government employees. In case of private employees the balance amount payable to an employee was to be utilised in the manner as the government would direct.

This created a lot of problems for the employees and employers in the public and private sectors and caused considerable dislocation in management and production. The confusion in both the sectors continued for a while and ultimately the maximum salary in the public sector was raised to Tk. 2000/- on the recommendation of a national commission but in the private sector both the employers and the employees started to ignore the government directives till the law was repealed.

This pay-cut had far-reaching consequences. Not more than 3 months had expired, the prices of essential commodities were rising fast and the sense of sacrifice and austerity in the newly born country lost its meaning as far as the government employees were concerned. The government decision not only affected the higher salaried employees but a large number of middle and lower-middle range employees who were already stuck down by the rising cost of living. The rise in prices also affected the lower salaried groups who started raising demand for the increase in their wages and salaries. That there was a difference between reducing the gap of higher and lower salary scale and random salary cut was perhaps not realised in the right perspective as a result of which a great amount of dissatisfaction continued to prevail amongst all sections of employees particularly in the public sector. With rising inflation this ultimately led to a large-scale corruption in the public sector, corroded the moral standard of the functioneries and had a decaying effect on the very foundation of the new country.

Besides the question of this austerity measure, equally if not more consequential, was the question of deciding who was or was not a 'patriotic' civil servant. Those who crossed the border and joined the government in exile took the upper hand in the state affairs undermining those who remained inside the country and the conflict arising out of this attitude was nothing but disastrous. Encouraged by the political leaders and workers of the Awami League those officers who returned from India took over the charge of the administrator in Dhaka[86]. But soon it was discovered that many of them were not competent enough to run the administration and those who did not join the war directly had to be inducted. This resulted in a division of the civil servants between those who crossed the border and those who did not[87].

In this way, the grouping within the administration continued. Besides treating some senior officers as collaborators : the government removed 53 public servants on the ground that they were conferred civil awards by the Pakistani Military Regime during the period from March 26 to December 16, 1971[88]. This action caused further deterioration of discipline and cohesion in the civil service as a whole. The situation was further worsened when the government failed to face the impact of such an action as it took back some of the officials the next day and almost all of them later on. This action and its withdrawal directly affected the credibility of the government.

Nevertheless, keeping in line with their earlier commitment and assuming that following the war it now represented a 'revolutionary government', the Awami League proceeded to reorganise the entire system of administration in order to establish a machinery which could effectively meet the urgent task of national reconstruction. With these objectives in view the government introduced a law popularly known as the President's Order No. 9 of 1972[89].

Contrary to the provision of the Laws Continuance Enforcement Order, Article 5 of the President Order 9 now declared that no person had any claim to employment in the service or any other claim whatsoever against the Government on the basis of having been employed at any time in the service of Pakistan. In other words, the terms and conditions of service of any government employee kept in tact under the Continuance Order were made non-existent and they were all now holding their jobs at the sheer mercy of the ruling Government. Besides the direct employees of the government, persons employed by the statutory corporations and autonomous bodies were also brought within the purview of the law by expanding the definition of the "government servant".

Article 6 of the President's Order No. 9 provided that if in the opinion of the government employees of the government or any corporation were not required in the interest of the Republic, the government could remove such persons "without assigning any reason notwithstanding anything to the contrary contained in any law or in the terms and conditions of the service". This power was not to be exercised only upon those who were previously in the service of Pakistan but also on all those who are newly recruited and were in the service of the Government or any statutory corporation.

The law provided that no legal action would lie against the government arising out or in respect of an order made under order (Article 7).

This was a short law with the most serious consequences in the administration of the country. While the government with the Laws Continuance Order took the position of a successor government it now changed into a revolutionary one. According to the preamble however these provisions were required "to give effect to the reorganisation of the entire administrative system to meet effectively the urgent task of national reconstruction".

While there was no reorganisation in sight, the law took its own course. The blanket-cover it provided, only brought in more uncertainty in the administration of the country. Since the British rule, the government servants were enjoying certain defined privileges, the most important one being the security of employment. No one could be deprived of his job without due process of law and there used to be elaborate service rules and regulations covering every aspect of the terms and conditions of service of any person employed by the government. These added to the social prestige of a person so employed. During the Pakistan period the same system continued and both the constitutions of 1956 and 1962 guaranteed special provisions for the government servants to protect their rights according to the terms and conditions of their service.

It was true that the new revolutionary achievement of independence for a better order of life, without any doubt, demanded a new approach to the problem of administration by a colonial power. That the newly independent country would need to reorganise the administrative machinery was not to be questioned. But whether the President's Order No. 9 was the answer could only be ascertained on examining how the law was implemented at the end. Ironically it would be evident that the law was put into operation without any plan for reorganisation. It was like having a carriage before the horse and the consequence was disastrous.

Whatever might have been the objectives or the intention of the government, the immediate reality was that the plea for reorganisation of administration for national reconstruction was only a cover. The action taken by the government in pursuance of the law proved that the underlying purpose was to establish total political authority over the bureaucracy and civil administration. The removal of the collaborators and the political opponents in the quickest possible time could now be legalised. Anyone who was not conforming or was reluctant to carry out any order of the Awami League elite, good or bad, could be removed without any legal hindrance, likes and dislikes of the political leaders became more important than efficiency or experience and consequently, the entire civil service out of insecurity, turned subservient to its political masters. The victims of the law could be anyone from a senior secretary to a thana development officer, from an engineer in a workshop to a driver or a conductor of a BRTC bus[90]. It was not so much a question of actual removal but it was the fear of being removed that shook the confidence of the government officials. Although no removal of any employee during this period had anything to do with the reorganisation of the administration but the government continued to claim that actions under the law were taken in order to facilitate the reorganisation of the administration.

With regard to the President's Order No. 9 even the superior courts could not come to much assistance. Although the Supreme Court could assume the jurisdiction under its inherent power given in Article 102 of the Constitution despite Article 7 of the Order, the court was constrained to take a restricted view because of the specific provisions laid down therein. Although the same initial orders were issued by the court on the ground that the law denied the established principle of natural justice and that the Constitution being the supreme law was to prevail over the President's Order No. 9 but at the end the court did not intervene in the implementation of the law. In other words, the law took its own course in the literary sense denying the opportunity to question its vires.

In Md. Rezaul Haque v. Government of Bangladesh[91], although the Court held that there was no check whatever to wrongful exercise of the power given under President's Order No. 9 it was not possible for the Court to intervene because of Article 47(2) which provided a protective shield over all the statutes specified in the First Schedule of the Constitution. As President's Order No. 9 was one of the laws protected and included in the First Schedule of the Constitution, the principle of natural justice could not be made available to an employee although Article 135 of the Constitution provided for a show cause notice prior to the termination of service of such an employee. The Court however, remarked that "a legislation like P. O. 9

might have been necessary but retention of it for an indefinite period is hardly justified."

The Bangladesh Public Servants' (Retirement) Order, 1972

The government promulgated two more laws in 1972, one relating to retirement age of public servants and the other for screening corrupt officials, 'collaborators' and others. By the first one the government regulated the retirement age of all public servants including those who were in the service of autonomous, semi-autonomous bodies, corporations and local bodies constituted under any law. The retirement age was fixed at 55 years with provision for extension under re-employment of those who were considered to be doing work of specialised or technical nature and whose replacement were not readily available. Under the law the government retained the authority to terminate the service of any person who was already on extention beyond the age of superanuation without leave or prior notice. It meant that the employee of the public sector who had passed the age of 55 could be removed by the government. Although it put a considerable number of senior employees out of work it helped the government to employ the young persons who were qualified but unemployed, providing a scope for the younger employees to rise through promotions.

The major amendments made to the laws were contained in President's Order No. 121 of 1972 Ordinance XXVI of 1973 and Act XII of 1974. The most interesting provision was related to an option for the retirement both from the side of employee and the government. Besides other provisions, the amendment consistently maintained a retirement option allowing a public servant to seek retirement on the completion of 25 years of service and similarly, a power was given to the government to retire a public servant at any time on completion of 25 years of service without assigning any reason.

Like the cases under President's Order No. 9 the courts took a restricted view of this law of retirement also in view of certain provisions laid down in the Constitution. In Abdur Rashid v. Government of Bangladesh Justice Ruhul Islam held that the Parliament being the supreme law-making body was competent to regulate the time of retirement of the government servants notwithstanding the terms and conditions of service which were applicable immediately before the commencement of the Constitution. In view of the provisions made in paragraph 10 of the Fourth Schedule of the Constitution, the Court held that section 9(2) of Act XII of 1974 relating to retirement of public servant without assigning any reason could not be ultra vires of the Constitution. It further held that the provision relating to compulsory retirement was not protected under Article 135 of the Constitution although the Court left an opening on the question of compulsory retirement by the government if made by way of punishment.

It would be evident that the Awami League was determined to reorganise the services and keeping that in view adequate provisions were made in the Constitution to empower the Government to bring necessary changes in the terms, conditions, appointment and re-organisation of the services. Paragraph 10 of the Fourth Schedule of the Constitution clearly indicated this intention of the ruling party. It not only protected President's Orders 9 and 67 of 1972 it also empowered the Government to make laws varying the terms and conditions of service.

The other law was somewhat of a more serious nature[92]. The law was made for establishing an administrative machinery whereby corporations, nationalised enterprises, local authorities and government aided institutions would be free from corrupt persons, collaborators, official and other employees wedded to the ideology of Pakistan and for effectively carrying the urgent task of national reconstruction[93]. Here also like in the President's Order No. 9 the definition of the government servant was broadened and included all persons who were in the service of the government or any corporation or local authority and anyone purporting to claim a right to employment in the service of Bangladesh having been at one time in the service of Pakistan. In this case the law went further to include the persons who were in the service of the nationalised enterprises and any govt.-aided institution meaning any organisation receiving any kind of financial assistance from the government. The law however excluded the members of the armed forces, persons holding office created by a President's Order. If there was any inconsistency with any existing law or rules or the terms and conditions of any service, this law or any rule made thereunder would prevail. In other words, any employee of the government or any institution mentioned would come within the framework of the law, no matter what the terms and conditions of their service would guarantee them (Article 2A).

The scheme was to have atleast 2 screening boards, the First Screening Board and the Second Screening Board (Article 3) with one Chairman, one member and one member-Secretary in each (Article 4) to examine the case of any government servant as defined above with reference to his activities, records or such reports of allegation on any reference made to it on such person by any agency of the government or any information received in writing from any other source (Article 5). The allegation could be in respect of (1) corruption, or corrupt practices or even having reputation of being corrupt like having assets beyond known and ostensible income and would include assets of wife, dependents and other relations also, (2) conduct or activity while exercising power or discharging duties manifesting ardour or zeal amounting to collaboration which could be considered as aid, assistance or support to any activity directed against the liberation struggle or creation of Bangladesh or any ardent faith or support were exhibited to the ideology of Pakistan or in support of the Pakistanis and inimical to the liberation struggle or creation of Bangladesh, particularly the occupation forces, (3) conduct or behaviour of any kind showing opposition or hostility towards the declared objectives, programmes, policies and decisions of the government or the principles underlying them or any tendency to undermine the implementation of such policies etc., (4) anti-social activities or conduct involving moral turpitude amounting to misconduct as defined in the Government (Efficiency and Discipline) Rules, 1960.

For the purpose of examination of a case on allegations mentioned in Article 5, the Board could call for any evidence or record or statement from any person and all the executive authorities would assist the Board in the discharge of its functions. The Court by an appointed officer could conduct an enquiry or investigation of its own and for this purpose could enforce attendance of any person or compel production of any record etc. and the Board would enjoy the same power in this respect as are vested in a civil court under the Code of Civil Procedure. The Board would also have power to examine cases of employees of any university, association, institution or any other organisation if such institution through their executive body passed a resolution to that effect and the government had declared that the order would be applicable to such person and in such event the employees of any such institution would be deemed to be 'government servant' for the purpose of this Order.

The Board on examination of each case could make one of the three recommendations to the government. (1) Dismissal from service and in cases where charges of corruption or collaboration were proved, forfeiture or property in full or part. (2) Removal from service with or without retirement benefits. (3) Discharge or compulsory retirement with or without retirement benefits or stoppage of increment or reduction in rank. The Government could however while giving effect to the recommendation of the Board award reduced or enhanced punishment as provided in the Order. Before making a recommendation, the Board would however hear the person concerned without being accompanied by any formal adviser or legal practitioner. In the interest of an impartial enquiry, the Board could recommend to place a government servant under suspension.

This law also provided, interestingly enough, an opportunity to review an order of dismissal or removal or any other order made under MLR Nos. 58 and 59 of the Yahya regime if such matter was referred to the Board by the Government on receipt of a representation by an aggrieved person (Article 9)[94]. The Board on examination of a case could recommend variation or amendment of the earlier order or confirm the same or could recommend further penal action.

No court could call into question any action taken under this order or its rules which meant that any action of the Board could only be challenged under the extraordinary writ jurisdiction of the High Court Division. The government framed rules for the functioning of the two Boards and on such framing of the Rules the Board started functioning.

As it would be evident, it was a self-contained law and in line with the President's Order No. 9 the law excluded the force of any other law, rules or terms and conditions relating to service which would otherwise give an employee a certain protection. The established principles relating to the removal, dismissal or disciplinary punishment particularly with regard to government servants were done away with. However, as the President's Order No. 67 provided a procedure for punishment including a right to be heard, it was certainly an improvement over the harsh and arbitrary law called President's Order No. 9 but the interesting point was that both the laws continued to be in operation simultaneously.

Similarly another interesting point was that the collaborators could also be punished within the purview of this Order. Despite the more compact law of the Collaborators Order, the government felt the necessity of introducing another law to handle and punish them. It appears from the reading of all these laws that the government did not want to leave any loophole with regard to the supervision and control of the employees of the government and public sectors.

The President's Order No. 67 also served as a weapon for the Awami League to eliminate corruption from the administration. This aspect of the law was acclaimed by the people as corruption was so widespread and the pressure was mounting on the government to do something about it. A large number of cases containing allegations of corruption initiated both by the government and by members of public were handled by the two Boards and a sizeable number of employees were punished under the law on charges of corruption.

Although not very many cases were filed on charges of collaboration the main purpose of the law was to create a deterrant rather than serve for actual punishment of government servants. This kept the government servants who were serving inside the country during the war period terrified and psychologically subdued for fear of being harrassed or blackmailed. In most cases, this led to victimisation and humiliation, as the law was such that anyone could be said to have aided or assisted the occupation army by just being in office under their orders or by just carrying out the normal function.

As far as the courts are concerned they did not challenge the vires of this statute. Like in cases concerning President's Order No.9 no remarkable judicial pronouncement was made in respect of President's Order No. 67. The court of course intervened whenever there was any violation of any rules made under the law with regard to the functioning of the Boards or punishment of the empolyees.

Although the declared objectives of these laws could not be questioned, the effect of their implementation reflected an inherently weak position of the government so far as the allegiance of the total population was concerned. To enact multiple laws to deal with the collaborators demonstrated a sense of insecurity in the members of the Government because of the fact that the number of officers and employees who crossed the border were comparatively much smaller than those who remained inside the country during the war period. This created an atmosphere of psychological warfare between the two groups. So, a general distrust of those who remained inside the country was reflected through the provisions of these laws arising out of the fear that the vast majority of the government servants who did not cross the border or joined the government in exile were now opposed to the government.

Exemption of Taxes and Land Ceiling

Along with these laws, some of which were of repressive nature and provided scope for widespread corruption and appropriation of public properties, the government took certain other actions to maintain its electoral commitments and general popularity. The government moved to hold its popularity by showing some fruits of independence for the common men[95].

In order to maintain its credibility and image, one of the first things the new government did was the suspension of the realisation of land revenue from the people which gave relief to a large section of rural population[96]. Later the land revenue was exempted for holdings not exceeding 25 bighas of land. The law also remitted all arrear taxes for the same land holdings. In the same law, the State Acquisition and Tenancy (Third Amendment) Order, 1972 which was created for the purpose of this exemption 'family' was defined to include husband, wife, son, unmarried daughter, son's wife, son's son and son's unmarried daughter[97]. This was in line with the Awami League's election commitment that the land revenue for land holding upto 25 bighas ($8\frac{1}{3}$ acres) would be exempted from revenue with the ultimate aim for total abolition of land revenue[98]. On the same day on 5th August, 1972 their commitment for land ceiling was translated through the P.O. 98 which for the first time fixed the land ceiling ownership to 100 bighas of land[99]. The law defined the land and the family in the same line as in the P.O. 95/1972 and provided penalty for not complying with the provisions of the Order. Although these laws produced limited benefit in the over all context of the burning issues like the land tenure system and landlessness that was prevailing in the country and despite the fact that the implementation of the law limiting the ceiling would not be made effective[100], the actions earned the government some popularity. The Government also distributed 100 million Taka of Taccavi loan and 160 million Taka under Test Relief Schemes. The government granted amnesty to all who were convicted by military courts before 16th December, 1971. It even commuted all death sentences to 14 years rigorous imprisonment with provision for special remission at the rate of 3 months per year[101]. By promulgating the Legal Proceedings Order, 1972 on 7th February, 1972 the government also made null and void all judgements, decrees and orders by any court or tribunal which were passed exparte due to default in any legal proceeding at any time after March 1, 1971 till the Order was made[102]. In the education sector in order to please the students the government exempted tuition fees payable by students of all educational institutions both government and non-government for the period from March, 1971 to December, 1971[103]. Further, government in order to unfold before the students an academic life free from set backs and hindrances decided to remit the unexpired portion of the period of punishment of the SSC and HSC examinees[104]. The government in the same month decided to provide free books for all students in all primary schools upto Class V[105]. Within 5 months of independence, the new government appointed an Education Commission for the purpose of initiating reforms in this vital sector and to enunciate a "pro-people education policy"[106]. The government abolished the excise duties on salt and in doing that met a long standing demand of the salt producers.

Industrial Workers

As for the industrial workers who constituted the vaneguard of the independence struggle, impression was given to them by the political leaders that on nationalisation of industries they would now become the owner of these industries. The ministers and other leaders continued to make statements without understanding their implications. The Labour Minister announced that shares of industrial concerns would be alloted to workers. He later on confirmed that 30% of shares of an industrial concern would be alloted to workers, 30% to employers and 40% would be held by the goverment[107]. In his first anniversary statement when he declared the nationalisation of all major sectors Mujib assured the workers that perennial conflict that had divided the labour and capital would be eliminated and the workers would participate in the managment of the industrial concerns[108]. When he addressed the workers' representatives on 3rd April, 1972 Mujib told them that the government was firmly committed to establish a socialistic economy for the welfare of the people and sought their co-operation in implementing the programmes. He reiterated that the workers representatives would be taken into the management boards of the nationalised industries[109].

Although these statements and assurances made the workers happy temporarily at the end they were frustrated when a labour policy was announced without giving them any share in the industries. The policy further narrowed the scope of collective bargaining on the ground that the industries now belonged to the public sector and it recommended for the constitution of a National Wage Board to formulate a wage structure for all the workers categoriwise. For public sectors, Management Boards and Management Councils were to be constituted for the efficient running of the industries. The opposition parties rejected the policy on the principal ground that the policy did not ensure the right to bargain and strike. In any case, the first labour policy of the Awami League government could not take off the ground not because of the rejection of the policy by the opposition parties but because of the highhandedness of the labour leaders belonging to the Awami League. Most of the industries were already in the hand of the proteges of the Awami League who were unwilling to sacrifice the privileges they were enjoying in the name of protecting the right of the workers.

Despite the enactment of all these laws and the measures taken the situation on the law and order and the economic front did not improve. In many ways the situation continued to deteriorate. Industries were incurring loss, inflation was shooting up, the price of essential commodities was rising[110] and smuggling across the border could hardly be checked. A grave sense of insecurity continued to prevail in the mind of the ordinary people; civil servants lost the security of their service[111]; banks[112], bazars and police stations were being looted; secret killings[113], kindnapping, hijacking[114], robbery and dacoity[115] became a daily affair.

This trend in the law and order situation continued till the last day of the Mujib regime. In the entire period of the Awami League regime almost every day newspapers were full of stories of loot, killing and sabotage. The characteristic feature of the lawlessness was that whenever a police station was looted, the adjacent bazars were also looted and generally the miscreants would do so by imposing a 'curfew' in the area.

Politically, within less than six months since independence the Awami League through its various organisation took over the control of almost every agency and forum upto the grassroot level having socio-economic relationship with the people. Starting from the Relief Committees and local councils to the Managing Committees of hats and bazars the omnipotent position of the Awami League workers was more than established. All the managing or governing committees of the Schools and Colleges of the country were also dissolved and new ad-hoc committees were constituted through the Awami League Members of the Constituent Assembly[116]. Hundreds of industries and other properties, abandoned or nationalised went into their hands or administrative control. Thousands of permits and licences for trade and business dealership and agencies were issued to the favourites of the Awami League[117]. The Awami League did it alone and they would not allow anyone else to take the responsibility of nation building task. Moulana Bhashani's call for a national government was completely ignored[118], and the Awami League failed in associating any other political party or groups to take part in their programme for "national reconstruction". With all possible agencies and committees within their control and a government led by a leader like Sheikh Mujibur Rahman, they had all the opportunities to provide the people with a new sense of direction and materialise their cherished goal of establishing a 'Sonar Bangla' for the 75 million Bengalis. During these months there was hardly any political opposition to the Awami League and yet they failed to show any tangible progress towards achieving their 'cherished goal'.

Along with issues like law and order and the problem of reconstruction, the government faced another deadly issue and that was food. Bangladesh was already a food-deficit area and now ravaged by war the production in 1971 went down compared to the past years. Added to this was the large scale smuggling across the border causing a sharp rise in price of rice on which depends the popularity of any regime in this country. So the Government was faced with a gigantic food deficit created both by man and nature. Experts were already warning[119] about the possible threat of famine when the country was engaged in war but it seemed, no adequate measures were taken to meet the situation. This development will be discussed in detail in Chapter 4 below.

FOOTNOTES

1. See appendix 'D' on "problems to be faced by the present Government".
2. See appendix 'D'.
3. From author's discussion with Tajuddin Ahmed immediately after the independence.
4. Other members were A.H.M. Kamaruzzaman, Moulana Abdul Hamid Khan Bhashani, Monoranjan Dhar, Prof. Muzaffar Ahmed, Moni Singh, Tofail Ahmed, Abdur Razzak, Rafiquddin Bhuiya, Gazi Golam Mostafa and Capt. (Retd.) Sujat Ali.
5. It is not known whether the Moulana was really consulted or he had his consent to be a member of this committee.
6. The word 'Gonobahini' was used to include all categories and groups of freedom fighters.
   Accordingly, national militia camps were set up for the purpose.
7. See Mujib's statement on January 17, 1972.—*The Morning News*, January 18, 1972, Dhaka.
8. A few days later the government issued a press release outlining the objectives in the same line and ended by saying "Let us all unite to shape our motherland into a real Shonar Bangla".—*The Morning News*, Dhaka, January 25, 1972.
9. There was an arms surrendering ceremony held at the Dhaka Stadium on January 30 on behalf of the Mukti Bahini loyalists. The arms and ammunition surrendered were insignificant in quantity compared to the actual accumulation in the hand of the people and many of those surrendered were obsolete.
10. No comprehensive statement of actual arms recovered has been made available by any government.
11. *The Morning News*, February 25 and 29 of 1972.
12. No one knew the exact number of Freedom Fighters. Certificates which were to identify freedom fighters were sold in the streets at one time, as many people were issued false certificates as a part of political patronage.
13. The Bangladesh (Freedom Fighters) Welfare Foundation Order, 1972 (President's Order No. 94 of 1972), 7th August, 1972.
14. Mujib knew about it and made concessions to his partymen on the question of arms surrendering.
15. Al-Badars was another armed gang of persons who were trained by Pakistan Government to apprehend the freedom fighters.

16. Mujib alleged in his statement issued on 17th January, 1972 that members of Al-Badr, Razakars and Al-Shams organisations were masquerading themselves as members of the Gonobahini and posing a threat to the life and property of the people.—*The Morning News*, Dhaka, 18.1.1972.
17. See newspaper reporting on these occurances almost everyday from mid, 1972 to end of 1974.
18. The Awami League leaders however continued to allege in many of their statements that conspiracies were still going on to undo Bangladesh. Mujib in his address to the members of the Mukti Bahini on the arms surrender ceremony on 30th January, 1972 at the Dhaka Stadium warned that "the imperialists and their leckeys are still conspiring against the independence of Bangladesh".
19. On December 14, only two days prior to the surrender of the Pakistan Army, members of the Al-Badr killed 9 eminent teachers of the Dhaka University besides many other men of letters. See for more details on the question of killing, kidnapping etc. of the intellectuals.—*The Morning News*, February 21, 1972.
20. The Bangladesh Collaborators (Special Tribunals) Order, 1972. (President's Order No. 8 of 1972), 24th January, 1972.
21. This generally meant officials and employees of the Government including judiciary and other agencies.
22. The punishable offences were :

    PART I

    Offences under sections 121, 121-A, 302, 304, 307, 376, 396 of the Penal Code and attempts to commit or the abetment of the commission of any of such offences.

    PART II

    Offences under sections 308, 325, 326, 328, 329, 330, 331, 333, 354 363, 364 365, 367, 368, 369, 380, 382, 386, 388, 389, 392, 393, 394 395, 397, 435, 436, 437, 438, 449 and 450 of the Penal Code and attempts to commit or the abetment of the commission of any of such offences.

    PART III

    Offences under sections 148, 324, 332, 338, 343, 346, 348, 355, 356, 379, 384, 427, 428, 429, 430, 431 and 440 of the Penal Code and attempts to commit or the abetment of the commission of any of the offences.

    PART IV

    (a) Offences under sections 143, 147, 336, 337, 341, 342, 352, 357, 374, 426, 447 and 448 of the Penal Code and attempts to commit or the abetment of the commission of any of the offences

    (b) Any act which is mentioned in Clause (b) of Article 2 of this Order but which is not covered by any item under any of the parts of this schedule.
23. The Bangladesh Collaborators (Special Tribunals) (Second Amendment) Order, 1972 (President's Order No. 60 of 1972) lst June, 1972.
24. The complaint used to be made largely by the Awami League workers and supporters. Amendment was introduced by the President's Order No. 103 of 1972.
25. The President's Order No. 60 of 1972.
26. The Bangladesh Collaborators (Special Tribunals) (Third Amendment) Order, 1972 (President's Order No. 103 of 1972, 29th August, 1972.
27. *Ibid.* Trial in absentia which had been unknown under the original Code of Criminal Procedure thus made it appearance in Bangladesh law, to be extended later to the Special Powers Act (Ordinance XL of 1977 Sec. 2) and to the Code of Criminal Procedure itself (Ordinance XXIV of 1982, sec. 24).

28. 27 DLR 1975, p. 437. In another case a similar view was held by the court and the entire proceedings were quashed on this particular ground.
29. 27 DLR 1915, p. 77
30. The Bangladesh Collaborators (Special Tribunals) (Third Amendment) Order, 1972 (President's Order No. 103 of 1972), 29th August, 1972.
31. Transaction in somebody else's name—a Benami transaction. See 1956 SCR 691 AIR 1957 SC 49.
32. The implication of this provision had serious consequences causing harrassment, victimisation and unlimited suffering to a section of people.
33. 27 DLR 1975 AD, p. 16
34. 25 DLR 1973 HC, p. 207
35. 26 DLR 1976, AD, p. 1.
36. 25 DLR 1973 HC 335.
37. 26 DLR 1974 HC 241.
38. 27 DLR 1975, p. 334.
39. The Bangladesh Collaborators (Special Tribunals) (Third Amendment) Order, 1972 (President's Order No. 103 of 1972), 29th August, 1972. Ironically, while the law was made to apprehend those who filed nomination paper for the bye-election during the war as collaborators, the person who conducted all such elections as the Chief Election Commissioner of Pakistan and the only person who took oath under the Pakistan Consititution in 1972 was not considered as a collaborator by the Awami League government. On the contrary, on his return from Pakistan, Justice Abdus Sattar who subsequently became the President of Bangladesh, was appointed as the Chairman of a state owned insurance corporation. This highly discretionery law was therefore used mainly for political purposes.
40. 26 DLR 1974 HC, p. 1.
41. 26 DLR 1974 HC, p. 183.
42. 26 DLR 1974 AD, p. 14.
43. The first list included

    (1) Mr. Nurul Amin, (2) Mr. Hamidul Huq Chowdhury, (3) Mr. Khan A. Sabur, (4) Mr. Mahmud Ali, (5) Mr. Wahiduzzaman Khan, (6) Khawja Khairuddin, (7) Mr. Kazi A. Kader, (8) Prof. Ghulam Azam, (9) Mr. Shah Azizur Rahman, (10) Mr. A. Q. M. Shafiqul Islam, (11) Mr. A. Jabbar Khaddar, (12) Mr. Raja Tridib Roy, (13) Prof. Shamsul Huq, (14) Mr. Obaidullah Majumder, (15) Mr. Aung Shwe Prue Chowdhury.—*The Morning News*, 10.2.1972.

    There was a second list which included prominent amongst others

    (1) Maulana Abdullah A. Kafi of Dinajpur, (2) Maulana Abdur Rahim of Barisal, (3) Mr. Zulmat Ali Khan of Mymensingh, (4) Mr. A. Sattar Khan Chowdhury of Rajshahi, (5) Mr. Saiyid Ashqar Hossain Zaidi of Pabna, (6) Mr. A.K. M. Musharraf Hossain of Mymensigh, (7) Mr. A.T.M.A. Main of Comilla, (8) Mr. Shamsul Huda of Dhaka, (9) Mr. Md. Shahidullah of Dhaka, (10) Mr. A.N.M. Yusuf of Dhaka, (11) Mr. Saiyid Kamal Hossain of Dhaka, (12) Mr. Raisuddin Ahmed of Rangpur, (13) Mr. Saidur Rahman of Rangpur, (14) Mr. Jabanuddin Ahmed of Rangpur, (15) Maulana Tamizuddin of Dinajpur, (16) Mr. Maziul Azam alias Islam of Bogra, (17) Mr. M.A. Matin of Pabna, (18) Maulana A. Sobhan of Pabna, (19) Mr. Jasimuddin Ahmed of Rajshahi, (20) Mr. Afazuddin, of Rajshahi, (21) Mr. Afiluddin of Kushtia, (22) Mr. Azmat Ali of Kushtia, (23) Mr. M. A. Rashid of Jessore and others.—*The Morning News*, 18.2.1972.
44. *Deshbangla*, a Dhaka Weekly, November 1972.
45. No foreign lawyer was allowed to defend any of the accused persons. Sir Dingle Foot, Q.C. who came from London to defend one of the accused persons was turned away from

the Dhaka Airport during the Ayub Regime only four years ago at the Agartala Conspiracy case trial, when Mujib was the principal accused charged for conspiring to secede East Pakistan through an armed revolt and treated as enemy number one of Pakistan was allowed to be defended by Thomas Williams, another Queen's Counsel of England.

46. Gonobahini included all categories of freedom fighters. Mujib's statement on January 17, 1972 calling for the surrender of arms. See *Bangabandhu Speaks,* a collection of speeches published by the Ministry of Foreign Affairs.
47. This suited the plan of the Indian authority also. Now that Bangladesh had a friendly relationship with India it was not necessary for her to have a regimental army. In such a situation India would not have to deploy any armed forces along with Bangladesh border and as a result, they could either reduce the military expenditure or deploy the same force in other border, like China and Pakistan.
48. Rakkhi Bahini are Bengali words meaning a Force for protection or defence.
49. The Jatiya Rakkhi Bahini Order, 1972 (President's Order No. 21 of 1972), 7th March, 1972.
50. The Jatiya Rakkhi Bahini (Amendment) Ordinance, 1973, 30th October, 1973.
51. Mohsin Sharif vs. The State, 27 DLR 1975 HC, p. 186 became known as Shahjahan case It was argued in Court by the author.
52. This is a normal practice that suspects relating to the civilian matters are handed over to the police. In the absence of this General Diary entry the case would have been much weaker since the Rakkhi Bahini did not use to make any entry of any person they arrested. Sec. 54 CCP persuits arrest without warrant by Police Officer of persons suspected of any cognizable offence, and in certain other cases.
53. FIR is a formal complaint required to start a criminal case.
54. Read Enayetullah Khan, Face of Terror, Bangladesh Syndrome, *Holiday*, May 13, 1973.
55. 27 DLR 1975, HC 186.
56. *Ibid.*
57. *Ibid.*
58. *Ibid.*
59. *Ibid.*
60. *Ibid.*
61. "miscreants" would include political opponents too.
62. Mrs. Aruna Sen v. Government of Bangladesh, 27 DLR 1975, p. 122.
63. The *Ittefaq*, February 27, 1974.
64. This case was conducted by the author as the General Secretary of the Committee for Civil Liberties and Legal Aid (see below).
65. As the detenues were released unconditionally, the case became infructuous and the court proceeding ended there. At a subsequent stage Aruna Sen herself filed a separate writ petition on behalf of her son, Chanchal Sen in a similar Habeas Corpus matter conducted also by the author.
66. BSF stands for Indian Border Security Force.
67. The opposition parties claimed that in its first 2 years the Rakkhi Bahini killed 30000 young political workers who were opposed to the Government.
68. The Jatiya Rakkhi Bahini (Amendment) Ordinance, 1975 (Ordinance No. IX of 1975) which subsequently became Act No. XVIII of 1975. The Rakkhi Bahini was designed to be raised in the style of an Army. Mujib felt the necessity of raising a strong army soon after the first year of independence had past but he could not do anything as he feared that it would have annoyed India and secondly, there was pressure from within the party not to organise army on a large scale as reasoned by them earlier on political grounds. Having failed to strengthen the Army, Mujib went for strengthening the Rakkhi Bahini to substitute the Army. According to an interview with a family member of Mujib who is still alive, the author was told that Mujib was forced to

strengthen the Rakkhi Bahini as he felt frustrated for not being able to raise a large-scale Army.

69. Offences mainly taken from the Army Act.
70. There were widespread speculations and comments on the issue of printing currency notes in India by Bangladesh.—Daily *Ittefaq*, April 18, 1973. Taken from Bangladesh *Bahattar Theke Pachattar*, (72-75), Muniruddin Ahmed, Khoshroz Kitab Mahal, Dhaka, p. 61.
71. Bangladesh Scheduled Offences (Special Tribunals) Order, 1972 (President's Order No. 50 of 1972).
72. Read Article 3a(i) as added by the President's Order No. 123 of 1972 and Article 3(2) of the President's Order No. 18 of 1973.
73. Article 3(4)(5) of President's Order No. 50 of 1972 and Article 3(4) of the President's Order No. 105 of 1972.
74. 25 DLR 1973, p. 335. By that time although the Constitution came into operation but President's Order No. 50 was saved by it.
75. See the discussion on saving clause in Chapter IV.
76. Solicitor, Government of Bangladesh vs. A.T. Mridha, 26 DLR 1974, SC 17.
77. 27 DLR 1975, p. 93.
78. 27 DLR 1975 HO 334.
79. In the 21-Point Programme, one of the demands was democratisation of administration.
80. Manifesto of the All-Pakistan Awami League published by Abdul Mannan, publicity Secretary, All Pakistan Awami League, 51, Purana Paltan, Dhaka-2, June, 1970.
81. *Ibid.*
82. Point 12 of the 21-Point Programme. In Pakistan, in 1960s while a Secretary to the Central Government would draw a salary of about Rs. 4000/- per month, a sweeper would draw about Rs. 85/- per month.
83. The All Pakistan Awami League Manifesto, June, 1970.
84. The Awami League's election pledge, 1973.—Daily *Ittefaq*, 21.9.1972.
85. The following arrangement was made—
    (a) Employees drawing salaries upto Rs. 350/- per month — full pay
    (b) Employees drawing salaries exceeding Rs. 350/- but not exeeding Rs. 500/-, 20% less subject to a minimum of Rs. 400/-
    (c) Employees drawing salaries exceeding Rs. 500/- but not exceeding Rs. 1000/-, 30% less subject to minimum of Rs. 450/-
    (d) Employees drawing pay exceeding Rs. 1000/-, 40% less subject to a minimum of Rs. 700/- and maximum of Rs. 1000/-.—*The Morning News*, Dhaka, 29.12.1971.
86. Only 11 CSPs joined the government in exile other than those who joined abroad from different diplomatic missions.
87. Statement of Ataur Rahman Khan.—*Desh Bangla.*
88. Mujib's address to the officials on 1.2.1972. The same day he removed 53 government officials—*Bangabandhu speaks*, published by the External Publicity Division of the Ministry of Foreign Affairs.
89. The Government of Bangladesh (Service) Order, 1972, President's Order No. 9 of 1972.
90. BRTC—Bangladesh Road Transport Corporation, a state-owned corporation for public transport. The author himself conducted cases of 24 bus conductors who were removed under P.O. 9 but they could get no relief.
91. 28 DLR, 1976, HC, p. 38.
92. The Government of Bangladesh (Service Screening) Order, 1972 (President's Order No. 67 of 1972).
93. The Government of Bangladesh (Service Screening) (Amendment) Order, 1972 (President's Order No. 92 of 1972).
94. Yahya Khan removed 303 government officials on charges of corruption under

Martial Law Regulation Nos. 58 and 59. Many of these officers were Bengalis and it was alleged that some of them were victimised for their support to Bengali nationalist movement. Mujib however had already appointed some removed officers who had lost their jobs under the above MLRs to high posts after the independence.

95. Mujib asked people to allow him three years before he could bring any fruit of independence to them.
96. Bangladesh (Collection of Taxes) Order, 1971 A.P.O. No. 1 of 1971. It was a long standing demand from 1954 to reduce the burden of taxes from the largest section of the rural population.
97. The State Acquisition and Tenancy (3rd Amendment) Order, 1972 (President's Order No. 95 of 1972).
98. All Pakistan Awami League Manifesto 1970. See also 11-Point Programme of 1969 of the students when similar demand was incorporated.
99. The Bangladesh Land Holding (Limitation) Order, 1972, P.O. 96/1972.
100. Only 76000 acres of land were surrendered under this Order.—*The Bangladesh Observer*, 8.12.1973.
    The leaders and the land owning class supporters of the Awami League were reluctant to implement this Order.
101. The Bangladesh Legal Proceedings Order, 1972 (President's Order No. 12 of 1972).
102. *The Morning News*, 19.1.1972.
103. *The Morning News*, 1.1.1972.
104. *The Morning News*, 17.2.1972.
105. *The Morning News*, 22.2.1972. The government estimated that it would have cost 10 million Taka and benefitted students of 25000 primary schools.
106. *The Morning News*, 19.5.1972.
107. *The Morning News*, Dhaka, 2.2.1972.
108. *Bangabandhu Speaks*, Ministry of Foreign Affairs.
109. *The Morning News*, 4.4.1972.
110. From January to October, 1972 the price index rose from 208 to the 297 nearly 50%, Rounaq Jahan, *Bangladesh Politics*, University Press Limited, Bangladesh, p. 74.
111. See President's Order No. 8, 9 and 67 of 1972.
112. In 1972 alone 31 banks were looted.—*Ganakantha*, January 29, 1973.
    In February, 1973 within 28 days 20 Awami League workers were killed. —Daily *Ittefaq*, March 2, 1973.
    During this time an unaccountable number of bazars were looted.
    19 Police Stations and sub-stations were looted. —Daily *Ittefaq*, September 25, 1973.
    In the first 18 months 400 fire arms were looted.—Parliamentary Report : *Ganakantha*, February 2, 1974.
    In October 1973 alone, 11 Police Stations and sub-stations were looted. —Daily *Ittefaq*, November 1, 1973.
113. In the first 16 months of the independence, the number of secret killing reached 2035. —Statement of the Home Minister in the Parliament, Daily *Ittefaq*, July 7, 1973.
114. In the first year of independence, 17341 cases of hi-jacking took place—*Ganakantha*, January 29, 1973.
115. In first 2 years of independence, 10280 decoities took place—Source : Parliamentary Proceedings, *Ganakantha*, February 2, 1974.
116. *The Morning News*, Dhaka, 21.1.1972 and 6.2.1972.
    For the Managing Committees of hats and bazars, see also Bangladesh Government Hat and Bazars (Management) Order, 1972 (President's Order No. 73 of 1972).
117. In 1973, 14000 fake importers were detected out of 29044 issued. 78 fake factories only handloom sector were blacklisted.—*The Bangladesh Observer*, 27.6.1974 and 3.3.1974.

See also JSD on permits and assets of MPs—*The Bangladesh Observer*, 14.5.1973. Rounaq Jahan's book, on the improved condition of the MPs, *Bangladesh Politics*, University Press Limited, Bangladesh, p. 100.

118. Moulana's public meeting on 31.12.1972, 7-Party Action Committee.

119. Mujib's statement on the first anniversary, 26.3.1972.

CHAPTER FOUR

THE CONSTITUTION-MAKING PROCESS

The image and credibility of Mujib's Government although was in decline but his personal popularity was still very high and the Awami League was still in command of the political field to contain the new rising opposition forces. Mujib went ahead with his programme of establishing a political and economic system for the new country. The most important of all those was the constitution-making which was to provide the country with a parliamentary political system reflecting his own commitments and the people's long standing aspirations.

Demand for a New Constituent Assembly

While the people had welcomed the intention of Sheikh Mujib for taking measures aiming at establishing a Parliamentary system, the formation and legalisation of the Constituent Assembly comprising of MNAs and MPAs elected for Pakistan created a good deal of political controversy in the country. A section of the people and some politicians opposed to the Awami League challenged the authority of such a Constituent Assembly to frame the constitution of a sovereign independent country. Their argument was that the election in 1970-71 was held for the National Assembly of Pakistan which was to function under the Legal Framework Order and so was the Provincial Assembly. The members elected to the National Assembly were elected to frame a constitution for the whole of Pakistan and people voted them on a mandate on the 6-point programme to frame the constitution within the framework of Pakistan. They argued that with the emergence of Bangladesh as a sovereign independent country election of 1970-71 under the Legal Framework Order became infructuos and for all practical purposes the representatives became functus officio. In the new circumstances, once Bangladesh was born, a new Constituent Assembly would be necessary to frame a constitution of the country, otherwise the authority of the Constituent Assembly so formed would suffer from illegitimacy.

Some of them further argued that with the paramount change after 1971, the Awami League had no legitimate right to form the government. Some even went to argue that even the elected representatives who assembled in

Calcutta and issued the Proclamation of Independence and declared Bangladesh as independent had no authority to do so as they were never voted to create an independent Bangladesh and they had no 'mandate' from the people which they claimed to have in the Proclamation of Independence.

It was further argued that Mujib's switch to a so-called parliamentary democracy without a Parliament was a political bluff and the fact that his newly formed Constituent Assembly was not given any legislative power proved his true intention[1] to rule the country as a dictator.

While challenging the Proclamation of Independence itself would have been self-defeating and unrealistic, the argument for the creation of a fresh body to frame a constitution of the country in the new and changed circumstances could not be said to be absolutely unreasonable. As the days passed by and the economic conditions deteriorated, the opposition to the government gained more ground and the politicians became more vocal in raising the above arguments. Other than the Awami League, all other political parties raised the same question[2]. The opposition consensus was that in those circumstance the country ought to be governed not by one single party but by a national government and there ought to be a new Constituent Assembly elected through a fresh election. Only then, they argued would the country achieve a legitimate government and a constitution.

The most effective of all the politicians raising these demands was the veteran left wing mass leader of the NAP, Moulana Abdul Hamid Khan Bhashani. He addressed a series of public meeting raising these demands. On 3rd September, 1972 the Moulana led a procession demanding resignation of the government and formation of an all-party national government to run the country under a 20-point programme prepared by him. At one stage the Moulana demanded a national convention of students, youths, labourers, peasants, lawyers and intellectuals to discuss the future Constitution[3]. Nevertheless, Sheikh Mujib continued to enjoy a massive popular support and therefore, the opposition demands went without consideration. The Awami League argued that they had the mandate of the people and it is through their government that Bangladesh achieved her independence. In view of the fact that they still enjoyed the confidence of the overwhelming population of the country, even a fresh election if held would have gone in their favour. It was argued by the Awami League that a fresh election would be an unnecessary waste of time and money and the constitution-making process would be delayed further. The bitter experience of Pakistan's early years of constitution-making reminded them not to plunge the country into another phase of uncertainty. It is true that a fresh election if held in 1972 would not have made any difference and ultimately the Constitution would have been framed by the Awami League in any case. But in that event the credibility of the constitution-making would have certainly increased. The interesting point is that no political party declared its opposition to the four State Principles enshrined in the Constitution and none came forward with any concrete alternative suggestion to the basic feature of the Constitution. It is however to be noted that the religion-based political parties were either banned or were in the background, otherwise demand for certain Islamic provisions certainly would have been raised and the principles of secularism would have met with some opposition.

However, the Constituent Assembly entrusted with the making of the Constitution for an independent Bangladesh sat first on 10th April for two days when it formed a 34-member Constitution Committee to draft a constitution headed by Dr. Kamal Hossain as the Law Minister. Its second and final session was a longer one commencing on October 12.

At this session the Assembly adopted Rules of Procedure for its own functioning and on October 18, a 91-page draft Constitution Bill was placed for discussion. Although the Constitution was originally drafted in English, its Bengali translation was to have precedence over the English version in its interpretation in case of any conflict. The Assembly discussed the 153-Article Bill for about 3 weeks and on November 4, 1972 it adopted a constitution for the new country.

As it would be evident, with the 9-month war in the background and virtually no opposition in the Assembly, the scope to debate on the major issues was limited and the Constitution was enacted without any provocative or analytical discussion. The Constituent Assembly comprised the representatives elected to the then National Assembly of Pakistan from East Pakistan and those who were elected to the Provincial Assembly in East Pakistan in 1970-71 for the functioning of the Constituent Assembly, constituted under the Proclamation of Independence of 10th April, 1971[4]. The interesting point was that the Constituent Assembly was not given any law-making power other than framing the Constitution. During the period from the 16th December, 1971 to 15th December, 1972 although the country was run in the line of a parliamentary system with the Prime Minister as the head of the cabinet under the Provisional Constitution Order, the system operated within the framework of the Proclamation of Indepedence. While the Constituent Assembly had no other function save the framing of the Constitution[5] the law-making power remained vested in the executive and the government which, although claiming to be elected, remained unanswerable to any body or forum. The Proclamation of Independence continued to be the supreme law till the Constitution took effect from 16th December, 1972[6].

The 1972 Constitution : Basic Principles

The Constitution contained 11 parts with 4 schedules and a preamble. Part I contained provisions relating to the character of the Republic. Part II stated the fundamental principles of state policy. Part III narrated the

Fundamental Rights, Part IV described the nature of the Executive, Part V the legislature, Part VI the Judiciary, Part VII the election, Part VIII the Comptroller and Auditor-General, Part IX the Services of Bangladesh, Part X the amendment of the Constitution and Part XI contained the Miscellaneous items. The Part IV contained 5 Chapters (Articles 48 to 64) while Part V contained 3 Chapters (Articles 65 to 93) and Part VI contained 3 Chapters (Articles 94 to 117) and Part IX 2 Chapters (Articles 133-141).

The Preamble emphasised the ideals for which the people of Bangladesh had struggled for 'national Liberation' such as nationalism, socialism, democracy and secularism. It cited them as the fundamental aim of the state "to be realised" through a democratic process—a socialist society free from exploitation". It envisaged "a society in which rule of law, fundamental human rights and freedom, equality and justice-political, economic and social would be secured for all the citizens". Unlike the Pakistan constitution of 1956 and 1962 the constitution proclaimed secularism and not the Islamic tenets to be the guiding principle of the constitution. Both the constitutions of 1956 and 1962 expressed in their preamble that the sovereignty over the entire universe belonged to the Almighty Allah and emphasised the Islamic principles of social justice and the teachings and requirements of Islam as set out in the Holy Quran and Sunnah. The Indian Constitution adopted in November, 1949 in its preamble neither mentioned any religion nor secularism as guiding principle. Insertion of secularism instead of Islam in the Constitution of 1972 had a long background in the political movement and tradition of the people against the attempt of the ruling elite of Pakistan to establish an Islamic State. The Awami League and other major political parties in East Pakistan propagated secularism as one of their aims[7]. The fact that East Pakistan where a substantial Hindu population to the extent of nearly 13%-15% exists was also an important factor for preaching secularism by the major political parties. It was not only the question of drawing political support but also recognising a long tradition of sharing a common way of life. Now with the active association of India established through the war, the question of security of the Hindu community in Bangladesh assumed more international significance.

Although the format used for the Constitution is the same as that of India and Pakistan based largely on the British Commonwealth model, it varied in content and characteristics in some of its significant features.

In Part I of the Constitution, the significant feature is the fact that Bengali was establised as the only state language of the country[8] and that it inscribed "Amar Sonar Bangla" a song written and composed by Rabindranath Tagore as the national anthem. It also provided the description of the national flag and the emblem (Article 4) and proclaimed that the citizens of Bangladesh would be known as "Bangalees" (Article 6). The Constitution being the solemn expression of the will of the people was made the supreme law of the Republic and it declared that any law inconsistent with it would be void to the extent of such inconsistency (Article 7). Unlike the earlier 2 Constitutions of Pakistan, the question of national anthem and citizenship were given significant importance in the Constitution. The most significant one was the assertion of making the citizens known as 'Bangalees'[9]. This was done due to some historical reasons. In the context of Pakistan the entire nationalist movement was based on the assertion that the people of East Pakistan constituted a separate nation and they were first 'Bangalees' and then Pakistanis. The selection of 'Shapla' a flower so commonly seen in the waters of riverine Bangladesh as the national flower also reflected the nationalistic thoughts of the ruling class.

Part II of the Constitution dealt with the principles of state policy contained separately prior to the chapter on fundamental rights. In the Indian Constitution the state principles were named as the Directive principles of State Policy but were incorporated in the same Part with the fundamental rights. In the 1962 Constitution of Ayub Khan, the same style was applied naming the whole as "Fundamental Rights and Principle of Policy". In the 1956 Constitution they were dealt with separately but were titled "Directive Principles of State Policy" as the Indian one and contained in Part III following the Part on the fundamental rights. In this Constitution the "Fundamental Principles of State Policy" were made more elaborate and comprehensive. They were contained in 18 Articles (Art. 8 to 28) as compared to 16 Articles in the Indian Constitution, 9 Articles in Pakistan's 1956 Constitution.

The state principles, although do not constitute any law by themselves nor confer any legal right, represent the ideals and objectives set to be achieved by the people for a better future. This has been a common feature in almost all the modern Constitutions of the world and particularly in the Constitution of the Sub-continent with features reflecting an established tradition of constitution-making in the line of the Irish Constitution. The state principles embodied in the 1956 and 1962 Constitutions were identical to a large extent giving emphasis on Islamic Principles and Islamic way of life, but the objectives set in the 1962 constitution were written in a different form. Some of the objectives were also similar to those laid down in the Indian Constitution. The Indian law makers however avoided laying down objectives based on any particular religion.

The objectives set forth in the state principles in Bangladesh constitution are generally identical in content to those embodied in the constitution of India and the two constitutions of Pakistan. The essential features of the Bangladesh Constitution which make it different in character are (i) that some of the principles set forth are more emphatic in nature and (ii) some of the objectives particularly relating to achieving socialism are not found in the other constitutions. The Indian constitution conceived of a welfare state whereas the constitution of Pakistan conceived some kind of Islamic state with a general welfare concept. It is interesting to note that the Awami League did not propose any amendment to the state principles set in 1962 Constitution when it drafted a Constitution Amendment Bill in March, 1969 to incorporate the 6-point Programme in the same Constitution[10].

In the Constitution of Bangladesh, nationalism, socialism, democracy and secularism—these are embodied as the fundamental principles of state policy. These principles will be applied by the state in making laws and they will be a guide in the interpretation of the Constitution and other laws. Although they are not to be enforceable, these principles would form the foundation of the state (Article 8). In Article 9, 10, 11 and 12 these state principles are elaborated. In the elaboration of nationalism the emphasis of 'Bangalee' nationalism is predominent. The unity and solidarity of the Bangalee nation which derives its identity from its language and culture and attained a sovereign and independent Bangladesh through a united and determined struggle in the war of independence is to be the basis of the Bangalee nationalism. Here an attempt has been made to join the ethnic nationality with the political nationhood leaving a wide scope for controversy over the concept of 'Bangalee nationalism'. The conception was primarily derived from the long struggle of Bengali nationalists within the context of Pakistan as one nation with its consequent geo-political development and cultural suppression. Although there should be no doubt left of the fact that the struggle for autonomy was based on Bengali nationalism and the people who now constitute the population of Bangladesh due to their common ethnicity, language and culture are Bangalees, the concept of the "Bangalee nation" and "nationalism" as embodied in the constitution perhaps require a careful consideration in a separate study[11].

On the question of socialism, the elaboration has been clear and almost unequivocal. The objective was to establish a "socialist economic system with a view to ensuring the attainment of a just and egalitarian society free from the exploitation of man by man" (Article 10).

On democracy it said that the "Republic would be a democracy in which fundamental human rights and freedom and respect for the dignity and worth of the human person would be guaranteed and in which effective participation by the people through their elected representatives in administration at all levels would be ensured" (Article 11).

Although in Article 10 while socialism has been elaborated as an objective, the process through which it could be achieved has not been mentioned, the third paragraph of the preamble provided a guideline in this respect. In view of the commitment for democracy and human rights made in Article 11 on the one hand and establishment of a "socialist economic system" on the other in Article 10, one has to read both the Articles together to understand the true import of the objectives laid in the preamble. It would lead to the conclusion that the objective of establishing a socialist economic system was to be achieved through a democratic process.

The principle of secularism as contained in article 12 was to be realised by eliminating (a) communalism in all its forms, (b) by not granting political status by the state in favour of any religion, (c) avoiding the abuse of religion for political purposes and (d) any discrimination against or persecution of persons, practicing a particular religion. This was considered to be a bold and significant state principle embodied in the Constitution, and it was as progressive and idealistic as it could be in the prevailing political context. Since the time the party dropped the word 'Muslim' from its nomenclature in 1955 the Awami League struggled as a secular political party and was opposed to linking religion with politics. Consequently, the historical tradition of the Bengali nationalist movement developed without religious ferver, and secularism as such emerged as a more acceptable political thought. The Indian involvement during the war of independence and their concern for the Hindus in Bangladesh perhaps further cemented the thought to shape Bangladesh as a secular state. This objective bears a clear note to eliminate the abuse of religion for political purposes. However progressive it might sound, enacting secularism as a state principle raised scores of controversial political issues centering round the main question whether religion could be left aside from politics totally in Bangladesh where political institutions were yet to reach a mature stage of development for a proper appreciation of the issues involved. Bangladesh had not yet reached any appreciable stage of development to enable it to leave religion totally aside from politics.

Some critics would however say that the insertion of the concept of secularism in such an emphatic term was made to please the Indian authorities. This was done to remove any possibility of having another 'Pakistan' on the eastern side of the Indian border and make India's influence secure for good both politically and militarily. Secondly, it was argued that elimination of the abuse of religion for political purposes was in itself a political issue and hence was used as a devise to ban opposition political parties on the ground that they preached religious ideologies[12]. Thirdly, the concept of democracy itself has embodied the principle of secularism and so the insertion of secularism as a state principle was redundant[13]. Nevertheless, the principle of secularism embodied in the constitution has opened a wave of controversy not so much for the principle itself but in its political motivations both in national and international context[14].

Another important feature of the State Principles was the question of ownership of the wealth of the state on which all the other Constitutions were silent. It declared that the "people shall own and control the instruments and means of production and distribution" and with this end in view three forms of ownership was visualised : (1) State ownership of the key sectors of the economy through an efficient and dynamic nationalised public sector ; (2) Ownership by co-operatives within such limits as would be prescribed by law and (3) Private ownership by individuals within limits as would be prescribed by law. Keeping in line with the objective of establishing a 'socialist economic order' emphasis has been given more on the state and co-operative ownership. It would be interesting to note that in the Constitution of the Socialist Republic of Sri Lanka the objectives for achieving a socialist order was put in a much milder form giving almost equal treatment to both public and private sector[15].

In this Part the Constitution also emphasised on rural development and agricultural revolution as a fundamental objective of the State. It maintained that the State would adopt effective measures to bring about a radical transformation in the rural areas "through the promotion of an agricultural revolution" to remove progressively "the disparity in the standard of living between the urban and the rural areas". Unlike other documents and in the context of the past movement for cultural autonomy, a special emphasis has been laid on the national culture, tradition and heritage of the people and on fostering and improving the national language, literature and arts. On the question of dignity of labour and work as a right and duty, payment for work has to be made on the basis of the principle "from each according to his abilities, to each according to his work".

On the question of international peace, security and solidarity the objective has been made much more comprehensive and emphatic in nature. It has pledged to strive for general and complete disarmament and support for the oppressed people throughout the world "waging a just struggle against imperialism, colonialism and racialism." The other objectives contained in the Constitution are similar to those in other Constitutions of the sub-continent and they were on emancipation of peasants and workers, provisions for basic necessities, free and compulsory education[16], public health and morality, equality of opportunity, duties of citizens and public servants, protection of national monuments and lastly the separation of judiciary from the executive.

The state objectives set in the Constitution largely reflected the hopes and aspirations of the people nurtured through a series of political movements culminating in the war of independence. It is to be noted that the manifesto with which the Awami League contested the election in 1970-71 was framed in the context of Pakistan and could not be considered now as a wholesome document in the context of an independent Bangladesh. So it was the combination of the earlier pledge made before independence and the hopes raised during the war that led to create a high degree of idealism in respect of the future of the country. However, what the Constitution makers ignored or failed to perceive was the low level of economic and political infrastructure not fully capable of carrying out the objectives of such candid nature. It is true that the state principles and objectives are generally set out to be the ultimate goals of the state but the objectives for which immediate action was necessary ought to have been examined from the point of view whether adequate political institutions were in existence and whether the people were prepared to accept such changes.

Besides the contradictions between the preamble and the State principles on the one hand, on the question of achieving a socialist economic systems and the variation in the Awami League election programme and their subsequent commitments made through the manifesto on the other, another important fact needs to be noted ; the Awami League was not engaged as it sometimes tended to claim, in any revolutionary struggle in a classical sense. Although the fundamental principles set out were not contradictory to the aspirations of the people, the over-emphasis on certain issues and actions taken thereon without adequate preparation had put the Awami League into great difficulties at a later stage.

The Fundamental Rights

Part III contained the fundamental rights guaranteed in the Constitution and almost all the rights traditionally incorporated in a modern constitution have been embodied in this constitution. Most of the rights guaranteed are identical to those embodied in the Indian Constitution, the Pakistan Constitutions of 1956 and 1962 and the Sri Lanka Constitution, 1972. As far as the fundamental rights are concerned the traditional practice of subjecting some of the rights to certain restrictions have been maintained and the Constitution do not offer anything new or dynamic in this regard excepting those discussed below.

The rights incorporated in the Constitution are equality before law (Article 27), discrimination on grounds of religion etc. (Article 28), equality in public employment (Article 29), right to protection of law (Article 31), protection of right to life and personal liberty (Article 33), safeguards against arrest or detention (Article 33), prohibition of forced labour (Article 34), protection in respect of trial and retrospective punishment (Article 35), freedom of movement (Article 36), freedom of assembly (Article 37), freedom of association (Article 38), freedom of thought and conscience and speech (Article 39), freedom of profession or occupation (Article 40), freedom of religion (Article 41), right to property (Article 42), and protection of home and correspondence (Article 43).

As in other Constitutions, in Article 44, a right has been guaranteed to move the Supreme Court for the enforcement of all the rights conferred in this part of the Constitution. In the Sri Lanka Constitution such right was guaranteed in Article 17, in the Indian Constitution by Article 32, in the 1956 Constitution by Article 22 and in the 1962 Constitution through the amended provision of Article 98 of the Constitution[17].

Another common feature in all these Constitutions excepting the Sri Lanka one has been to guarantee the supremacy of the fundamental rights in the Constitution. Keeping in line with other constitutions, Article 26 read as follows :

> 26. (1) All existing laws inconsistent with the provisions of this Part shall, to the extent of such inconsistency, become void on the commencement of this Constitution.
>
> (2) The State shall not make any law inconsistent with any provisions of this Part, and any law so made shall, to the extent of such inconsistency, be void[18].

Nevertheless the Constitution of Bangladesh has contained some distinguishing features relating to the fundamental rights which are not found in other constitutions. In Article 26, although laws inconsistent to the provisions of fundamental rights were to be void, Article 47 introduced not only some contradiction in the concept itself but tended to negate to a large extent the effectiveness of the fundamental rights claimed to have been guaranteed. Although it is not unusual to provide a saving clause for certain laws made in the interim period prior to the framing and commencement of a constitution[19] the Article 47(2) paragraph 1 has drawn critical attention on two major grounds : (1) saving of certain laws and (2) saving of amendments of such laws with retrospectivity. Firstly the provisions to save certain laws were there in the Indian Constitution in Article 31B also. But some of the laws contained in the First Schedule of Article 47 vitally affected the basic fundamental rights of the citizens. The provisions in the laws like the President's Order No. 8, President's Order No. 9, President's Order No. 50 and President's Order No. 67 of 1972 were not only inconsistent to the enjoyment of fundamental rights but they took away some of the established rights enjoyed by the citizens for a long time. Secondly and the most controversial was the inclusion of any amendment of any such laws including amendments made after the commencement of the Constitution and amendments giving retrospective effect.

Similar in line with the provisions of the Indian Constitution (Article 31C), Article 47 (1) also excluded the provision of Article 26 with regard to laws made which were inconsistent with or took away or abridged any of the rights guaranteed by that part of the Constitution. The ground of making such laws would have to be made out to give effect to any of the fundamental principles of state policy set out in the Constitution[20].

This brings us also to the question of right to property. The Indian Constitution and the two Constitutions of Pakistan guaranteed right to property subject to laws made for compulsory acquisition or requisition. Similar right has been guaranteed in Article 42 of the Constitution, the difference being that while the other three Constitutions provide that such laws would provide compensation for acquisition or requisition, under Article 42(2) the provision for compensation was made optional only[21].

Provision relating to Preventive Detention and Emergency

The most significant features of the 1972 Constitution have been : one, the absence of a provision for preventive detention in Article 33 and two, absence of provisions for emergency and suspension of fundamental rights. It has been a common practice in the constitution-making of the sub-continent to include provisions in the constitution for detention without trial and to make provisions for proclaiming emergency in the country not only to handle a situation of war or threat of external aggression but also to combat internal disturbance with the power to suspend the fundamental rights. This pattern was set more candidly in 1935 Act by the British to perpetuate their colonial design and the provisions continued to have place in the subsequent constitutions in the sub-continent although freedom was achieved and the countries became independent sovereign states. In the management of the colonial state these provisions were considered necessary weapons to crush opposition and perpetuate the rule. Hundreds and thousands of Indians both Muslims and Hindus and almost all their leaders had suffered imprisonment or rigours of these laws in some way or other. Particularly a detention without trial was considered by all during the Indian independence movement as a crime against humanity.

The Indian Constitution contained provisions both for preventive detention and proclamation of emergency. Although that constitution, framed and adopted in 1949, guaranteed the fundamental right of protection against arrest and detention, the right was excluded in cases of preventive detention.

In Artcle 7 of the 1956 Constitution similar provisions were embodied, so also in Article 6(2) of the 1962 Constitution.

But in the Bangladesh Constitution enacted in 1972 the right of protection from arrest or detention has been guaranteed without the proviso for preventive detention.

Provisions for preventive detention without trial as contained in laws like the Security of Pakistan Act, 1952 or the East Pakistan Public Safety Ordinance, 1958 could no longer be applicable. The desire to fulfil the political commitment of repealing all the black laws in order to establish a 'living democracy' was admirably noticeable[22]. It was a remarkable achievement on the part of the Awami League to have done away with the menacing provisions of detention without trial from the Constitution of the country. But unfortunately, this was not to remain for a long period.

On the question of provisions for emergency, keeping in line with the 1935 Act, the Indian Constitution in Article 352 provided as follows :

> "352. proclamation of Emergency.—(1) If the President is satisfied that a grave emergency exists whereby the security of India or of any part of the territory thereof is threatened, whether by war or external aggression or internal disturbance, he may, by Proclamation, make a declaration to that effect.

Following the same line, the 1956 Constitution of Pakistan contained the emergency provision in Part XI and Article 191 read as follows :

> If the President is satisfied that a grave emergency exists in which the security or economic life of Pakistan, or any part thereof, is threatened by way of external aggression, or by internal disturbance beyond the power of a Provincial Government to control, he may issue a Proclamation of Emergency.

The 1962 Constitution also carried almost identical provision for emergency with some more power to the President than usual. Article 30 of the Constitution read, as follows :

> "30.—(1) If the President is satisfied that a grave emergeny exists—
>
> (a) in which Pakistan, or any part of Pakistan, is (or is in imminent danger of being) threatened by war or external agression ; or
>
> (b) in which the security or economic life of Pakistan is threatened by internal disturbances beyond the power of a Provincial Government to control, the President may issue a Proclamation of Emercency.

The common features and the implications of the emergency provisions are that once the emergency is proclaimed by the President not only would the fundamental rights be suspended, the power of the superior courts to issue any writ for the enforcement of such right would also be suspended. The emergency could be proclaimed for the whole country or a particular province or state where the constitutional machinery in the opinion of the President/Central Government has collapsed and this applies to both India and Pakistan. As a result, in an emergency assumption of all the powers of such state or provincial government and assumption of legislative powers in certain cases with or without authorisation would be the natural sequence.

The experience of the application of the emergency provisions in Pakistan were extremely bitter. In its 23-year long history, Paksitan witnessed a series of action taken by the ruling elite or some time by one individual in the office of the President under the garb of these emergency provisions, not only to perpetuate themselves in power but also in effect to destroy the existing institutions and the integrity of the country as a whole. The exercise of such powers in the most arbitratory fashion crushed the prospect of Pakistan developing into a coherent state and such exercise by the rulers of Pakistan began even before the Constitution of 1956 came into effect. The unconstitutionalism set in by Ghulam Mohammad and Iskander Mirza in 1950s through use of emergency powers under the 1935 Act never allowed the country to build a normal democratic system[23]. The emergency imposed by Ayub Khan in 1965 war was not lifted till 1969 when he was forced to leave power. The constitutional history of Pakistan was a history of arbitrary exercise of power by the chief executive followed by proclamations of emergency and Martial Law and almost all the actions taken under these instruments ultimately weakened the political institutions. This led to suppression of opposition and putting hundreds and thousands of citizens into jail without any trial, sometime for years together[24]. Almost all the political leaders of Pakistan particularly the prominent ones in the former East Pakistan were extremely critical of these harsh laws including those on preventive detention[25]. The Awami League in particular was committed since the formation of the United Front in 1954 to repeal not only the black laws but also to remove any scope or prerogative enabling an individual or retard the process of democracy. The experience of Pakistan showed that whenever such power was enshrined in the constitution, however well intentioned the laws might have been the tendency to use or in most cases misuse them was overwhelmingly predominant. These authoritarian powers were therefore considered contradictory to the concept of nourishing a living democracy.

With these experiences in mind, the Awami League Government did not want to leave any scope for such exercise of power by the President. (1) Firstly, they were establishing a parliamentary system and as such, giving such power to the President who was only a titular head could lead Bangladesh back to the cycle experienced in Pakistan and frustrate the system as a whole, (2) they were considered as undemocratic provisions tending to create a conflict between the Parliament and the President, (3) they would be contradictory to commitments the Awami League made to the public for the repeal of the black laws, and (4) lastly the Awami League thought that in view of the fact that there was hardly any opposition in the country and having had a strong friendship with India there was not much necessity for such provisions in the constitution.

As a result in the constitution of Bangladesh no provision or article was embodied for any emergency situation. The decision was bold and courageous. Of all the features for which Bangladesh constitution is distinguishable from others in the sub-continent—the absence of any provision relating to (1) preventive detention and (2) proclamation of emergency were the most significant and outstanding ones. But like the change made in article 33, the constitution was also amended to include provisions for emergency sooner than a year had passed. The cynics or even some critics would say that dropping these provisions in the original constitution attributed no idealism or motivation on the part of the constitution-makers. They simply forgot to include them.

The fast growing opposition in the country and the deteriorating law and order situation shook the confidence of the ruling class and the stark realities of political management of a state led them to take certain measures to bring the situation 'under control'. At the end the Awami League Government moved to take refuge to the 'colonial instruments' of sustaining power. On the 22nd September, 1973 when hardly 9 months had gone, the Constitution (Second Amendment) Bill was passed to amend Article 33 and to add a new Part to the Constitution for incorporating the emergency provisions. Article 33 was substituted in line with Article 22 of the Indian Constitution so as to allow for laws of preventive detention. But as compared to Indian constitution, the initial period of detention was increased from 3 to 6 months, and the detention could go on for an unlimited period if the Advisory Board would think in its opinion that sufficient cause existed for such detention. Like under the Indian Constitution, Parliament could make laws prescribing the procedures to be followed by the Advisory Board.

To incorporate the Emergency provisions a new Part IXA was added to the Constitution by the same Amendment Bill. The new Articles 141 A, 141 B and 141C showed not only improved draftmanship but also more candidness compared to the provisions of the other three constitutions, although the contents remained more or less the same.

The interesting features were that they were closer to the provisions of the 1956 and 1962 Constitution than to the Indian one. The Indian Constitution provided that the duration of such emergency could not exceed two months unless before the expiry of that period the Proclamation was approved by both the Houses of Parliament. In both the 1950 and 1962 Constitutions there was no mandatory time limit for the expiry of the Proclamation. Under these Constitutions the Proclamation was to be laid before the National Assembly "as soon as practicable". In the 1956 Constitution once the National Assembly disapproved the Proclamation it would cease to operate but in the 1962 Constitution even the National Assembly had no power to disapprove the Proclamation (Article 30(6)). The Bangladesh Constitution fixed the time limit at 6 months and the Proclamation would cease to exist if it was not extended by the parliament for its continuance before that period. Another distinguishing feature not contained in any of the other constitutions was the proviso to Article 141A(1) that the proclamation "shall require for its validity the counter-signature of the Prime Minister". This was incorporated in order to safeguard the misuse of power as had been experienced in the past by the President under a Parliamentary system. It also, however, meant that the power to proclaim emergency in reality rested with the Prime Minister. By

Article 141B, certain arcticles relating to the fundamental rights could be put under suspension and laws inconsistent to Article 36, 37, 38, 39, 40 and 42 could be made during the emergency period. As in other constitutions, by Article 141C provisions were made to have the enforcement of fundamental rights through the law courts suspended during such emergency period.

Westminister-type Parliamentary System

The Constitution of Bangladesh envisaged a Westminister type of Parliamentary system reflecting the aspirations of the people nurtured for nearly 2 decades. The Awami League's commitment since its inception for the establishment of a "real living democracy" for which they struggled and suffered for so many years could now be fulfilled because of the absolute power of the government. Accordingly, the President was put into a titular position, being only a conventional figure-head. A considerable precaution was taken to limit the scope of the President increasing his power to disrupt the political process. In view of the bitter experiences with the Presidential form of government in undivided Pakistan and the clear public commitment made, all measures were taken to pave the way for a parliamentary democratic system to take its firm root in the country. The scheme provided that the government would be run by a cabinet of Ministers headed by the Prime Minister collectively responsible to the Parliament and would remain in power so long it enjoyed the confidence of the majority members of the Parliament.

One significant feature of this Constitution was that excepting appointing the Prime Minister pursuant to clause 3 of Article 56, the President in all and every other matter in the exercise of his functions was to "act in accordance with the advice of the Prime Minister" (Article 48(B)). The President would be elected by the members of Parliament (Article 48) and the provisions relating to his age and qualification were similar to those in other constitutions. He would not be less than 35 years of age, qualified for election as a member of the Parliament and could be removed from the office of President by impeachment under the Constitution (Article 148 (4)). As in other Constitutions the President enjoyed the prerogative of showing mercy and immunity from court Proceedings (Article 49 and 51). In the absence of the President for any reason, the Speaker would act as the President in the same line as Provided in 1956 Constitution. No person could hold the office of the President for more than 2 terms, more in the line with the 1956 Constitution. The Indian Constitution as well as the Pakistan Constitution 1962 provided eligibility for re-election with no bar on the term of holding office. In the Bangladesh Constitution the term was limited deliberately to curb an over-ambitious President. On the question of removal of the President on ground of incapacity or illness and or inability by way of impeachment, the procedure in all the Constitutions continued to remain more or less in the same form.

The most important aspect of the Bangladesh Constitution as far as the position of the President is concerned was the provision expressly made : the President to act in accordance with the advice of the Prime Minister[26]. The Prime Minister would however keep the President informed on matters of domestic and foreign policy and submit for consideration of the cabinet any matter which the President would request him to refer to it. In a Parliamentary system the relationship between the President and the cabinet and the Parliament and the President is generally governed by convention and tradition. As an example, the Indian Constitution also envisaged a parliamentary system but it did not write in such emphatic terms that "in exercise of all his functions, the President would act according to the advice of the Prime Minister." It even went to the extent of vesting all the executive powers in the President. In the Indian Constitution, the Council of Ministers headed by the Prime Minister was to aid and advise the President in the exercise of the latter's function[27]. It also Provided that the Ministers would hold office during the pleasure of the President[28]. But in reality the council of ministers is the most important executive organ headed by the Prime Minister as the most important person. It is not the exact words or their literal meaning but democratic practice and convention which dominate the functioning of Indian Constitution.

Whereas in the 1956 Constitution of Pakistan words similar to those in the Indian Constitution were used but in practice the words were taken more literally and ultimately the President became the most dominent figure. In this Constitution the word cabinet instead of council of Minister's was used[29] and the executive authority of the Federation was to "vest in the President"[30]. Here too the Prime Minister was to hold office during the pleasure of the President and other Ministers could be removed by the President. In a Parliamentary system whether it is written or not the custom is that the President would be a titular head and would act according to the advice of the Prime Minister and he would not do anything against the wishes of the cabinet. The only time the President or the head of state would exercise power was when no person was able to command a clear majority in the Parliament for appointment as the Prime Minister. Once this issue is resolved the President becomes a functional head only. However, although the Constitution of 1956 was supposed to provide a parliamentary system its practice and effect was different. Articles 37 and 34 of this Constitution gave adequate scope for the President to intervene and exercise his discretion and in the absence of developed political institutions, the President tended to take the powers and exercise them literally. Therefore, although both the Indian Constitution and the Pakistan Constitution of 1956 were parliamentary in nature in real practice one succeeded and other failed. The 1962 Constitution stands on a different footing as it was meant to provide a strong centralised Presidential system.

Considering these experiences, the Awami League in 1972 did not want to leave any scope for the exercise of any discretion by the President and preferred to have all the basic matters recorded in writing. They avoided giving any discretionary power to the President. Accordingly, it provided not only that the President would act in accordance with the advice of the Prime Minister (Article 48(3)) but by Article 55(2) provided that the executive power of the Republic was to be "exercised by or on the authority of the Prime Minister". In Article 56 it provided that the President would appoint as Prime Minister a member of Parliament who appeared to him to command the support of the majority of the members of Parliament. As indicated earlier, excepting this power, the President was to act in all other matters on the advice of the Prime Minister. Unlike the other Constitutions including the Indian one, such provisions, as the council of Ministers would hold office "during the pleasure of the President" or they would "aid and advice the President" were not incorporated in the Bangladesh Constitution. So although the other Ministers were to be appointed by the President, who and how many were to be appointed was to be determined by the Prime Minister (Article 56 (1)). No person could be appointed as a Minister unless he was a member of Parliament. Anyone who was not a member of Parliament would cease to be a Minister if he was not elected as a member within 6 months of his appointment (Article 56 (4)). The office of the Prime Minister would become vacant if the Prime Minister resigned or ceased to be a Member of Parliament, or lost the support of the majority in the Parliament. If the Prime Minister had ceased to retain the support of the majority of the members of Parliament, he would either resign or advise the President to dissolve the Parliament (Article 57). A Minister would vacate office if he resigned or ceased to be a member of Parliament or if he was requested to resign by the Prime Minister or terminated by the President on request by the Prime Minister, or if the Prime Minister had resigned or ceased to hold office for any other reasons.

The Defence Services

Chapter IV dealt with the Defence Services and as in many other Constitutions[31] the supreme command of the Defence Services was to be exercised by the President (Article 61). Parliament was to make laws to regulate raising and recruiting the personnel of the defence services and their reserves, grant commission, appoint chiefs of staff of the defence services and determine their salaries and allowances and the question of discipline and other matters relating to those services.

The most interesting feature of this chapter was the provisions relating to war contained in Article 63 of the Constitution. In the original Constitution it read as follows:

(1) War shall not be declared and the Republic shall not participate in any war except with the assent of Parliament,

(2) In case of actual or imminent invasion of Bangladesh by land, sea or air, the President may take whatever steps he considers necessary for the protection and defence of Bangladesh, and Parliament if not sitting shall be summoned forthwith.

(3) Nothing in this Constitution shall invalidate any law enacted by Parliament which is expressed to be for the purpose of securing the public safety and preservation of the State in time of war, invasion or armed rebellion.

By a subsequent amendment in September 1973 while on the one hand provision for emergency and preventive detention were made, on the other hand clauses 2 and 3 of the Article were omitted. In other words, no war could be declared nor could the country participate in any war except with the assent of the Parliament. This again reflected a new democratic thinking which was not found in other Constitutions of the sub-continent[32]. The interesting point, was that the power of the President to declare war was excluded. The provision that the Republic would not participate in any war "except with the assent of the Parliament" was indeed notable[33].

Local Government

Another important aspect of the 1972 Constitution was that it attached much importance to decentralisation and functioning of local government. Keeping in line with the objectives set in the State Principles, a separate chapter under this Part was devoted to this subject. Article 59(1) of Chapter III provided that the local government in every administrative unit would be entrusted to bodies composed of persons "elected in accordance with law". In order to fulfil the Awami League's promise of establishing "a real and living democracy" the law envisaged that each such local body would perform within the appropriate administrative unit such functions which would include administration and the work of public officers, the maintenance of public order and the preparation and implementation of plan relating to public services and economic development. For this purpose, in order to give full effect to the idea visualised by Article 59, Parliament was to confer by law powers of imposing taxes for local purposes, on preparing their budgets and maintaining their own funds. This chapter was however completely omitted by the Awami League when they passed the Fourth Amendment Bill to introduce a one-party system in January, 1975[34]. Prior to that the article was never implemented.

Legislature

Part V of the Constitution dealt with matter relating to the Legislature. It envisaged a unitary, one-house Parliament vested with all the legislative powers of the Republic. It was to consist of 300 members to be elected from single territorial constituencies by direct election. In addition to this, for a period of ten years, there was to be 15 seats reserved exclusively for women who were to be elected in turn by the directly elected members. Both the Constitutions of 1956 and 1972 made the President a constitutional part of the Parliament. The Indian and the Bangladesh Constitutions maintained the same form except that no seats were reserved in the Indian Constitution exclusively for women—although some seats were reserved for schedule castes and tribes. In the 1962 Constitution there was no provision for direct election in the National Assembly as it was elected by an electoral college based on basic democracies.

With regard to the qualifications and disqualifications for members of the Parliament similar provisions were made in all constitutions except that the Bangladesh constitution disqualified a person from being elected to Parliament if he was convicted by any offence under the Collaborators Order whatever might have been the duration of the sentence (Article 66(c)). But the most distinguishing feature of this part of the Constitution was Article 70 which read as follows :

> "A person elected as a Member of Parliament at an election at which he was nominated as a candidate by a political party shall vacate his seat if he resigns from that party or votes in Parliament against that party."

This was a new provision not incorporated in any other constitution, not even in the Constitution of 1962[35]. A section of politicians called it to be contradictory to the principle of democracy and the right of conscience as guaranteed by the Constitution. They claimed that it would encourage the establishment of party dictatorship and lastly, it infringed the sovereignty of Parliament. In no other country where democracy is in practice has such provision been seen in operation. Neither the 1956 nor the 1962 Constitution contained any provision like that. It was argued that democracy could not flourish if members of Parliament were to be blackmailed by the party hierarchy. It tended to place the party above the interest of the nation. Although in practice members are to go along with line of the party through which they get elected to implement its programme etc., to impose a constitutional condition on the freedom of the members in case the party deviated from its declared policies and programmes could have impaired the functioning of the Parliament itself. Members were elected for a period of five years making pledges to their respective constituents on the basis of a political programme and therefore, it was, undemocratic to tie them down to the dictates of a political party[36].

But the historical background on which this article was incorporated did not make the provision less justified either. The past experience of the parliamentary system in Pakistan and India both at the Centre and the States showed that members once elected tended to cross the floor for their selfish ends rendering the parliamentary system unworkable on many occasions. They would defy party decisions and ignore party commitments made to the electorate and once elected would not subject themselves to any party discipline through which platform he got elected to the Parliament—resulting in splitting party and destroying inner cohesion. This generally encourages factionalism and ultimately disrupt the stability of the government and smooth functioning of the entire system. It is with this end in view that the Awami League committed itself since long to stop this possible anarchy within the Parliament. As long back as in 1969 when a Constitution Amendment Bill was drafted for the National Assembly of Ayub Khan amending the 1962 Constitution, the Awami League incorporated such a provision[37]. It provided that :

(4) (a) If any person, having been elected to a Legislature as a candidate or nominee of a political party—

(i) withdraws himself from it ; or

(ii) is expelled by his political party for violation of the party's mandate in respect of any matter relating to his activities as a member of the Legislature ;

(iii) votes, or abstains from voting against the direction of such political party upon any legislative measure or on any motion put to vote in the Legislature, he shall cease to be a member of the Legislature for the unexpired period of his term unless such member is re-elected at a bye-election occasioned by the vacancy created by such cessation of membership

It will be evident from the above provision that the thought-process of the Awami League leaders was working for a long time on this line and therefore, in the 1972 Constitution they maintained the same views with some leniency but once the one-party system was introduced in 1975, the original provision of 1972 was amended and almost the full effect of the 1969 provision was incorporated. Notwithstanding whether such provision was democratic or not or whether it affected the sovereignty of Parliament or not, such provision reflected two aspects as far as its incorporation was concerned. It reflected a genuine wish to stabilise the system within the Parliament. It emerged through a history of bitter experience. But on the other hand, its application and subsequent amendment in the context of the Awami League's introduction of a one-party system bringing a total change in the Constitution, frustrated the credibility of that genuine desire. Consequently, it justified the criticism of the opponents that such provision was only made to subject the members of Parliament to threat and blackmail.

On the question of the sessions of Parliament, like in all other constitutions of the subcontinent, the President as contained in Article 72 was to summon, prorogue or dissolve the Parliament. But the President of Bangladesh was empowered to take such action only in accordance with the advice of the Prime Minister and therefore, the danger of the President exercising the power to dissolve the Parliament on any pretext was removed. The Indian Constitution, as mentioned earlier, however depended on practice of democratic conventions and its President continued to act on the advice of the Prime Minister although no such provision was made. In the 1956 Constitution, although the provision was the same, the President was ensured of a dominant role and as there was no check the President exercised more discretion in these matters[38]. In the 1962 Constitution under Article 23 the President could dissolve the Parliament at any time unless the unexpired term of the National Assembly was less than 120 days[39] or any proceedings was pending before the Assembly on impeachment or removal of the President.

The Parliament would sit in sessions and the gap between two sessions would not exceed 60 days. This provision in the Constitution indicated that the Parliament would sit frequently and almost continuously to transact its business as a sovereign body and strengthen the institution of democracy in the country but the attitude of the Government changed and article 72 was later on amended to substitute the words "sixty days" by the words "one hundred and twenty days"—the intervening period could be now 4 months instead of 2 months[40].

Article 72 also made provisions to deal with war vis-a-vis the sessions of Parliament. If the country was at war the normal term of 5 years could be extended by an Act of Parliament upto a period of one year at a time but not beyond six months after the termination of the war. If a war broke out at a time between the dissolution of Parliament and the holding of the next general election, the President if it was necessary to recall the Parliament could do so and in such event the Parliament that was dissolved was to be summoned.

Ombudsman

Another important feature was the provision for the office of an Ombudsman. In order to maintain the supremacy of the Parliament and to provide a machinery to overview the activities of the civil bureaucracy the Parliament could by law provide the establishment of an office of Ombudsman. Although no other country in the sub-continent made such provision and very few countries in the world have such office as that of Ombudsman, the incorporation of a provision for such a sophisticated office reflected the desire of the Awami League to strengthen the functioning of democracy in the country[41]. The powers and functions of Ombudsman were to be determined by the Parliament which would however include the power to investigate into any action taken by a Ministry, or an Officer or a statutory public authority (Article 77).

Law-making Procedure : Supremacy of Parliament

The procedure to make laws was provided in Article 80 of the Constitution. It provided that when a Bill was passed it would be presented to the

President for assent and he would do so within 15 days but he could in a case other than a Money Bill return the same to the Parliament with a message requesting for the reconsideration of the Bill or any of its particular provision along with any amendment specified by him but if the President did not do so within 15 days it would have been deemed that the President had assented to the Bill. In case of a bill so returned by the President, the Parliament would consider the same along with his message and if it passed the Bill with or without the amendment again, the President would assent to it within seven days failing which it would be deemed to have been assented by him.

The chapter relating to the legislative and financial procedure was drawn in line with the Act of 1935 shown by the British and then followed by the Indian Constitution and the Pakistan Constitutions of 1956 and 1962. The former followed the rules of procedure adopted by the British in the House of Commons with regard to placing of the annual financial statement, the Appropriation and Finance Act, etc.[42].

On the question of the ordinary law the procedure regarding assenting to the Bill as embodied in Article 80 was in substance similar to the provision in the Indian Constitution except that in the Indian Constitution no time limit was put for the President to assent[43] and that the country had a bicameral legislature. In the Pakistan Constitution of 1956 a third element was introduced i.e. the President could declare that he withheld his assent to the Bill and in such event the Parliament had to pass the same Bill by two-third majority to make it a law[44]. In the Constitution of 1962 however, the provisions were somewhat different, in such a case even if the Parliament had passed the Bill again it would require the assent of the President. If the President disagreed, the question whether the Bill was or was not to be assented to was to be decided by a referendum under Article 24 of the Constitution. However, if the Bill was not sent for a referendum within 10 days, it would become a law[45].

As in all other Constitutions of the sub-continent no Money Bill could be introduced in the Parliament except on the recommendation of the President (Article 82) and no tax could be levied or collected except by or under the authority of an Act of Parliament (Article 83). Although the legislative practice of introducing these bills being recommended by the President was maintained, the 1972 Constitution retained fully the supremacy of the Parliament in this regard and left very little scope for the President to exercise any discretion on the legislature. The provisions made in this regard in the Constitution were clear and precise and powers were defined appropriately.

In respect of each financial year a statement of estimated receipts and expenditures of the Government for that year in the form of an Annual Financial Statement was to be laid before the Parliament. The statement would show and distinguish expenditure on revenue account from other expenditures (Article 87). The part of the statement relating to expenditure charged upon the consolidated fund could be discussed in the Parliament but no vote was required, for the assent of the Parliament was imperative and such assent could be subject to reduction of the amount specified. Subject to the provision of the Constitution no money could be withdrawn from the consolidated fund except under an appropriation made by law (Article 90).

In matters of finance the 1962 Constitution offers major variation and this was mainly due to the fact that the Constitution itself was conceptually a different one—more centralised and presidential in nature and form. In the 1972 Constitution it was made clear in Article 82 that in respect of any Money Bill no recommendation of the President was required for making an amendment for the reduction or abolition of any tax whereas in Article 47 of the 1962 Constitution recommendation of the President was required for any amendment and the National Assembly without the consent of the President could not reduce a demand for grant.

Another common feature of the Constitution was the Ordinance-making power of the President during the time when the Parliament was not in session or stood dissolved. In such circumstances when immediate action was necessary the President could make an Ordinance but no ordinance could make any provision which could not be lawfully made by an Act of Parliament, nor alter or repeal any provision of the Constitution, nor continue in force any provision or an Ordinance previously made. On the question of time-limit for laying such Ordinance before the Parliament the 1972 Constitution provided that unless such law was repealed earlier it was to be placed at the first meeting of the Parliament following the promulgation of the Ordinance for approval within 30 days from the day it was so laid. Otherwise, the law would expire. In the 1956 Constitution the time was 6 weeks and in the 1962 Constitution 6 weeks after the first meeting of the National Assembly or 180 days from the day of the promulgation of the Ordinance.

If Parliament stood dissolved the President, as in 1956 Constitution could make an Ordinance authorising expenditure from the Consolidated Fund whether charged by the Constitution upon that fund or not but necessary adaptations were to be complied with in regard to the financial procedures as contained in the relevant article within 30 days of the reconstitution of Parliament.

It will be evident from the constitutional development that the gap between the sessions continued to widen and frequency of parliamentary session continued to be reduced. From the gap of 60 days between two sessions in the original constitution it was widened to 120 days in September, 1973 by the Second Constitution Amendment and then by the Fourth Amendment the time gap was altogether abolished with a provision of minimum of two sessions in one year. So the Parliament was sitting less and less and the Ordinance-making power assumed more and more significance.

Judiciary

One of the fundamental principles of State policy as contained in Article 22 of the Constitution was to ensure the separation of Judiciary from the executive organ of the State. Inspired by the concept of rule of law and the lofty idealism inculcated through a system primarily contributed by the British, the demand for the separation of judiciary from the executive organ of the state gained a political momentum in the history of the sub-continent[46]. Almost all the political leaders and parties who advocated democracy pledged to ensure the independence of judiciary in order to establish the rule of law in the country. How much the separation as well as independence of the subordinate judiciary could be achieved in the complex system of the state administration was a different matter but an objective principle of the same nature was adopted by all the constitution-makers of the sub-continent. Even the iron rule of Ayub Khan had to ensure the independence of judiciary. The format used to achieve this objective reflected a common pattern in all the constitutions, the form and structure being almost identical with that originally conceived by the British[47].

Unlike India and Pakistan, Bangladesh established itself as a single unitary homogeneous state and therefore the immediate question was to decide whether the country needed two separate establishments as Supreme Court and High Court and to determine their respective functions in a country with no federal problems or issues. Secondly, even during the Pakistan period it was widely felt that the seat of the High Court at Dhaka could be permanent but the Judges of the High Court ought to sit in circuit at least in the major district towns of East Pakistan to make justice available to all the litigants, particularly to the poor ones who did not have financial resources to travel upto Dhaka. Keeping these two major issues in view, the structure of the superior branch of the judiciary was to be determined.

Bangladesh not being a federal state, the judicial structure was also to be rationalised. The idea of having a Federal or Supreme Court is primarily linked up with a federal form of government where the major function of such court besides the interpretation of law and constitution was to resolve the rights, obligations and disputes between the centre and the states and between the states themselves. So the major function of the Supreme or Federal Court as envisaged in the U.S.A., Germany, Australia, India, Pakistan, etc.—all being federal states was not required for the Supreme Court in Bangladesh. Its primary function was to hear appeals from the courts below and decide the law points involved in cases which would come before it for hearing. Accordingly, in the Bangladesh Constitution only one superior court was established to avoid unnecessary expenses and hierchical duplicity, to be known as the Supreme Court with two Divisions, one Appellate and the other High Court,—the Appellate Division was to act as the highest court and the High Court Division to exercise the functions of the former High Court.

In other words, to administer justice there was to be one establishment for the entire country and there would be one Chief Justice of the Supreme Court as a whole. The Chief Justice and the Judges appointed to the Appellate Division would sit only in that Division and the rest of the Judges were to sit in the High Court Division.

As an objective of establishing an independent judiciary the Constitution proclaimed that "subject to the provision of this Constitution the Chief Justice and the other Judges shall be independent in the exercise of their judicial functions" (Article 4(4)). The Chief Justice and the other Judges were to be appointed by the President. Once the Chief Justice was appointed, the other Judges could only be appointed after consultation with the Chief Justice (Article 95). Once a Judge was appointed he could not be removed unless the Parliament passed a resolution supported by a majority of not less than two-thirds of the total number of members on the ground of proved misbehaviour or incapacity (Article 96 (2). The Supreme Court would be a court of record and would have all the powers of such a court including the power to make an order for the investigation of or punishment or a contempt of iteself (Article 108) and all the authorities, executive and judicial in the Republic would act in aid of the Supreme Court (Article 112). The appointments to the staff of the Supreme Court would be made by the Chief Justice or any other Judge or Officer he would direct, in accordance with the rules made with the prior approval of the President (Article 113). The Supreme Court would also make rules for regulating the practice and procedure of each Division and any court subordianate to it with the approval of the President (Article 101).

The most distinguishing feature of the 1972 Constitution is Article 116 which extended the authority of the Supreme Court as follows :

> "The control including the power of posting, promotion and grant of leave and discipline of persons employed in the judicial service and magistrates exercising judicial functions shall vest in the President and shall be exercised by him in consultation with the Supreme Court".

This control was provided in addition to the High Court Division's superintendence and control over all courts and tribunals subordinate to it[48].

While both the Constitutions of 1956 and 1962 retained such power of superintendence and control for the High Court, none provided such extraordinary power to their Supreme Court to determine the posting, promotion and grant of leave and control and discipline of persons employed in the judicial service and magistrates exercising judicial functions. Further, with regard to the appointment of persons to offices in the judicial service or as magistrate exercising judicial functions the President would make the appointment but in case of District Judges the appointment would be made on the recommendation of the Supreme Court and in case of other Judges in accordance with rules made by the President after consulting the appropriate Public Service Commission and the Supreme Court. In order to maintain the integrity of judiciary it further provided that no person would be eligible for appointment as a District Judge unless he held a judicial office for atleast 7 years or had been an Advocate for not less than 10 years. All these mandatory and constitutional provisions were not made available in any other constitution of the sub-continent. Despite the complexities of state management and the realities confronted in the governmental system there is no doubt that the constitution of 1972 provided for more institutional opportunities and independence for the members of judiciary in the exercise of their judicial functions. The Supreme Court was provided with much more power and authority in developing the institution as an independent organ of the State.

The Writ Jurisdiction

As in other constitutions of the sub-continent the High Court Division was provided along with others an extraordinary original jurisdiction for the enforcement of fundamental rights and the power to issue writs in the form of mandamus, certiorari, quowarranto, habeas corpus, etc. under Article 102[49]. One major exception made in Article 102 was however that the power would not apply to matters to which Article 47 applied[50].

Subject to this restriction relating to Article 47, the High Court Division was provided with wide power under Article 102 of the Constitution. Besides the enforcement of fundamental rights the Court could issue writ of mandamus and certiorari against person performing any function in connection with the affairs of the Republic or of a local authoriy which included a statutory public authority or any court or tribunal. Again such writs could not, however, be issued against a court or tribunal established under law relating to the defence services of the country. In other words, the proceedings of any court or tribunal established under the Army Act or any Act relating to the defence services could not be called in question by the Supreme Court under its original jurisdiction[51]. The writ jurisdiction was also excluded with regard to the administrative tribunals if established under Article 117 of the Constituion.

Administrative Tribunals

In order to provide quick relief and avoid lengthy proceedings of litigation the constitution provided for the creation of Administrative Tribunals in Article 117. Such Tribunals would exercise jurisdiction in matters relating to or arising out of (1) terms and conditions of persons in the service of the Republic i.e. broadly government servants, (2) the acquisition, administration, management and disposal of any property vested in or managed by the government, including operation and management of any service in any nationalised enterprise or statutory public authority and (3) any action in relation to any law relating to Article 47 of the Constitution. Once an Administrative Tribunal was established no court including the Supreme Court could interefere in respect of any matter falling within the jurisdiction of that Tribunal and in particular, the writ jurisdiction under Article 102 was excluded. Parlimnent could, however, by leave provide for an appeal or review. Although no Administrative Tribunal was established by the Awami League Government the inclusion of such an enabling provision for creating the Tribunals was considered as a step in the right direction.

The writ jurisdictin of the High Court Division re-established by the Constitution of 1972 was wide enough to extend the jurisdiction of the court over almost all possible wrong or injustices that might be committed by the public functioneries against the citizens. As the High Court was without this jurisdiction for about a year re-introduction of writ jurisdiction by the Constitution was a significant change in the field of administration of justice. Under the writ jurisdiction the High Court continued to have power to interfere not only for the enforcement of the fundamental rights but also in matters of executive excesses and judicial errors. With regard to judicial errors of Courts and Tribunals subordinate to it the High Court Division's jurisdiction to issue writs was excluded in 2 exceptional cases. (1) With regard to court or tribunal established under a law relating to the Defence Services of Bangladesh or any disciplined force like Police, Ansar, etc. and (2) Administrative Tribunals established under Article 117 of the Constitution. Apart from these 2 areas, the jurisdiction of the High Court under the writ jurisdiction was considered to be comprehensive in the arena of law and administration of justice.

It would be interesting to note that the Awami League in their constitutional proposals to Ayub Khan contained in the Constitution Amendment Bill 1969 did also not offer any amendment to Article 98 of the 1962 Constitution excepting that a definition of "local authority" was embodied. In the 1969 Amendment Bill a direct remedy for the enforcement of fundamental rights was made available also through the Supreme Court.

The Hight Court Division was also provided with the power of superintendence and control over all courts and tribunals subordinate to it (Article 109). It was also empowered to transfer cases from subordinate courts to the High Court Division if the case involved a substantial question of law as to the interpretation of the constitution or a point of general public importance. Similar provisions were made in both the Constitutions of Pakistan. In both the 1962 and 1956 Constitutions, a judge could be transferred from one High Court to another with the consent of the judge concerned and after consultations with Chief Justice. In Bangladesh naturally the provision could not apply but the interesting point is that the Awami League in their 1969 Constitution Bill proposed to delete Article 94 of the 1962 Constitution[52].

Another interesting feature of 1972 Constitution was Article 100 which related to the permanent seat of the Court and its sitting at different places from time to time. Although the provision was not a new one and was similar to those in the 1956 and 1962 Constitution, it was in a different context that the provision was incorporated in 1972 Constitution. Article 100 read as follows :

> "The permanent seat of the Supreme Court shall be in the capital, but sessions of the High Court Division may be held at such other place or places as the Chief Justice may, with the approval of the President, from time to time appoint".

The point was that while the seat of the Supreme Court was to be at Dhaka, the sessions of the High Court Division could be held at other places. As indicated earlier this provision reflected a political desire of having the High Court Division sittng in all the major towns of the country. According to the Awami League, to have all the courts of both the Appellate Division and the High Court Division sitting in Dhaka for a small, contiguous and unitary country like Bangladesh with poor litigants living in far away rural areas could hardly be justified[53].

But the Government faced stiff opposition both from the Bench and the Bar. From the Bench, the objection was not raised against the objective or principle involved in the matter, it was raised more on logistical points such as, residence, staff, library and other facilities. But the opposition from the Bar was much more vocal and vehement both on grounds of logistics and principles. They raised the point that in the absence of adequate logistical facilities and with the low standard of advocacy in the district headquarters, the standard of judgement would be affected and dispensation of justice would become weak. They argued that the charm and dignity of the office of a Supreme Court Judge would not diminish and qualified persons would no more be available to accept the job of a judge. They feared that corruption which had not yet reached the corridors of the Supreme Court would now possibly have an access to travel to that level once the courts were moved to the Districts. All these would lead to a considerable credibility gap in the administration of justice in superior courts, the only institution left in which the public had yet not lost all their confidence. Their final argument was that the litigants would have to pay more to engage good lawyers from Dhaka and so it would cost them more in taking a lawyer from the capital than it would if they come to Dhaka to have the case settled. As most of the litigants were poor, sitting of courts in other towns would cause more financial burden on them if they were to engage good lawyers. Although these arguments might have had some substance the political parties who committed to establish an egalitarian society criticised the Dhaka lawyers as being selfish and argued that the lawyers were mainly opposed to the plan for the fear of losing their briefs and clients and a large number of Dhaka lawyers would have to live without many of their traditional clients. As far as the good lawyers are concerned and the well-to-do clients, the sitting of the courts in other towns would not have made any difference. And yet the Government could not put through the programme due to the opposition mainly from the Bar and for the fear of losing political support of a conscious urban community. The Awami League faced opposition from within itself also since a large number of the influential Awami League lawyers residing in Dhaka opposed the programme for their own professional reasons.

The jurisdiction of the Appellate Division was to hear and determine appeals from judgments, decrees, order and sentences passed by the High Court Division. The Appellate Division would also have the power to review any of its own judgements pronounced (Article 105). The Appellate Division like the Supreme Court of other countries in the sub-continent also enjoyed an advisory jurisdiction by reporting its opinion to the President on a question of law of public importance if the latter referred the matter to it for such opinion (Article 106). In order to ensure the supremacy and independence of judiciary, like in other constitutions, it was provided that the law declared by the Appellate Division would be binding on the High Court Division of the Supreme Court and binding on all courts subordinate to it (Article 111).

Election

Part VII of the constitution contained provisions relating to election. It had been a part of the tradition in the sub-continent to have an independent body to hold national elections in order to ensue their fairness. The Indian Consitution and both the 1956 Constitution (Article 137-47) and the 1962 Contstitution of Pakistan (Article 147-54) contained similar provisions for the constitution of an Election Commission. Similar salary, status and position were offered to the members of the Commission and in order to gain public cofidence the Chief Election Commissioner and other members of the Commission were invariably drawn from the judiciary. Their remuneration and status etc. were also to be the same. Like the Judges of the High Court and Supreme Court an Election Commissioner once appointed could not be removed by an executive order.

In case a Parliament was dissolved, a new Parliament was required to be elected within 90 days. Similarly, in case of any particular seat in the Parliament falling vacant, a bye-election was to be held within 90 days of the occurence of the vacancy.

The most interesting aspect of this chapter was the age of voters. Article 122 provided qualifications required for the registration as a voter in line with other constitutions referred to. But the distinguishing feature was the reduction of voting age to 18 years. Throughout its struggle, the Awami League received maximum support from the students and youths and at many stages of their survival, the younger generation dominated by the students of schools, colleges and universities maintained the strength of the party and in this process in order to secure their support, the party was also committed to reduce the voting age. As far back as in 1969 when the Awami League prepared the Constitution Amendment Bill it used the opportunity of reducing the voting age to 18 years[54]. In all the other Constitutions the voting age was fixed at 21 years.

The other interesting feature of this Article was that it defranchised those persons who were convicted of any offence under the Bangladesh Collaborators Order, i.e. convicted collaborators. This provision was criticised on the ground that it took away the voting right of a collaborator for the entire life without considering the length of sentence or gravity of offence. Secondly, such exclusion after having gone through a punishment by a collaborator, was considered to be too harsh. On the other hand, the exclusion reflected the public sentiment of the relevant time.

As far as the actual functioning of the Election Commission is concerned, the experience has not always been a good one. On the theoretical plane the Commission has been retained as an independent body to be impartial in conducting election. In reality, however, it has been seen that the ruling party tends to influence the Commission and on many occasions the Commission becomes helpless in the face of the highhandedness of the ruling party[55].

The Services

It has been a practice in constitution-making to embody provisions relating to services in the civil sector and to incorporate principles of the terms and conditions of service and recruitment etc. Provisions tended to provide security to the persons employed in the service of the Republic and enable the bureaucratic machinery to develop its own mechanism into an institution in running the administration of the country. The basic concept centered round the creation of Public Services on the basis of tests and examinations and to provide adequate safeguards for their service condition in order to infuse a sense of confidence, prestige and security in those who entered the services.

Pakistan followed the British colonial practice of creating a strong elitist bureaucratic machine in order to provide a "good administration' for the country. Consequently, unlike India which had strong political leadership, bureaucracy in Pakistan where political leadership lacked strength and cohesion played an important role in the political arena of the country. Since the death of Quaid-e-Azam Jinnah and Liaquat Ali Khan, the bureaucrats led by persons like Gholam Mohammed, Iskander Mirza and Chowdhury Mohammad Ali dominated the political scene. This enabled the creation of elitism in Pakistan bureaucracy maintaining the British tradition of safeguarding the interest of the civil servants as a separate class. The British created the civil service in order to rule India and they felt the necessity of providing extraordinary protection to those who were to work for the perpetuation of their rule. The principles for creation and maintenance of their Civil Service were fully reflected in the Government of India Act, 1935 (Article 240-268).

But as Pakistan never witnessed any democratic Government till it broke up, the Civil Servants whether under civil or military rule played the most important role and this was reflected both in 1956 and 1962 Constitutions as far as constitutional provisions for Services were concerned. No attempt was made to introduce a system or a structure to suit the needs of its own people, no fresh element was introduced in the Constitution to meet the new situation and the emerging geo-political dimension of Pakistan. If not in its format but in its content, the 1956 costitution followed almost in totality what was provided in the 1935 Act. On the question of Services, terms and conditions and their safeguards, creation and constitution of Public Service Commissions and the recruitment procedures, similar provisions were retained. A similar line was followed also in the 1962 Constitution. In this context it would be interesting to read Article 241 of the 1935 Act and Article 182 of the 1956 Constitution and Article 178 of the 1962 Constitution. These Articles provided that whether the rules relating to the terms and conditions of service of persons employed in the central or provincial affairs were made by the President or the Governors, such rules would be so framed to ensure that the terms and conditions of service relating to remuneration and age fixed for superannuation would not be varied to his disadvantage. If an order was made, (1) punishing or formally censuring a person, (2) altering or interpreting any rule affecting his terms or conditions of service or (3) terminating the employment of a person, he would have a right of appeal and if the orders were passed by the President or the Governor, he could file an application for review. These advantages and provisions for further protection of service conditions were in addition to what they would enjoy under other Articles of the Constitution. These were made to ensure permanancy of service.

The Bangladesh Constitution, although it followed the general format adopted by the other constitutional documents, attempted a departure in its content. The Awami League committed itself to rebuild the administrative machinery so that it could "meet the needs and aspirations of the people"[56]. They pledged to establish a "pro-people administration" in place of a colonial system. It is in this context that the Awami League rejected the concept of rigidity and permanency in the service conditions and instead made provisions for the reorganisation of services. Although constitutional provisions for seeking remedy for unlawful dismissal, removal or reduction in rank were retained, the permanency of terms and conditions of service were not guaranteed. Article 133 provided that the Parliament would by law regulate the appointment and conditions of services of persons appointed in the service of the Republic and till such law was made the President would make rules regulating them. In Article 136 it was provided that "provisions may be made by law for the reorganisation of the service of the Republic by the creation, amalgamation or unification of services and such law may vary or revoke any condition of service of a person employed in the service of the Republic". This was a fundamental devlation of far-reaching consequences from the established principles.

More interesting point is that although the Fourth Schedule guaranteed the continuation of service and other authorities in paragraph 10, it made certain categorical exceptions to such continuation as enshrined in Para 10 (2).

Para 10(2) contained saving clauses with respect to Presidential Orders 9 and 67 of 1972 and also for future legislation reforming service conditions. It would be evident that although the P.O. 9 and P.O. 67 were already saved by Article 47(2) of the Constitution as read with the First Schedule and the authority for the reorganisation of service continued in Article 136, these provisions were again re-emphasised in paragraph 10 (2) of the Fourth Schedule. It showed, beyond any doubt, that the Awami League was determined to reorganise the salary and service structure of the government employees and that all constitutional precautions were taken to give effect to such programmes. It envisaged not only the continuation of the P.O. 9 and 67 but kept open the provision to make laws varying or revoking the condition of service including remuneration, leave, pension, right and rights relating to disciplinary matters[57]. The political motives behind these provisions were more than evident.

But on the other hand, as in other constitutions of the sub-continent, in Article 135 remedies were also provided against any unlawful dismissal, removal or reduction in rank. The operative portion of Article 135 illustrates this. It contained the traditional twin guarantee that a person holding a civil post in the service

(a) could not be dismissed, removed or reduced in rank by an authority subordinate to that by which he was appointed ;

(b) could not be dismissed without prior hearing.

For the purpose of maintaining such services through an institutional mechanism, the system of having an independent Public Service Commission was maintained. A Commission would consist of a chairman and such other members as would be prescribed by law (Article 137). Provision was made so that at least one-half of the members of a Commission were persons who held office for 20 years or more in the service of the Government at any time within the territory of Bangladesh [Article 138(1)].

The Amendment of the Constitution

Part X of the Constitution laid down provisions relating to the procedure for amendment of the constitution. The principle applied in formulating this Article was comparatively more simple but at the same time rigid and straightforward in its content. In the Indian Constitution a bill for amendment would become an Act if it is passed in each House of the Parliament by a majority of the total membership of that House and by a majority of not less than two thirds of members of that House present and voting; it is then presented before the President who "shall give his assent to the Bill". For certain Articles and part of the constitution the amendment would require ratification by the legislatures of not less than one-half of the states before presenting to the President for his assent. The 1956 Constitution of Pakistan followed similar principles on the voting procedure but no "shall" was used for the President to assent to the Bill. Nothing was indicated as to what would happen if the President refused to assent to the Bill or just kept silent for an unlimited period.

The 1962 Constitution being Presidential in nature gave even more power to the President enabling him ultimately to take the matter to a referendum if he did not agree to any amendment. Firstly, the Bill would require votes of two-thirds of the total number of members of the National Assembly. Similarly, within 30 days, the President could either assent to the Bill or withhold such assent or return the Bill with amendments. When the President would withhold the Bill the National Assembly could pass the Bill again with votes of the three-quarters of the total number of members and again place it for the President's assent. If the Bill was again passed by three-fourths of the total number with or without his amendments, the President could still have power to either give his assent or cause the Bill to be referred to a referendum. In other words even with the support of the three-fourths of the total number of members of the National Assembly an amendment could not be effected to the Constitution of 1962 as the President held enormous powers in relation to legislation.

In the Bangladesh Constitution Article 142 read as follows:

(1) Notwithstand anything contained in this Constitution—

(a) any provision thereof may be amended by way of addition, alteration, substitution or repeal by Act of Parliament:

Provided that—

(i) no Bill for such amendment shall be allowed to proceed unless the long title thereof expressly states that it will amend a provision of the Constitution;

(ii) no such Bill shall be presented to the President for assent unless it is passed by the votes of not less than two-thirds of the total number of members of Parliament;

(b) when a Bill passed as aforesaid is presented to the President for his assent he shall, within the period of seven days after the Bill is presented to him assent to the Bill, and if he fails so to do he shall be deemed to have assented to it on the expiration of that period.

It will be evident that the constitution did not leave any scope for the President to stop or create obstruction to any amendment once the Parliament had passed it with votes of two-thirds of the total number. After the presentation of the Bill if the President failed to give his assent within 7 days, the Bill would become a law. From this point of view the provision in the Bangladesh Constitution was an improvement over all others on the question of maintaining the sovereignty of Parliament. The second interesting point to note was that while it did not contain any restriction or exclusion and gave an absolute power to bring any amendment to any provision of the Constitution, it did not exclude Article 26(2) of the Constitution which read as follows :

"The State shall not make any law inconsistent with any provisions of this Part, and any law so made shall to the extent of such inconsistency, be void."

The two Articles 26 and 142 appear to be contradictory as far as Part III of the Constitutions was concerned which related to provisions on fundamental rights. On the other hand, the fundamental rights were guaranteed to the extent that they could not be changed even by the Parliament but on the other hand, Article 142 gave an unequivocal power to the Parliament to bring an amendment and indicated that the Parliament was sovereign in changing any provision of the Constitution. However, this contradiction was removed in 1973 by the Constitution (Second Amendment) Act in which a new clause was added to Article 26 and Article 142[58]. The new clause in Article 26 read as follows :

"(3) Nothing in this Article shall apply to any amendment of this constitution made under Article 142."

In Article 142 the new clause read as follows :

"(2) Nothing in Article 26 shall apply to any amendment made under this Article."

In other words, the sovereign authority of the Parliament was secured on the question of amending any part or provision of the Constitution including the fundamental rights[59].

But again although the amendment removed any possible contradiction between the two Articles and apparently established the absolute authority of the Parliament to amend any provision of the Constitution, it indirectly provided more power to the party controlling the government. In other words, the executive office through the party in power could now bring any amendment to suit their administration. In a way the amendment took away the inherent power of the Parliament to retain the fundamental rights and destroyed the balance that existed between the permanent nature of the Constitution and the amending power of the Parliament with regard to the most important part of the Constitution—the fundamental rights. The point bears special importance in the Bangladesh Constitution in view of the fact that this amendment of Article 142 which excluded the impact of Article 26 enabled the Parliament at a later stage to change the basic structure of the Constitution when it introduced a one-party system[60].

On the question of changing the basic structure of the constitution by the Parliament having absolute authority to amend any provision of the constitution, we have series of precedents to understand the real import of such an amending power of the Parliament. When the Awami League government on January 25, 1975 passed the Fourth Constitution Amendment Bill to introduce a one-party monolithic system, it changed the very basic structure of the Constitution but there was no scope to challenge the validity of such a change in the circumstances prevailing at that time. In India however, there has been a series of judicial decisions on this vital question whether the Parliament having absolute power to amend any provision can change the essential features of the Constitution. The Supreme Court of India at different stages enunciated the 'doctrine of basic structure' and the most celebrated of all the cases is known as the Fundamental Right Case (Kesavanda Bharati v. State of Kerala, AIR 1973 SC 1461) where the court overruled the decision in Golaknaths case[61]. and upheld the validity of the 24th Amendment. In this case the court held that the power of amendment extending to all part of the Constitution was at the same time subject to inherent or implied limitations and it could not be used to change or affect the basic structure of the Constitution, Parliament was still constrained from changing the essential features of the Constitution[62].

Interesting provisions were made with respect to laws existing on the day of commencement of the Constitution. While Art. 149 kept existing laws in force generally, Art. 151 specifically repealed laws earlier made since the declaration of independence in March, 1971[63]. Then again under Article 47, twenty seven laws, all excepting one made during the same period, were not only protected but were provided with the status of fundamental laws having equal force as the Constitution itself. These laws contained in the First Schedule of the Constitution, enjoyed to some extent a super constitutional status in the sense that any amendment made to any of these laws would also be protected even if such amendments were made to give retrospective effect[64]. It is true that in the extraordinary circumstances of the country certain special laws were required to be made and they had to be saved but these had 2 very significant elements. One, the saving excluded the application of Article 26 of the Constitution. Two, it went further to save their subsequent amendments too.

Bengali Text of the Constitution

The Constitution adopted by the Constituent Assembly on November 4, 1972, was to come into force on December 16, 1972 on the first anniversary of the victory day of the country. The Constitution would have an authentic text in Bengali and an authentic text of an authorised translation in English. Both were certified to have same effect but in the event of any conflict between the Bengali and the English text the Bengali text would prevail. It is to be noted that the constitution was originally drafted in English and then translated into Bengali. But in the Constitution the translated Bengali version was given the status of an original and the original English text was to be considered as an authentic text of an authorised translation in English. This somewhat unnecessary arrangement was made, in order to uphold the status of the state language of the country.

The Constitution contained 4 Schedules. The first Schedule contained the laws saved under Article 47 of the Constitution as already discussed. The Second Schedule provided the procedure relating to the election of the President under Article 48 of the Constitution. The Third Schedule contained the terms of Oaths and Affirmations of the President, Prime Minister and Ministers, Speaker, Deputy Speaker, Members of Parliament, Chief Justice and Judges of the Supreme Court, Chief Election Commissioner and other members, Comptroller and Auditor General and Members of the Public Service Commission as envisaged under Article 148 of the Constitution.

The Fourth Schedule contained the transitional and temporary provisions as provided under Article 150 of the Constitution. Under this Article and Schedule provisions were made for the dissolution of the Constitution Assembly on the commencement of the Constitution. Paragraph 2 laid provisions as to how the first election would be held after the commencement of the Constitution. It provided for electoral rolls and delimitation of constituencies for the general election. In order to ensure a smooth transition, all necessary legal precautions were taken by removing every possible inconsistency that could arise in making the constitution operate effectively from the day of its commencement. In this context, any time before the first meeting of the Parliament after the general election, the President under paragraph 17 was empowered for the purpose of removing any difficulties in relation to this transition, to direct by an order that the Constitution would have effect subject to such adaptations, whether by way of modification, addition or omission as he would deem necessary or expedient. The President was also empowered, for the purpose of bringing the provisions of any law to conform with the Constitution, to amend or suspend the operation of such provisions by an order within a period of two years from the commencement of the constitution and any such order could also have retrospective effect.

In order to maintain the continuity of laws and actions taken thereunder, the constitution in paragraph 3 of the Fourth Schedule ratified and confirmed all the laws made between 26th March, 1971 and the commencement of the constitution, all the powers exercised and the things done under the authority of the Proclamation of Independence. From the time the Constitution commenced and till the first meeting of the elected Parliament, the executive and the legislative powers including the power of the President to legislate by order on the advice of the Prime Minister were to be exercised in the way they were exercised before the commencement of the Constitution, notwithstanding the repeal of the Provisional Constitution of Bangladesh Order, 1972. During this period the President could also legislate in respect of any matter under the Constitution which required Parliament to legislate.

Another interesting feature contained in the Fourth Schedule related to the liability or obligation of the government prior to independence. In paragraph 16(3) of the Fourth Schedule which carried lot of implication immediately after the creation of the country read as follows :

> "No liability or obligation of any other government which at any time functioned in the territory of Bangladesh is or shall be a liability or obligation of the Republic unless it is expressly accepted by the Government of the Republic".

Immediately after independence the Government started receiving thousands of claims from individuals, corporations, loan agencies and other institutions from abroad who were in transaction with former East Pakistan. By this provision in the Constitution the Government retained the right of scrutinising such claims and accept or reject the same. The Government took this stand on the question of liabilities and obligations in line with international practice of state succession. By removing the presumption of being bound as a successor government it adopted the same principle on the question of accepting or rejecting obligations as recommended by the International Law Commission in the International Draft Convention on State Succession. Accordingly, although the Awami League Government took the stand that it came to power through an armed struggle and revolution, in matters of liabilities and obligations of the previous governments it did not stick to it always depending on the kind of claim it faced. Sometime it behaved as a successor government by accepting the past liability and sometime as a revolutionary government by not accepting such past liability. Anyhow, such provision was necessary to enable the Government to handle a complicated area of financial obligations particularly when it related to foreign countries and international agencies. The option contained in paragraph 16(3) helped the government during the interim period in settling the claims with a constitutional weapon in hand.

Summary and Conclusion

For the entire rule of the Awami League, one of its greatest achievements was to write a constitution for the country. It is true that compared to the complexities which India and particularly Pakistan had in their constitution-making, Bangladesh faced no such problem because of her political homogeneity and geographical contiguity. But even then, the Awami League's effort of giving the nation a constitution within a year should not go uncommended. It was a full, comprehensive and well written document—precisce and straight—much improved over all the existing constitutions of the subcontinent[65]. Although there were some weaknesses and contradictions the constitution to a large extent reflected the aspirations of the people. If one looks back and recapitulates the long struggle and sufferings of the Bengalis in East Pakistan in the context of the colonial rule of Pakistan, it would not be difficult to affirm that the demands raised at different stages and commitments made by the Awami League leaders were largely reflected in various part of the constitution and the Awami League made an effort to give expression to the sentiments of the people raised at different stages of political struggle in the country. The most notable of its features were : (1) introduction of a parliamentary democratic system, (2) guaranteeing fundamental rights, (3) exclusion of any provision for preventive detention, (4) exclusion of any provision for proclaiming emergency and suspension of fundamental rights, (5) provisions for a socialist economic system including nationalisation of property with or without compensation, (6) re-organisation of civil bureaucracy with the power to change the conditions of service, (7) a sense of Bengali nationalism, (8) provision for the emancipation of peasants and workers, (9) decentralisation in administration, planning, implementation and maintenance of public order by local bodies composed of persons elected by people, (10) no declaration of or participation in war of the Republic, without the consent of the Parliament, (11) exclusion of right of Members of Parliament to change parties or to vote against the Bill introduced by the party, (12) empowering the Supreme Court with the authority to control and discipline persons employed in the judicial service and magistrates exercising judical functions, (13) provision for administrative Tribunals and, (14) reduction of voting age to 18 years. Each of these features has a political background and each was a result of the demand made by people at different stages in the past.

As a matter of fact, the constitution provided a little bit too much of a parliamentary system in the sense that it attempted to ensure a perfect system so that democracy and nothing else would flourish in the country. Within the constitutional framework the check and balance that was required even for the balanced growth of a parliamentary system was not thought to be necessary. The attempt was more to establish a parliamentary system by writing down the laws than depending on practice or convention. The President was to perform all his functions on the advice of the Prime Minister and he could not declare war or do anything on his own. The quality of democracy which are generally achieved through practice, maturity and experience was expected to be acquired through writing in the book, eliminating all scope for any kind of interference from the office of the President. The relevant point here was that the past experience of attempting to establish a democratic system in Pakistan was a tragic failure and the Awami League leaders were not prepared to take any chance. Moreover, as a new country maturity and experience were yet to be gained and so it was found advisable to write down the scheme in a relatively rigid form so that the Parliament did not have to depend on the ingredients of tradition or norms for its functioning. The question of the President assenting to a Bill could be cited as an example. The President's action was restricted to a time schedule and he could exercise no authority even in the remotest possible way to create any obstruction in the passage of a Bill. While India being a Federal Union and having 2 Houses, its Constitution provided an inbuilt mechanism of check and balance within the system but Bangladesh being unitary required no such mechanism.

A section of politicians would argue that by writing down everything, the Awami League only secured its own position as it assumed that Bangladesh was created only for the Awami League to rule. The argument was, however, not tenable in the sense that the precautions taken mainly reflected the bitter experience of the past. If one only looks at the history of Pakistan, one can see how at different stages the interventions from the Presidents ruined the sustenance of constitutional government in that country. The suspicion about the President intervening in matters which otherwise were not his job in a parliamentary system was not without any background or foundation. One could however argue that in view of the fact that the Awami League enjoyed so much strength in the Parliament and that no person could be elected as President without their support, those rigid provisions were not required. No such President would do anything against the wishes of the ruling party. This only justified the contention of the Awami League that those provisions were made to ensure a smooth growth of a parliamentary system in the absence of tradition and political maturity of the country as a whole and had nothing to do with the strength in Parliament of a particular political party.

The Awami League claimed to have achieved the independence "through a historic struggle for national liberation" and all through that period they maintained this emphasis. According to them it was a government which emerged through a revolution and they were to frame the constitution in that context. But the fact is that the Awami League was neither a revolutionary party nor had it any specific revolutionay ideological bias in any classical sense. So while making the constitution, the Awami League had to combine the revolutionary urges emerging through the armed struggle and their long standing commitments for a traditional development. It is from this point of view that the evaluation of the Constitution framed by the Awami League was to be made. No one was to expect a revolutionary constitution from the Awami League. In the given context and circumstances, the constitution produced by the Awami League was a fine book of law and it remained to be so till the time they themselves destroyed it.

The main thrust of the Constitution was to make provisions to realise a socialist society through a democratic process. At an early stage prior to independence the Awami League leadership was influenced by the political aim s of the British labour party to adopt certain socialist measures through laws to be made in Parliament. The aim was to establish a kind of a welfare state conceived by the Fabians. But in the process of the struggle and political development of two long decades, the position of the Awami League shifted considerably on the question of socialism and it went to the extent of establishing a "Socialist society free from exploitation of man by man". On the other hand it also did not deviate from its commitment to "establish a society in which the rule of law, fundamental human rights and freedom and dignity of man would be secured and administration at all levels would be run by elected representatives of the people based on universal adult franchise".

This ultimately led to the creation of certain contradictions in the constitution and the principal manifestation of it was found in Article 26 and Article 47 of the Constitution which we have already discussed. Besides the basic contradictions that arise out of attempting to establish two systems together, a socialist and a democratic, there were other features also which the Awami League failed to reconcile. The two aims could be complimentary to each other and could go together upto an extent but not beyond a certain point when it could become contradictory, depending on the scale of socialist measures aimed to be achieved.

In order to achive the two objectives together rights were given with one hand and taken away by the other. Fundamental rights like freedom of movement, freedom of assembly, speech, expression and press were guaranteed subject to restrictions made by law. While Article 42 guaranteed right to property, at the same time it also took away that right by making provision for acquisition, nationalisation or requisition with or without compensation. Further, the impact of Article 47 and its far-reaching consequences had borne a deeper contradiction within the framework of the Constitution. The judiciary with the kind of independence envisaged in the Constitution and the powers contained in Article 116 within a democratic system of conventional type also posed a threat to achieving a socialist economic order. Anyhow an attempt was made to strike a balance and reconcile the two socio-economic forces in one Constitution. While there was nothing wrong in the intent of achieving socialism through a democratic order as such, the question remained as how much it could achieve and to what extent. It is true that adequate provisions were maintained to adopt socialist measures through the mechanism of a parliamentary democracy, but the point was how much the dynamics of a socialist order could be met through the passage of law passed in a Parliament of the kind envisaged in the Constitution.

To make a correct evaluation of the point at issue one has to undertake a deeper study to determine how much the Awami League committed to establish a "Socialist economic system" and of what brand. If their aim was to establish only to the extent of that socialism which could be achieved through a bourgeois mechanism of law, the provisions made in the constitution were quite adequate to achieve that objective. But if their primary objective was to establish "a society free from exploitation of man by man" in the strict socialist sense and if they had meant so, the situation would call for a serious re-thinking. It was known to the Awami League leaders that in no country as yet a true socialist economic system could be established through a bourgeois mechanism, no matter what strong words or provisions were incorporated in the Constitution. So the question arose in a logical sequence as to what was the real intention of the Awami League leaders. Were they proceeding towards the path of socialism with a genuine conviction or the whole thing was an eye-wash. Was it a reflection of their own inner-contradictions or were they simply deceiving the people ?

Finally, it should be kept in mind that the Constitution making process in Bangladesh during the era of Mujib really could be divided into 3 parts. The first part was the period between December 16, 1971 to Decmber 15, 1972. During this time although by the Provisional Constitution Order, a kind of parlimentary structure was introduced but for all practical purposes the country was run in a dictatorial manner. The Constituent Assembly was not allowed to function as a legislature during this period nor was the Government made accountable to it. The fundamental rights were not restored and the court's jurisdiction to issue writs was excluded by Article 4 of the President's Order No. 5 of 1972.

The second part ran between December 16, 1972 to January 24, 1975. During this period the Constitution of Bangladesh came into operation. The fundamental rights were restored and the courts jurisdiction to issue writs to enforce the fundamental rights was guaranteed. The Government was made accountable to the Parliament in line with a Westminister-type Parliamentary system.

In the 3rd phase, during the period between January 25, 1975 to August 15, 1975 a new one-party monolithic system came into existence. Under the new scheme the court's jurisdiction to enforce fundamental rights was excluded, all the existing political parties were banned and all privately owned newspapers were confiscated. The fundamental rights continued to remain suspended under the Emergency, In other words, parliamentary system introduced by the new Constitution in 1972 was completely reversed and democracy was substituted by a monolithic dictatorship.

FOOTNOTES

1. It is still not known why the newly formed Constituent Assembly could not be allowed to work as a legislature.
2. The Muslim League (all factions), Jamat-i-Islami, Nejam-e-Islam—all right wing political parties continued to remain banned but privately they were supporting the opposition views.
3. Weekly *Satyakatha*, October 27, 1972.
4. The Constituent Assembly of Bangladesh Order, 1972 (President's Order No. 22 of 1972).
5. Article 7 of the Constituent Assembly of Bangladesh Order. 1972 (President's Order No. 22 of 1972).
6. The Constitution was authenticated by the Speaker on 14th December, 1972 and was signed by 357 members.
7. The Awami League in its draft Constitution Amendment Bill prepared in 1969 agreed to retain the Islamic character of the Constitution includig the title "Islamic Republic of Pakistan".
8. Article 3. See also the background of the state language movement. Author's book. *Bangladesh : Constitutional Quest for Autonomy*, Dhaka, p. 29.
9. The tribal groups of the Chittagong Hill Tracts and other areas who have different language and cultural background were opposed to calling themselves Bangalees although they constitute only about 1% of the total population. The controvery arising out of this assertion needs a separate discussion.
10. See the Appendix in Author's Book, *Bangladesh : Constitutional Quest for Autonomy*. Dhaka, p. 279.
11. It is interesting to ascertain in such a study what actually motivated the constitution makers to be so emphatic about this despite the fact (1) that a section of the Bengali nation resides in West Bengal within the territory of India and their position vis-a-vis the 'Bangalee nation' of Bangladesh as embodied in the constitution ; (2) although Bangladesh is largely a homogenous country both ethnically and geographically it has some minority ethnic groups and tribes living in Chittagong Hill Tracts and other areas who are not Bangalees ; (3) it creates a conflict between an ethnic nationalism and a political nationalism.
12. Such political parties continued to remain banned from December, 1971.
13. Seo the manifesto of the Awami League in 1970-71 elections.
14. Radical changes were introduced in the chapter on fundamental Principles of State Policy after the assassination of Sheikh Mujibur Rahman and in a gradual process the character of the objectives originally laid were almost entirely changed.
    See Proclamations (Amendment) Order, 1977.
    Proclamation Order No. 1 of 1977 dated 23rd April, 1977.
15. See the Directive Principles of State Policy, Article 27 Chapter VI, Constitution of the Socialist Republic of Sri Lanka.
16. The Indian Constitution pledged to provide free and compulsory education for children upto 14 years of age within a period of 10 years from its commencement (Article 45).
17. In 1969 Article 98 was amended to add a new paragraph C to the Article in this regard.
18. Article 26 corresponds to the Indian Articles 31A and 31C read together.

19. Both Articles 26 and 47 were amended subsequently to remove this contradiction.
20. See also Article 15 of the 1956 Constitution and Article 6(14) of the 1962 Constitution of Pakistan whereby certain laws were saved.
21. The original 31C Indian Constitution gave protection to laws made in furtherance of 2 specific principles only. When the 42 Amendment tried to enlarge the protection so as to cover any and all directive principles, the later addition was struck down in the Minerva Mills case.
22. Inspite of the laudable attempt one ought to remember that extensive provision for arrest without warrant and any right to bail were maintained under President's Order No. 8 and President's Order No. 50 of 1972 protected by Article 47 of the Constitution.
23. Tamizuddin Khan's case, PLD Federal Court, 1955, p. 240 ; Asma Jilani's case PLD 1972, SC 139.
24. The most relevant laws under which preventive detention could be ordered were :
    (a) The Security of Pakistan Act, 1952 5th May, 1952
    (b) The East Pakistan Public Safety Ordinance, 1958 25th November, 1958.
    In India :
    (a) Preventive Detention Act, 1950
    (b) Maintenance of Internal Security Act, 1971
25. See the Special Powers Act, 1974 and the discussion below, Ch. V p. 310. The discussion of the Indian Constitution has been based on its original form and the subsequent amendments have not been taken into consideration.
    In the entire life of Pakistan the only period when no one was kept in jail in East Pakistan on political ground was the time when Ataur Rahman Khan was the Chief Minister of the province.
26. Article 48 (3) of the Bangladesh Constitution.
27. Article 74 of the Indian Constitution.
28. Article 75 of the Indian Constitution.
29. Article 39 of the 1956 Constitution.
30. Article 37 of the 1956 Constitution.
31. Article 39 of the 1956 Constitution.
32. The Basic Law of the Federal Republic of Germany gives the supreme command of the Defence services to the Defence Minister in the peace time (Article 65 a) and to the Chancellor in War time (Article 115 b).
33. In contradistinction to the British system, in U.S.A. the war power vests with the Congress ; in Federal Republic of Germany with the Parliament (two houses concurring Article 115 a), in France also the authority of the Parliament is required (Article 35).
34. See also the legislation made by the Awami League Government at the initial stage of the independence in Constituent Assembly of Bangladesh Order, 1972 (President's Order No. 22 of 1972) as discussed, *supra* Chapter II.
35. A similar provisions was however incorporated in the Political Parties Act III of 1962 in which withdrawal or resignation from the party would cause loss of membership in the Parliament but it had little significance at that time as the system itself was based on an indirect election.
36. The classic example cited was the passing of the Fourth Amendment which was contrary to what they pledged to the electorate and yet the members had to vote for the Bill to retain their seats under this provision of the Constitution. On this issue 2 members of Parliament belonging to the Awami League formally dissented and lost their seats. They were Gen. (Retd.) M.A.G. Osmani and Mr. Mainul Hossain, a leading Barrister of the Supreme Court.
37. See Amendment 50 to substitute the clause of Article 104 of the 1962 Constitution. Author's book, *Bangladesh : Constitutional Quest for Autonomy*, Dhaka, p. 305.

So in 1969 the Awami League's proposal was much worse. It provided that a member of Parliament would cease to be Member if he was just expelled by the party. The proposal tended to establish a more extreme party dictatorship than the subsequent provisions.

38. The Parliament under the 1956 Constitution survived only about 2 years when it was dissolved in 1958 at the behest of President Iskander Mirza when Ayub Khan took over power.
39. All the Constitutions of the sub-continent provided a term of 5 years for the Parliament.
40. When the Awami League introduced the 4th Amendment in 1975, the time limit between the two sessions was completely abolished. The amendment provided "at least two sessions of Parliament in every year".
41. But the Awami League Government never passed any law for creating an office of Ombudsman.
42. There were however differences in their application and methodology both in content and substance.
43. See Article 111 of the Indian Constitution.
44. Article 57(b)(2) of the 1956 Constitution.
45. See Article 27 of the 1962 Constitution.
46. This whole problem cannot be understood by a reader not familiar with the colonial structure. At District level (subordinate courts as distinguished from the High Courts) the British had introduced a fusion of administrative and judicial functions i.e. the Deputy Commissioner was also the District Magistrate, and there was some fusion in the services also between judicial and administrative branch. The demand for separation refers to this system of subordinate court—because it is a peculiarity of the colonial British Indians system and at variance with general standards of the time as accepted in Great Britain as well as continental Europe. The independence of Higher Courts is a different problem and ought to be clearly distinguished.
47. In view of recent developments (Pakistan 1977, and 1978 ; Bangladesh 1982) I should like to see the point showed a little more : that the independence of the High Courts and Supreme Court had remained sacrosanct on the subcontinent even through the dictatorship of Ayub Khan and Yahya Khan, let alone India.
48. Courts below the two Divisions of the Supreme Court are generally termed as subordinate courts.
49. In the Indian Constitution it is contained in Article 226, in the1956 Constitution in Article 170 and in the 1962 Constitution in Article 98.
50. It is not understood what the constitution-makers meant by saying that the High Court Division would have "no power under Article 102 to pass any order in relation to any law to which Article 47 applies". The only plausible explanation could be that under Article 102 the Court could not strike off a law or question the view of such law made under Article 47. Other than this restriction, the court could always examine the veracity of the application of such laws or their misuse or malafide use. This was the outcome of the Indian Fundamental Rights case (Kesavananda Bharati case): that the determination of Parliament as to whether a law had a nexus to the purposes stated, was subject to judicial scrutiny.
51. It is because of this proviso that proceedings of the military tribunals created at different stages of Bangladesh's short history could not be called in question under the writ jurisdiction of the Supreme Court. The latest case dismissed by the Appellate Division was the one related to the death sentence ordered by a military tribunal against 12 army officers following the killing of President Ziaur Rahman in 1981. The Supreme Court upheld the view of the High Court Division that it had no jurisdiction to challenge the validity or authority of the Military Tribunal established under the Army

Act and the writ jurisdiction could not be extented to such proceedings of a military tribunal (See BCR 1982, Vol II, p. 61). The officers were hanged to death.

52. See Author's book, *Bangladesh : Constitutional Quest for Autonomy*, Dhaka, Appendix, Draft Constitution Amendment Bill, 1969, Amendment No. 46, p. 304.

53. The conflict continued *and still exists*. After the political change in 1975 the matter was taken to another extreme position. Two distinct courts with two Chief Justices were created i.e. the Supreme Court and the High Court. Again the question was raised since the High Court was a separate entity it ought to be in a better position to go round in circuits. The Bar did not agree and consequently, the two Courts were integrated into one Supreme Court again. In the Fourth Amendment, Mujib contemplated to reduce the traditional power and status of the Supreme Court and intended to establish courts at the Thana level bringing a radical change in the judicial system of the country.

54. Author's Book. *Bangladesh : Constitutional Quest for Autonomy*. Dhaka, p. 315.

55. See what happened in 1973 election in Chapter IV showing the inadequacy of Election Commission as a safeguard. During that time the independence and impartiality of the Election Commission was seriously challenged by the opposition political parties following the massive rigging done by the ruling party.

56. See the discussion in Ch : III.

57. In 1973 when the Government went for reorganisation of salary and services and subsequently, implemented the same, such action enjoyed the protection of the Constitution.

58. Compare Article 13 of the Indian Constitution with Article 26 of the Bangladesh Constitution when analysing Article 368 and Article 142 of the respective Constitutions.

59. In India similar clauses had been added by the 24th Amendment to Article 13 (corresponding to Article 26, Bangladesh Constitution) and Art. 368 (corresponding to Article 142 Bangladesh Constitution) after the Indian Supreme Court had held in Golak Nath vs. State of Punjab (AIR 1967 SC 1643) that Art. 13 prohibited Parliament from making any amendment to fundamental rights.

60. See the change in the basic structure of the Constitution introduced by the Fourth Constitution Amendment Bill in Chapter XI.

See also the series of Indian Supreme Court decisions on this subject and particularly on the question of Parliament's authority in curbing the fundamental rights guaranteed in the constitution.

61. Golak Nath v. State of Punjab. AIR 1967 ; SC 1643.

62. The other leading cases on this point are :

(a) Smt. Indira Nehru Gandhi v. Raj Narain, AIR 1975 SC 2299

(b) Minerva Mills v. Union of India, AIR 1980 SC 1789

(c) Wamanrao v. Union of India. AIR 1981 SC 271

In Pakistan the Courts have at various stages enunciated similar doctrines with respect to Presidential powers of amending the constitution ; see

(a) Fazlul Quader Chowdhury v. Muhammad Abdul Haque, PLD 1963 SC 486. PLD 1963 Dhaka 669

(b) Darwesh M. Arbey v. Federation of Pakistan PLD 1980 Lahore 206

(c) Suleman v. President, Special Military Court, National Law Reporter, 1980 Civ. 873

63. The following laws were repealed, the subject matter of which was mostly covered by the Constitution :

(a) The Laws Continuance Enforcement Order, made on 10th April, 1971 ; (b) The Provisional Constitution of Bangladesh Order, 1972 ; (c) The High Court of Bangladesh Order, 1972 (P.O. No. 5 of 1972) (d) The Bangladesh Comptroller and Auditor-General Order, 1972 (P.O. No. 15 of 1972). (e) The Constituent Assembly of Bangladesh Order, 1972 (P.O. No 22 of 1972) ; (f) The Bangladesh Election Commission

Order, 1972 (P.O. No. 25 of 1972) : (g) The Bangladesh Public Service Commissions Order, 1972 (P.O. No. 34 of 1972) ; (h) The Bangladesh Transaction of Government Business Order, 1972 (P.O. No. 58 of (1972).

64. The State Acquisition and Tenancy Act, 1950 (E.B. Act XXVIII of 1951).
The Bangladesh (Taking over of Control and Management of Industrial and Commercial Concerns) Order, 1972 (A.P.O. No. 1 of 1972) ; The Bangladesh Collaborators (Special Tribunals) Order, 1972 (P.O. No. 8 of 1972) ; The Government of Bangladesh (Services) Order, 1972 (P.O. No. 9 of 1972) ; The Bangladesh Shipping Corporation Order, 1972 (P.O. No. 10 of 1972) ; The Bangladesh (Restoration of Evacuee Property) Order, 1972 (P.O. No. 13 of 1972) ; The Bangladesh Public Servants' (Retirement) Order, 1972 (P.O. No. 14 of 1972) ; The Bangladesh Abandoned Property (Control, Management and Disposal) Order, 1972 (P.O. No. 16 of 1972); The Bangladesh Banks (Nationalisation) Order, 1972 (P.O. No. 26 of 1972) ; The Bangladesh Industrial Enterprises (Nationalisation) Order, 1972 (P.O. No. 27 of 1972) ; The Bangladesh Inland Water Transport Croporation Order, 1972 (P.O. No. 28 of 1972) ; The Bangladesh (Vesting of Property and Assets) Order, 1972 (P.O. No. 29 of 1972) ; The Bangladesh Insurance (Emergency Provisions) Order, 1972 (P.O. NO 30 of 1972) ; The Bangladesh Consumer Supplies Order, 1972 (P.O. No. 47 of 1972) ; The Bangladesh Scheduled Offences (Special Tribunals) Order, 1972 (P.O. No. 50 of 1972) ; The Bangladesh Nationalised and Private Organisations (Regulation of Salary of Employees) Order, 1972 (P.O No. 54 of 1972) ; The Bangladesh Jute Export Corporation Order, 1972 (P.O. No. 57 of 1972). The Bangladesh Water and Power Development Boards Order, 1972 (P O. No. 59 of 1972) ; The Government of Bangladesh (Services Screening) Order, 1972 (P.O. No. 67 of 1972); The Bangladesh Government Hats and Bazars (Management) Order, 1972 (P.O. No. 73 of 1972) ; The Bangladesh Government and Semi-autonomous Organisation (Regulation of Salary of Employees) Order, 1972 (P.O. No. 79 of 1972). The Bangladesh Insurance (Nationalisation) Order, 1972 (P.O. No. 95 of 1972) ; The Bangladesh Land Holding (Limitation) Order, 1972 (P.O. No. 98 of 1972) ; The Bangladesh Biman Order, 1972 (P.O. No. 126 of 1972) ; The Bangladesh Bank Order, 1972 ; (P.O. No. 127 of 1972). The Bangladesh Shilpa Rin Sangstha Order, 1972 (P.O. No. 128 of 1972). The Bangladesh Shilpa Bank Order, 1972 (P.O. No. 129 of 1972).

65. Almost the entire credit of producing such a document goes to Dr. Kamal Hossain, the then Law Minister.

CHAPTER FIVE

MOVE FOR POLITICAL CONSOLIDATION : THE GENERAL ELECTIONS, 1973

On the commencement of the Constitution on the 16th December 1972, the Constituent Assembly was dissolved and the government announced the date of general elections to be held on March 7, 1973. Moulana Bhashani had already formed his 7-Party Action Committee with a 15-point Charter of Demands, one of them, being the demand for resignation of the government. At a large public meeting held at the Race Course (Suhrawardy Uddayan) on 31st December, 1972 the Moulana announced that he would oust the government through election and the same line was followed by other political parties. The Jatio Samajtantrik Dal which was formed earlier was also gaining strength fast but almost all the political parties reconciled themselves to the new situation and gradually showed their readiness to participate in the election under the provisions of the new Constitution. With the law and order situation deteriorating and the economic life of people becoming hard, the opposition parties were calculating to take advantage of the growing public resentment against the government.

Soon after the announcement of the election date political activities started intensifying and of all the political parties the Jatio Samajtantric Dal and the National Awami Party (B) adopted a more militant line in opposing the government. The National Awami Party (M) and the Communist Party of Moni Singh adopted a more conciliatory line because of its support for the government mainly arising out of Bangladesh's warm relationship with the Soviet Union and their close association with the Awami League developed during the war in 1971. Excepting the little rupture and the set-back suffered by these two parties in the first week of the new year of 1973[1] they constantly collaborated with the government either through active co-operation or infiltration which ultimately culminated in the formation of the new single party BAKSAL created at a later stage by Sheikh Mujib.

The incident of police firing on the New Year's Day exposed the weaknesses of the ruling party in handling the opposition. It also showed the extent of resentment that had already accumulated in the urban areas against the government. Within little over a year after independence the Awami

League demonstrated a high degree of impatience and their intolerance of the oppositions grew. As discussed earlier the overall situation, instead of improving, was deteriorating and the effect of the bad implementation of earlier laws was fast tarnishing the image of the government. But the Awami League stalwarts were not ready to accept the fact that their popularity could start declining so soon and this feeling bred more and more intolerance in them, showing its ultimate manifestations in the election that was coming soon.

Mujib however, in the meantime, had already started blaming the opposition for trying to foil the election and at a public meeting at Pirojpur on January 2, the day after the firing took place, he called upon the people to resist those who were trying to create disruption in the election process, obliquely referring to the *hartal* by the opposition[2]. The next day at Barguna he maintained that foreign conspiracy was at work in Bangladesh and some people were trying to create disorder in the country[3]. The next day at Dhaka he asked people to keep a watch on foreign agents who were trying to create chaos in the country. He went on saying: "Do not be misled by any insinuation of the agent provocateurs who are trying to tarnish my image to the outside world to fish in the troubled waters."[4] In many countries, particularly in the developing world ruling politicians generally blame the opposition by making such statement, although the entire government machinery to hold and punish such offenders remain in their own hand. The manifestation of such weaknesses or intolerance in the entire Awami League rank and file was becoming evident. When people started criticising Sheikh Mujib for not being able to restore peace or economic order to control the price spiral of essential commodities, the Awami League leaders started discovering conspiracy in such criticisms. Following the firing incident and a successful strike in protest, the Awami League leaders issued a statement in newspapers alleging that a conspiracy was going on to undo the independence and said, "the conspirators are trying to-day to confuse the world by even resorting to malign Bangabandhu"[5]. The arrogance over the issue extended to chopping of an ear of a person when he attempted to tear down a picture of Sheikh Mujib in a Dhaka neighbourhood on the day of the strike. It was claimed to have been done as a punishment for showing "disrespect to the Father of the Nation". But the opposition claimed that as a Prime Minister and a leader of a political party, if not as the Father of the Nation, he could not remain above criticism in a highly politicised country like Bangladesh.

Anyhow the atmosphere during the week further deteriorated when the Awami League stormtroopers destroyed the dias of a public meeting of the 7-party Action Committee, set fire to the office of Jatio Samajtantrik Dal headqurters at Dhaka and launched a physical attack on Ataur Rahman Khan. When such terror was created, the opposition again demanded resignation of the government and formation of a national government to ensure a free and fair election. They claimed that if a fair poll was held, the Awami League would lose majority seats in the Parliament. Mujib was still confident about his own popularity and ignored that. At the Silver Jubilee function of the Students League at Ramna Green on January 4, 1973 Mujib in his address rejected the suggestion of an all-party government[6]. He even refused to grant the status of a "political party" to the opposition parties and continued his attacks on the opposition[7]. At Gopalganj on January 6, he again maintained that the vested interests were trying to create chaos and conspiring against the interest of the new nation. He blamed the opposition for conspiring to malign him and the country and for working against the unity of the nation.

The opposition, on the other hand, continued to condemn the terror, intimidation, repression and fascist activities of the ruling party and demanded a congenial atmosphere for holding elections. The Moulana at a Paltan Maidan public meeting called upon the people to form committees in every village to resist the fascist activities of the ruling party. He claimed that the Awami League comprised of forces which were enemical to democracy and justice, and he asserted that about 700 workers were killed in Khulna, Mongla and Chittagong over last few weeks. He warned that if in future any meeting of the opposition was disturbed or their offices were burnt, he would go for retaliation. At the same meeting Ataur Rahman Khan alleged that the opposition political workers were being oppressed by the supporters of the ruling party and he challenged that if the elections were held freely and impartially, most of the Awami League candidates could not return[8].

Against this volatile backdrop, the campaign for the first general election of Bangladesh began. In addition to what happened in the first week of January, the excessive power used by the Rakkhi Bahini and the secret political killings that was going on, frightened the opposition parties. Arrogance of the ruling party and the lack of confidence in the opposition parties in handling the situation dominated the election scene. Despite the fact that the popularity of Awami League was declining, the opposition parties were divided and could not forge any unity against the government. With all the points in their favour, the opposition still failed to gather sufficient strength to retaliate. They were no match for the massive political organisation of the Awami League especially when they failed to operate unitedly. Moreover, with the entire government machinery backing the Awami League, the opposition appeared to be helpless at times.

Manifestos

It would be interesting to study the programmes of various political parties participating in the election of a newly born country. In view of a long political background of movements and struggles and an 'armed war for independence' the manifestos reflected the thoughts and aspirations of both the people and the political leaders of the country. For a proper evaluation of the political process and development the manifestos constituted without any doubt an important guideline particularly in the light of the changes in the political thinking produced by the war of independence.

The rightist parties having been banned, the election manifestos so far as the economic programmes were concerned showed a more progressive and leftist tendency. The Awami League committed itself to establishing a socialist economic order through a peaceful and constitutional process. They advocated socialism and democracy side by side but compared to their earlier manifesto they committed themselves more towards a socialist transformation. The National Awami Party (M) and the Communist Party of Bangladesh were already committed to establishing socialism in the country and accordingly they explained their position in their respective manifestos. The Jatio Samajtantrik Dal went further and pledged to organise a revolution to establish scientific socialism. The National Awami Party (Bhashani) pledged for nationalisation of basic, heavy and large industries but advocated to leave the rest in the private hands. It was in favour of generating national capital by introducing a production oriented economy to achieve self-reliance but the party also pledged for equitable distribution of national wealth. So, almost all the major political parties who took part in the election made radical pledges to the people and promised to bring change in the quality and conditions of the ordinary people of the country.

On the basis of their respective programmes, the political parties including the Awami League entered the electioneering battle. Seeing the weaker position of the government and its inability to cope with the situation of law and order and the general economy of the country, the opposition parties aimed at taking the fullest advantage of it. It was an opportunity for them to consolidate their respective position and gain strength in the electoral race. Seeing the large crowds in their public meetings, the major opposition parties gained more confidence about their victory. The opposition parties like the National Awamy Party (M) and Moni Singh's Communist Party of Bangladesh having identified themselves with the ruling party were not taken seriously and the public did not take much notice of their political stand or statements. Among the opposition parties the real challenge was put forward by the National Awami Party (Bhashani) and the Jatio Samajtantrik Dal and with their increasing strength demonstrated in huge public meetings they became a threat to the ruling party.

Besides the programmes contained in the respective manifestos the main thrust of attack of the opposition on the ruling party was that : (l) it had failed to restore law and order in the country. According to them the rule of law had vanished and people were not able to sleep peacefully at night. Shooting, robbery, dacoity, hi-jacking, kidnapping, increased beyond any control. The government had failed to protect the life and property of citizens, (2) the government had failed to check the price spiral of essential commodities. Almost 100% rise in almost all the essential commodities within one year of independence pushed the people against the wall. The price index went beyond their purchasing capacity. While their cost of living went up drastically the income of the people particularly those in fixed income group went down because of government legislation[9] causing enormous hardship to the middle and lower middle class families, (3) it had failed to check smuggling, black-marketting, hoarding and other social menaces.

The opposition alleged that the government could not do anything to check them mainly because their own people were involved in such activities. They alleged that every day a bulk of national wealth including paddy, gold, silver, medicines, spare parts, jute, hide and skins, machineries and industrial raw materials were being smuggled across the border to India and the government lost control over such activities, (4) it was guilty of mismanagement and corruption in the administration and particularly in the nationalised sector and abandoned industries. They alleged that the members of the ruling party were involved in the wide-spread loot and plunder of the nation's wealth from thousands of industries and the extent of corruption and political patronisation went beyond any limit of past record, (5) the ruling party adopted undemocratic means to suppress the opposition by way of disturbing their public meetings and attacking and burning down their offices. They cited arrest of hundreds of political workers and repression of people through the black laws like P.O. 8, 9 and 50. The torture and repression inflicted by the Rakkhi Bahini exceeded all limits and the secret killings of political opponents by the Jatiyo Rakkhi Bahini was no longer a secret, (6) the opposition criticised the government for making the country a client state of India and they substantiated their argument on the following major grounds ; (i) the Indian Army took away millions of Taka worth of war machines and other capital goods of the country immediately after the independence but the government failed to bring them back ; (ii) the large scale smuggling across the border in favour of India went unchecked at the connivance of the government authorities and the party henchmen ; (iii) the signing of the Friendship Treaty with India in March, 1972 providing a scope for intervention was against the national interest of the country[10] ; (iv) allowing the Indian government to perpetuate its influence on the national affairs of Bangladesh under the Treaty and the various commercial, cultural, credit and trade agreements.

The ruling party's main propaganda strategy was to emphasise on how the independence was achieved and the Awami League's role in achieving it. They glorified the independence war and narrated at length the atrocities the Pakistan Army had committed and used to elaborate in detail the extent of damage done to the country during that period. Emphasis was laid on what state the country was left after the war and how the country and administration was restored by the Awami League in a war-ravaged country[11].

Although the Awami League's popularity as a political party was in decline, Mujib's position as an individual was still not questioned and it is on his personal popularity and image that the Awami League continued to enjoy the edge over the opposition parties. It was still Mujib's charisma and personal touch and appeal which dominated the election scene and that the Awami League would win with a majority was not in doubt. Although the public in general was not happy and they nursed lot of resentment on various matters, Mujib still enjoyed their confidence and they were willing to give him a chance to retrieve the country from the existing chaos.

Yet the Awami League took a course of intrigue and intimidation. The leaders of the Awami League plunged into a competition to prove their popularity to impress their leader. A rage of arrogance dominated their thoughts and an element of intolerance crept in their mind and they maintained an egoistic jingoism that they and they alone had the right to rule the country. So when the election strategy was worked out, democratic practices and norms were disregarded and sometime deliberately violated on petty personal motivations with a general but erroneous notion that there was actually no opposition in the country. With the entire administrative machinery on their side, the government utilised daily newspapers, the media like Radio and Television, transport, patronage and other facilities for the purpose. They became irritant, intolerant and arrogant despite all the advantages they had on their side for a sure victory.

The Elections

Despite all these advantages inherent in a ruling party the opposition parties particularly the Jatio Samajtantrik Dal and the National Awami Party (Bhashani) were drawing large crowds at their public meetings, a barometer to determine popular support practised in Bangladesh. Despite the fact that Mujib and other Ministers were using the helicopters meant for relief operations in their election campaign, the opposition parties were gaining support and the nearer the day of election came the more impatient became the Awami League candidates and their workers towards the opposition. The first conflict between the ruling party and the parties in opposition arose when the time came for submitting nomination papers. Election of a person unopposed or uncontested is considered as a prestigeous matter in the sub-continent. If someone returned in an election uncontested an extra point was added to his credentials for holding an office in the government or party.

So on February 5 when the nomination papers were received, in 6 seats the Awami League candidates had no contestants and they were as follows :

(1) Mr. M. Sohrab Hossain,
(2) Mr. Tofail Ahmed,
(3) Mr. Md. Motaharuddin,
(4) Sheikh Mujibur Rahman,
(5) Mr. K. M. Obaidur Rahman,
(6) Sheikh Mujibur Rahman.

Excepting perhaps the case of Sheikh Mujib, in all other cases, allegations were made by the opposition parties that the respective Awami League candidates or their supporters just did not allow anyone else to file any nomination. Threat of life. intimidation, kidnapping and every other coercive measures were taken to see that none could come near the office of the Returning officer to file any nomination. Further on the date of withdrawal of candidature 5 more Awami League candidates were found without contestants and they were as follows :

(1) Mr. AH.M. Kamaruzzaman,
(2) Mr. Rafiquddin Bhuiya,
(3) Mr. Monoranjan Dhar,
(4) Syed Nazrul Islam,
(5) Mr. Zillur Rahman.

A reign of terror prevailed in some of these areas. In order to compete with some of their colleagues earlier declared elected unopposed, some others now set out to prove their 'great' popularity in their respective areas. The method applied was the same and in most of the cases nomination papers were withdrawn forcibly.

The opposition made a great noise out of these incidents and condemend the actions of the ruling party as manifestations of their fascist attitude. The Jatio Samajtantrik Dal demanded refixation of date for submission of nomination papers and so did the other parties. They expressed their apprehension about what would happen on the election day. In a public meeting held at Baitul Mukarram, A. S. M. Abdur Rab of JSD alleged that the present situation was not congenial for free and fair polls as the Government had adopted a policy of intimidation. He claimed that many JSD nominees were prevented from submitting nomination papers and the government was not maintaining even a minimum decency. He challenged the neutrality of Chief Election Commissioner and demanded his resignation. It is true that in the given circumstances, even if they were allowed to contest in most cases, the Awami League candidates would have won the election in any case but the methodology and the attitude they adopted caused a sense of fear in the mind of the people and earned a bad name for the ruling party.

Ironically the same attitude was maintained throughout the election campaign and it reached its elimax on the election day. Despite all the constraints and disadvantages the opposition faced, in about 2 dozen constituencies the opposition leaders and candidates showed a solid edge at the polls over the Awami League candidates and when the counting started in certain areas some of the opposition candidates were unofficially declared by the local officials as elected. But this was not to be allowed at the end. The opposition candidates like Dr. Alim-al-Razee (NAP-B) in Tangail VI against sitting Minister Mr. A. Mannan, Shahjahan Siraj (JSD) in Tangail IV against Abdul Latif Siddiqui, Abdur Rahman (NAP-B) against Mirza Tofazzal Hossain in Tangail V, Major M.A. Jalil (JSD) against Abdul Mannan and Harannath Bain in Bakerganj V and XII, Rashed Khan Menon (NAP-B) in Bakerganj IX and VIII against Mr. Fazlul Huq and Nurul Islam Manzur, Suranjit Sengupta (NAP-B) against Minister Abdul Samad Azad in Sylhet II, Prof. Muzaffar Ahmed (NAP-M) in Comilla XII against Capt. Sujat Ali, Mostaq Ahmed Chowdhury[12] (NAP-M) in XIV against M, Siddique were all leading at the polls upto the last stage and names of M. A. Jalil, Shahjahan Siraj and Moshtaq Ahmed Chowdhury were announced by the television commentators as having been elected. Besides these persons, some other candidates like Nuruddin Zahid (JSD) in Chittagong VII, Mokhtar Ahmed (JSD) in Chittagong XV, A.K.M. Hammad Chowdhury (Ind) in Noakhali XIII, Nurul Islam Master (JSD) in Noakhali VIII, Md. Ismail Mia (JSD) in Noakhali V. Abdur Rashid (Ind) in Comilla IX, Murtaza Hossain Molla (Ind) in Comilla VIII, Fazlul Huq Khondker (Ind) in Dhaka XXIV, Harun-ur-Rashid in Mymensingh IV, S.M.A. Sabur, (NAP-M) in Khulna III, Ahsan Ahmed (NAP-B) in Rangpur II were close to their Awami League rivals. They along with about a dozen others claimed that they would have won the election if the polls were not rigged in their constituencies and had the Awami League not adopted unfair means.

The central leadership of the Awami League took it as a prestige issue particularly on the question of allowing the prominent opposition leaders winning the election. The party stalwarts argued that victory in election of persons like Ataur Rahman Khan, Mashiur Rahman[13] M.A. Jalil, Shahjahn Siraj, Rashed Khan Menon, Dr. Alim Al-Razee, Muzaffar Ahmed and Suranjit Sen would cast a direct aspersion not only on the party but on the "Father of the Nation". How could these people win when Bangabandhu was still alive and was the chief of the party and the government ? The election of such persons would confirm the decline of the party popularity and it would mean victory for the opposition. With these personalities in the opposition it would be difficult to manage the Parliament the Awami League feared. Moreover, many of them were considered 'unpatriotic' persons who according to the Awami League were opposed to the independence of Bangladesh. If they had won in the election it would have cast another kind of aspersion on the whole spirit of the independence movement. Election of a few persons not politically known would not bother them much but the key personalities from the opposition were not acceptable.

The loss of seats by 2 senior Ministers Abdul Mannan and Abdus Samad Azad (in one of the two constituencies) would have been disastruous, or at least this is how the Awami League leadership looked at it.

Being convinced by all these considerations the central leadership of the Awami League had moved promptly once the news started pouring in that they were losing some important seats and more so that most of them belonged to some prominent opposition leaders. The Central Election Campaign Committee constituted earlier to handle the election affairs was completely by-passed and the responsibility of formulating strategies and actions were taken over by the control room at the Gonobhavan. When frantic telephone calls started pouring in from the candidates who were likely to be defeated, the government machinery including the Jatio Rakkhi Bahini was alerted and orders were sent to help out those candidates who were in trouble. As the counting of votes started indicating sure victory for some of the oppostion candidates, helicopters were flown out to render assistance and at least in half a dozen constituencies entire ballot boxes were removed and replaced with new ones.

It is true that the Awami League would have won the election with an overwhelming majority in any case. At the most if the central leadership of the Awami League had not intervened, the opposition would have won an additional 20 seats over the 9 they had already won. It is still difficult to determine what attitude worked in the ruling party to behave in such a manner and what loss the Awami League would have suffered if they had, say 30 members in the opposition instead of 9 out of the total 315. What ultimately happened was that it created a credibility gap. It had sown the seed of a deeper resentment and distrust between the parties in opposition and the ruling party. It created a genuine suspicion in the minds of the people about the bonafide of the whole election result. A conservative estimate in the government newspapers suggested that the opposition could secure at least 30 seats[14].

Anyhow excepting the few mentioned above in almost all the constituencies the Awami League candidates won with a wide margin and in many cases the deposits of their rivals were forefeited. In the constituencies where the opposition or independent candidates had won, the margin was not very wide, in most cases varying within 5000 votes. Ataur Rahmam Khan in Dhaka XIX won by 3917 votes. Abdus Sattar of JSD in Tangail won by 4389 votes and the independent candidates Syed Quamrul Islam Mohammed Salehuddin in Faridpur III by 1817 votes, Chai Thowai Roaza in Chittagong Hill Tracts II by 4850 votes, Md. Ali Ashraf in Comilla XI by 5790 votes, Manabendra Narayan Larma in Chittagong Hill Tracts I by 41967 votes, Md. Abdullah Sarker in Comilla XXV by 3702 votes[15]. The Awami League candidates won with much larger margins varying generally from 1000 to 50000 votes. When the election results were being announced there was a competition noticed as to who had more votes cast in one's own favour to demonstrate individual popularity. This was particularly noticed between Abdur Razzak who in Faridpur XVI secured 95114 out of total 129251, Shah Muazzem Hossain in Dhaka, securing 107689 out of total 130111 votes. Gazi Golam Mustafa 110284 in Dhaka XIII out of total 285120 (total votes cast was 162306). Later when it was found that Sheikh Mujib secured 105958 votes in Dhaka XV which was less than what Gazi Golam Mustfa managed to secure, his (Mujibs) votes were increased and recorded to be at 114928 in Dhaka XI (total votes cast was 138417)[16]. Never before in any election including the highest poll-sweeping election in 1970-71 were so many votes cast in these constituencies. The reasons, as discussed above, were so obvious.

In the election, as officially announced, the Awami League secured 282 seats out of 289 contested and the opposition including the independent candidates secured 7 seats. Only two political parties secured one seat each, Ataur Rahman Khan BJL[17] at Dhamrai and Abdus Sattar of JSD at Tangail—all the other five seats were won by independent candidates who were not much known politically. The result revealed the miserable condition of the opposition parties. Excepting those seats, the opposition failed to show any brighter aspect in any other constituency. On the other hand, although it was assumed that the NAP(B)[18] and the JSD[19] were the main challengers, the results showed that the NAP(M)[20] secured second position with 1569299 votes in their favour consisting of about 8.3% of the votes cast. They had more candidates who secured second position to Awami League in the poll than the NAP(B) and JSD. This happened mainly due to the fact that NAP(M) had a good number of workers all over the country and they polled more votes mainly because of their candidate's personal qualities.

The NAP(B) although secured less votes than the JSD but with only 169 candidates compared to JSD's 237 and NAP(M)s 224, it secured 10,02,777 votes constituting 5.32% of the votes cast. The NAP(B) although a very old party with some grass root base, suffered set backs due to its politics and the role of individual leaders including the Moulana at different stages of history.

So although the opposition parties attracted crowds and seemingly gained support of the people, they proved at the end weak and disorganised. Despite repeated attempts, no unity could be achieved amongst them. The Seven-Party Action Committee led by the Moulana at last quarrelled on the issue of selecting candidates and failed to contest the election under one leadership[21]. The JSD was overwhelmed by their sudden popularity and were not ready to share the victory with anybody else. However, although the JSD was the new political party it was able to put up 237 candidates and secured 12,29,110 votes constituting 6.52% of the votes cast.

It would be interetsing to note that the independent candidates performed better than the opposition party candidates in the sense that there were 120 of them securing 9,89,884 votes withe 5 seats in the Parliament.

Of the total 3,38,96,777 registered voters in 289 contested constituencies 1,93,29,683 votes were polled and the total valid votes polled represented 55.62% of the total registered voters[22]. Of the 3 political parties other than the Awami League, none secured more than 10% of the total votes cast. Although the NAP(M) did better than the other two parties, it did not secure any seat in the Parliament. It is to be noted that the religion-based political parties were banned and deprived from participating in the election but their supporters had exercised their franchise mostly in favour of the opposition parties. An analytical study of the whole election pattern in the country since 1954 would reveal that even if those parties were able to participate in the election, it would not have made any difference in the overall election result[23].

As no member could retain more than one seat in the Parliament, Sheikh Mujib decided to represent only Dhaka XII and vacated the other 3 constituencies and Kamaruzzaman and Abdus Samad Azad vacated one each. In the bye-election the Barisal seat went uncontested to the Awami League candidate and out of the 4 seats the Awami League won 2, one went to JSD and the other to an independent candidate showing that the popularity of the government was further declining. The final result including the reserved women seats was as follows :

Awami League	306
Jatio Samajtantrik Dal	2
Bangla Jatiyo League	1
Independent	6

So, following the bye-elections with only 9 opposition members and independents elected, the Awami League began its journey to govern the country within the framework of a democratic parliamentary system under a well-defined constitution. Mujib at a post-election press conference on March 8 claimed that there was no opposition in Bangladesh. From the point of view of numerical strength he was correct but it was forgotten that this was the worst that could happen to help the growth of a democratic system in the country. The government carried a stigma of highhandedness in depriving the opposition from gaining at least some more seats which they would otherwise have won. The loss of credibility of the government in the election was far more serious than the loss of seats to the opposition would have been. The effect of thunderous victory of the Awami League in the election proved to be counter-productive at the end.

The Lal Bahini

Through this massive victory in the election the Awami League not only gathered more political strength but a monopoly of power in the newly born country. The manifestation of a corresponding state of mind was found in the behaviour of its workers all over the country. Instead of regretting what happened in the election the party leaders moved in the opposite direction posing to be more powerful and boisterous than ever before. In less than a month after the election the labour front of the Awami League launched a campaign to drive out all other trade union leaders and workers from the industrial areas of the country. According to them, in view of the fact that the Awami League had won a "total victory in the election and since the industries were nationalised for the benefit of the workers and the government was establishing a socialist economy" there was no need for any other trade union. On April 5, 1973 at Tongi Industrial Area, Dhaka they began their first attack on the workers of the Bangla Sramik Federation, a powerful left wing national trade union, resulting in assault and death of workers. When a delegation of the affected workers reached Dhaka and met the Prime Minister, Mujib assured them that "justice" would be done, but no action was taken by the Government. On the contrary, in a meeting the Sramik League, the Awami League's labour front resolved to get rid of the "wrong type of trade unionists" and expressed their determination to expel them from all the industrial areas of the country[25].

The labour wing of the Awami League headed by Abdul Mannan had earlier formed a "Lal Bahini"[26] to help the government to establish "socialism and economic emancipation of the working class". The Bahini was to get rid of the "bad elements" in the indusrial areas and the "corrupt officials" of the government controlled industries, although the area of their "operations" extended beyond the industrial sector and sometime into the life of private citizens of the country. Under the patronage of the ruling elite, they grew in strength and in the process the discipline that was required to run the nationalised industries profitably was destroyed. Innocent workers were made victims and in many places, in order to establish their authority, they raised a 'local and non-local' issue, an element which intorduced "districtism" more than ever before in the working community of the country. Earlier at Tongi and then at Kalurghat and finally at R. R. Jute and Textile Mills at Barabkunda in Chittagong a large number of workers coming from districts other than Chittagong who had been working in the same factories and mills for years were killed in riots instigated and supported by the Bahini members[27]. A large number of industries also went into the hands of the Sramik League leaders or their proteges.

With the law and order situation still not improving, the production sliding down and the food deficit increasing, the country entered into another year of economic depression. The expectation of the people that the situation would improve once the election was over was frustrated further by the ruthless behaviour of the ruling party. The excesses perpetrated by the Lal Bahini, Shecha Shebak Bahini[28] and the Rakkhi Bahini created fear and terror amongst the people. The Lal Bahini and other agencies of the ruling party launched a 'movement' "to straighten the black marketeers, hoarders, smugglers and fake dealers and industrialists". The attempt was to handle the situation 'politically' and so all the frontal organisations of the Awami League were geared up for this task. Being organisations of the party in power they even called for a general strike on May 3 to further their 'cause'. But this campaign against the social evils failed because (1) the evil doers enjoyed the patronage of the ruling party ; (2) indiscriminate treatment produced innocent victims amongst ordinary people ; (3) lack of orientation and discipline among the "purifiers" turned some of them into "profiteers" ; (4) The police and the civil administration did not co-operate as they were by-passed, and the judiciary was helpless as the legal course was dishonoured[29] (5) engagement of the Rakkhi Bahini without any rules of procedure or code of conduct resulted in its use of power in excess causing public resentment ; (6) the campaign was used to victimise the political opponents.

As a consequence the public became more frightened. Not only the campaign failed to produce any result or helped in improving the situation, it created lawlessness in the spheres of production and distribution. The whole operation turned out to be counter-productive. When the government started by announcing that it had detected 67 fake dealers in cement, textile and other profitable items and 1277 industries of various descriptions in April, 1973 the hope was raised that perhaps the government had meant business this time. But as the days passed it was discovered that the government failed to take any action against them as most of them either belonged to the party or enjoyed its patronage in some form or other.

With this scenario in the background, the bye-election for the uncontested constituencies, earlier vacated by the leaders took place in which the government lost 2 seats, in Rajshahi XI to Moinuddin Ahmed of JSD and in the other, Sylhet IV to an independent candidate. Within less than three months of the general election, these results in the bye-ecletion reflected the negative mood of the people towards the performance of the government. It was an early warning which the Awami League did not seem to take too seriously in view of their commanding position in the Parliament.

Amendment of the Constitution and Enactment of certain Laws

In the meantime in order to cope with the deteriorating law and order situation, the President Order 50 was further amended on March 11 to bring some more offences under the purview of the law and to provide summary trial for them. They included among others robbery, dacoity, hi-jacking, kidnapping, abduction, rape, arson, adulteration of drugs, medicines and foodstuff, offences punishable under the Eoreign Fxchange Regulations Act, blackmarketing, smuggling and hoarding. The punishment prescribed for these offences was 3 to 14 years rigorous imprisonment. The law only reflected the offences which were being committed in the country at that time.

So the Awami League tried both ways, a strategy which they thought would produce result. On the one hand harsh laws were made with the Jatiyo Rakkhi Bahini to implement them and on the other hand the political organisations were used to bring the situtation under control. But even then the situation did not improve. The stark realities of state management of such an impoverished country soon led the Awami League leaders to adopt a course which they were so averse to. As the political opposition grew more in strength and the ruling party's popularity declined, like any other Government of the sub-continent the Awami League proceeded for more harsh laws and political repression.

In order to consolidate their political position further the high degree of idealism embodied in the 1972 Constitution was at last sacrificed. They now felt the necessity of incorporating the provisions relating to preventive detention and proclamation of emergency. The Government thus proceeded to reverse the process and introduced the Constitution Second Amendment Bill in September, 1973. Article 33 was substituted by a new Article in order to make provision for preventive detention, and a new Part IXA was incorporated to include new emergency provisions in the constitution.

With such a meagre number of members in opposition, the Amendment Bill was passed within a short time without much debate. The opposition's proposal including that of Mr. Ataur Rahman Khan to refer the Bill to elicit public opinion was rejected. The new law Minister, Monoranjan Dhar however attempted to make out a case arguing that these provisions for preventive detention and proclamation of emergency were in the constitution of all democratic countries of the world and they were being kept to meet the emergency situation of the country. He argued that these provisions were not incorporated in the constitution when it was framed and that now this amendment was introduced to fill up that "omission". What the Minister implied was that either the entire Constituent Assembly forgot to incorporate them or Dr. Kamal Hossain did not do so by mistake.

The Law Minister however further assured the Parliament that the emergency power would never be used by the present government unless the government was compelled to do so. The Minister tried to convince the Parliament that the provisions for emergency including the suspension of fundamental rights were retained to control the activities of the 'enemy aliens'. He argued that in the situation existing in the country the provision for preventive detention law was required to deal with the 'miscreants, anti-social elements, smugglers and profiteers'.

Ataur Rahman Khan strongly criticised the new provisions and reminded the Parliament that the Awami League over the last 25 years was opposed to this kind of law because they were always used against the political opponents. He apprehended that the same would be used against the political oppenents in Bangladesh also. He alleged that the provision for proclamation of emergency for internal disturbance revealed the weakness and failure of the administration. He argued that the Awami League had won the election on the basis of the present constitution and amendment of this kind of fundamental nature could not be effected without the approval of the people. He argued that in view of the already existing Article 63 with regard to war or external aggression, the making of provisions for emergency was not justifiable nor had the suspension of fundamental rights during the pendency of the emergency any reasonable basis. He alleged that the motives of introducing these provisions now were highly political and that they would primarily be used for repression of political opponents. From the side of the government none made any sincere attempt to repudiate the charges. The Law Minister did not elaborate in what kind of internal disturbances the emergency could be proclaimed nor did he explain why enforcement of fundamental rights would be suspended in the case of Bangladesh citizens during the emergency. The Law Minister's justification for preventive detention laws to deal with the smugglers, miscreants, etc. ignored the fact that adequate provisions were there to handle such criminals under the P.O. 50 and preventive detention law was generally not used against such offences. The opposition members including the independents led by Ataur Rahman Khan walked out of the House in protest against the making of such provisions and the Bill was passed to become an Act only by the ruling party[30].

Whatever might have been said by the Law Minister or the Government it was known to all why the Constitution had to be changed. The cherished dream of Sheikh Mujibur Rahman that in a democratic Bangladesh none would be detained without trial and the fundamental rights would not be suspended to suppress political opponents was thus frustrated. It was realised by the Government that it was becoming increasingly difficult to cope with the situation. They had now reached a point where they required preventive detention and proclamation of emergency to combat internal disturbance. The political strength and support they claimed to have was not strong enough to keep them away from making such provisions of law. It is to be noted that the provisions to make law for preventive detention was invoked within less than 6 months of the amendment and the power to impose emergency and suspension of fundamental rights was invoked before the year was over.

Press and Publication Ordinance

During the same session before the Constitution Amendment Bill was passed another law of great significance was voted into an Act by the Parliament. The Press and Publication Ordinance was originally promulgated by Ayub Khan in 1960 and the law was widely criticised and condemned as a black law. As freedom of press was one of the major issues in Pakistan, it naturally featured high in the democratic struggle of the country. The Awami League was committed to establish freedom of press and repeal of all related black laws including the Press and Publication Ordinance, 1960.

In order to keep its commitment, the Awami League repealed the law of 1960 and introduced a new law called the Printing Press and Publications (Declaration and Registration) Ordinance[31]. But once the new law was published it was found that it was in essence a duplication of the other. The whole purpose was to control the declaration and registration of media service. The tone of the Home Minister who moved the Bill in the House was harsh when in defence of the Bill he attacked the irresponsibility of the press. He warned that opposition to the state principles enshrined in the Constitution would not be tolerated[32].

The law provided for obtaining declaration for possession of printing press and for the printing and publication of newspapers. The Home Minister told the House that the government was determined to uphold the rights and privileges of the Press. He asserted that the Government had initiated the Bill keeping the above in view and claimed that all the black laws of the old Ordinance had been deleted from the Bill. The law was not intended to curb the functioning of printing presses or newspapers as was apprehended by the independent and opposition members. The Minister criticised the role of certain newspapers and cited certain examples of "irresponsible journalism". Hinting at "Holiday", an opposition weekly, he went to the extent of saying that some newspapers "went so far as to cast aspersion on the sovereignty of the country." He accused that some newspapers were publishing false and motivated stories and said that the government would not allow any such role by any newspaper. The Minister argued that the mushroom growth of newspapers was to be stopped and that there was no malafide behind introducing such a Bill. It was therfore evident that the Awami League government also, like the past ones, felt the necessity of adopting some kind of measures for regulating the press.

The law and the statement made by the Home Minister reflected the overall attitude of the government towards the press and newspaper. The opposition pointedly rejected the law outright as one which was repressive and black both in content and nature. They claimed that many of the black provisions of the earlier law of Ayub Khan were kept intact in the Bill. According to them the Bill violated the basic principles of parliamentary democracy and the law was made to gag the press and suppress the freedom of the journalists. It would however be evident from the reading of the law that the Awami League government did not really come forward with any new approach towards the problem of press and publication in the country. But if there were any necessity of regulating the operation of press, publications and newspapers, the statement of the Home Minister marred that spirit and instead demonstrated an authoritarian attitude. It exposed clearly the political intention of the government.

Enayetullah Khan, the Managing Editor of the holiday called the Home Minister's statement a "wild speech" for questioning "the parentage of freedom loving journalists, holding the judiciary in contempt and telling the most unbelievable lies about the editors and journalists working in the opposition"[33].

It was obvious that in the given circumstances when the opposition was growing fast and their own popularity declining, the Awami League government thought it wise to retain some of the provisions of the old law. They realised that the over all situation of the country was not yet settled and the press was the single most important institution which would play a significant role both for and against the government.

The Special Powers Act, 1974

Further, with the power now derived from the amended Article 33 the Parliament in February 1974 enacted a law called the "Special Powers Act" to make provisions, among others, for preventive detention.

Section 3 of the Special Powers Act provided for preventive detention. A person was to be detained if the Government was satisfied that it was necessary to do so with a view to preventing him from doing any prejudicial act. In defining "prejudicial act" the Act consolidated the definition found in the East Pakistan Public Safety Ordinance, 1958 which was repealed. In the Public Safety Ordinance the prejudicial act was defined in 16 paragraphs under section 2(4). This definition in the old law covered many other offences which have now been dealt with separately[34].

Once a person is detained, the authority making the order of detention would communicate the grounds on which the order was made at the time of his detention or within 15 days from the date of detention to enable the detenu to make a representation in writing against such order (section 8). An Advisory Board was created by section 9 to examine the grounds on which the order was made and the representation of the detenu within 120 days from the date of detention (section 10). The Advisory Board after considering the materials placed before it and calling for such further information as necessary from the government and after affording the detenu an opportunity of being heard in person was to submit a report to the Government within 170 days from the date of detention. The Board was to submit its opinion as to whether or not there was sufficient cause for the detention of the person concerned (section ll). If the Advisory Board reported that there was sufficient cause for the detention of a person, the government could confirm such detention. Otherwise such cases would be reviewed once in every 6 months from the date of such detention order. If however, there was no sufficient cause found by the Advisory Board, the Government was to revoke the detention and cause the person to be released (section 12). Under section 13 the government however, could revoke an order of detention at any time or release the person for a temporary period under section 14.

Section 15 dealt with sabotage and section 16 with prohibition of prejudicial acts including publication of any prejudicial report. Sections 17 and 18 dealt with prescription etc. of certain documents made, printed or published and regulation of publication of certain matters. These 3 sections from 16 to 18 were provided mainly to control the media in various ways and forms. Section 19 and 20 curtailed the freedom of association and under these provisions the Government was authorised to impose control over such associations which would "act in a manner or be used for the purpose prejudicial to the maintenance of public order" and after hearing the person or persons concerned the Government would "direct the Association to suspend its activities for such period not exceeding six months".

Under section 24, the Government could also impose curfew within a particular area or areas.

Under section 25, penalties for hoarding or dealing in black market were provided. By an amendment in 1974 section 25 was broadened and some more offences were brought within the purview of the Special Powers Act, along with the enhancement of maximum punishment. Besides the offence of hoarding or dealing in the black market (section 25), some more offences and penalties were introduced, such as, counterfeiting currency notes and government stamps (section 25A), smuggling (section 25B), adulteration or sale of adulterated food, drugs and cosmetics (25C) and attempt to or abatement of any offence punishable under this Act (25D).

By the amendment in 1974 penalty of death by shooting was provided for certain offences and the general period of sentences against any offence was made much higher than those under the ordinary law. In case of sabotage, black-marketing, hoarding, counterfeit of currency notes and government stamp, adulteration, sale of adulterated food, drinks, drugs or cosmetics, smuggling—for all such offences the amended Act in 1974 provided punishment by death. Even any attempt in or abetment of any such offence was made punishable with death.

Another aspect of the Special Powers Act was that all the offences triable under the Act were made cognizable any no person who was accused or convicted for an offence punishable under any of the penal provisions of the Act could be released on bail by any Magistrate, Special Tribunal or Court (Section 32). The Act also excluded the jurisdiction of the court to challenge any order made under the Act except as provided in the Act itself.

For the purpose of trial of the offence under the Act, Special Tribunals were created with every Sessions Judge, Additional Sessions Judge and Assistant Sessions Judge in their respective Sessions Division and such Tribunals were to have all the powers conferred by the Code of Criminal Procedure on a Court of Sessions exercising original jurisdiction (Sections 26 to 29). In the original law an appeal from the judgement of the Special Tribunal lied with the High Court Division but by an amendment made in 1974 the jurisdiction of the High Court was taken away. Instead, an appellate Tribunal was created and such Appellate Tribunal was also authorised to confirm any death sentence passed by such Tribunal (Section 30).

It would be evident that although the Special Powers Act dealt with anti-social offences, it had a lot of political content in it. Individual liberty and freedom of press and association were all brought under the perview of this law. In its application also it was found that the law was more used against the political dissidents than the so-called anti-social elements. Although adequate measures were taken to handle the offences but they were not implemented in the right direction. Although penalty of death by shooting was imposed with a great amount of enthusiasm, in reality no one was put before any firing squad. The Rakkhi Bahini was employed frequently and the Army was also called in at times, but their exercises failed because of the involvement of the Awami League members or their proteges in the very activities which the Act was to check and forestall. In those days it was found that the Army had to be called back under the pressure from within the ruling party and the Rakkhi Bahini in its operation took a partisan view by sparing the Awami Leaguers in most of the cases.

The offences like hoarding, black marketing, smuggling and subotage which were destroying the economy of the country and making the life of the ordinary people miserable could not be checked despite the introduction of such a harsh and comprehensive law. The law could neither bring to book any Awami League leader nor any influential person known to have been involved in such activities. At the end, the wrath of the law fell mainly on those who were poor, living near and around the border and on such persons who had no political backing or patronage.

Court Decisions

In view of the fact that the law was a special one it was both restricted and stringent in its content. The cases with specific charges of offence like hoarding, black marketing, sabotage. etc, were dealt with before the Special Tribunal. The jurisdiction of the High Court to hear an appeal was ousted within several months when the Act was amended in August, 1974. So, for all practical purposes the jurisdiction of the superior court having been ousted the scope for interpretation of the law was extremely limited. On the question of bail, the jurisdiction of the court was taken away with regard to the offences enumerated in section 32(b) of the Act. In other words, any person who was simply accused of such an offence could not get bail even if the charges were vague or flimsy. In practice, it was found that in describing any complaint in the FIR a simple inclusion of the words "and under Special Powers Act" could deprive a person of his right to bail. In Yar Ahmed vs. State[35] the

High Court Division held that "section 32 of the Special Powers Act puts a total bar in granting bail in connection with a matter as enumerated in clause (b) of section 32''.

The High Court's jurisdiction under section 561A of the Criminal Procedure Code to quash proceedings pending before a Special Tribunal was also ousted particularly after the amendment of the Act in August, 1974. The High Court Division in Salimuddin vs. State[36] held that "the High Court Division has no jurisdiction under Section 561A of the Criminal Procedure Code to quash proceedings pending before a Special Tribunal under the Special Powers Act, 1974 particularly after its amendment". The same view was taken by the Court in Nurul Bepari vs. State[37].

In Shahar Ali v. Sessions Judge, Mymensingh[38] the High Court Division dealt in depth with its own constitutional position vis-a-vis the Special Powers Act particularly on the question of reviewing a judgement or sentence passed by the Appellate Tribunal under the Act. The court discussed Article 114 and Article 109 of the Constitution and Sections 26 and 30 of the Special Powers Act. The provision that "no Court shall have authority to review any judgement, order or sentence of the Appellate Tribunal under the Special Powers Act and the decision of the Appellate Tribunal shall be final". Justice S.M. Hossain observed as follows:

> "Any judgement or sentence of the Appellate Tribunal shall not only be final but no Court including the Appellate Division of the Supreme Court shall have any such normal power to revise any appellate judgement and sentence even when it involves the confirmation of a death sentence. This is an unprecedented innovation in the history of common law countries. There is no Commonwealth country where a sentence of death has been normally kept out of scrutiny by the highest constitutional court of the country. This was evidently an attempt not only to exclude the supervisory and superintending jurisdiction of the High Court Division of the supreme Court but at the sametime it was also an attempt to create a Court parallel to the High Court Division of the Supreme Court outside the pale and purview of the Supreme Court as such because of the fact that even under Article 103(4) of the Constitution, the Appellate Division of the Supreme Court has no jurisdiction over any judgement and order of the Appellate Tribunal which is for all practical purposes exercising the function of the High Court Division in this regard".

The Court analysed Article 114 and Article 109 of the Constitution and elaborated the powers and functions of the High Court Division and the Appellate Division with relation to Subordinate Court. The Court finally held:

> "In view of the aforesaid constitutional position of the Supreme Court and its High Court Division with regard to its authority over other Courts

established by other law including any judicial tribunal exercising the function of a court of law like the Appellate Tribunal under the Special Power Act and considering the implications of Article 114 along with Article 109 of the Constitution of Bangladesh, it must be held that the prosecution and trial of the petitioner under the Special Powers Act can proceed before a Special Tribunal or an additional Special Tribunal and therefore, also before the Appellate Tribunal but any judgement, order or sentence of any such Appellate Tribunal shall be subject to a revision short of an appeal under the normal procedural law before the High Court Division and in any event even directly under Article 109 read with Article 114 of the Constitution of Bangladesh, being quite separate, distinct and independent from the extraordinary prerogative jurisdiction the of High Court Division under Article 102 of the Constitution of Bangladesh".

Since the case involved substantial question of law as to the interpretation of article 109 and Article 114 of the Constitution, it granted a certificate for leave to appeal before the Appellate Division for further adjudication of the points raised.

The High Court Division, however, entertained application under writ jurisdiction against orders passed by the Appellate Tribunal in such cases where the Appellate Tribunal or the Special Tribunal acted beyond their jurisdiction or outside the purview of the Act[39].

With regard to Section 3 of the Special Powers Act which relates to preventive detention, there have been a series of decisions. The Court as in the past tended to construe the provisions of preventive detention liberally based on a number of precedents laid down in all the courts in the sub-continent. The tradition of protecting the right of the individual citizen was maintained in almost all the cases that came before the Supreme Court of Bangladesh.

The 2 most illustrious judgements dealing with the entire ambit of preventive detention and its laws and precedents were (1) Abdul Latif Mirza vs. Government of Bangladesh[40] and (2) Mrs. Aruna Sen vs. Government of Bangladesh[41]. In both these cases, particularly in the case of Aruna Sen, the whole history of preventive detention has been touched upon and the decisions referred to in both the cases will perhaps offer almost all the case laws of England and the sub-continent on the subject of preventive detention and liberty of citizens. In both the cases the detenu was set at liberty by the order of the Court. Based on these two judgements there has been hardly any case where a person could be kept in custody on any political ground under Section 3 of the Special Powers Act[42].

FOOTNOTES

1. On the US's renewed bombing in North Vietnam these parties organised demonstrations on 1st January, 1973 in front of the Dhaka USIS where police opened fire and 2 students were killed. As the Awami League and NAP (M) were on best of terms no one could explain why or how the incident took place. A section of the Awami League claimed that it was an act of a sabotage from within the government machinery. All the opposition parties condemned the killing of students by police firing, first of its kind since independence, and tried to take full advantage of it. Next day a country wide general strike for 9 hours was a complete success. Having realised the general resentment and impact of the strike the Awami League went for political counter-action, attacked the offices of NAP (M), CPB, held processions in favour of the government.

   As the opposition held Sheikh Mujib as the head of the government responsible for killing the students, the Awami League took it up as an issue that the opposition was trying to malign the Father of the Nation. To demonstrate their strength they held a massive public rally with bamboo sticks and fastoons. They were trying to say that Mujib could not be blamed for the incident as it must have occured due to the conspiracy of some people within the government opposed to independence and they condemned the killing themselves. They also raised slogans such as, Rab-Bhashani-Muzaffar Banglar Mirzafar (Traitors of Bengal). They also organised a Resistance Day on January 10 and held a public meeting at Paltan. Anyhow, although the opposition was united on this issue and despite the fact that the office of the NAP (M) was attached by the Awami League supporters, the agitation soon died down as the main victims of the government attack retreated. For national and international reasons the NAP (M) and its allies withdrew from the battle and surrendered to the Awami League to continue with their close association.
2. *Bangladesh Observer*, January 3, 1973.
3. *Bangladesh Observer*, January 4, 1973.
4. *Bangladesh Observer*, January 5, 1973.
5. *Bangladesh Observer*, January 4, 1973.
6. *Bangladesh Observer*, 5.1.73.
7. *Bangladesh Observer*, 7.1.73.

   As discussed earlier, the Awami League considered all the opposition parties as non-patriotic excepting the National Awami Party (M) and the Communist Party of Bangladesh. In their dealings this attitude towards the opposition was demonstrated all through.
8. *Bangladesh Observer*, 23.1.1973
9. The government fixed Tk. 2000/- as the maximum salary in public sector.
10. See discussion of that treaty, Ch. VII.
11. Dr. Mazharul Islam, *Sheikh Mujib*, p. 974-978.
12. The election of Mustaq Ahmed Chowdhury (NAP-M) was published in Government owned newspapers also. —*Bangladesh Observer*, 9.3.1973
13. Mashiur Rahman Jadu Mia of NAP-B contested the election from prison where he was detained on political grounds and was not allowed to come out even on the election day. He secured 28870 votes against his nearest rival Abdur Rouf, Awami League securing 39056 votes. Jadu Mia claimed that he would have won even from prison if the Awami League candidate did not adopt unfair means.
14. A political correspondent of the Government owned English daily made this assessment based on views gathered from different quarters. See his account in *Bangladesh Observer*, 4.3.73.

15. Bangladesh Election Commission Report on the election, 1973.
16. Sheikh Mujibur Rahman filed nomination for four constituencies. In two, he was elected uncontested and in other two, both in Dhaka, he was contested. Also see *Bangladesh Observer*, March 10, 1973.
17. Bangladesh Jatiyo League (National League)
18. National Awami Party (Bhashani)
19. Jatyo Shamajtantrik Dal
20. National Awami Party (Muzaffar)
21. Enayetullah Khan, the Editor of *Holiday* who contested in Dhaka XIII constituency made repeated efforts to unite all left-democratic forces but in vain. His appeal "let us not fight each other but fight the enemy" went almost unheeded. —*Bangladesh Observer*, 12.2.73.
22. The highest number of votes ever cast in Bangladesh was 57 6% in the 1970-71 election.
23. *Report on the First General Election to Parliament in Bangladesh*, 1973. Bangladesh Election Commission, p. 53.
24. See below for further discussion.
25. Badruddin Umar, *Holiday*, April 8, 1973.
26. "Red Force", a special corp of Industrial workers.
27. *The author himself* as a lawyer led several delegations to the Prime Minister during this period against atrocities committed to workers of other districts in Chittagong.
28. Volunteer Corps.
29. The Dhaka District Bar Association in a meeting called for taking action against the law breakers. They expressed their grave concern over the deteriorating law and order situation. They condemned those who took the law into their own hand.—*Bangladesh Observer*, 15.5.73.
30. See for detail the parliamentary proceedings. September 1973 and the *Bangladesh Observer*, 21.9.73.
31. The Printing Press and Publications (Declaration and Registration) Ordinance, 1973. 28th August, 1973.
32. *Bangladesh Observer*, 20.9.73.
33. *Holiday*, September 23, 1973.
34. The "prejudicial act" has been defined in the Special Powers Act as follows :
    "prejudicial act" means any act which is intended or likely—
    (i) to prejudice the sovereignty or defence of Bangladesh ;
    (ii) to prejudice the maintenance of friendly relations of Bangladesh with foreign states ;
    (iii) to prejudice the security of Bangladesh or to endanger public safety or the maintenance of public order ;
    (iv) to create or excite feelings of enmity or hatred between different communities, classes or sections of people ;
    (v) to interfere with or encourage or incite interference with the administration or the maintenance of law and order ;
    (vi) to prejudice the maintenance of supplies and services essential to the community ;
    (vii) to cause fear or alarm to the Public or to any section of the public;
    (viii) to prejudice the economic or financial interests of the State.
35. 27 DLR 1975, p. 575.
36. 28 DLR 1976, p. 187.
37. 31 DLR 1979, p. 241.
    But see also Bangladesh vs. Shahjahan Siraj, DLR 1980, AD 1.
38. DLR 1980, p. 142.

39. 28 DLR, 1976, p. 371.
40. 31 DLR (AD), 1979, p. 1.
41. 27 DLR, 1975, p. 154. See discussion above Ch. III.
42. Almost in every case of preventive detention within the knowledge of the author, detenu was set at liberty by the Court especially after the pronouncement of the judgement in the two cases mentioned above.

CHAPTER SIX

ECONOMIC PLANNING AND REORGANISATION

In the field of economic policy, the Awami League government took two steps of great significance and national importance. They were the preparation of the First Five Year Plan for 1973-1978 and the implementation of certain recommendations of the National Pay and Services Commission. In the midst of all chaos and post-independence difficulties the action in these two vital areas demonstrated the political will of the Awami League leadership to govern the country in a methodical way. Notwithstanding the weaknesses and the defects of these exercises and the rush in preparing them which we will discuss in due course, the fact that such measures were adopted in such a short time and in an atmosphere of near-anarchy prevailing in the country, calls for a careful analysis of the sense of direction the political elite was adopting for the future.

The First Five Year Plan :
A Move for a Socialist Transformation

One of the first steps the government took soon after the independence was the constitution of a Planning Commission. Unlike the traditional practice of creating a full fledged bureaucratic machine for the purpose, the government looked for technocrats and economic experts to head the body and appointed a Deputy Chairman and other members of the Commission from outside the civil service. The members were distinguished economists, all of whom were associated with the Awami League and the national movement of the country and so the formation of such a Planning Commission was acclaimed by the people at the beginning. But on the other hand recruitment of experts from outside the civil service for the coveted posts of the Planning Commission created an immediate hostility between the technocrats and the bureaucrats within the government machinery. As a result a fierce tension continued to grow between the members of the Planning Commission and the senior bureaucrats, which in effect produced a strained relationship between the commission and other Ministries and agencies of the government. In the prevailing political context the bureaucrats were pushed aside by the political elite and the fact that the members of the Planning Commission were academics and not civil servants raised the image of the government for the time being. The members of the Commission also enjoyed the confidence of the political leaders and maintained a close liaison with the political machineries of the country. Consequently the Planning Commission emerged as the most powerful agency of the government.

The entire economic Planning was left in the hand of the Planning Commission. It was vested with the responsibility of assisting preparation of development projects by the Ministries. It would scrutinise the technical and economic aspects of the projects before their approval for inclusion in the Plan and would also evaluate the performance of the economy and the progress of project implementation. It was also responsible for negotiation and allocation of foreign and economic assistance between sectors and projects[1]. Besides these, the Commission was involved in all aspects of economic policy-making, programmes and projects and their co-ordination. So the Planning Commission was not only involved in preparing a development plan for Bangladesh. It was performing also some traditional works of other Ministries and agencies of the government as it was entrusted with "wideranging" functions[2].

Besides the planning aspects and those mentioned above, the entire administrative machinery seemed to have gone under the supervision of the Planning Commission. It assumed the responsibility of being the watch-dog over all other Ministries. Starting from evaluating or approving a project of a Ministry down to the question whether a loan for an industry received during the Pakistan period would be accepted by the Bangladesh Government or not was to be determined by the Planning Commission. Every file of any question of a complicated nature used to be referred to Planning Commission for its opinion by the Ministries. In the process, the Planning Commission itself grew into a big bureaucratic machine to dominate the civil administration of the country.

However, having began virtually from scratch the Planning Commission was able to complete its primary task of preparing a Plan for the nation within a relatively shorter period. In preparing the Plan the Commission adopted more or less the same format as used in Pakistan. A plan for a period of 5 years was prepared with the Annual Plan cut out of main plan. With the country still in chaos, the law and order situation deteriorating every day, prices of essential commodities rising and the rate of inflation soaring, the nation embarked on its journey for a planned economic growth in the style practised before the independence of the country. With the Annual Plan for the year 1973-74 already set in motion, the Cabinet approved the 5-year plan on October 13, 1973.

Philosophical base of the Plan

The Plan was aimed at laying a programme for 'a socialist transformation' of the economy in Bangladesh; as the ideal of socialism, according to the Commission, still remained a "vision and a dream." Since socialism was laid down as one of the four Principles on which Bangladesh was founded, the Plan was directed towards achieving this objective through peaceful means within a democratic farmework. For analysing the social and political perspectives of a planned development in Bangladesh, the Commission relied also on certain provisions of the Constitution of the country which according to them was meant to ensure the establishment of an exploitation-free society. For this, (a) conditions were to be created to emancipate the toiling masses from all kinds of exploitation; (b) every citizen was to enjoy the right to work ; (c) all citizens were to be assured equal opportunity so that an egalitarian society could be established ; (d) enjoyment of unearned income was to be discouraged and (e) there would be limits to private ownership of means of production as prescribed by law.

Preconditions for a Socialist Development

The Commission discussed the preconditions required for a socialist development and considered that the "removal of the capitalist system of income distribution of the private ownership of means of production and of the pre-capitalist mercantile as feudal forms of production relation" was a necessary precondition for socialist development. The process of such removal of the existing economic structure could be done in stages depending on the objective conditions of the society but the necessity of fulfilling such preconditions could not be ignored. The Commission thought that in a country where more than 80 per cent of the economy was dependent on agriculture, it was inconceivable "to bring socialism without the socialisation of agriculture".

The Commission also emphasised the need for production and austerity in order to achieve a socialist transformation of the economy. It required growth of productive forces, basic discipline from labour and management and hard work from the population. It would be necessary to remove forces which hampered productivity or growth of productive forces and dissipated the meagre resources of the counry in unproductive activities and unnecessary consumption. As an egalitarian distribution of social income would be an essential feature of a socialist development, the phenomenon where every one was trying to reap benefits guided by sectarian economic interest was to be discouraged. Therefore, a "national income policy was a must which would apply to all members of society irrespective of whether an individual was engaged in the public or private sector". All forces of unproducive consumption were to be removed from the economic sytem. In the transittion period "consumption was to be reduced to the essential minimum and unnecessary luxury and conspicuous consumption were to be eliminated''. It would require "the will and determination of the government and the ruling party to transform the existing society with traditional values and habits generally antagonistic to the norms of productive work into a production-oriented society where work, discipline and savings would be the basic tenets of economic activity."

The Commission emphasised the essential need for cadres for an effective evolution of a socialist society. It recommended adoption of radical measures to free the masses from their "age old bondage of traditional values and customs as well as from their exploiters". No amount of socialist policy adopted by the government could usher in socialism unless the broad masses were able to accept the norms of behaviour necessary for a radical transformation of society. Before socialism became a reality, the task was to educate the public about the need for social change and "revolutionary thinking must precede revolutionary action by the masses". And this required catalytic agents who would totally identify themselves with the people. The government functioneries with their training and expertise could only function effectively where their duties and scope of work were clearly outlined and rules of business and code of conduct were properly laid down. They could neither be innovators nor catalytic agents for social change. The Commission realised that formation of "political cadres" was essential for this purpose. It was only "a political cadre with firm roots in the people and motivated by the new ideology and willing to live and work among the people as one of them" that could mobilise the masses and change their pattern of behaviour. Unlike a government servant whose primary attraction for a job lay in the material incentive, the effort and compensation of a cadre lay in the realisation of his ideals. The "cadres would be the principal instruments through which the task of building a socialist society was to be carried out." The Commission was aware that whenever a party "had failed to be vigilant and immediate remedial measures were not taken, the cadres have deviated from their goals and resorted to self-indulgence". The performance of the party workers had to be constantly reviewed so that neither complacence nor self-indulgence could over take them. The cadres who were successful were to be rewarded by conferment of higher responsibilities and those who failed were to be punished with the door for rehabilitation open. For a successful growth of a socialist society the highest level of party functioneries "must subject themselves to self-criticism and be aware of the fact that they must personally set examples for the party workers to emulate".

The Objective Conditions Prevailing in Bangladesh

Then the Commission analysed the objective conditions prevailing in Bangladesh and tried to relate them, to the pre-conditions earlier indicated for a 'socialist transformation' as this was necessary 'if a viable strategy for development towards socialism is to emerge'. While discussing the subject, the Commission mentioned both the positive factors and the constraints in building socialism in Bangladesh. As constraints, it observed (1) in a multi party state the administration tend to maintain its identity separately from the ruling party and therefore, the party cadres could not be automatically injected into the machine to supervise its operation. This had to be done only from outside under the prevailing conditions. (2) The number of political cadres with adequate understanding, motivation and training to control and direct the bureaucracy as well as mobilise the people was not sufficient. (3) Ideological orientation to the bureaucracy could partially mitigate the problem but as they were a product of the colonial srtucture their attitude was to be replaced by their positive identification with the common man. (4) As the cadres were yet to emerge and the bureaucracy was not sufficiently motivated, the survival of the exploitive elements would continue to remain as a serious problem. (5) The feudal forms of production-relations reflected an unequal land ownership which perpetuated the subjugation of the village poor through dependence for land, work, credit and other necessities for production and consumption on the affluent farmers must go. (6) Private enterprise was still dominant in the distribution system and it was active in the construction field and indenting for foreign suppliers. There was no adequate mechanism to subject them to social control or to collect adequate taxes from them and their high living standard was creating social tension in a situation of acute scarcity having an undesirable effect on the rest of the society.

The positive factors in favour of a socialist transformation noted by the Commission were : (1) The 'war of liberation' had heightened the consciousness of the people and made them aware of the need for political struggle to realise a better life. The demand for social justice underlying the political struggle had transformed into a widely held consensus to build a socialist economic order. (2) All the political parties were more or less inclined to work for socialism though their interpretation and strategies varied. (3) The indigenous private capital received a major setback as a result of the nationalisation policies. (4) With regard to land system, although feudal form of production still survived, large scale feudal land ownership was absent and the land ownership pattern was more equal than in most developing societies. (5) The rural poor were also more aware of their strength and the advantages of the collective action. (6) Given proper orientation, motivation and leadership some of the Government servants could use their skills to manage the economy more efficiently. (7) A whole generation of young men thrown up by the 'liberation war' were willing to dedicate themselves to the transformation of the society and the political leadership and organisation could mobilise their talent and energies towards productive goals and finally (8) Bangladesh had a socially homogeneous population where linguistic, religious, tribal and cast differences were not serious constraints to the development process.

The Commission however expected that the political leadership would dedicate themselves to the ideals of socialism and would provide leadership in bringing about a social transformation. The party leadership would shoulder the obligation and responsibility to set examples in social behaviour and cope with bold new ideas for social action giving them the moral authority to effect disirable changes.

Socio-Political Assumptions of the Plan

Based on their analysis of the 'preconditions required for building socialism' and the 'objective conditions prevailing in the country' the Commission prepared the plan. They took into account "the realities and capabilities" of Bangladesh. Although it did not assume that within 5 years it could approximate to the social structures prevailing in other socialist countries the Plan recognised the urge for social transformation among the masses. It also assumed that the experience of the post-liberation period "did not disqualify them from all attempts to organise the productive forces more efficiently with a view to realising the socialist objectives". All these led the Commission to draw up the socio-political assumptions underlying the plan summarised as follows :

(1) Due to resource constraints the plan did not hope to meet the full expectation of the people. The investment strategy was made biased towards meeting the consumption needs of the masses and expanding employment opportunities both through labour intensive investment strategy and unconventional measures to mobilise labour. The investment strategy was directed to achieve a substantial decline in the degree of dependence on external assistance which according to the Commission restricted the size of the Plan. (2) The Plan aimed at "reducing the elements of exploitation" in phases because of the prevailing circumstances. In order to achieve the socialist goals under this strategy, the Plan laid emphasis on the need for land reforms along with extention of co-operatives for particularly small farmers and landless labourers. The investment strategy in the industrial sector was aimed at securing the ascendency of the public sector leaving small and cottage industries largely for private initiative and enterprise. In the field of both domestic and foreign trade the state and co-operative enterprises were to play an increasingly dominant role leaving retail trade primarily in the hands of private traders. State agencies like the Consumers Supply Corporation would seek to provide some safeguards to the consumers by distribution of some essential items. In the public sector, the role of the State and the co-operatives would be expended considerably while a ceiling on urban property and a limit on the capital gains on property would be imposed. In the transport sector the strategy would be to place ownership of transport facilities with state agencies and co-operatives

of drivers and operators. (3) The Plan emphasised the need for material incentives for those who worked for productive enterprises at all levels in order to ensure hard work and efficiency to increase production. The Commission did not agree with the existing policy of the government in power for limiting the remuneration from work without making any difference in skill and performance. On the contrary it required at the early stages to provide high regards in order to attract the flow of expertise into areas where supply was short. The Plan was critical of the Pay Commission and the wages Commission and contended that arbitrary cuts in income from work without reference to present supply of skills, level of responsibility and the social value of the productive fuctions performed could create disequilibrium in the supply and demand for skills and jeopardise the fulfilment of the Plan target. The Commission also assumed that "the Plan was not merely a technical and an economic document but also a socio-political document. It had to enthuse, mobilise and motivate people. It was to provide a vision and perspective for the nation". It was therefore essential that people and their representatives played a role in setting their socio-economic objectives and in its formulation. The Planning Commission was mainly to work elosely with the political leaders in the Government seeking their guidance and instructions and advising and making recommendations to them on a day to day basis. The Commission thus thought it was necessary to maintain contact with the various groups in society such as Members of Parliament, students, representatives of peasants and workers and other economic groups. It was therefore, advisable to constitute regular advisory panels where various interest groups and the Planning Commission could exchange views and experiences. (5) The Commission emphasised that the "role of the cadres and the political leadership" would be the most important factor in achieving the "goals of a socialist economy". As the cadres were to be identified as an essential element in the "revolutionary transformation of the society", a programme to train cadres in the initial phase of the development efforts was to be immediately taken up. They were to be carefully chosen for their motivation, personal integrity, courage and willingness to work and make sacrifices—they were to undergo a rigorous training process in ideology and policies to be implemented. (6) The Ministers and party leaders were to personally supervise the implementation of development projects in the field and give guidance and leadership to the people as it was necessary that the people had confidence in the "integrity and commitment of the political leadership". Economic development in the context of the acute poverty prevailing in Bangladesh "required sacrifice all round particularly from the political elite of the society". (7) In order to ensure that people did not regard corruption as an acceptable feature of the society, detention and punishment of offenders involved in corruption, irrespective of their personal and political affiliations was necessary.

External and Domestic Resource Target

The total amount of external capital inflow was estimated at about Tk. 1800 crores or about 40% of the total financial development outlay. The annual inflow of aid was estimated to an average of Tk. 360 crores per year. The absolute amount of external capital inflow required was not expected to increase over the Plan period. As a percentage of total financial Plan outlay, external capital inflow was expected to decline from over 62% in 1973-74 to as little as 27% in 1977-78[3].

It was aimed that the planned growth and acceleration of development outlay would be financed by additional domestic resource mobilisation as the Plan proceeded. As part of the effort, the average rate of domestic monetised saving for the Plan period was estimated to be about 9.2% and by sustained efforts it was to close the foreign exchange gap. The Plan aimed not only at a considerable raising of the rate of saving but also at channelising a large part of total savings into public investment.

GDP and per Capita Income

The Plan aimed at both reconstruction and development. It integrated the short term task of economic recovery with the development programme of the plan as a whole. On the one hand it aimed at a quick economic recovery to the bench mark levels of 1969-70 and on the other, attain the general goals set to achieve at the end of the terminal year of the Plan. The Plan aimed at an increase in the rate of growth in GDP at 5.5% per annum appreciably exceeding the rate of growth in population (at about 3% per annum) which would enable a net per capita growth at the annual modest rate of 2.5%. As 1969-70 instead of 1972-73 was fixed as the bench mark year, it meant that over the levels of 1972-73 the Plan aimed at a much higher rate, about 8.8% in GDP and 5.7% in per capita growth[4].

Bangladesh was born with an extremely poor economy. With floods in 1968, 1969 and early 1970 already causing a colossal damage to the agriculture on which the bare survival of its people depended, the November cyclone of 1970 again took not only more than 2,00,000 human lives it had cost more than 1.1 billion Taka worth of properties and innumerable cattleheads[5]. Then came the 9-month long war of 1971 resulting not only in death and killing but in destruction of railway lines, bridges, roads, telecommunications, mills and factories and the total economy of the counrty. The Pakistan government did not even leave behind the ships and aeroplanes which could be of some help to the newly born state. The per capita income in 1970-71 went down about 22% compared with 1969-70 in prices of 1972-73 and in 1972-73, the first year of the country's independence and prior to the launching of the Plan, the country had hardly seen any progress. In 1972 the rice production was about 15% lower than that of 1969-70, industrial output lower by about

30% jute industry's output by about 28%, textile by about 23% and 3% in cloth and in 15 months from its independence the money supply was increased by 83%[6].

The Plan

So the objectives of the Plan presented in 1973 for a long term development was a modest one and it claimed to have been made taking into account "the inexplicable political, social and economic realities of Bangladesh[7]." The Government decided to launch the Plan early because it felt the "cogent need to provide a sense of direction" for a coherent planned development. The Plan did not set unduly high sights in case "it generated greater expectation than it was able to fulfil."

While this approach seemed to be realistic, the Plan itself appeared to have been framed on some contradictions of fundamental nature. As far as the technical or economic aspect of the plan is concerned it would be up to the economists to investigate and judge its merits. The fundamental premises of the Planning Commission and its political leaders would, however, need some analytical discussion in order of find out whether such a plan was a realistic one in view of the country's prevailing economic and socio-political conditions. Even if the Plan had gone through the process of full implementation without any interruption in the government, it would be worth while to examine as to how far and how much it could have achieved in its basic objectives of attaining a socialist transformation.

It was not the economics of the Plan but its politics that dominated the thoughts of the Planners. Although the Commission was chaired by either the Finance Minister or Prime Minister, the two most important political personalities of the ruling party, the task of formulating the plan rested on the members of the Commission. It would also be apparent from the Plan itself that the Planning Commission took up this responsibility with all earnestness.

The Planners did not therefore play the role of 'pure technocrats.' They took in view the constitutional commitment of the government for the establishment of an exploitation-free society. They outlined the pre-conditions for socialist development and the objective conditions prevailing in the country. The Plan was claimed to be not only a book of planning but a "socio-political" document. In its entire investment strategy maximum emphasis was laid on reducing the areas of exploitation, more investment in public sector and reducing dependence on foreign assistance. For the success of the implementation of the programme and for achieving a socialist transformation it relied on the formation of political cadres and the political leadership of the country.

In the process of doing this exercise the Planners sometimes played the role of doctrinaire theorists, sometime as preachers and sometime as politicians[8]. They not only emphasised the need for cadres for the "revolutionary transformation of society" but also dealt with question as to how the cadres were to be chosen, where they should be drawn from, what kind of training they ought to undergo and how their activities were to be supervised and controlled. The Commission also suggested what the functions of the cadres would be in respect of mobilising the people for preventing pilferage and wastage, assisting in distribution of scarce commodities and collecting revenues in areas where evasion was considerable; in informing and educating the peasants and workers and organising various groups and co-operatives etc. They also specified how the Ministers and political leaders ought to behave and the sacrifices they ought to make and how corruption in a society tended to misallocate resources leading to maldistribution of income and its adverse moral consequences.

It is not that these points were in any way irrelevant for implementing or achieving a socialist transformation nor that they were anything new for the purpose laid down but the intriguing aspect of it was that it revealed the point that either the Planning Commission considered itself to be a superior body completely isolated from the rest of the Government or that it deliberately ignored to recognise what was happening in the country at that time. They expected the political leadership to dedicate themselves to the ideals of socialism without analysing their class character ; they expected the cadres to pursuade people to contribute land and materials for projects under the Plan without examining whether the ruling party was capable of forming such cadres.

The positive factors on the basis of which the Commission expected that the Plan would succeed were largely presumptions and they were not based on any in-depth study of the situation. The socio-political assumptions underlying the Plan were more hypothetical than real.

A better understanding of the objective conditions of the country could be achieved if the Commission reviewed the overall socio-economic situation of the country. The decline in production both in agriculture and industry, the general mismanagement of state affairs, the economic anarchy created by the ruling party and the deteriorating law and order situation in the country, represented an atmosphere which was not even conducive for any kind of planned economic growth, not to speak of achieving a 'socialist transformation'. Instead of saying what the political leadership ought to have done, it was necessary to find out what they were really doing.

The planners ignored certain important points before drawing their socio-political assumptions or analysing the objective conditions of the country. Such as : (1) The class character of the Awami League was petty bourgeois in nature. (2) The Awami League was neither a doctrinaire socialist party nor had it any socialist leadership. (3) The party leaders and workers at various levels and a section of the hierarchy were involved in nepotism, favouritism and corrupt practices (4) A section of the Awami League frontal organisations did not surrender arms and they were using those arms for their selfish ends. (5) The Awami League's commitment to socialism had no ideological basis and the leadership of the Awami League did not know what kind of socialism they really perceived or how to go about to achieving that goal[9]. (6) The Awami League's public commitment to socialism developed through a process of struggle mainly dominated by the sentiments of the urban and rural youths and not by any ideological conviction. (7) The Awami League leaders' public commitment to socialism was contradictory to their private habits and behaviour. (8) Most of the Awami League leaders and members of Parliament came from middle class background; lawyers, businessmen, landed gentry and other professionals[10] who constituted the main stream of the party and they hardly represented the class interest of any other class or economic interest groups below them. (9) It was only Sheikh Mujib and Tajuddin Ahmed in the leadership of the Awami League who spoke or thought with some seriousness about establishing an exploitation-free society or a scientific socialist order[11] or a socialist economy but it was doubtful whether the rest were with them. (10) When they talked of socialism or socialist transformation the Awami League excepting a very few "did not mean business". They used it as a tactical slogan. (11) The factions within the party and contradictions within the party leadership were too acute to withstand the pressure of the conservatives and vested interest groups.

Added to these, it is also necessary to examine how much interest the Awami League as a party took in the preparation of the Plan or in the planning process as a whole with the object of achieving a socialist transformation of the economy. How serious was the Awami League really in its endeavour for achieving the goals of an 'exploitation-free society?" The Awami League's rank and file, their student leaders, youth and labour leaders, the Lal Bahini and the Shecha Shebak Bahini were not involved in producing this "socio-political document". The party itself had no role to play in its making, even less in its implementation process. There was no deliberation or discussion on the objectives of the Plan or on the preconditions of a 'socialist transformation' of economy. The party's role was only limited to writing in the manifesto and saying in speeches that an 'exploitation-free socialist economic order' was its political objective and the recommendations made in the Plan were therefore not subject to serious scrutiny in any political forum. As a result there was also no public debate or discussion on the objectives, priorities and strategies set in the plan. The Plan was never presented to the Parliament for any debate or discussion—in fact it was not even exhaustively debated by the Cabinet[12].

There were also some serious contradictions in the Plan's objective, in the constitution itself and in its implementing process. Although the planners were right in mentioning the constitutional obligations for a socialist economy as basis of the social and political perspectives of the Plan there was another aspect of the constitution which related to democratic principles generally practiced in a society more congenial for a free economy. There is hardly an example where an 'exploitation free society' has been established within the framework of a Westminister-type democratic system. The Fabians had their idealism and the British Labour Party could at best go to the extent of thinking of a welfare state with nationalisation of steel and the Indian Congress to the extent of nationalisation of some banks and insurance companies. None could create a cadre to implement and overview the operational aspect of socialist transformation while retaining the enjoyment of fundamental rights of individual citizen. There are inherent contradictions between the eastern socialism and the western democracy and those contradictions would invariably cause a back-lash as the one fails to contain the other. As long as they contained each other as social forces they could exist together. In other words, there are inherent limitations in transforming a traditional society into a true socialist order through a western type democratic system. Socialism or even a socialist transformation could not be achieved by mere nationalisation. Within a democratic framework, nationalisation of certain sectors of economy is possible and there are many examples even in the western world where both can function. But this cannot be said of the kind of socialism which the Planning Commission of Bangladesh envisaged.

The point here is that knowing all these weaknesses and inner-contradictions why did the Commission go so far in expecting to realise a socialist transformation through such a constitutional mechanism and with such a political party like the Awami League? Although the constitution provided certain provisions to specially safeguard the transition to socialism – such as Article 47, 42, etc. the fact remains that the constitution also guaranteed fundamental rights and the right to enforce such rights throuh the courts of Law. In such circumstances it has to be assumed that the Planning Commission members were carried away like any others believing that the Awami League leadership would be able to deliver a socialist economic order to the people. It is however true that the objectives of the Plan and the way it was presented would have received much greater significance if the country was really moving towards socialist transformation and the ruling party was competent to carry out the implementation of such a programme. But unfortunately, the Plan could not be adequately appreciated by the ruling elite itself as they were not capable of fulfilling their commitment of establishing 'an exploitation-free society'. The Commission, therefore, made a serious error in their socio-political assumptions and in the analysis of the positive factors of the objective conditions prevailing in the country.

The members of the Commission, the economists and other professionals who were involved in the 'presentation of the Plan' could however argue that they were working as technocrats and professionals and they placed a Plan the way they were asked to do having no other involvement, social or political. It was a 'made-to-measure' plan as the politicians desired it to suit their political objectives. But since a plan for a socialist transformation would essentially be a political exercise by itself, this argument would not go without any challenge. On the other hand, the Plan did not have a complete run mainly because of the political change of the government in August, 1975 which along with the change introduced a different directive for the economic development of the country. So it is difficult to say how much of its objectives would have been ultimately achieved if it had been given the full contemplated time of the 5 years cycle.

Performance of the Plan

The Plan achieved neither its economic targets nor its political objectives. The performance during the first two years when the Awami League was still in control was poor and unsatisfactory. The size of the Annual Plan of 1973 was fixed at 5250 million Taka but the actual expenditure was 4000 million Taka which in real terms was lower than in 1972-73. The size of the Annual Plan in 1974-75 was also fixed at the same amount of 5250 million Taka because of resource constraint but the expenditure in real terms was almost the same as in 1973-74 although for both the years the estimated size was much higher than actually fixed[13].

Although the major target of the first Annual Plan was mainly to go for 'revival' of the economy rather than development and to achieve the production level which existed in 1969-70, the Government failed to achieve that target. Although there was substantial recovery both in agricultural and industrial sector, in the first year of the Plan the total output in the industrial sector was 25% lower and in the agricultural sector 12-13% lower than in 1969-70[14]. In 1973-74 the food grain output reached a figure of 11.8 million tons compared to 9.8 million tons of the previous year and also higher than 11.2 million tons of 1969-70 but it was short of the target which was fixed at 12.5 million tons[15]. In fertilizer, engineering and food procuring the 1969-70 level was surpassed but the industrial sector in general continued to lag behind. The targets in power, housing and roads and highway construction were not achieved and the achievement in education, health, family planning and other social sectors fell far short of the targets[16].

The balance of payment situation also reflected the same trend of shortfall it surpassed the projected deficit by 23%. The import bill was higher than the projected estimate by Tk. 635 million (79m. dollars) and the export receipts fell short of the projection by 220m. Taka ($ 27m.), as a result the gap between the import bills and export receipts only widened further. In the face of this enhanced deficit on current account, foreign aid flow fell from the projected amount of Tk. 3700m. to Tk. 3070 million ($ 463 million to

$ 348 million). As a result there had to be short term borrowing and drawing from the resources to the tune of $ 217 million[17].

Although the import bills were higher than the projected estimate, the real volume of imports was much less as the world prices of both food and non-food items rose sharply due to the rise in oil price, world food stock shortage and the general inflation. For Bangladesh it meant a rise of 91% in the price of food and 74% in the price of non-food imports in 1973-74, Although there was a slight rise in the price of raw jute and jute goods, the export volume failed to reach the targets. No more than 2.7 million bales of raw jute were exported compared to a target of 3.6 million bales[18]. The low volume of imports not only affected the foreign exchange and aid position but seriously jeopardised the internal revenue receipts and domestic resource mobilisation. Despite the fact that the revenue increased substantially compared to the year before, the actual revenue and capital receipts fell short of Taka 1003 million from the original estimate of Tk. 4501 million. On the other hand, despite the short fall in revenue receipts the non-development expenditure of Tk. 3308 million (exclusive of railway deficit or food subsidy) exceeded the budget provision by Tk. 354 million. As a result the revenue surplus (exclusive of food operation) fell from Tk. 1547 million to a meagre Tk. 190 million. Since a large sum was spent on unexpected food subsidy, the surplus in revenue turned into a deficit one ultimately affecting the overall development. The ever-increasing price situation of essential commodities in 1972-73 got worsened in 1973-74 for the reasons stated above. The overall impact of the performance in 1973-74 was that the prices of essential commodities during the year rose about 40% over the average price of the previous year.

In the Annual Plan for 1974-75 the size of expenditure was fixed at the level of 1973-74 as mentioned earlier and due to resource constraint adequate measure could not be taken to make up for the short fall in the development performance in 1973-74. While it was estimated that the gross domestic product would increase 5 to 6% over 1973-74, the actual increase was estimated only at 2% over the previous year[19]. The total production of food grains was 11.5 million tons which was lower than the previous year and was 12.6% less than the target set for the period. Consequently, a huge food deficit continued and an estimated import of 2.64 million tons was arranged. The production of jute decreased to 4 million bales from the production of 6 million bales of the previous year, although production of other crops such as tea, sugar cane, potatos and vegetables increased considerably.

In the industrial sector, although production in suger, yarn, cloth, engineering products, cement and petroleum products increased the over all industrial production declined. The sector of jute products which earns foreign exchange declined by 8% and the production of urea fell by 77% due to the closure of the Fertiliser Factory at Ghorasal[20].

The balance of payments position worsened during that period. While the import requirement was estimated to be at 7660 million Taka, the actual imports were at Tk. 9710 million and yet the volume of actual import continued to remainl ow because of the rise in world price and increased import of food grains and fertilizer. Like the previous year, on the other hand, the exports lagged far behind the targets. The value of actual export was estimated to be Tk. 2960 million while the target was Tk. 3480 million. Only 1.5 million bales of jute as against a target of 2.7 million was exported and only 3.9 lakh tons of jute products was exported as against a target of 4.4 lakh tons.

During this year also, the non-development expenditure increased from an estimated Tk. 4900.8 million to Tk. 5310.1 million. It was estimated that the price levels in 1974-75 increased by about 35% over the previous year[21].

At the end the food situation became so acute from the beginning of that period that the estimated 2.6 million tons of foodgrain could not be procured on time and the country was gripped by a famine killing thousands of people.

In other words, neither in the agricultural nor in the industrial sector the targets set in the Plan of 1973-74 and 1974-75 could be achieved. On the contrary in some areas the performance lagged for behind and the country plunged into such a serious balance of payment crisis that the whole economic target of the Five Year Plan was in serious jeopardy. The most important factor was that neither in the agricultural nor in the industrial sector could the country reach the 1969-70 levels of production in the first 2 years of the Plan although it was envisaged to achieve it in only the first year of the Plan. The national income during these two years also did not exceed the level of 1969-70[22].

It is true that the Plan suffered serious set backs right from the beginning. It started its operation under dismal economic conditions following the war in 1971 and bad drought in 1972. In 1973-74 the world faced the worst inflational crisis since the second world war mainly due to the rise in price of oil and general food shortage and consequently the price of almost all the import items, on which the country's economy heavily depended, increased at a phenomenal rate upsetting the entire strategy of the Plan targets. For climatic reasons the production of foodgrains also continued to suffer causing a huge loss each year and diversion of substantial resources for procurement of food grains from abroad. All these directly affected the balance of payment situation. Besides the drought in 1972 there was a serious cyclone in December, 1973 and the country had the worst flood of the century in 1974.

While there ought not to be any denial of the fact that the economy of the country suffered very badly due to some reasons beyond the control of the political leadership of the country or that of the Planning Commission and that the Government just had ill-luck all round, these factors alone should not be held fully responsible for the failure of the Plan. Besides the ideological objectives and the wrong assumptions of the Commission discussed earlier, some man-made factors also contributed to the failure of the Plan. The continuous labour unrest mainly led by the Awami League's own labour front, printing of currency notes in India and the tendency to run the country by increased money supply which increased 83% by the end of March, 1973 and by June, 1974 over 100%, the widespread corruption in nationalised and abandoned industries, indiscipline in the political machinery, massive patronisation of the party workers and leaders at the cost of national wealth, large scale smuggling, hoarding and black-marketeering and overall mismanagement of the administration and economy of the country—all these contributed further to the upsetting factors of inflation and natural calamity.

Dependence on Foreign Aid

Moreover, the sense of direction and the setting of priorities constituting the underlying theme of the First Five Year Plan were also frustrated right from the initial stage. The realisation of one of the major objectives set in the Plan for a socialist transformation of economy largely rested in gradual reduction of dependence on foreign assistance. The political leadership made numerous speeches on this issue and Tajuddin Ahmed, the first Prime Minister of Bangladesh once declared immediately after independence that Bangladesh would not seek foreign assistance for its development. Accordingly, the Plan was also designed to reduce drastically and in an unrealistic manner dependence on foreign assistance from 62% of the total financial development outlay to 27% in the terminal year of 1977-78. Emphasis was laid on increasing the domestic resources and reducing the gap between imports and exports without examining the real factors of national life. Due to this attitude the Government did not make any serious effort for a long time to initiate the constitution of the Aid to Bangladesh Consortium, the principal forum through which western donor countries channelise their aid. To keep in line with the socialist development scheme, private enterpeneurship was discouraged and was limited to a "ceiling of only Tk. 2.5. million".

But what was seen later was that the dependence on foreign assistance only increased further, the gap between import and export only widened and Bangladesh had to surrender before the Aid Club in 1974 with a decision to encourage private investment raising its ceiling by 12 times. In the Development Budget made for 1974-75 fixed at Tk. 5250 million, the foreign aid component was shown as Tk. 4420 million which was more than 80% of the total amount[23]. The balance of payment situation also showed an opposite trend with the phenomenal rise in the gap and a consequent increased dependence on foreign aid. The shortage in the balance was shown as $ 113 million[24] and net gap of $ 573 million. The earlier thinking of the Government that the country would survive without foreign assistance was no longer considered a practical view in the face of the hard realities of the national economy.

Private Sector

In the private sector there was hardly any investment with a ceiling of only 2.5 million. In July, 1974 the ceiling was raised to 30 million Taka and the Government allowed foreign investment in both public and private sectors with various incentives. The Government also gave the undertaking that there would be a moratorium on nationalisation for a period of 15 years for such industries where investment would be made from the date of going into production of the unit. Also in the event of nationalisation of any industry after that period compensation would be paid on fair and equitable basis.

So the deviation took place from all sides. The failure of the political leadership in accepting and implementing the Plan as a first step for a socialist transformation of the society in the direction of establishing a new economic order, only reflected their inherent weaknesses. This attempt to aim for a socialist economic order without understanding the depth and dimension of the subject and without an appropriate political vechicle had far-reaching consequences not only in the country or in the Awami League itself but for the prospect of establishing any socialist economic order in future in Bangladesh. Knowingly or unknowingly the Awami League and the ruling class including the Planning Commission in effect had sabotaged the future of 'socialism' in Bangladesh and along with that the hopes and aspirations of millions of people who struggled, suffered and died for the independence of the country. The over-commitment of the party without a deeper study led to produce a counter-productive result. The leaders might have been optimistic theoretically that a socialist economic order was the only answer for removing miseries of the masses and establishing social justice, but an attempt to implement such a theory without adequate preparation was bound to produce a counter-reaction. Mere theoretical or emotional commitment in a society basically traditional, under-developed, illiterate and poor could not be fulfilled without political indoctrination of the masses and a well-organised political party thoroughly oriented to implement such a theory or commitment.

The irony of politics in the third world countries is that the more under-developed the country is the more radical commitments are made by the politicians because, the people being poor are to be given a hope of removing all their miseries in one go and possibly overnight. The more under-developed a people is, the more such emotional appeals tend to carry the masses who are invariably helpless and strive for security. The more-under-developed a society is, the higher the number of political parties exist in that country. The number of political parties goes on increasing mainly because of poverty and unemployment. With poverty and misery all around, some get inspired to do something for the people and as nothing much can be done, it becomes a continuous process of frustration which in turn breeds more political parties as a counter-process. For some it is an occupation or an employment or a source of income or a self-employment to acquire some status in the society. Parties also multiply for reasons of personality cult or conflict in thoughts—individuals becoming more important than the ideological doctrines. The ultimate object of the majority of the parties or leaders of course remains to be the seizure of power, authority and prestige.

The Awami League's experiment of establishing "an exploitation-free society" and a "socialist transformation" should work as a lesson to all the political leaders and parties of Bangladesh irrespective of their ideological thinking—socialist, non-socialist, revolutionary or for even social democrats and advocates of free enterprise. The advocates of free enterprise would also face the same problem as its experiment in socio-economic context of Bangladesh may produce an equally disastrous result. In the present Bangladesh context the more dependence on foreign assistance would increase, the more is wealth likely to concentrate in the hands of the few because the poorer a society is, the more easily can wealth be accumulated. The more insecure a society is the more capital would generally go out of the country. Again, the poorer a society is, the more immoral earnings would there be and the more wealth concentrates in the hand of a few, the more repression and landlessness would occur. With that will come more anarchy and convulsion, more restlessness and instability in the society.

Reorganisation of Salary Structure

Along with the national planning of economy, another very significant and major step the Awami League government took in 1973 was the attempt to reorganise the administrative and salary structure of the Government. The Awami League pledged to restructure the services and the existing bureaucratic machinery in order to make it 'a people-oriented system' discarding the old colonial set up. Earlier in 1972, the government appointed an Administrative and Services Reorganisation Committee along with a committee to recommend the pay structure of the employees of the government and autonomous agencies. In April, 1973 the Administrative and Service Reorganisation Committee submitted its recommendations and suggested radical structural changes in the administrative machinery of the government with the removal of the bureaucratic elitism existing previously. It divided the services into general and development cadres. The Pay Committee Report submitted soon after, recommended 10 National Pay Scales reducing them from over 2000 scales for all the employees of the government, autonomous and government-financed bodies. The report primarily aimed at rationalising the pay structure and reducing the gap between the low income group and the high income group of employeees in the government. Therefore, the salaries of the lower income group were generally raised and the higher income groups were generally reduced from the scales that existed earlier. The minimum pay was fixed at Taka 130/- from Tk. 55/- and the maximum was reduced to Tk. 2000/- from Tk. 4000[25]. While implementing a part of the Pay Committee Report the fundamental basis of rationalisation of pay scales was "same pay for same work". The number of pay-scale was higher before because almost each office had a pay-scale of its own. The employees having same qualifications doing the same work were earning different pay just because they were working in different offices, Ministries, Directorates or Autonomous bodies. It was an extremely complicated task of a monumental nature to bring all categories of employees from over 2000 scales to a bare 10 in number. Although it created a lot of chaos at the initial stage and notwithstanding the quantum of salary and other reservations, its adoption as a whole was considered to be a bold and pragmatic step. Many countries of the world could not do what Bangladesh government did within such a short time with regard to having a National Pay Scale for all who work for it. The other recommendation with regard to the reorganisation of the service structure was however not implemented. The government started implementing the National Pay Scale Programme with effect from 1st July, 1973[26].

FOOTNOTES

1. Professor Nurul Islam, *Development Planning in Bangladesh*, 1979, p. 5, University Press Limited, Dhaka.
2. *Ibid*
3. **Shares in percentages for selected years**

	1973-74	1977-78
Gross financial development outlay as per cent of GDP	11.9	18.7
Gross domestic monetized saving as per cent of GDP	4.5	14.2
External capital inflow as per cent of GDP	7.4	5.1
External capital inflow as per cent of total financial development outlay	62.2	27.0

4. Prof. Nurul Islam, *Development Strategy of Bangladesh*, Pergramer Press Oxford, p. 4.
5. Mohiuddin Alamgir, *Famine in South Asia*, 1980, Oelgeschlagew, Guan & Hani Publishing Limited. Cambridge, Massachusetts, p. 112.
6. *The First Five Year Plan*, 1973-74, Planning Commission, Government of Bangladesh, p. 26.

7. **Development outlay and its financing**

In crores of Taka for Plan Period	Monetized	Non-Monetized
Development outlay :		
Public	3,952	..
Investment	3,298	..
Non-investment	654	..
Private	503	585
Investment	471	585
Non-Investment	32	..
Total Development Outlay	4,455	585
Investment	3,769	..
Non-investment	686	..
Domestic Resources	2,698	585
Public Saving	1,618	..
Private savings and loans from the banking system	1,080	585
External Capital inflow	1,799	..
Domestic resources equivalent of capital inflow	1,757	..

8. See *The First Five Year Plan,* Government of Bangladesh, p. 1 to 8.
9. It was because of this reason perhaps the Planning Commission had to take the role of party theoriticians and had to give some direction as how to achieve a socialist order. If the party was a socialist one this would not have been necessary.
10. Rounaq Jahan, *Bangladesh Politics : Problems and Issues,* University Press Ltd., Dhaka, 1980, pp. 99, Table 1.
11. Sheikh Mujib's speech on Nationalisation, *The Bangladesh Observer,* March 26, 1972.
12. Professor Nurul Islam, *Development Planning in Bangladesh,* University Press Limited, Dhaka, pp. 6-7.

13. The phasing of the financial development outlay in the 5-year plan was as follows :

(Taka in crore)

Year	Total	Public Sector	Private Sector
1973-74	595	525	70
1974-75	725	645	80
1975-76	870	775	95
1976-77	1040	925	115
1977-78	1225	1082	143

14. Professor Nurul Islam, *Development Strategy of Bangladesh,* Pergramer Press Oxford, p. 4.
15. *First Five Year Plan,* Planning Commission, Government of Bangladesh, p. 91.
16. *Memorandum for the Bangladesh Consortium,* 1974-75, Planning Commission, Government of the People's Republic of Bangladesh, October, 1974.
17. *Ibid,* p. 9.
18. Government of the People's Republic of Bangladesh, Planning Commission, *Memorandum for the Bangladesh Consortium,* 1974-75, October, 1974.
19. Government of the People's Republic of Bangladesh, Planning Commission, *Economic Review,* 1974-75.
20. *Economic Review,* 1974-75, Planning Commission, Government of the People's Republic of Bangladesh, 1975, p. 6.
21. *Ibid.* p. 8.

22. *Arthanaitic Shamikhan*, (Economic Review), 1975-76 Planning Commission, Government of Bangladesh, p. 4. In the industrial sector the production even in 1975-76 still continued to remain lower than the level in 1969-70.
23. *Economic Review*, 1974-75, p. 20-21.
Even this amount of Tk. 4420 million shown was much less than the amount entered in the balance of payment account.
24. *Economic Review*, 1974-75, p. 19.
25. Since independence no government servant drew any salary higher than Tk. 2000/- as it was reduced right at the beginning. In view of the inflation and other factors, the real income of all the employees went down considerably creating lot of resentment particularly in the higher income groups.
26. The Pay Scales were raised to 21 subsequently by the Zia government as 10 scales were considered too few to accommodate all the earlier scales but the principles followed were same.

CHAPTER SEVEN

THE BANGLADESH-INDIA RELATIONSHIP

In order to fully understand the dimension of this complex and somewhat sensitive subject one must trace the thousand year's history of the sub-continent and that of Bengal. India was partitioned in 1947 not so much for the 'two-nation theory' but more for economic reasons. The Moslems of the different regions of the sub-continent wanted to have autonomous states to determine their own destiny as they were 'exploited and dominated' by the economically powerful Hindu community[1].

However, once Pakistan was established the dream of achieving autonomous and independent states enshrined in the Lahore Resolution did not materialise[2]. The colonisation within the country resulted in exploitation of the resources of East Pakistan by the ruling coterie of West Pakistan and this continued for nearly two decades. The country could not adopt a political system for itself. Out of 24 years, more than half the country was under military rule and there was never a national election till 1970-71. With the economic exploitation and cultural suppression by a rich minority over a poor majority having no democratic right to take part in the policy-planning of the country, the Bengalis continued to struggle to establish their right to live. When all the constitutional means failed, the movement for autonomy turned into a movement for independence, an internationally recognised path for establishing the right of self-determination.

During all these years since the partition, the relationship between India and Pakistan was never good. The Indian Congress Party was opposed to the concept of Pakistan. Pakistan continued to oppose the Hindu domination in the sub-continent. They fought 3 wars in the first 18 years and maintained a competitive and hostile attitude to each other all through. Since Bengalis did not constitute the ruling elite of Pakistan they had little participation in national affairs and had no significant role to play in this relationship and consequently, developed no enthusiasm for having a "thousand-year war" with India[3]. While Pakistan emerged as India's enemy number one and vice-versa, the Bengalis in East Pakistan were struggling for their democratic rights. In the context of the sub-continental power-balance, for her own strategic reasons India was soft towards the cause of the Bengalis right from the time when the left and the progressive forces first initiated the nationalist movement in East Pakistan.

Because of the Sino-Soviet conflicts, the left forces in East Pakistan got divided and a part of it continued to support the Soviet line in international polemics. As India moved towards the Soviet Union, the pro-Soviet forces in East Pakistan developed closer ties with their counterparts in India. On the other hand, the groups led by Moulana Bhashani lent support to Ayub Khan for his China policy. In this process both India's position and the position of the leftist forces changed and consequently a dominant section of the Indo-Soviet forces infiltrated into the Awami League.

By 1966 through the 6-point programme the Awami League was able to capture the mind of the Bengalis and Mujib emerged as the leader of the nationalist cause. In the Agartala Conspiracy Case, the role of the Indian government in supporting the nationalist cause was revealed and it was alleged that Mujib and 34 others with the help of India conspired to separate East from West Pakistan by armed revolt[4]. In 1968-69 during the great mass upsurge, the Awami League emerged as the strongest nationalist force and Mujib became the undisputed leader of the Bengalis. The emergence of the Awami League as the nationalist front for the Bengalis suited its Indian counterpart and the government. During the 11-point movement in 1968-69 the pro-Soviet lobby through the Students Union worked hard and were able to establish a working relationship with the Student's wing of the Awami League[5].

When the Pakistan Army cracked down on the Bengalis on 25th March, 1971 all the Awami League leaders except Mujib crossed the border kept open by India. With the assistance of the Indian government, the Awami League leaders formed a government-in-exile and the Indian government provided shelter, food, training, equipment, materials and the finance for the Bangladesh government to gain independence. Though the Indian government was cautious in helping anybody other than those who had allegiance towards the leadership of the Awami League, many other political parties and nationalist cadres took part in the war and used India as a sanctuary.

When the independence war broke out, India's desire to weaken her enemy No. 1 coincided with the aspirations of the Bengali nationalist forces. India wanted to increase her influence in the sub-continent and maintain her superiority in the region and the Bengalis wanted to win the war and gain their independence. It suited both sides and more so because the two governments were represented by two political parties of the same character and social classes. In the absence of Sheikh Mujib, the Awami League leadership was weak and submissive which helped India in establishing a complete control over the government in exile[6]. In the course of the nine-month struggle the bond between the Awami League and the Indian Government grew further and they developed a deeper understanding. It was therefore only natural for India to see that the 'armed struggle' remain within their control and that they had a government of their own liking installed in Bangladesh.

India, therefore, pursued a policy of employing strict methods in matters of recruitment, training and logistics to those who joined the Mukti Bahini. It was not easy for any young man to join the fighting force without proving complete allegiance to and recommendation from the Awami League leaders[7]. India's total reliance on the Awami League raised bitter criticism amongst other nationalist forces and the policy was considered ill-conceived in view of the fact that an independence war of that magnitude could not be kept confined to one political party and the fact that all other political parties or individuals had the right to participate in the war should not have been undermined[8]. In the war field, control and authority which were assumed by the Indian Army in respect of operations conducted by the Bengali freedom fighters created a lot of resentment amongst the Bengali Army officers and members of the Mukti Bahini. The Indian Army's control of war logistics and interference in the operation in many cases were considered unnecessary by the freedom fighters who gradually developed into an independent group. During the war, the freedom fighters were openly critical of both the Awami League leadership for not taking part in the war and of the Indian government for too much interference and highhandedness. While the war carried the seed of friendship between the government of India and the government of the Awami League, it had also sown the seed of discord from within and outside. This discord only deepened further by the Indian Government's raising another cadre of freedom fighters under the name and style of Mujib Bahini[9].

However, once the war was over on the surrender of the Pakistan Army, the Indian government achieved the twin objectives, a weaker Pakistan by destroying its military strength and an increase in her influence in the region. The people of Bangladesh were happy for what the Indian Army had done for them and consequently, the relationship between the two countries could not be any better.

The Indian Army and the technical experts and advisers continued their presence to assist and guide the government of Bangladesh. But for reasons not known, or most possibly as a victorious force, the Indian Army soon after the surrender of the occupation forces, started taking away the arms, ammunitions, equipments, machineries and even furniture and household goods in convoy of trucks across the border[10]. Kamal Uddin Siddiqui a freedom fighter and a civil servant, as the Deputy Commissioner, Khulna sent a protest note to India alleging that an estimated Tk. 600000 worth of goods were taken by the Indian Army from the city and port area of that district[11].

Smuggling across the East Pakistan and Indian border was nothing new but soon after the independence the scale of such smuggling took a gigantic form as the border between the two countries remained open for a long time[12]. More so in such a situation, one of the first steps the Bangladesh government took was to withdraw the ban on export of raw jute and jute goods to India which helped in increasing the volume of smuggling since the border was now open following the independence. On the same day, on 1st January, 1972 the government devalued Taka bringing the rate of currency at par with India and simultaneously the government declared all foreign sale contract for raw jute and jute goods entered into by exporters or Mills before the 16th December, 1971 as null and void[13]. When the Bangladesh Government refixed the price of jute after the devaluation, smuggling became more profitable than the normal trade. So jute, the golden fibre and the life line of Bangladesh foreign exchange earning suffered a great set-back both in terms of foreign saving and domestic production[14]. Following the independence right through 1974 for causes unknown, a series of act of sabotage took place in Bangladesh most of which entered round the jute mills and jute godowns. Widespread outbreak of fire in jute godowns became almost a daily affair causing a further damage to the economy of jute[15]. As a result, both the Jute Marketing Corporation and the Jute Trading Corporation incurred heavy losses in 1972-73.

As an effect, the Border Agreement signed earlier was substituted by smuggling as it did not produce anything good for Bangladesh and consequently, it was dropped in October. Bangladesh signed 4 credit agreements and one bilateral trade agreement with India within May, 1972. In 1973 it signed 500/- Taka barter agreement with India on limited repayment basis and this agreement also failed due to non-purchase of Bangladesh goods by India. India also printed some currency notes for Bangladesh which either due to forging or leakage created embarrassment for both the governments and caused an enormous damage to the economy of Bangladesh.

Soon the reactions of all these and their effect on the economy of the country started accumulating, raising a considerable amount of suspicion in the mind of the people. The country was already ravaged by the Pakistan Army and now the people started having fears over the presence of the Indian overlords. With prices of essential commodities already soaring high and smuggling going unchecked, the country was gripped with the menace of flight of capital and inflation. The more the economics of scarcity began to hit the daily life of the ordinary people, the more smuggling, hoarding and black-marketing became a profitable trading, causing a serious breach of trust between the people and the government on the one hand and the people of Bangladesh and the Government of India on the other.

The transfer of the country's properties by the Indian Army, the influence of the Indian bureaucrats in the administration, large-scale smuggling across the border, withdrawal of the ban on export of raw jute and jute goods to India, the printing of currency notes in India, the raising of the Rakkhi Bahini, devaluation of currency and the presence of the Indian Army—all this only helped in increasing the distrust of the people. The seed that was sown during the war due to the mistakes made by the Indian government in relying on the Awami League government now began to take its roots in what was termed as the "Indian exploitation" of the Bangladesh's resources. Due to the carelessness of both the governments no effective measure was taken to remove this distrust created by the action mentioned above. These had far reaching political and economic consequences and with the law and order situation fast deteriorating, the confidence that grew in the mind of the people in the Indian Government and the Army were shaken considerably within the first year of the independence. All the political parties other than the Awami League raised criticism against some or all of the actions of both the government of Bangladesh and India. The right-wing communal forces which were banned were not inactive either. They took the full advantage of this situation and from behind the scene continued a vigorous campaign against the domination of the 'Hindu India' over Bangladesh and they tried to hold India responsible for all the miseries the people were suffering from. Added to this was the fact that the Awami League, because of its highhanded behaviour, alienated people who did not cross the border and yet suffered, constituting a vast numerical majority over those who crossed. These 3 factors had led to worsen the relationship between the two countries right from the beginning. So while the formal relationship between the two governments remained strong and friendly, as far as the people of Bangladesh were concerned it started to flow in the opposite direction from the day the Indian army started taking away the properties of Bangladesh and allowed the border to remain open.

The Friendship Treaty

In the first few months the presence of the Indian Army in Bangladesh was an important factor that led to raise a lot of misapprehensions both at home and abroard. It constituted a challenge to the new Government's ability to run and manage its own people and its capacity to hold the honour and sovereignty of the new state. Pakistan and her allied countries were claiming that Bangladesh was under the occupation of Indian forces and India was forcefully occupying a part of Pakistan. In the international arena a large number of countries was withholding their recognition to Bangladesh because of the presence of the Indian Army. At home, although Mujib had to praise "the impeccable behaviour of the Indian troops during their brief stay in Bangladesh"[16] ; the people became frightened at their taking away the national wealth of the country and were suspicious about their future intention. Mujib felt these pressures but was unable to take any quick step due to his sense of gratitude for what India did for the creation of Bangladesh and for himself[17]. Once Mujib was released, the Indian Government was subjected to embarrassment in the world forums to continue to have her troops in Bangladesh. From the Indian side, she being a spokesman of non-aligned and the Panchashila principles and in the face of worldwide pressure created by Pakistan and her allies, sought an alternative. Consequently, at the end, an arrangement was made to sign a Treaty and as a bargain Mujib was able to effect the withdrawal of the Indian Army. Accordingly, by a prior arrangement, the Indian Army was formally withdrawn on March 12, 1972 with Mujib's message to the departing Indian soldiers in a farewell address "to carry love from the people of Bangladesh"[18]. In return, just a week later, Bangladesh received Mrs. Indira Gandhi on its soil and signed the Joint Declaration and the Friendship Treaty.

The relationship that developed between the two governments during the war led them to follow "common policies in matters of interest to both the countries" but this understanding which many alleged took its roots through some secret arrangement made earlier, could not be substantiated till now[19].

In order to formalise this relationship which was "cemented through blood and sacrifice"[20] the two governments signed a Treaty of Friendship, Co-operation and Peace for a period of 25 years with a provision for renewal under a joint Declaration signed by Sheikh Mujibur Rahman and Mrs. Indira Gandhi when the latter came to pay her first visit to Bangladesh on March 17, 1972. The Treaty was signed between the countries on being "inspired by the common ideals of peace, secularism, democracy, socialism and nationalism" with 10 objects declared in the preamble and 12 articles incorporated in the operative body of the Treaty[21].

The objects and reasons as contained in the preamble made emphatic assertion about the two countries having struggled together for the realisation of the above ideals and cxpressed the determination of the two countries to "transform their border into a border of eternal peace and friendship" and safeguard peace, stability and security "through all possible avenues of mutual co-operation." Both the governments were convinced that further development and co-operation would meet the natural interest of both states as well as the interest of lasting peace in Asia and the world and that the present-day international problems could be solved only through co-operation and not through conflict or confrontation.

Article 1 of the Treaty declared that the two peoples having struggled and made sacrifices together, there would be lasting peace and friendship between them and each side would respect the independence, sovereignty and the territorial integrity of the other and refrain from interfering in the internal affairs of the other side. In Article 2 both the states condemned colonialism and neo-colonialism in all forms and manifestations and pledged that they would strive to eliminate them and lend co-operation to those who were struggling against colonialism, racial discrimination and for national liberation. In Article 3 the two sides reaffirmed their faith in the policy of non-alignment and peaceful co-existence.

The important and more relevant items on foreign relations, defence and economy were in Article 4 to 10 of the Treaty. In Article 4 it was stipulated that both sides "shall maintain regular contacts with each other on major international problems affecting the interests of both states" and they would hold meetings and exchange views "at all levels". Article 5 provided that they "shall continue to strengthen and widen their mutually advantageous and all-round co-operation in the economic, scientific and technical fields." The two countries "shall develop mutual co-operation in the fields of trade, transport and communications between them on the basis of the principle of equality, mutual benefit and the "most favoured nation principle". By Article 7, it was also stipulated that both the countries "shall promote relation in the fields of art, literature, education, culture, sports and health".

One of the most significant clauses was contained in Article 6 of the Treaty. By this Article both sides agreed to make joint studies and "take joint action in the fields of flood control, river basin development, the development of hydro-electricity, power and irrigation".

Articles 8, 9 and 10 were of paramount importance as they relate to both foreign and defence policies of the countries. Article 8 stipulates that no country "shall enter into or participate in any military alliance directed against the other party" and each "shall refrain from any agression against the other" and "shall not allow the use of its territory for committing any act that may cause military damage to or constitute a threat to the security of the other". Article 9 stipulated that each party shall refrain from giving assistance to any third party taking part in an armed conflict against the other party". In case either party is attacked or threatened with attack, the parties "shall immediately enter into mutual consultations in order to take appropriate effective measures to eliminate the threat and thus ensure the peace and security of their countries". Article 10 stipulated that "no party shall undertake any commitment, secret or open, towards one or more states which may be incompatible with the present Treaty".

The Indo-Bangladesh Treaty was part of a Joint Declaration of the two Prime Ministers signed on the concluding day of Mrs. Gandhi's visit on March 19, 1972[22]. Besides the Treaty, the Declaration incorporated certain other significant decisions touching the relationship of the two countries. The two Prime Ministers declared that the Indian Ocean area would be kept free of great power rivalries and military competition and they expressed their determination to endeavour to make the Indian Ocean area "a nuclear free zone". In order to strengthen the cultural relation between the two countries concrete steps were to be taken by signing a bilateral agreement to cultural, scientific and technological co-operation.

They took three most important decisions. Firstly, revival of transit trade and the agreement on border trade. Secondly, they decided that in order to strengthen co-operation between the two countries, regular consultation "shall be held between the officials of the Ministries of Foreign Affairs, Defence, Planning Commissions and the Ministries and Departments dealing with economic, commercial, cultural and technical affairs of the two governments". They decided that such consultations would take place periodically "atleast once every six month's". Thirdly, they also decided to establish a Joint Rivers Commission "to carry out a comprehensive survey of the river systems shared by the two countries" and "formulate projects concerning both the countries in the fields of flood control and to implement them". They further directed to formulate detailed proposals on advance flood warnings, flood forecasting, study of flood control and "irrigation projects on the major river system and examine the feasibility of linking the power grids of Bangladesh with the adjoining areas of India"[23], so that the "water resources of the region can be utilised on an equitable basis for the mutual benefit of the people of the two countries".

The Joint Declaration and the Friendship Treaty envisaged the evolution of an integrated system between the two countries on all vital national and international issues. According to the Indian Prime Minister the Treaty embodied the "will of the two governments to pursue common policies in matters of interest to both countries" and solemnised "the close ties of friendship between our two countries and peoples cemented through blood and sacrifice[24]." With regard to the Joint Declaration she said, "it emphasises the importance of close co-ordination and co-operation between the two countries in trade and payments, economic development and transit". The Indian Prime Minister invited the attention of the members of her parliament to that portion of the Declaration "which deals with the existing prospect of harnessing the waters of Brahmaputra, Meghna and the Ganges to the benefit of the two peoples".

The Indo-Soviet and Afgan-Soviet Treaty

The treaty which was meant "to cement the bond between the two countries" covered almost all spheres of national and international policies. In its features and content it had similarities with some other treaties signed in this region. Two treaties can specially be mentioned ; one between India and the Soviet Union and the other between Afganistan and the Soviet Union.

The Soviet Treaty of Friendship with India contained the same words in the title, "Peace, Friendship and Co-operation" instead of the "Friendship, Co-operation and Peace". In their spirit and context both the Treaties carry identical stipulations. Article 2 of the Indo-Bangladesh Treaty is the same as Article 3 of the Indo-Soviet Treaty dealing with colonialism and racialism. Article 4 is the same as Article 5 of the latter binding the parties to maintain regular contacts with each other on major international problems excepting that in the former the word 'shall' has been used in place of 'will'. Article 5 of the former is the same as Article 6 of the latter stipulating about co-operation in the field of economy, sciene and technology and trade, transport and communications, Article 7 relating to the provisions for co-operation in the field of art, literature and education are indentical in both. The most important clauses relating to defence and foreign relations contained in Articles 8, 9 and 10 are not only similar but almost identical in both the Treaties with the use of the word 'shall' in all of them. Even the construction of the words and phrases are mostly the same. While the Indo-Bangladesh Treaty is signed for 25 years initially, the Indo-Soviet Treaty is signed for an initial period of 20 years.

It will also be interesting to compare these treaties with the one signed between the Soviet Union and Afganistan about one year prior to the actual Soviet invasion of Afganistan with Nur Mohammad Tarakki as the President. The Afgan-Soviet Treaty signed on December 5, 1978 was titled as "Treaty of Friendship and Co-operation". This Treaty also by Article I recognises the equality, respect for national sovereignty, territorial integrity and non-interference in each other's internal affairs. Although the Treaty reflects a much deeper mutual involvement arising out of their existing relationship and talks about the creation of an "effective security system in Asia" the Articles 6 and 10 have identical provisions, the former being identical to Article 8 of the other 2 Treaties and the latter being identical to Article 4 of the Indo-Bangladesh and Article 5 of the Indo-Soviet Treaty. The other provisions also carried similar features for co-operation in various fields of economy, science, technology, etc. excepting that, unlike the other two Treaties Article 4 of the Afgan-Soviet Treaty envisaged that both the countries "shall" continue to develop co-operation in the military field on the basis of appropriate agreements concluded between them".

With regard to the circumstances leading to the signing of treaty between Afganistan and the Soviet Union not much elaboration is required in this discussion. The Soviet interests in Afganistan and its global strategy pursued for a long period in Afganistan led the two countries to sign the treaty with more direct military content in its overall implications.

India signed the treaty with the Soviet Union in August, 1971 at a time when she had to take international precaution against a possible threat from China or the United States over the critical situation arising out of the Bangladesh issue. She needed a guarantee of a military support to defend her sovereignty and territorial integrity and by signing the treaty with the Soviet Union she achieved her immediate objective of striking a balance against any outside interference.

On the other hand, for Bangladesh, once it became independent, the situation was different from those which led to the signing of the Indo-Soviet treaty or the Afgan-Soviet treaty. Bangladesh being in the best terms with India who surrounds her from almost all directions was not under threat of external aggression. The gentle and friendly people of Burmah and the Bay of Bengal on the south did not pose any threat to her. In such circumstances it was argued that

Bangladesh was not required to sign such a treaty involving defence or foreign relations. Articles 8, 9 and 10 of the Treaty in the absence of any threat or absolute necessity as mentioned above, seeking military protection to defend the sovereignty of the country could mean the acceptance of subservient position in her relations with India.

The provisions relating to economic co-operation implied that India having an advanced industrial economy could provide Bangladesh with the technology, technical know-how and assistance, machineries and raw-materials for building its infrastructure both in the industrial and agricultural sectors. As India is a producer of almost every industrial item and Bangladesh was hardly producing any basic industrial item to meet her demand, the economic co-operation between the 2 countries only lead to one turning the other into a market.

The desire of harnessing the waters of Brahmaputra, Meghna and Ganges carries far-reaching and deeper consequences. Under any agreement or treaty for co-operation and assistance between 2 unequal states, between a large and powerful country on the one hand and a small and weak country on the other, the benefit would generally go in favour of the powerful one. It is on this very point of view that a sizeable section of the Awami League was not in favour of such a treaty. But they were over-shadowed by the dominant Indian lobby inside the Government.

Almost all the opposition parties raised the demands to rescind this treaty and Moulana Bhashani was the first person to raise such a demand. This was the first of the 15-point demand raised by the 7-Party Action Committee under the leadership of Moulana Bhashani formed on 29. 12. 72. They apprehended that the Treaty was signed not in the interest of Bangladesh but to guarantee India her influence and domination over the future course of Bangladesh. It was pointed out that India had this treaty signed in order to extend and establish her own sphere of influence over the sub-continent.

The Conflicting Interests between Bangladesh and India

Bangladesh has conflicting interest with India in areas of sovereign importance[25]. Besides the land boundary sphere[26], the maritime boundary will take a long time to finalise in view of the position taken by each side on the economic zone[27] and territorial waters. The new territories arising in the mouth of the Bay of Bengal has given rise to a new dispute[28]. The most important of all, on which depends the life line and survival of Bangladesh and 90% of its inhabitants, is the question of water that flows in numerous rivers through the heart of the new country. All the major rivers of Bangladesh originating from the Himalayas and the adjacent areas come to her piercing through the north east region of India and emptying into the Bay of Bengal. The Ganges is only one of those rivers. The mighty Brahmaputra, the Meghna,

Teesta, Jamuna, Gomoti, Muhuri, Surma, Khoai, Kushiara and Padma constitute the ecological life for the people of Bangladesh. India has constructed the Farakka Barrage causing an irreparable damage to the life and economy of Bangladesh. The sharing of water of the Ganges being most unsatisfactory and the need on both sides being so high, the dispute will go on denting the relationship of the two countries. In the absence of any respect for Bangladesh's requirement, the relationship could even turn bitter. India has already constructed the Teesta Barrage and there is no agreement till now on the quantum of water to be shared. Bangladesh will get less water than she was getting before the barrage was commissioned and as a result at least 4 northern districts will be severely affected. Similarly. India is constructing Barrages over the Gomoti, Khoai and at least 10 other rivers which will certainly reduce the flow of water into Bangladesh in the dry season when the water is required most.

The "exciting prospect of harnessing" the water of Brahmaputra, Meghna and Ganga by India include her proposal to build a link canal to transfer water from the Brahmaputra Basin to the Ganges at the mouth of the Farakka Barrage. On this the Bangladesh Government has a definite negative stand.

Again, although the Treaty envisaged that the border of the two countries would be transformed "into a border of eternal peace and friendship", its implication could be interpreted in a different way both from military and economic points of view. The Awami League's earlier political commitment for not having a large army for a poor country like Bangladesh coincided "with the integrated defence objective" of India for her entire north east region. The best possible way to turn the border into a border of eternal peace and friendship "could be achieved by eliminating all possible means of any military confrontation between the two countries". This could be ensured if Bangladesh did not have an Army as she could neither afford to have one nor did she need one in view of the support assured by India through the Treaty. It is however, difficult to ascertain the actual import of such an assurance since the real intention of the two governments needed a deeper scrutiny. The only known position made public was that of the Awami League and their argument for having only a ceremonial army.

The second aspect has deeper economic implications in the sense that due to the imbalances that exist between the economies of the two countries and the price differences in many commodities, smuggling across the border has always gone against the interest of Bangladesh. So any "border of peace and friendship" could not have meant an open border without BSF or BDR[29]. The BDR or the BSF could only be withdrawn if the two countries had a fully integrated economy complimentary to each other. Unfortunately, none of the two conditions exist between the two countries and from the Bangladesh point of view even a liberal border would immediately cause large-scale smuggling ruining the economy of the country.

It is not that the conflicting interests between the two countries should not or could not be resolved peacefully to mutual benefit nor it ought to lead to any kind of confrontation. It would require mature political leadership in both the countries to adopt a pragmatic and human approach to the problems—no sense of domination or deprivation on the part of either would help resolving the issues. On the contrary any such attitude would only take the two countries further apart.

FOOTNOTES

1. See author's book, *Bangladesh : Constitutional Quest for Autonomy*, University Press Limited, Dhaka, 1979.
2. *Ibid*, p. 2-6.
3. A phrase voiced by Z.A. Bhutto.
4. See the detail on the Agartala Conspiracy Case in author's book, *Bangladesh : Constitutional Quest for Autonomy*, p. 99-131.
5. In drafting the eleven-point programme, the Students Union played an active role.
6. When the war broke out, the two pro-Soviet parties, Moni Singh's Communist Party and Muzaffar's National Awami Party rendered full support to the Awami League. They were members of the consultative committee constituted in India by the Government in exile during the war period.
7. For the role and character of the Awami League, see author's book, *Bangladesh : Constitutional Quest for Autonomy*, Dhaka, pp. 272-276.
8. Although the pro-Soviet NAP and the Communist Party rendered full support to the Awami League they were not a part of the government in exile. See for control employed by the Indian Government, author's book, *Bangladesh : Constitutional Quest for Autonomy*, Dhaka, pp. 272-276.
9. Mujib Bahini was established at the instance of Serajul Alam Khan and Sheikh Moni who claimed that they had a letter of authority from Mujib and they were his real successors meaning that Mujib trusted them more than he did Tajuddin and others. At the end, both the Bahinis were critical of Tajuddin and they became a threat to the government in exile.
10. According to Aneek (Bengali), December, 1974, p. 80 the Indian Army took away capital goods, industrial raw materials and military hardware worth $ 1000 m.
    In the *Guardian* of June 21, 1972, Martin Wollacott wrote : Systematic Indian army's looting of mills, factories and offices in Khulna area has angered and enraged Bangladesh civil officials here. The looting took place in the first few days after the Indian troops arrived in the city on December 17".
11. In November, 1972 a Bangladesh Defence Ministry delegation to Delhi raised the question of returning the captured arms but received a cool response.—*Holiday*, August, 1975.
    At a later stage, in reply to a written question in the Parliament from an Awami League Member, the State Minister for Information and Broadcasting said that India had already returned a substantial quantity of arms and ammunition which she had captured from the occupation forces and the transfer of those arms and ammunition was still in progress. In reply to another question the Minister however refused to disclose the full figure of those arms and ammunition "in the interest of the State".—*The Bangladesh Observer*, 18.6.1974.

12. Moulana Bhashani claimed that smuggling and confiscation of goods transferred to India by the Indian army accounted to a total approx. Tk. 6000 crores. According to Aneek, December 1974, p. 81 the value of goods smuggled from Bangladesh to India between 1972-75 was estimated to be not less than $ 2000 million.
13. *The Bangladesh Observer*, 2.1.72.
According to the business and financial experts all the three steps had gone to the advantage of India and it was alleged that these decisions were taken at the instance of the Indian advisers.
14. For several decades India was neither able to export raw jute nor produce enough jute to feed her own industries. The position dramatically changed after the birth of Bangladesh. In 1973 India had exported 1 million bales of raw jute and by 1974 not only her existing mills were running at full capacity but they had also started to to setup more jute mills.
—Kamal Uddin Siddiqui, *The Political Economy of Indo-Bangladesh Relations*, 1971-75. A part of the thesis submitted at the London University.
15. The Jute Minister told the Parliament in 1974 that jute worth Tk. 139.2 million was destroyed due to fire incidents since independence.
16. Joint Indo-Bangladesh Declaration dated 19th March, 1972.
17. Mujib described how Indira herself requested the Heads of States of all the countries of the world to plead for his release.
18. Mujib's address to the Indian Army, on March 12, 1972,—*Bangabandhu Speaks*, published by the Ministry of Foreign Affairs, Government of Bangladesh, Dhaka, p. 53.
19. The Awami League government has constantly denied that there was any secret pact with India. The present government which is opposed to the Awami League also could not disclose whether there was any secret pact as claimed by the opposite political parties.
The Bangladesh Foreign Minister refused the claim of Moulana Bhashani that there was any secret pact between India and Bangladesh.—*The Bangladesh Observer*, 14.1.73.
The Indian Foreign Minister while addressing the Press on 23. 1. 73 at New Delhi said that there was no secret document or pact with Bangladesh. He claimed that the Treaty was a public document and there was no secret clauses or secret arrangement between the two countries.
20. Mrs. Indira Gandhi's statement at the Indian Parliament on March 20, 1972. *Bangladesh Document*, p. 648, published by the Govt. of India.
21. Text of the Friendship Treaty. See appendix E.
22. In the Joint Declaration signed on 19th March, the reason of signing such a Treaty was mentioned in paragraph 8 as "to give concrete expression to the similarity of views, ideals and interest between India and Bangladesh".
23. On 4.1.73 an Indo-Bangladesh Agreement was signed for setting up a Joint Power Co-ordination Board to study the possibility of exchange of surplus power of the two countries.—*The Bangladesh Observer*, January 5, 1973.
24. The text of the Treaty and the Joint Declaration were placed on the table of the Indian Lok Shaba and Mrs. Gandhi made a statement on the floor of the House on the same day.—Mrs. Gandhi's statement in Parliament, *Bangladesh Documents*, Volume II, published by the Government of India, p. 648.
25. In 1975-76 following the assassination of Sheikh Mujib, India gave sanctuary to a large number of Mujib followers who with the assistance from the Indian authorities used to attack Bangladesh border posts and such attacks continued for almost a year. This was clearly a violation of Article 8 and 9 of the Treaty on the part of India.
26. In 1974 Bangladesh and India signed a border agreement with regard to the demarcation of some disputed areas. Bangladesh ratified the agreement the same year making it a part of its constitution but India till today has not ratified the Agreement.

India's position is that on the conclusion of the demarcation the ratification would be done, which is not reconcilable with the terms of the agreement.

27. Due to the position taken by India on the maritime boundary and economic zone the Ashland Oil Company, one of the six companies who signed Production Sharing Contract with the Bangladesh Government in 1973-74 to explore oil off shore could not do their drilling although they paid for it under the Contract.
28. The new island called South Talpatti rising at the mouth of Hariabhanga river was once taken over by force by the Indian marines in contravention of an agreement between the two countries that a joint survey would take place before the ownership of the island is determined.
29. BSF—Border Security Force ; BDR—Bangladesh Rifles.

CHAPTER EIGHT

THE PRISONERS OF WAR

A Central Issue in Foreign Relations

By mid 1973, although a vast number of countries including the United States of America had recognised Bangladesh as a sovereign state, she was unable to get her admission to the United Nations. Although she became a member of several international bodies like World Bank, International Monetary Fund, United Nation's Educational, Scientific and Cultural Organisation, World Health Organisation, etc. she was unable to take her seat in the comity of Nations. Saudi Arabia had still not given recognition and China exercised her veto against the admission of Bangladesh[1]. Despite the backing of Soviet Union and its entire block and the full support of India and the majority members of the non-aligned Conference, Bangladesh was still not comfortable with her relationship with the Western donor countries, the rightist Muslim states and the People's Republic of China. It is not that the ruling government was not making efforts to establish relationship with countries which had yet not given recognition to Bangladesh but they were not yielding any positive result as the major hindrance in its way centred round the 90 thousand Prisoners of War now held in the Indian camps and the Bangladesh's relationship with Pakistan, the country she once belonged to and fought against to earn her independence.

At the beginning as the victors, the Awami League government took a very strong stand on the question of punishing the Prisoners of War on grounds of genocide and inhuman torture. In every possible public meeting the people were reminded of the atrocities committed by the Pakistan Army and the people cheered when they were assured that trial would be held to punish the Pakistani soldiers. Being carried away with the victory for independence and the fresh memory of repression committed by the Pakistan Army, the ruling party was naturally self-confident and boisterous in its attitude towards Pakistan. They always gave a firm impression that the trial would be held and they did not care about the reaction of Pakistan or other countries. Mujib considered that it was their moral obligation to punish the offenders of genocide and Abdus Samad Azad the Foreign Minister rejected on June 9,

1972 at Singapore an Indonesian suggestion for a summit meeting between Sheikh Mujibur Rahman and Zulfiqar Ali Bhutto[2].

On the other hand, Pakistan, split in half and with a vanquished army and a low morale was now led by Zulfiqar Ali Bhutto. His main responsibility was not only to restore the morale and faith of the people and put the country back to the economic rails but also to get back all the troops held in India and without further humiliation. He therefore, employed all his energy to convince the powerful nations that India had no right to hold the prisoners and there could be no trial of the prisoners of war as (1) India was the aggressor and (2) the Pakistan Army was only carrying out orders for quelling a rebellion in East Pakistan which was an integral part of the sovereign state of Pakistan. Bhutto's personal prestige and the right to stay in power depended on the safe return of the troops. Bhutto was aware that he could not achieve his immediate objective without coming to terms with India and on the question of the return of POWs he realised that it was not Bangladesh but India who would play the key role.

For India, the ultimate victor in the war, it was time to pause. Now that she had established her superiority in the region beyond any doubt, normalisation of relationship with Pakistan was the most desirable objective for her to achieve in both national and international context. It had to repel also the allegation of Pakistan that India wanted to destroy West Pakistan too. The only conceivable concession India could aim for was a formal renunciation of her claim over Kashmir by Pakistan and with 90 thousand of Pakistani troops in her hand the pressure she could exert was not a meagre one. On the other hand, however, the international pressure on India was also mounting everyday for the return of the Pakistani troops on the ground that the troops were taken away from the territory of Pakistan and as they did not commit any alleged crime in India, she had no right to withhold them once the war was over. It was also propagated by Pakistan that withholding her troops so long after the war was violative of the Geneva Convention.

Simla Agreement

A modern war is generally followed by a 'peace settlement' by the contending parties irrespective of any victory or defeat for any side. So following an intensive diplomatic manoeuvre and a visit of a high level Indian delegation to Pakistan, the two heads of governments of India and Pakistan met at a summit level. This had not occured in the last 15 years between the two countries. Indira Gandhi and Zulfiqar Ali Bhutto met at Simla from June 28 to July 2, 1972.

Bhutto desired to make 'a new beginning' and Indira Gandhi agreed to 'forget the past and look to the future'. According to the agreement both the countries agreed to settle all their differences through bilateral negotiation or any other peaceful means. The steps necessary for restoration of communication including air links, travel facilities and trade and economic transactions would be taken by both countries.

Both the leaders gained diplomatically without losing anything. On the psychological plane, Bhutto perhaps gained more in the sense that although the question of POWs did not figure in the official document the impression the people got was that the Simla Agreement was the first step for obtaining the return of the POWs. Besides, the agreement was a historical one for the normalisation of relations between the three countries in the subcontinent. Although India pursued a 'package deal' which would ensure Pakistan's recognition of Bangladesh and a 'no-war pact'[3], Bhutto keeping an eye on his internal situation decided to proceed carefully. In response to India's D.P. Dhar's earlier proposal for a "bouquet of flowers" Bhutto's reply "a flower at a time" was a sufficient indication of his cautious mood[4]. Bhutto was also happy to go back home with 600 sq. miles of territory India agreed to return, which was occupied during the war[5].

The Bangladesh Government, however, continued to stick to its own stand. What annoyed the Bengali nationalist leaders most was the showing of Bangladesh as a territory of Pakistan in the latter's constitution[6] and a Pakistani attempt to bypass Bangladesh undermining its sovereign existence. The government continued to prevail upon India to withhold the troops so that they could be tried. When suspicion grew that India would hand over the troops to Pakistan after the Simla summit, Mujib refuted the charge saying that India could not have done so as the "criminals surrendered to the joint command of Indo-Bangladesh forces". At the beginning, the government leaders were asserting that they would put all the POWs on trial. Later however having discovered that it was not physically possible to do so, the number was fixed at 1500. During the entire election campaign from December, 1972 to March, 1973 the Awami League leaders at every public meeting made political use of the issue by arousing sentiments of the people for the trial of Pakistani troops for committing atrocities[7].

As it became clear that only a limited number of POWs would be tried attempts were made at different levels for the early solution of the humanitarian aspect of the problem which involved the repatriation of civilians from one country to the other i.e. Pakistanis from Bangladesh and Bengalees from Pakistan, the families of the POWs and the very sick soldiers. As a gesture Bangladesh and India offered to let 1000 Pakistanis return home in addition to an earlier offer of 6000 family members of POWs in exchange of 1000 Bengali women and children stranded in Pakistan[8]. But Pakistan showed no response and on the contrary as a counter-pressure prepared for the trial of a large number of Bengali civil and military officials held in Pakistan custody on charges of treason and espionage[9]. This deteriorated the situation further and led the Bengali leaders to condemn the attempt to have such a trial. They considered that any trial of innocent Bengalis stranded in Pakistan would jeopardise the normalisation of relationship between the countries in the sub-continent[10]. Bangladesh's stand on the trial of the war criminals on its soil and Pakistan's persistent refusal to recognise Bangladesh before securing the return of all the POWs continued to keep the tension unresolved.

The relationship between Bangladesh and Pakistan now centred round the following issues : (1) The return of the POWs, (2) The return of the Pakistanis from Bangladesh, (3) The return of the Bangladeshis from Pakistan,[11] and (4) The sharing of the assets and liabilities of united Pakistan.

As the pressure was increasing both within and outside the three countries—Bangladesh, India and Pakistan to resolve the issues arising out of the war in 1971 each country was faced with its own commitment. India having won the supremacy of the region wanted to hand over the POWs as soon as possible but could not do so without offending Bangladesh, her new ally in the sub-continent. Having settled the immediate issue through the Simla Agreement, India reached a more advantageous position but did not wish to antagonise the Bengali sentiment. They were no more interested in carrying the burden of feeding and maintaining such a large number of foreign troops on their soil and facing the embarrasment in the world forums for detaining Pakistani troops. They adopted a policy of reconciliation and advised Bangladesh not to insist on the Pakistani recognition before the settlement of other issues particularly relating to the POWs.

Out of the four issues, excepting the question of trial of 195 prisoners of war, the return of the rest of the POWs and the repatriation of the respective citizens from both the countries were largely humanitarian in nature. The question of sharing of assets and liabilities of united Pakistan could not be solved at this stage as it was basically an issue between Bangladesh and Pakistan.

Bangladesh's stand was that 195 POWs would have to stand trial on her own soil "not for vengeance but for justice"[12]. What Bangladesh insisted upon was quick repatriation of all the Bengalis from Pakistan and of the Pakistanis including the Biharis from Bangladesh, only then could the return of the rest of the POWs take place. Bangladesh, at the initial stage did not think too seriously about the recognition whereas the question of recognition turned out to be the most crucial point at issue. As a matter of fact the Awami League leaders at the beginning thought it would come without much of a problem. Sometime they even thought they could do without Pakistan's recognition. In a speech at a public meeting at Pirozpur in January 1973 Mujib made a sarcastic remark on Pakistan's putting condition on giving recognition. "It makes me laugh when Bhutto talks of recognition of Bangladesh. The question rather is whether I recognise you"[13].

In course of time, however, Bangladesh realised that (1) without the recognition of Pakistan, she could not participate in any discussion. India and Pakistan were holding talks on issues essentially involving Bangladesh. (2) recognition of nearly 50 countries including that of China was not forthcoming unless these issues were settled. Bangladesh now, therefore, took the stand that recognition of Bangladesh was a pre-condition to the initiation of any meaningful talks with Pakistan[14]. So from Bangladesh point of view the crisis boiled down to a trial of only 195 POWs and recognition of Pakistan.

Pakistan on the other hand considered all the four issues together and applied a political approach to the whole situation. Having already obtained some concessions in the reduction of the member of prisoners to be put on trial and Bangladesh and India agreeing to return the rest of the POWs along with the Pakistanis stranded in Bangladesh, Pakistan adopted a dilatory policy in order to put further pressure on Bangladesh and India for putting off the proposed trial and the return of all the POWs. It not only launched a world-wide propaganda to achieve this objective, she started humiliating the Bengalis who were stranded in Pakistan. Threat of a counter-trial and rounding up of the Bengalis, raiding their homes and taking them to various camps in isolated places, were tactics deliberately employed as counter-pressure on Bangladesh. When in April, 1973 Bangladesh officially announced its decision to try 195 POWs for crimes against humanity, Pakistan retaliated by humiliating and torturing the innocent stranded Bengalis. When Bangladesh and India jointly offered a settlement base, Pakistan went to Hague World Court. When Bangladesh proceeded to make the law, Pakistan ordered freezing of all bank accounts of the stranded Bengalis.

When Bangladesh proceeded to frame a law for the trial, Pakistan formally filed a petition before the International Court of Justice protesting against the proposed trials and claimed that there was no ground in international law to justify the handing over of the POWs to Bangladesh by India[15]. So Pakistani policy was to try to stop the trial by any means and withhold recognition till Bangladesh had decided to put off the trial[16]. Although the issue, mellowed down considerably through passage of time but it became a matter of national prestige for both the countries.

Joint Settlement Offer by Bangladesh and India

Bangladesh continued to pursue the humanitarian line separating the issue of trial from the rest of the problems. At the instance of India it even gave up the stand that it would not talk to Pakistan without recognition[17] but kept India convinced on the question of trial. As a part of a diplomatic move and to secure the return of the stranded Bengalis for which pressure was building up within the country after the election, Bangladesh and India made a joint settlement offer to Pakistan by signing an agreement in April, 1973[18]. It offered a simultaneous repatriation of the Pakistani POWs and civilian internees other than those 195 POWs required for trial, repatriation of Bengalis forcibly detained in Pakistan and the repatriation of Pakistanis in Bangladesh including those who opted for Pakistan, In the agreement however Bangladesh asserted that she could not participate in any discussion with Pakistan at any level except on the basis of sovereign equality which meant recognition[19].

Reply of Pakistan

Pakistan did not want to make any hasty response. Not only that, in order to offset any diplomatic advantage India and Bangladesh could have gained out of the joint offer, it decided to go to the World Court at the Heague claiming that the handing over of the POWs by India to Bangladesh would be illegal[20]. But however at the end, a lengthy reply was sent by Pakistan after raising points which did not hasten the materialisation of the offer made by Bangladesh and India. It raised the provisions of the Geneva Convention saying that India had no right to hold back the POWs who were to be released "without delay after cession of hostilities". It also refused to recognise Bangladesh and asserted that Pakistan "cannot recognise the competence of the authorities in Dhaka" to try the POWs on criminal charges. The Pakistan Government argued that since the alleged crimes were committed in a part of Pakistan and the alleged offenders were citizens of Pakistan, according to established principles of international law only a "competent tribunal of Pakistan could have jurisdiction over this matter and it would be repugnant to Pakistan's sovereignty to surrender its exclusive jurisdiction in this regard". It reiterated the Pakistan Government's readiness to constitute appropriate judicial tribunals to try persons charged with the alleged offences.

The note of the Pakistan government contained a threat also saying that if the authorities in Dhaka began to hold the trials of 195 POWs it would not only "poison the atmosphere" for peace and reconciliation but would make it impossible for the Pakistan Government to continue with the restraint shown so long in respect of trying Bengalis in Pakistan charged with the offence of subversion, espionage and high treason. On the question of the repatriation of the non-Bengalis also who owed allegiance to and had opted for Pakistan, the Pakistan government termed them as victims of prejudice and bigotry and urged "the international community to pursuade the authorities in Dhaka to protect the basic human rights to which these unfortunate people are entitled."

The Government of Pakistan however retained the position that it was willing to solve the humanitarian problem and to fully participate in the efforts of alleviating "their human plight" and it was prepared to fully cooperate with arrangements for all Bengalis to leave Pakistan if they so desired.

On the other hand it maintained that the normalisation of the situation in the sub-continent would be accelerated by India promptly fulfilling its "international obligations under the Geneva Convention".

Athough the reply of the Pakistan government was ambiguous and sometime contradictory, the message was clear. They were not ready to accept the proposal made by India and Bangladesh but at the same time kept the door open for negotiation. Although Bangladesh not being able to communicate directly, could not reply to the legal points raised by the Pakistan government on the question whether the POWs could be tried by Bangladesh or whether Pakistan was obliged to take back those who owed allegiance to her, the intention of Pakistan was still to ignore the status of Bangladesh and maintain a line of negotiation with India keeping within the purview of the Simla Agreement. It also continued to maintain a direct threat of retaliation in case Bangladesh staged a trial of 195 POWs. Soon after the reply was sent, the Pakistan government also moved the International Court of Justice against the proposed trial with a request for an interim injunction against transfer by India of the 195 POWs for war crimes trial in Bangladesh.

In the meantime, however, Bangladesh leaders continued to demonstarte its determination to put 195 POWs on trial and preparation for collecting evidence and the transfer of the POWs from India to Bangladesh was in the process of being finalised. A law for the trial of the POWs was also ready for introduction before the Parliament. As opposed to these measures Bhutto now referred the issue of recognition of Bangladesh to his own Parliament and sought its authority to accord recognition at a time suitable to the "interest of Pakistan". The strategy was to obtain the authorty of the Parliament in order to use it at a politically suitable time. Bhutto while addressing the Pakistan Parliament on the 'authority resolution' for recognition pleaded that peace could not be established by "evasion of reality, the reality of Bangladesh". Bhutto however made it very clear that the authority of recognition would not be exercised at a time when the "POWs were in captivity".

At the Hague no dispute of this nature would be entertained by the International Court of Justice till both parties agreed to the adjudication and the Court refused to grant the request of Pakistan for an interim injunction against the transfer of 195 POWs from India. In the same month, in July, 1973 the Bangladesh Constitution was amended to exclude certain fundamental rights in respect of detention, prosecution or punishment of prisoners of war for genocide, crimes against humanity or war crimes[21]. Within less than a week the International Crimes (Tribunals) Bill was introduced in the Bangladesh Parliament to make provision for the trial of the 195 POWs[22]. The interesting coincidence was that both the actions namely authority for recognition in Pakistan and the law for the trial of the POWs in Bangladesh were moved almost at the same time. Although this affirmed in a way what Bhutto had earlier said that Pakistan would not grant recognition till the POWs trial was dropped but the fact that Bangladesh now really proceeded to make the law and hold the trial forced Bhutto to move faster towards the issue of recognition. This also perhaps quickened the solution of the other humanitarian problems on the basis of the offer made jointly by Bangladesh and India in April, 1973.

Delhi Agreement between India and Pakitsan

A series of discussions took place between India and Bangladesh since the reply of Pakistan arrived on the joint offer and Bangladesh was at least pursuaded to agree to authorise India to settle all the matters with Pakistan on its behalf with regard to the humanitarian aspect of the problem keeping the question of trial of 195 POWs open. Consequently, an Indian delegation went to Islamabad to resume the discussion in response to the Pakistan invitation and signed an agreement in Delhi later without the presence of Bangladesh[23]. Although the terms of the agreement were based on the joint offer made originally by India and Bangladesh Pakistan maintained that she had drawn the accord within the purview of Simla Agreement. Much to her humiliation Bangladesh had to remain content with the words of P. N. Haksar, the leader of the Indian delegation praising the "statesmanship" and the "great accomodation" shown by Sheikh Mujibur Rahman.

The two deligation of India and Pakistan first met from July 24 to 31 at Islamabad and finally at Delhi from August 18 to 28. Under agreement an arrangement for simultaneous repatriation of the POWs other than the 195 accused of charges by Bangladesh, the Bengalis in Pakistan and the Pakistanis in Bangladesh was to take place and details as to logistics etc. were worked out. The most important points however were : (1) Bangladesh was not a signatory to this agreement although it had its concurrence to it expressed through India and she had to carry out a lot of the obligations created under the agreement. In other words, Bangladesh was a party to the Agreement without being present or a signatory to it, (2) with regard to the Pakistanis in Bangladesh, the repatriation of the non-Bengalis who opted for Pakistan was not accepted by Pakistan as a legal obligation and Pakistan "guided by considerations of humanity" agreed to receive a substantial number of such non-Bengalis from Bangladesh,[24] (3) on completion of repatriation of the POWs, civilian internees in India, Bengalis in Pakistan and Pakistanis in Bangladesh as envisaged in the agreement or earlier Bangladesh, India and Pakistan would discuss and settle the question of the 195 POWs. It was however made clear that Bangladesh could participate in such a meeting only on the basis of sovereign equality. It is evident that for Bangladesh, besides the trial of 195 POWs another most important issue remained unresolved : the question of Pakistan accepting the non-Bengalis who owed allegiance to and opted for Pakistan. With the trial put on the shelve and the burden of feeding an uncertain number of non-Bengali Pakistanis, the only gain Bangladesh made was the repatriation of the Bengalis stranded in Pakistan. Accordingly, a massive 3-way repatriation programme started on September 19, 1973 which continued till April, 1974,

On the question of recognition Bhutto at last used his own choice of time. He was successful in making the issue of recognition the focal point and continued to threaten that China would again exercise her veto to block Bangladesh's admission to the United Nations[25]. When the date of the proposed Islamic Summit Conference to be held in Pakistan was getting closer new diplomatic moves were initiated to solve the crisis. Pressure was built up both within and outside the Conference to facilitate the attendence of Bangladesh the second largest Muslim country in the conference, which could not be attained without recognition of equal sovereignty between Bangladesh and Pakistan. On receiving and understanding that the proposed trial would be dropped, Bhutto posing to further the cause of Muslim solidarity declared his decision to accord recognition to Bangladesh on February 22, 1974. A goodwill mission of the Islamic Summit came to Dhaka with an invitation for Mujib and the next day an Algerian aircraft flew Mujib and his delegation on a historic flight to Lahore to be received by Bhutto at the airport to the annoyance of many Indians[26]. Mujib termed the recognition as a "triumph of truth" and Bangladesh entered into a new international role by attending the Islamic Summit.

Following the recognition and the Islamic Summit, the three countries now met at New Delhi in April, 1974[27]. to formally drop the proposed trial of 195 POWs in response to the appeal of the Pakistan Prime Minister to the people of Bangladesh to "forgive and forget the mistakes of the past" and the Bangladesh Prime Minister agreeing to that. According to a prior arrangement, in exchange of Pakistan government's request and condemnation of the crimes that might have been committed by its soldiers, the trial of the 195 POWs was at last dropped. On the question of the repatriation of the non-local Pakistanis, the Pakistan government insisted on treating them on humanitarian grounds rather than as a legal obligation. The Government of Pakistan agreed to take back without any limit three categories of those non-Bengalis who were (1) domiciled in former West Pakistan, (2) employees of the Central Government and/or their families and (3) members of the divided families.

The Pakistan government did not make any commitment for taking back the rest who did not fall within the above 3 categories only with the option of taking some on mercy as 'hardship cases'. So on this issue also the Bangladesh government received a raw deal in the light of its earlier stand[28]. The failure on the part of the Government to come to a clear agreement with Pakistan continued to have its effect in Bangladesh to this day also since the fate of these helpless people, nearly a quarter of a million who live in camps in utter poverty are still not known.

Apart from the success of being able to join the Islamic Summit and the new direction it introduced in the foreign policy of Bangladesh, the stand of the Awami Leage with regard to the POWs ended in a fiasco. In a case of not holding the trial, Bangladesh perhaps could get a much better deal and an enhanced prestige in the world community if she had directly negotiated with Pakistan from the beginning. While at the end, the world acclaimed the understanding reached between the two, the credit went to India, the total political gain to Bhutto of Pakistan and Bangladesh received only a pat in the back. The main reason however was that the Government had virtually no mobility in its foreign policy in the first two years of independence and it had to depend largely on India to determine its foreign policy. Joining the Islamic Summit was not only dramatic but was the beginning of a reduction of that dependence on India with far-reaching consequences.

More disappointing for the Awami League government was the veto exercised by the People's Republic of China in October, 1973 blocking the admission of Bangladesh to the United Nations. Although Bangladesh took her seat in the non-aligned Conference held at Algiers supported largely by the Indo-Soviet lobby, it could not take its legitimate seat in the United Nations. This stark reality of world politics led the Awami League leaders to realise that recognition of Pakistan was essential for them to reduce the possibility of a second rejection in 1974. The powerful Muslim countries like Turkey, Iran, Saudi Arabia were yet to recognise Bangladesh. The Awami League government's tilt towards the Soviet Union was not liked by the Chinese and its friendship with India led many Muslim countries to believe Bangladesh's subservience to a 'Hindu neighbour'. Although a section of the Awami League leaders was bitterly critical of the Chinese action, the vast majority could understand the solid reasons of China's backing Pakistan on the issue of the POWs.

Since the Delhi Agreement signed in August, 1973 the ruling party leaders did not make any more statements for the trial of the POWs for committing war crimes. The realities of world diplomacy and the strings in relationship with India brought a new experience for the rulers of Bangladesh. That strong and continued public statements and over-confident domestic postures in matters highly sensitive and complex in relations involving other countries could be counter-productive and in the long-run self-humiliating, was not now difficult to understand for the people of Bangladesh. What was considered to be a matter to 'laugh' at as Sheikh once said on Pakistan's recognition for Bangladesh and something to be taken for granted, became the most crucial issue in the relationship between Bangladesh and India. Bangladesh had to eat all her words mainly because she was not the master of her own affairs—it was India who played the most decisive role in this matter. The realities of the situation were such that on each point Bangladesh had to concede and accept a humiliating position.

Bhutto at last got away with what he wanted. He got back all the POWs, made Mujib attend the Islamic Conference at the displeasure of the Indians, accorded recognition to Bangladesh at his own time, had the trial postponed without compromising his position on the question for recognition and subsequently had the trial dropped in exchange of the recognition. Above all, he was able to avoid the responsibility of the non-Bengali Biharies who had opted for Pakistan. Although Bhutto at the initial stage appeared to be eager to get the POWs back which largely inspired him to go to Simla, later on he adopted a delaying tactics for political reasons. As against the stranded Bangalis in Pakistan, he raised the question of the collaborators Bangladesh government held in prisons and thereby rendered inspiration to those forces in Bangladesh who were opposed to the independence[29]. The retaining of the POWs in the Indian soil also helped him in maintaing the anti-Indian feeling within Pakistan and lastly it was used as an instrument to keep the Pakistan army constantly aware of their defeat and humiliation. This kept the Army demoralised and helped Bhutto in exercising his complete authority over an otherwise ambitious army and reorganise this mighty machine to suit his own political end.

FOOTNOTES

1. Upto June, 1973, 99 countries had accorded recognition to Bangladesh which meant that almost one-third of the countries had not yet accorded recognition.—Statement of Dr. Kamal Hossain in the Parliament, *The Bangladesh Observer*, 8.7.1973.
2. Pakistan's POWs in India : Col. S.P. Salunke, Vikas, New Delhi, p. 38.
3. Salmaan Taseer, *Bhutto : a Political Biography*, Ithaca Press, London, 1979, p. 142.
4. *Ibid.* p. 143.
5. See the Simla Agreement.
6. See *Interim Constitution of the Islamic Republic of Pakistan*, 15th April, 1972, Gazette of Pakistan, Extraordinary.
7. See Mujib's speech made at a public meeting at Pirozpur, Barisal, on 2.1.1973 and the series of public meetings he addressed during this time.
8. *The Bangladesh Observer*. Dhaka, 14.1.1973.
9. *The Bangladesh Observer*, Dhaka, 15.1.1973.
10. *The Bangladesh Observer*, Dhaka, 19.1.1973.
11. Col. S. P. Salunke, *Pakistani POWs in India*. p. 72 and 80. Break up of POWs : 73908 POWs—armed forces, para military forces and corps of the Merchant Navy, Civilians under protection 16413, Bangladeshis in Pakistan 3,00,000 Pakistanis in Bangladesh 2,80,000.
12. *The Bangladesh Observer*, Dhaka, 24.1.1973.
13. *The Bangladesh Observer*, Dhaka, 3.1.1973.
14. *The Bangladesh Observer*, Dhaka, 24.1.1973.

15. The Government of India however informed the International Court of Justice that the World Court had no jurisdiction and competence to adjudicate Pakistan's objection about India's handing over 195 prisoners of war to Bangladesh.
    The law for the trial of the POWs was passed in July, 1973. Sources close to the government disclosed that although it was difficult to collect evidence to prove cases against all the POWs, the government constituted a special cell for assisting and conducting the trial and sufficient evidential materials were collected against the 195 POWs who were being finally put to trial.
16. Bhutto in an interview with some American newsmen said, he would hold up the recognition of Bangladesh till the plan to try 195 POWs dropped.—*The Bangladesh Observer*, 6.7.1973.
17. It was first disclosed by the Indian Foreign Minister at New Delhi on January 21 that repatriation on POWs could be settled without recognition.
18. See the Indo-Bangladesh Settlement Offer to Pakistan April 16, 1973.
19. It showed a contradictory stand between India and Bangladesh. See *The Bangladesh Observer*, 23.1.1973 and the text of the Settlement offer April 16, 1973.
20. Bangladesh reaction to it was expressed by its Foreign Minister, Dr. Kamal Hossain as an "attempt to divert attention of the world and to shield those persons who committed the worst atrocities".—*The Bangladesh Observer*, 14.5.1973.
21. The Constitution (First Amendment) Act, 1973.
22. See International Crimes (Tribunals) Act, 1973.
23. Known as Delhi Agreement, August 28, 1973.
24. Primarily related to those popular known as 'Biharis'.
25. *The Bangladesh Observer*, 17.2.1974.
26. In Calcutta Indians burned the effigy of Sheikh Mujib for attending the Islamic Conference. On the same day Iran and Turkey also recognised Bangladesh.
27. See the text of the Tripartite Agreement between the three countries signed on April 9, 1974.
28. The Biharis stranded in Bangladesh were later deprived of their Pakistani citizenship by an ordinance of General Zia-ul-Huq in 1979.
29. Mujib released 30000 "collaborators" on the occasion of the 2nd anniversary of the Victory Day.

CHAPTER NINE

FOOD, FLOOD AND FAMINE

The worst crisis the Awami League government faced was food. On the supply, distribution and availability of food at a reasonable rate depended the political life of a government and it has always been considered as the barometer of political climate in the country. For decades, food has been scarce compared to the quantity required for the ever-growing population and so it has been and will continue to be the most important factor in politics of this country. The land-man ratio in Bangladesh is perhaps the lowest in the world and this makes the situation worse with a total cultivated area of only about 22.5 million acres for a population of 90 million. Rice being the principal foodgrain, on its production depends also the whole economy of the country. If the production of rice goes down, the deficit increases and with that the import of foodgrain costing a colossal amount of foreign exchange goes up. The effect is disastrous, the government has to cut down the development expenditure in other vital sectors in order to feed the people[1]. Even with a normal production yield foodgrains are imported every year and that also drains away a lot of resources. With the increase in population at the rate of about 3% per annum it has hardly been possible to reach the target of production since the independence[2]. As flood, drought and cyclone have been a common phenomenon of nature in Bangladesh, the production of rice remains unpredictable imposing an almost insurmountable constraint on the planners and politicians of the country to deal with it. In a year when there is a good crop, the face of the nation's economy changes and when it is bad, it bears a consequential effect in many other aspects of the economy.

When Bangladesh was a part of the colonial rule in Pakistan, the Bengali leaders had less to worry as it was the responsibility of the Central government to arrange the foodgrains and if there was any shortage or rise in price, they could put the entire blame on the rulers of the central government. During the great mass upsurge in 1968-69 and the election in 1970-71 when the Bengali nationalist movement was at its height, the Awami League cited the rising price of rice as one of the reasons why the 'Golden Bengal' was turned into a graveyard. They aroused public sentiment and gained support by pledging to bring down the price of rice to Tk. 20/- a maund from an average of Tk. 48/- in 1970-71[3]. With the emergence of Bangladesh the responsibility of managing its own people fell for the first time on Bengalis themselves and soon for the common reasons of population growth and natural calamities the leaders were faced with the realities of the new situation.

Deficit in the food production had been an age-old phenomenon. The country was hit by floods in 1968, 1969 and 1970 affecting 14400, 16000 and 16400 square miles of areas respectively with huge loss of human lives, homesteads and 2.2 million tons of paddy[4]. In addition to this, in November, 1970 the worst cyclone of the century hit the country causing a collosal damage to men and property with an unofficial estimate of 1 million people dead[5]. Consequently, combined, with the increase in population, the deficit of ½ million tons in 1950, increased to 1.5 million tons in late 1960s[6]. In 1971 when the war was on, another flood affected 14000 square miles with a loss of crop placed at over 300000 tons and in the same year the domestic availability of rice declined by 11 per cent[7].

Bangladesh was, therefore, born with a huge deficit in food and a history of government's handling the situation on a year to year basis in the past. During the 1971 war experts had already made forecast that Bangladesh would face a serious food crisis leading to a probable famine if adequate safeguards were not taken well in advance[8]. With the economy already shattered by the 9-month long war, it was not an unexpected fear that the country would plunge into a serious state of food shortage.

In 1971-72 the production fell by 2 million tons as against 1969-70 and in 1972-73 production was 25% below the projected target of 13 million tons necessitating an import of about 2.7 million tons although the per capita consumption was much less than the 1969-70 level[9]. In 1973-74 the original plan target was 12.05 million tons but the production was 11.83 million tons which was however slightly higher than the figure revised later on[10] (the revised estimate was 11.8 million tons). With the revision of the target however the import requirements were raised to 2.2 million tons. In 1974-75 the plan target was estimated at 13.22 million tons whereas the actual production was 11.23 million tons and the per capita consumption of foodgrains in 1974-75 was about 339 lb. the lowest in recent memory.

So the country was faced with an acute shortage of foodgrains requiring huge quantity in imports and diverting a substantial amount of resources from other major development sectors. It is true that the government was not favoured by nature which was largely responsible for the shortfall in food production. In 1972 there was a severe drought affecting the monsoon crop (*Aus*) and in December, 1973 the country was hit by a cyclone affecting 3 coastal districts of Barisal, Patuakhali and Khulna causing an estimated damage of Tk. 951 million[11]. In 1974 the country experienced two floods, one early flash flood in Sylhet and the other devastating country-wide flood in July-August considered to be the worst in the country's history. In the flash flood the entire *Boro* crop was destroyed, the total loss of which was estimated 149,695 tons. The *Beel* and *Haor* areas of the district where *Boro* is the only crop cultivated in the year suffered almost a total loss of crop[12]. In the mid-year flood excepting the District of Jessore the whole country was affected inundating an area of over 2000 square miles, more than one third of the country affecting nearly 30 million people and damaging crops over about 10 million acres of land[13] besides loss of human lives, cattle heads and homesteads.

While the threat of an imminent famine was existing at the brith of the country, the most crucial period was considered to be from January, 1973 to June, 1974 before the devastating floods occured. Experts and politicians were already warning the government about this threat. In 1972 the massive inflow of foreign assistance worth over a billion dollar for relief and rehabilitation saved the situation to a great extent although the level of consumption went down considerably. When the year of 1973 began, with such a difficult crisis, the government took the matter in routine fashion. When Moulana Bhashani in a desperate attempt tried to alarm the government of the urgency of the matter the cabinet discussed the "ways and means to make the country self-sufficient in food as soon as possible". When Kurt Waldheim in May, 1973 gave a call to the member nations of the United Nations for assistance to Bangladesh he warned that unless a serious food gap was met in 1973 before the autumn harvest, starvation in the country could not be avoided, although the Bangladesh leaders expressed satisfaction over the supply situation and on the movement of foodgrains from Chittagong to other districts[14].

Almost all the political parties warned the government during that time and all of them alleged that huge quantities of foodgrains were being smuggled across the border to India where rice price was much higher. The newspaper columns were full of stories of such smuggling. In the face of such criticism and having failed to check smuggling the government was forced to call in the Army to stop the smuggling. But this was resented by the members of the ruling party or their proteges themselves who were allegedly involved in many such smuggling operations. Although Mujib expressed satisfaction at the wonderful work done by the Army in stopping smuggling at the border,[15] the Army was eventually withdrawn before they could complete the work due to the pressure from within the party "on the ground that the Army was harassing people unnecessarily"[16].

In order to "relieve the suffering of the hungry people of the country", Moulana Bhashani resorted to a hunger strike with a pledge to 'fast to death' if the government did not take immediate steps to mitigate the situation. The Moulana warned, "never in the past came such a severe famine". In a statement issued on the 5th day of his fasting the Moulana claimed that

"86% of the peasants, workers, primary school teachers, fishermen, boatmen, blacksmiths, artisans and other poor people of the village did not have a full meal of rice in the last two months due to scarcity of rice or due to smuggling of rice across the border". Similar voices were raised by various political groups, members of the intelligentsia and newspapermen in their columns and editorials.

So it is not that the government was not warned about it in advance or that the government was not aware of such an acute problem in the supply and distribution of foodgrains. When the food procurement policy was announced on 3rd November, 1973 by the government, the Food Minister announed the decision of the Government to form people's committees consisting of representatives of the political parties with the members of parliament of the respective areas as advisers[17]. The Gano Oykka Jote, consisting of the three "patriotic political parties" of the country, the Awami League, NAP (M) and the Communist Party of Bangladesh of Moni Singh expressed their willingness to assist the government in checking border smuggling. Earlier the Prime Minister instructed to form Jatiyo Pratirakkha Committee (National Defence Committee) also. But as none of these produced any tangible result towards the end of 1973 the Army was again called in to intensify the anti-smuggling steps but the result was the same. They were to be withdrawn at the end for the same good reasons.

Despite the cyclone hitting 3 coastal districts in December, 1973 and the flash flood in Sylhet in April, 1974 the food production in 1s973-74 was slighty higher than the revised estimate of 11.8 million tons and ro the crop was not considered to be a total failure. And yet the procu ement drive was a total failure. Not even 10% of the target was procured largely due to the price differential between the market price and the government's procurement price. As people could not be mobilised, corruption was rampant in the procurement mechanism which in turn allowed the existing market mechanism to prevail[18]. While the government in the annual plan of 1973-74 reduced the target of food production, it increased the import requirement to 2.20 million tons. But the government failed to procure the required quantity as a result of which the actual import of foodgrains fell short by nearly half a million tons. This failure both in internal and external procurement had a devastating effect in the stock position, ultimately leading to the great crisis in mid-74 and after[19].

So the target requirement of foodgrains was not in hand and consequently the procurement having failed combined with the government's inability to check smuggling, the minimum stock the Food department was supposed to maintain drained away in meeting the day to day needs, result ing in a miserable stock position in the country by June, 1974. When the projected imports did not arrive on time the stock went further down in the crucial months of August, September and October.

With the shortage of foodgrains the prices of the essential commodities on the one hand were running upwards very fast and on the other-hand, the purchasing capacity of the common man was rapidly shrinking. With the rate of consumption lowest in decades the physical resistance capacity of the poor people had progressively declined. While the real income of the people went down in terms of salary and wages and the price of the essential commodities was shooting high, the suffering of the people only increased further. A maund of rice of medium quality which had cost 57.10 in 1971-72 now rose to Taka 244.40 in 1974-75. Masur pulse from 1.62 to 4.75 per seer, good fish from 4.19 per seer to 11.72 per seer, beef from 3.27 to 10.85, potato from .95 to 2.62, mustard oil from 6.87 to 31.17, chillies from 5.23 to 46.66, onion 0.78 to 2.57, salt 0.47 to 3.83, sugar 2.13 to 5.82, firewood 5.11 to 14.74 and kerosene 0.83 to 1.79 for 22 ounces[20]. Prices of almost all the commodities increased from 300 to 400% and in 1974 prices of all commodities increased almost 100% over the previous year. In some areas, rice was being sold at Tk. 10 per seer and dry chillies at Tk. 100 per seer and baby food at Tk. 80 to 90 per pound (milk powder). From September, 1973 onward prices were going higher at a much accelerated rate and from mid-1974 prices were going up almost everyday. A seer of coarse rice which was costing Tk. 3.90 in June was costing Tk. 4.87 in August, Tk. 6 in September and Tk. 7.16 in October.

So by the time the year 1974 began the people had already started eating "famine food". For lack of food people had already started starving particularly in those districts which were traditionally food-deficit areas and known to be famine prone like Rangpur and Mymensingh. As there was no employment and with no purchasing power amongst the poor, people started moving towards the town. When all this were happening, opposition politicians and newspapers raised alarm but the government claimed that the administration was in full command of the situation. When in March widespread starvation started in Rangpur,[21] the Food Minister assured the nation that the rising price of rice was only temporary and the government had sufficient stock in its depots. The government leaders blamed the traders, hoarders, smugglers and black marketeers for the "artificial rise in prices" and held the "anti-social" and "anti-state" elements responsible for creating such a situation. In April, although the Food Minister assured that every month 2,00,000 tons of foodgrains were being imported such quantity never arrived[22]. With the government stock position sinking far below the required minimum level, distribution of foodgrains through modified rationing system in many districts was drastically reduced[23].

It would be evident that the causes of the famine that stuck Bangladesh occured much before the flood. Although the famine took its major toll in September-October as soon as the flood water started receding, the flood itself was not the main cause of the death of people. The flood only hit the last blow by disrupting communications, washing away homesteads. spreading epidemics and increasing the miseries of the people who were already dying. From the beginning of the year a large number of poor people had started eating sweet potatoes. Kachu (Arunes), Kalar thor,[24] rice husk, rice water and all sorts of leaves. As famine is a result of a process of hunger, it started since the war broke out in 1971. A large section of people had less to eat and the consumption became lesser and lesser and ultimately they died on the soil of Shonar Bangla.

All the arguments which were forwarded to defend mass starvation and death in 1974 and after by the Awami League government, the Planning Commission and other agencies were not totally unfounded but death due to famine in the late 20th century could hardly be justified. It is true that Bangladesh met some of the worst natural calamities from 1968 to 1974, each year there was either cyclone of the worst kind or drought or floods. Then there was the nine-month long war and the consequent dislocation, world food shortage, phenomenal inflation and rise in import prices. But these alone were not responsible for the famine that took so many lives in Bangladesh[25]. Many economists, politicians, newspapers and members of the intelligentsia asserted that the famine was a man-made one and even if the flood had not occured, the people would have died. It was not only the incompetence, mismanagement or corruption of the government and the ruling elite but their carelessness and indifference which were equally responsible for such a catastrophe. It was alleged that large scale smuggling of foodgrains was one of the major causes which precipitated the process of famine.

In this modern world no matter how poor a country is or what ever natural calamity it faces, famine can always be avoided if (1) there is an advance warning and (2) the people in charge of the government of the particular country are competent enough to arrange the logistics. So, advance warning and arrangement of logistics are the two vitally important factors in combating famine in areas where such situation might occur. In Bangladesh, we will see that the government had a very early warning of such a possibility. Soon after the independence the political leaders, the Planning Commission, the Food Ministry and all other agencies of the government were well aware of the existing and the impending food shortage. Not only did they fail in procuring food grains from within and outside, they had no logistical plans for supply and distribution. The government was callous and indifferent, allowed large-scale smuggling and hoarding to go unchecked and depended heavily on foreign assistance. They took foreign assistance or commitment for food aid for granted and did not pursue a vigorous policy to actually procure them. They lacked the seriousness in mobilising the procurement internally and failed to adopt the mechanism required to mobilise the external procurement[26]. Heavy dependence on those countries which were otherwise under constant attack from the ruling leaders and who did not appreciate the domestic policies adopted by the government was also another reason why those countries themselves showed less seriousness and concern in meeting the food gap in Bangladesh. Corruption in gruel kitchens,[27] mishandling the distribution of food and relief materials, protection of hoarders, smugglers and blackmarketeers by the Awami League leaders and workers at different levels were the other causes why the number of deaths could not be minimised. The government's anti-hoarding measures taken in October, 1974 was too late to produce any worthwhile result[28].

By the end of November, the government decided to close down most of the gruel kitchens, although people still died thereafter. With the harvest season approaching and imports arriving, the situation tended to improve but the impact of the famine was phenomenal in the social and political context of the new country.

FOOTNOTES

1. In every year when the harvest is good, the strain on the economy has been less and progress of development work is better. There were good harvests in 1975 and 1980 and bad ones in 1972, 1973, 1974 and 1979. The economic review of these years will show what serious effects these had on the economy of the country.
2. In 1971 production was 1 million ton less than 1969-70. In 1972-73 the production was 25% less than the target fixed to achieve the 1969-70 level.
3. Imports in 1972-73 was about 2.7 million. *Statistical Year Book of Bangladesh*, 1979, p. 374. See also the Awami League election Poster published in 1970-71 election period.
4. Mohiuddin Alamgir, *Famine in South Asia*. Oelgeschlagew. Guan & Hani, Publishing Ltd. Cambridge, Massachusetts, p. 112.
5. Mohiuddin Alamgir, *Ibid*. 1 p. 114. Official figure was placed at 2,00,000.
6. Nurul Islam, *Development Strategy of Bangladesh*. p. 3.
7. Mohiuddin Alamgir. *Ibid*., p. 117. As the population to be fed was 14% lower because of their dislocation and taking refuge in India due to the war in 1971, the deficit did not make much difference and the price more or less remained the same.
8. Based on a position paper prepared by the Research Cell of the External Publicity Division of the Ministry of Foreign Affairs in which the cabinet Ministers were warned about the imminent food crisis once the refugees returned.
9. Nurul Islam, *Development Planning in Bangladesh*, p. 133. The per capita consumption of rice as shown for 1972-73 was 12.91 per day compared to 1969-70 as 15.41 per day. *First Five Year Plan*, 1973-78, Bangladesh Planning Commission, p. 21.
10. Nurul Islam, *Ibid*, p. 134.
11. Mohiuddin Alamgir, *Famine in South Asia, op. cit.*, p. 112.
12. *Ibid*, p. 122.
13. *Ibid*, p. 125.
14. The Government in March, 1972 reduced the quota of rice to 4/1 seer i. e. 12 chattacks and increased wheat to 2 4/1 sheers per adult—keeping the total quota of 3 seers same as before under the rationing system.
15. Report on a cabinet meeting held on 9.5. 1973. See *The Bangladesh Observer*, 10.5.1973.
16. *The Bangladesh Observer*, 10.5.1973.
17. This was the first and only time that the Awami League involved some political parties in food matter when the government announced constitution of People's Committee for

procurement of rice and paddy for the Aman season at every sub-divisional level. But the exercise did not work ultimately because of market economy and the price difference between what the government offered and the prevailing market price.—*The Bangladesh Observer*, 4.11.1973.

18. In 1973-74 the average procurement price of rice was 72.63 taka per maund whereas the average market price of a maund of rice in the year was Tk. 120.40. *Statistical Year Book of Bangladesh*, 1979, p. 372, 378.
19. In 1972 the deficit was 30 lakh tons but the government procured 2.56 tons.
    In 1973 the deficit was 2.5 million but the government procured 2.1 million tons.
    In 1974 the total deficit was 2.9 million tons out of which 1.2 was due to flood. The orginal deficit was estimated at 1.7 million tons.—*The Bangladesh Observer*, 23.11.1974.
20. *Statistical Year Book*, Government of Bangladesh, p.372.
21. *Economic Review*, 1974-75, p. 24. In Kurigram sub-division of Rangpur District where famine took the severest form, price of a maund of rice rose from Tk. 105-110 in January to Tk. 270-290 in October, 1974.—From a report of Mr. Ali Akbar under the title *Famine in Kurigram.*
22. The import figures between November, 1973 and June, 1974, showed that only in May 2,00,000 tons of food import arrived.
23. Mohiuddin Alamgir, *Famine in South Asia, op. cit.*, p. 121.
24. Softer portion found inside a banana tree.
25. The official estimate was 27500 declared in the Parliament but the unofficial estimate exceeds 100000. See also the statement made by the Food Minister in the Parliament on 22.11.74. *The Bangladesh Observer*, 23.11.74.
26. In 1979 when Bangladesh had experienced the worst drought of its history. Ziaur Rahman as President supervised the crisis himself and was able to avert an impending famine by importing about 2.8 million tons of foodgrains on emergency basis. President Zia proved that famine can be averted now-a-days if a government takes early warnings seriously and moves fast to mobilise the logistics.
27. In all 5862 gruel kitchens were opened.—*The Bangladesh Observer*, 23.11.74.
28. *The Bangladesh Observer*, 6.10.74.

CHAPTER TEN

ROLE OF THE POLITICAL PARTIES AND THE THREE-PARTY ALLIANCE

Following independence the country went under the complete control of the Awami League. There was no opposition as such excepting Moulana's occasional statements sometimes favouring Mujib[1] and sometimes opposing the government. There were two other parties, the National Awami Party (Muzaffar) and the Communist Party of Bangladesh. The extreme right-wing elements were in hiding and the leftist revolutionaries went for underground operations mainly because of their divided role based on ideologies developed during the war. The NAP (M) and the CPB were directly supporting the government and along with the Awami League they constituted the only three "patriotic" political parties in the country.

But, within the Awami League, particularly in the younger section and among those who took active part in the war, a different current was flowing. Disappointed with the performance of the Awami League and Mujibs' failure to rise to the nationalist aspirations culminated through an armed struggle, this section was already exploring the alternatives to vindicate their ideals and political hopes. This current was however not a new phenomenon. Although the Awami League was a middle-of-the road bourgeois political party drawing its strength initially from the middle class and Bengali business community, in its course of development its mass-base had spread. Being disappointed with other left political parties many radical nationalist youths joined the Awami League rank and file and created a new wave within the party. As long back as 1962 when the Students' League gained the leadership in the year-long students' movement against Ayub's new constitution and the Report of the Education Commission, a small group under the leadership of Serajul Alam Khan, the General Secretary of the Students' wing set this current of radical thinking within the party. Most of the leaders of the Awami League being in prison or in hiding, the students were dominating the political scene and this continued till 1971. When the left started supporting Ayub Khan for the latter's China policy, the nationalist movement was taken over by the Awami League and consequenly its support-base spread horizontally over the industrial workers and lower middle class urban and rural communities. By 1968-69, with the infusion of young people from such background, the Awami League had in itself considerable infiltration of nationalist elements with radical thinking. As the autonomy movement was gaining further momentum due to the socio-economic pressure of the masses, the youths adopted a more radical approach to realise their nationalist aspirations. Eventually these radical forces within the Awami League gained political control of the 1968-69 mass movement and maintained the same all through 1970-71[2]. Since the time Mujib was released in February, 1969 from military custody and until he was arrested in March, 1971 these youths played the most dominant role and Mujib led the people being under their constant pressure and influence.

The influence of this group also led the Awami League to shift from a 'welfare state' idea to a concept of 'socialist economic order'. The youths who were the vanguards of the Awami League argued in both open and secret meetings held in 1969-70 that bourgeois democracy was not the answer for the economic emancipation of the poor people of Bangladesh ; socialism was the only way to establish economic freedom. In 1970 in a special meeting of the Students' League a resolution was passed for forcing the party to proceed towards a scientific socialist revolution in order to produce a 'society free from exploitation'. The group was consolidating its ranks to launch a movement for an independent socialist country and according to them independence was not possible to achieve without an armed struggle which would in the process create opportunities to build up socialist cadres. Within the younger section, particularly in the Students' League, however, a moderate group also existed. This group kept itself in line with Mujib without adopting an independent course of thinking. The former group being militant and larger in number played the dominant role all through and had more influence over Mujib than the other[3]. Unlike some of the left ideological parties, this group held that national independence and social revolution were not contradictory, but complimentary to each other. They felt that it was not possible to establish socialism all over Pakistan at a time through a political movement because of its peculiar socio-economic and geo-political structure. Any attempt to divert the movement for establishing socialism all over Pakistan at this stage would cause a great set back to the nationalist movement in East Pakistan which had already gained a national consensus. This would mean that the exploitation of East Pakistan by the existing ruling class would continue for an indefinite period. So this young section wanted to advance the cause of revolution first through the nationalist movement for independence in East Pakistan. They did not want to make the mistake made by the Communist Party of India in 1940s which opposed the Indian National Independence Movement led by the Congress and the Muslim League.

Soon after independence the group gained command of the party but faced with the realities of power, Mujib's long submerged contradictions came to the surface. It was not possible for Mujib to go all the way for a 'scientific socialist revolution'[4]. The factionalism within the party and particularly within the Students' League took a deep and bitter turn. The moderate group led by Sheikh Fazlul Huq Moni, Abdur Razzak and Tofael Ahmed came close to Sheikh Mujib and started propagating "Mujibbad" as opposed to 'scientific socialist revolution'[5]. They were willing to accept a kind of democratic socialism but not the revolution. When the militants wanted Mujib to form a national revolutionary government and to go for radical socialist reforms, Mujib could only go upto nationalisation of industries and not beyond[6]. And thus the militants' attempt to advance the cause of 'revolution' by cashing in on the popularity of Sheikh Mujib failed[7]. As a result, the party moved for a split and the first crack came within the Students' League. In a bitter fight within the Students' wing, the militants got the majority and in April, 1972 two separate conferences of the Students' League were held. Out of the two groups Mujib opted for the group led by his nephew Sheikh Moni,[8] the more blunt and ruthless of all his proteges, in a struggle to uphold 'Mujibbad'. In the following month the peasants' wing of the party, Jatiyo Krishak League was broken into two and the next month in June the workers front Jatiyo Sramik League had also split. This process ultimately ended up in the formation of a new political party called the Jatiyo Samajtantrik Dal (National Socialist Party) with the announcement of a 7-member Convening Committee in October, 1972.

The emergence of the JSD from within the roots of the Awami League created a new volatile situation. A vast majority of the younger elements in the party broke away and in the absence of any substantial political opposition from the existing parties, the birth of this party caused a tremendous impact. It changed the existing political dimensions and with the economy sliding down and law and order situation fast deteriorating, the Jatiyo Samajtantrik Dal quickly emerged as a strong political party vindicating people's grievances against the Awami League government. Soon it started drawing crowds in its public meetings. The workers and supporters of the banned right wing parties attended their meetings to enlarge the crowd. Further, because of the Awami League's highhandedness in treating those who did not cross the border and claiming only three political parties[9] to be 'patriotic', the tacit support of a large section of the people who did not cross the border leaned towards the opposition and the JSD cashed in on that sentiment. Moreover, the JSD could not be called a non-patriotic party as most of their rank and file took part in the war. With its commitment to strive for a scientific socialist revolution led by front runner freedom fighters like Abu Taher, Serajul Alam Khan and others it also drew the support of many left wing workers spread all over the country. Before the first year was over, the JSD therefore, emerged as the single largest opposition party in the country.

Inspired by the thoughts of social justice and revolution, a few other groups armed with weapons also emerged. The Huq group of the Communist

Party gathered more arms and continued with their underground operations vigorously. In Rajshahi and Pabna area Matin, Tipu Biswas and Wahidur Rahman entered into direct confrontation with the government forces. But the most important and effective of all was the emergence of Purba Banglar Sharbohara Party[10] led by a brilliant engineer named Siraj Shikder. It started with a group of educated and highly motivated workers who gathered arms and received doctrinaire training during the war. The party was able to spread its roots fast among the freedom fighters and gained quick recruits from among those who were already operating from underground belonging to the various factions of the communist movement. Soon the Sharbohara Party developed into a very strong underground organisation with a more definite political programme[11]. Among the existing frontal parties although the NAP (B) was at a cross-road the Moulana did not sit idle. He continued to play his role in his own characteristic manner[12].

Within less than a year after the elections, the symptoms of an increasing opposition to the government were seen all over. Although the opposition parties lacked cohesion and they could not evolve any positive programme, the public dissatisfaction over the performance of the government was no doubt intensifying rapidly. The first recorded manifestation of their dissatisfaction was noticed at the local council election held in December, 1973. Although as a part of tradition, political parties did not directly come into the election campaign or officially nominated any person as their candidate, in the actual campaign support of a political party to a particular candidate at the local level or the candidate's bias to a particular political party played a significant role in the outcome. Despite the dominating role of the Awami League and the Government functioneries working in favour of the pro-establishment-forces, the local council elections in 1973 turned out a large number of representatives holding views opposed to the government[13].

So the public opposition to the government was taking different forms and the result of the union council election was a pointer to the opposition parties who were engaged in taking advantage of the situation. They were holding public meetings, processions and demonstrations raising popular slogans on price rise, food, corruption and mismanagement. In April, 1974 for the first time the Awami League government had to apply section 144 of the Criminal Procedure Code in Dhaka to prevent assembly of more than 4 persons and to ban processions, demonstrations and public meetings. This action was considered a 'defeat' for the government which claimed to be popular and democratic and was bitterly criticised by the opposition leaders. Inside the Parliament Ataur Rahman Khan termed the application of 144 as undemocratic and reminded the government that the Awami League was chosing a path which they had condemned for 25 years and he warned that their action of imposing 144 would be the beginning of the downfall of the government[14].

Role of JSD : the *Gherao* Movement

During this period both the NAP led by the Moulana and the JSD intensified their activities but the latter having a large following of younger radical elements emerged as a potential threat to the government. With largely attended public meetings in their favour all over the country, JSD was being considered as the largest opposition political party. On 17th March, the birth day of Sheikh Mujibur Rahman, after holding a largely attended public meeting, JSD went for a direct confrontation with the government. In the meeting they adopted a drastic programme of *gherao* against "the agents of exploiters in order to bring an end to the anarchy and repression of the government"[15]. This programme of "direct action" which was began at Dhaka included *gherao* of the Chairman of the Red Cross, Chairman of the Mahalla Relief Committees, illegal occupants of cars, houses, land and factories, the State Trading Corporation, fake licence holders, government import-export office, Freedom Fighters' Welfare Trust, Agricultural Development Corporation, Central Jail, the Secretariat, Planning Commission, offices and residence of Ministers, Deputy Ministers and Members of Parliament, Radio, Television and government owned newspapers and offices of the Rakkhi Bahini and all government and semi-government offices[16].

The JSD decided to launch their movement by first staging a *gherao* of the residence of the Home Minister at Minto Road the same day. A large procession led by the President and General Secretary of the JSD marched from the Paltan meeting to the home of the Minister to submit a Memorandum of Redemption. When they gheraoed the residence of the Home Minister, brick batting started between the processionists and the police on duty and at the end the Rakkhi Bahini was called in to resolve the matter by shooting with firearms. Although it was alleged that shooting took place from both sides, the demonstrators paid the toll. Although the official figure was six but more than a dozen people who took part in the *gherao* were killed, about a hundred injured with over 20 arrested on the spot which included both Jalil and Rab, the President and General Secretary respectively of the party.

The next day the Awami League took further revenge by staging a counter-attack on the JSD. While the government termed the JSD as anti-state political party involved in "destructive activities", the Awami League called them Sino-American agents engaged in undoing the rule of law and indulging in conspiracy to destroy the socialist programmes of the government. Branding them as enemies of independence, socialism and progress, the Awami League organised a procession in Dhaka that morning armed with all sorts of sticks demanding the punishment of the JSD followers and burned down the JSD central office situated at the Bangabandhu Avenue. The Rakkhi Bahini took over the party's newspaper (*Ganakantha*) office and seized all papers and materials in the middle of the night and its editor, Al-Mahmud was taken to prison.

In protest of the killings and attack on the JSD office, almost all political leaders and organisations condemned the government action. The government retaliated by imposing section 144 in almost all the districts and subdivisional towns and by throwing hundreds of JSD workers into prison the following day. As a result, with a large number of JSD leaders and workers in jail and the subsequent action by the Awami League on JSD launched in the name of a 'resistence movement', the party was demoralised. Once this upsurge subsided, the government moved quite mercilessly against the JSD and an organised mechanism of repression was put in motion against them, Besides the JSD, the underground marxist parties also intensified their activities. The Sharbohara Party led by Siraj Shikder, the different factions of the communist groups led by Toaha, Abdul Huq, Matin, Tipu Biswas, Wahidur Rahman and others in different areas of the country became more active. The massive attack on JSD led many of its young cadres to go underground resulting in the formation of more armed groups to join the political current of the country.

Role of the NAP (B) and Opposition Unity

Initiative was also taken to forge unity amongst some of the political parties from time to time. Prior to the election, Moulana Bhashani submitted a 15-point charter as a leader of the Action Committee comprising seven political parties but the Committee did not last long. As soon as the election neared, they fought over allocation of seats and finally broke up. In early 1974, Moulana formed a new political party called Hukumate Rabbania[17] of which he became the President. Almost simultaneously and after a series of discussions and negotiations, six political parties formd an "All Party United Front," comprising the National Awami Party (Bhashani), Bangladesh Jatiyo League, Jatiyo Ganamukti Union, Bangladesh Jatio League of Oali Ahad, Bangladesh Communist Party (Leninist) and the Bangladesh Sramik Krishok Shamyabadi Dal. The Front at its first public meeting held at Dhaka formulated a Four-Point demand which included release of all political detenues, restoration of peace and security of life, arrest of price spiral and full rationing in the village, confiscation of all illegally acquired property and scrapping of unequal treaties meaning the Friendship Treaty with India. Although the Moulana, while presenting the demand warned the government that he would launch a movement if the demands were not met within 7 days, the unity of the Front also did not last long. The Front failed to create any mass-based support and it never presented any positive programmes of its own. At a later stage Ataur Rahman Khan took the initiative to form a broad-based organisation and convened a national conference of "Democratic Forces" but before his efforts could produce any result, a state of emergency was proclaimed by the government and soon after that the Fourth Amendment was introduced to establish a one-party system in the country. As a result the proposed national convention could not be held.

So, although the public sentiment against the government was buliding up steadily, the opposition political parties were not able to consolidate their position. They were faction-ridden and disorganised and had nothing attractive to offer in terms of any positive programme. In the face of the Awami League's massive organisational machinery reaching down to the grass-root level, the opposition parties though many in number, were mainly city-based and had little support-base in the rural areas. Excepting JSD and the NAP and some individuals like Moulana Bhashani and Ataur Rahman Khan, the others were too insignificant in their role to determine the course of events. With relief committees in hand, the Awami League could provide substantial material support to all its workers in the villages and with licences, permits, abandoned properties and industries in control, they were able to build up a strong financial base for the party. Against the support of the Rakkhi Bahini, the opposition parties were no match for the Awami League as a political force. With the Lal Bahini and the Shechha Shevak Bahini on its wings, it still continued to be the largest political party in the country. Popularity and *modus operandi* notwithstanding, it was not difficult for the Awami League to take the upper hand at any time the situation so demanded.

The opposition had no alternative leadership to offer either. As far as the Moulana was concerned, his style of politics was different. He never contemplated to be a ruler in the country. The JSD leaders were young and required experience and maturity in order to enjoy respect of people. The other individual leaders without solid political parties to back them could not be considered as alternatives to take over power. The popularity of the Awami League might have declined but in the face of Mujib's towering stature which was Awami League's greatest asset during that period, the opposition leaders could only make limited headway.

Moreover, the NAP for a long time was singularly dominated by Moulana who always had his own way of doing politics. With a large mass-support in the rural areas based on his personal image, the role of Moulana was not always consistent. Being dissatisfied with the factionalism within his own party Moulana would sometime go on retiring from politics and live in remote rural areas for weeks. After Bangladesh was born, he had once announced his retirement from politics but soon joined again. Although on all basic issues Moulana would take a stand and advance the cause of the masses but he failed to sustain the same because of strifes within the party and weak organisational framework. All these factors made Moulana appear to be erratic on some occasions. His blending of socialism with Islam, slogan of greater Bengal, formation of Hukumate Rabbania and such views and ideas[18] without adequate elaboration or theoretical formulation tended to confuse his followers and the people at times.

On the other hand, Moulana's stand on India's exploitation of Bangladesh resources, cancellation of Friendship Treaty, return of arms, ammunition and capital goods taken by the Indian Army, smuggling and famine was extremely forceful and unequivocal both in content and substance. But again Moulana's relationship with Mujib and his affection for the latter played an important role too. Mujib used to maintain a constant touch with Bhashani which afterwards gave the impression of the Moulana adopting a compromising tendency. During the 1973 election and after, on many occasions there was tacit understanding between the two on national issues, one exerting pressure on the other. When the Islamic Summit was about to be held at Lahore in 1974 Moulana took personal initiative in seeing that Bangladesh could attend and he advised Mujib to go to Lahore. In other words, Moulana kept on supporting Mujib on the question of the 4 state principles Mujib had enshrined in the Constitution. As Moulana was suspicious about JSD's theoretical and political foundation, he kept on leaning towards Mujib. On the other hand, the sudden rise of JSD in opposition to the Awami League government kept the leadership in their hands and they would not allow Moulana to take the leadership over them. Besides many others, these were the main reasons why JSD and the NAP, the two major parties of that period could not forge unity to launch a common movement against the government.

The Committee for Civil Liberties and Legal Aid

In the vacuum of opposition politics and leadership, a cross-section of the intelligentsia played an important role by forming an organisation called the Committee for Civil Liberties and Legal Aid in March, 1974. It was a politically motivated forum created to raise voice against violation of civil liberties particularly in respect of political dissidents and members of the opposition. In their first meeting held at the National Press Club, attended by a cross-section of teachers, engineers, doctors, writers, poets, lawyers, journalists and others they demanded (1) withdrawl of laws not consistent with the constitution and termination of attack on fundamental rights by the various government forces and administrative machineries ; (2) immediate repeal of the undemocratic Special Powers Act ; (3) the repeal of the Rakkhi Bahini Act and withdrawal of the troops who were all engaged in brutal activities ; (4) release of all political prisoners detained in different jails of the country and (5) restoration of freedom of press and release of all newspaper workers including Al-Mahmud, editor of the daily *Ganakantha* and withdrawal of warrants against those wanted by the government for political reasons[19].

When the famine was on, the political resistance subsided since the people were too hungry to resist anything. The opposition political parties were as helpless as the party in power. Even the number of public meetings and demonstrations went down considerably during these months as the people were horrified at seeing the starving people dying on the streets. With the floods and starvation all around, the opposition political parties behaved like silent spectators and due to resource and organisational constraints they could hardly come to mitigate the miseries of the people. The Committee however organised a public meeting at Baitul Mukarram to express its solidarity with the suffering people and held the Awami League leaders responsible for such a man-made catastrophe. Once the main thrust of the famine was over, the opposition parties intensified their efforts and organised huge mass rallies criticising the incompetence of the government. They held smuggling and corruption to be responsible for the famine.

Despite the organisational superiority with the government machineries in hand, the Awami League proved to be weak as a political party in the face of so many challenges and particularly in implementing its programme of socialist transformation. In the face of the gigantic problems faced by the country following independence, the party having no ideological cadre was shaky and lacked confidence. Despite claiming the support of the entire population, the party leadership was jittery and intolerant of any criticism right from the beginning. With the independence won through an 'armed struggle' supported by the overwhelming majority of the people, the Awami League was still not sure about its actual position. So consequently, Sheikh Mujib and other leaders maintaind a common theme in their speeches growing out of a sense of insecurity which led them to continue with a negative approach all through[20]. They had found nothing better than narrating the atrocities of the Pakistan Army and the loss and damage suffered by the people and they would talk about the conspiracies afoot to end Bangladesh without explaining who they were and what action the government had taken against such conspirators. The speeches mainly contained sermons, advises, orders, threats and warnings without offering any new sense of direction or a guideline to the people needed to build a new society.

Three-Party Alliance

Because of its inherent weaknesses and lack of political perception, the Awami League succumbed to the theory initiated by the NAP (M) elements that there were only three "patriotic political parties" in the country—the Awami League, the NAP and the Communist Party of Bangladesh. The alliance of the trio had a long history originating in the student organs of the respective parties through the great mass movement in 1969-70 and since then the NAP and CPB did not leave the Awami League despite occasional jolts, abuses and humiliation. The CPB's link with the Communist Party of India (CPI) and their fraternity with the Kremlin was well known. On a simplistic plane the Moscow brand political parties in Bangladesh was following identical strategies followed by the CPI in India for several years. One was to infiltrate into the party in power or lend support to it in order to pressurise it to work towards the Soviet policies. On the Bangladesh issue, as the Soviet and Indian views were identical, the strategy of their Communist parties were also the same. So during the independence war, the CPB and the NAP (M) moved more closer to the Awami League. The alliance was not only for convenience but also for survival. After independence, although they maintained their independent entity and suffered occasional set-backs, the alliance gained both domestic and international strength. Although the CPB and the NAP (M), particularly the NAP (M) being a frontal organisation had to criticise the government from time to time, intrinsically they pursued the same policies both on the domestic and international fronts and their main motivation was to keep the Awami League on the 'right track'. They maintained close liaison with the Awami League leadership and the acceptance of Mohiuddin Ahmed, a member of the Communist Party in Bangladesh by the Awmai League indicated that all the three parties could work together on a broader plane. The CPB also maintained a very close link with Fazlul Haque Moni, a nephew who had the maximum influence on Sheikh Mujib. As Mujib sometime paid more heed to relations than political colleagues, concentration on Sheikh Moni was considered to be most worthwhile. Once Tajuddin on whom they depended heavily for a long time to represent their views fell from grace, Sheikh Moni assumed new importance from CPB's strategic angle.

Although on 1st January, 1973 the relationship between the Awami League and the allies got strained due to the police firing on the latter's students' demonstration protesting the renewed US attack on Vietnam in front of USIS, the misunderstanding was only temporary and healed sooner than the blood of the two persons killed could dry. Soon after the elections in which neither the CPB nor the NAP (M) could secure any seat in the Parliament, an attempt was initiated from this camp to go for a broader understanding. After a series of discussions and ground work, the alliance backed by their international supporters took a somewhat formal shape. The Awami League was initially reluctant as it had a tradition of 'going alone' politically and secondly, the conservative elements in the Awami League were very much opposed to such an alliance which they thought would allow infiltration of communist influence in the party. Thirdly, the CPB and the NAP (M) were insignificant as parties in terms of popularity or mass-base and therefore, any unity with these parties would hitherto confirm the diminishing strength of the Awami League in the public eye which was not considered politically prudent. Fourthly, a formal alliance with the CPB and the NAP (M) would push the Awami League more towards the Soviet block antagonising forces opposed to that both at home and abroad. At the end, the basis for a broader alliance was found to be stronger although Mujib wanted to proceed cautiously. It was argued by those who were in favour of such an alliance that (1) the Soviet Union actively supported the cause of Bangladesh when the other two super-powers supported Pakistan. (2) Since independence, the relationship between Bangladesh and Soviet Union strengthened further and they held identical views on world issues. (3) Bangladesh's Friendship Treaty with India and India's with Soviet Union placed the three countries on a common orbit in international relations. (4) Bangladesh and India pursued identical foreign policies and pursued common international interests. For a country like Bangladesh, in the context of the prevailing world situation, support of a super-power was essential for its survival. The strong ties that already existed with India would necessitate an alliance with the Soviet Union having identical interests in the global context. It was argued that Bangladesh could not afford to contain all the super-powers at the same time.

Equally important was that with regard to the domestic policies the CPB and the NAP (M) were in complete command with the Awami League, particularly after the latter's revised manifesto pledging to establish a socialist economic order. They now claimed to have almost the same social and economic programmes with similar understanding of the subjective and objective conditions of the country. They also held identical views with regard to the opposition parties inside the country. They lent complete support to the foreign policy pursued by the Awami League.

As a consequence of this calculated effort, the CPB and the NAP (M) were able to convince Mujib to understand about the necessity of a broader alliance with these two parties both from the domestic and international point of view. Mujib was made to understand by the Indo-Soviet lobby in Bangladesh that the Sino-American-Pakistan[21] forces were conspiring against him and he was continuously briefed on this line since he returned from Pakistan's captivity in January, 1972. The fear of these forces led Mujib to gradually seek protection and in this process, perhaps quite unknowingly, he geared the country into an arena of international polemics and block power politics. In many of his speeches Mujib kept on confessing that there was a conspiracy going on in the country to undo Bangladesh and the conspirators were engaged in sabotaging the economy of the country.

Mujib somehow developed a fear-complex and the more he tended to believe that there were conspiracies going on, the more he would lean towards those who were readily available to help him. As this aspect of Mujib's role and character would require a deeper analysis we will discuss the matter, later, but for the purpose of the present point in discussion it would be sufficient to say that conditions developed in such a manner that the CPB and the NAP (M) were gradually accepted as partners with all their international allegiance or ideology for political collaboration with the Awami League.

In October, 1973 the three parties sat officially for two days and prepared a joint declaration on their future programme. They reached a complete agreement with regard to the 'total programme' and 'structural pattern' and all other matters pertaining to the alliance of the three parties[22]. The representatives of the three parties prepared the declaration on the basis of the guideline earlier given by Sheikh Mujib. They determined the structure of the committees to be formed and their relation with the administration. Three days later Mujib held a discussion with Moni Singh and Muzaffar Ahmed and other leaders of CPB and the NAP (M) and approved the Declaration.

In the process of building this alliance the plan to turn the country into a one-party system also began to take its shape. In the two-year rule certain hard political facts led to dominate the thoughts of Sheikh Mujib, nurtured and advanced by the CPB and NAP(M) and a section of the Awami League close to him. These facts and arguments were : (1) the country did not make much progress as the economy was sinking and the law and order situation continued to deteriorate. (2) The 'conspirators' and the vested interest groups were active to frustrate all attempts of the government in bringing stability in the country. (3) The opposition political parties were behaving in an 'irresponsible' manner and a large section of people were still in possession of arms and were using them for dacoity, robbery, looting of bazars and banks and secret killing. (4) The Awami League was faction-ridden down to the grass-root level and corruption within the members earned a bad name for the party. (5) As Bangladesh was a young and poor country a Westminister-type parliamentary democracy would not help in bringing economic progress ; it needed a solid period of quiet stability to ensure development. (6) Sheikh Mujib was omnipotent and it was in his name the country was freed and the subsequent election was won—there was no reason why he should carry the bad name of the Awami League. (7) There was no real opposition or alternative in the country and so there was no necessity of allowing those 'non-existing' parties to create unnecessary chaos. (8) To achieve a socialist transformation, doctrinaire workers were necessary and a party like Awami League could not provide such workers. (9) To establish a socialist economic order strict discipline and doctrinaire cadres were essential requirements and a bourgeois parliamentary system was contradictory to such pre-requisite. With conflicting social interests a socialist transformation was not possible to achieve. (10) Nowhere in the world could a socialist economic order established under a multi-party bourgeois democratic system. As any socialist transformation would require radical structural changes, the bourgeois institutions and interests would have to be controlled and removed with an iron hand and this would be impossible to do under the existing system. (11) Parliamentary democracy was a luxury for a developing country like Bangladesh, when the entire people was behind Sheikh Mujib and were his supporters why not sustain the unity of the people by establishing one single political party in the country. (12) With all the commitments Mujib made to the people including the one to stop exploitation of man all these years, he was to act now to fulfil those commitments. (13) Mujib was taken to Moscow for treatment by a special Soviet plane and he stayed there for nearly three weeks where he was accorded a red carpet reception by the Kremlin leaders. Mujib as a leader of his people received better treatment in the East than in the West. (14) Mujib was born to be a reformer, "a liberator" for common people, a "nation builder" and a philosopher of "Mujibbad"[23] and therefore with his support and popularity the Bengalis now had a historic chance to redeem themselves from economic exploitation, bondage and slavery and this great task and responsibility now rested on Mujib's shoulders for realising that dream. It was only Mujib who could do it and that he ought not to miss this opportunity. It was "the demand of history that Mujib played the role of a messiah".

The opinion in favour of these arguments was gradually being built up in party caucuses and now with an official tripartite alliance, the mobilisation became easier to vindicate these thoughts. As the chaos and anarchy increased every day the strength of the arguments was getting brighter. When Mujib used to be told these points he tended to agree with them. He used to feel happy to hear about his omnipotence and 'statesmanship' and his future role as a 'liberator' of the common masses. But he moved cautiously as he had to resolve certain contradictions in himself and within his party which he would not be able to abandon totally. All-through his life Mujib was known to be a moderate politician believing in western democratic principles and he was still known to be so. He believed in independence of the judiciary and fundamental human rights and he framed the constitution incorporating all these principles. Within his party a vast majority belonged to a strong conservative lobby believing and practising all bourgeois habits of a liberal democratic set-up.

It was a crucial test for Mujib. He realised that the Awami League was no longer an asset to him and the party having earned a bad name was becoming redundant in the context of the changed needs and circumstances. It proved to be ineffective in meeting the challenges of the newly independent country. The party rank and file had lost their moral fibre. The pressure from the dissatisfaction of the people about their economic well-being and security of life and property was mounting on him. Every day members of his party were being killed by firearms and mostly by his own men, banks and bazars were looted, police stations ransacked and yet the party was helpless and unable to assist the government because of its own weaknesses. Although the opposition was not strong they were building up their strength, mobilising public opinion directly against him. As the 'Father of the Nation' he could not allow himself to go down in history as a failure.

So Mujib tended to move gradually in that direction which was thought by many to be inevitable. The design of the CPB and the NAP(M) coincided with his personal desire of ruling the country alone and to establish himself as a nation builder, a creator of a socialist economic order in Bangladesh. As everything was depending more on him than anyone else in the prevailing circumstances, he emerged as an arbiter, the omnipotent force to bring any change in the society.

It is difficult to say exactly when Mujib decided to go for a sweeping change in the constitutional structure of the country but the indications show that he moved slowly, allowed conditions to precipitate and waited for a suitable moment. With all cards in his hand and still the most popular individual in the country, Mujib decided to employ a democratic mechanism to bring the change. He first changed the constitution and assumed power to make laws for preventive detention and proclaiming emergency. With almost all the members of parliament on his side Mujib by the end of 1973 started taking constitutional measures to create a congenial situation in case he wanted to move for such a change.

The first step he took was to make Mohammadullah the President of the country. Justice Abu Sayeed Chowdhury was not happy being a titular President under the dominating shadow of Sheikh Mujib and other political leaders[24]. He was virtually holding a non-functional post and when the Second Amendment to the constitution was passed he could see what was coming. He was disappointed at the way the country was run but being in his position as the President he could not say anything. So the exit of Justice Chowdhury might not have been inconceivable but the induction of Mohammadullah as the President was both interesting and intriguing. By sending Justice Chowdhury to Geneva as a special representative Mujib removed any fear of obstruction that could come in his way for any future constitutional action and by appointing Mohammadullah, a simple, loyal, docile and a much lessor personality, Mujib now had on his side a President who would obey him all the time. So on December 24, Mujib took the opportunity of accepting Justice Chowdhury's resignation and Mohammadullah from the position of the Speaker assumed the responsibility of the President. Then in January, 1974 he was formally elected as the President by the members of parliament.

In the meantime, however, although the Joint Declaration of the Tripartite Alliance was approved and the Gana Oykka Jote[25] was formed, the Jote did not gain much importance in political terms. This was so because the Awami League workers were not prepared to give much importance to the members of the other components. At the top leadership level however a basic working relationship between the leaders of the three parties developed and for their own strategic reasons the CPB and the NAP(M) continued to keep the alliance alive for whatever it was worth. Within the framework of the Alliance, one of the major tasks of the CPB and the NAP was to keep Mujib away from the influence of the conservative forces of the Awami League who by then had come to be castigated as 'reactioneries'. They continued to put pressure on Mujib and others to get rid of these elements of the party who were standing in his way of implementing a 'socialist transformation'.

The year 1974 was the worst year for the Awami League government. The cumulative effect of the mismanagement of the economy, shortfall in foodgrains in successive years, the deteriorating law and order situation, the greed and factionalism within the Awami League leaders and workers at different levels and the ultimate tragedy of the famine, all led to a disastrous failure for the government. The strain of such failure was noticed in the revision of the 5-Year plan to its virtual extinction, resorting to firing on public and widespread repressive measures of the Rakkhi Bahini, making of harsher laws like the

Special Powers Act, controlling of medias by the News Print Control Order and the Printing Presses and Publications (Declaration and Registration) Act, 1973 etc. The year was the final year of Mujib's 3-year grace period which he had sought from the public to improve their lot. It expired with only more insecurity and less food to eat. On the political front, although an all-out attempt was made to crush the JSD, Bhashani continued with his political stride and his 'fasting to death' in May in sympathy with the people dying of hunger kept the political arena active and alert. The intensive guerilla activities of the underground parties continued almost unabated. The more the Rakkhi Bahini killed the young political dissidents and victimised the innocents, the more political strength the guerillas gathered in the country-side. The government was unable to stop the secret killings.

FOOTNOTES

1. Moulana blessed Mujib when the latter visited him on January 24, 1972 at Tangail.
2. Read author's book *Bangladesh : Constitutional Quest for Autonomy*, Dhaka, p. 224.
3. This group played the most vital role in the ll-point Movement and in issues like preparing and hoisting the Bangladesh flag, declaration of Independence, construction of slogans, selecting national anthem and in raising the Mujib Bahini in India. Read author's book, *Bangladesh : Constitutional Quest for Autonomy*, Dhaka, pp. 223-4, 251.
4. At the first anniversay of independence while Mujib announced the nationalisation programme he also mentioned that the party was pledged to establish a 'scientific socialist economy' and 'national social revolution'.
5. The promoters of Mujibbad at first did not know what it stood for. Later Mujibbad was defined to be a combination of nationalism, socialism, democracy and secularism without any philosophical thesis. It was more used as a slogan to boost up an independent image for Mujib.
6. It is not known whether this group had any definite programme for revolution. There is no document available to prove in the affirmative.
7. The leaders of this group were aware that a stage would come after the independence that either they would go into the leadership for a 'revolution' keeping Mujib in the front or they would have to leave and create a separate stream for their 'revolution'. Source : from the discussion the author had with Serajul Alam Khan in March, 1972. Serajul Alam Khan denied that there was any personality clash or rivalry for leadership between him and Sheikh Moni or between Rab-Shahjahan and Razzak-Tofael.
8. In Sheikh's family, blood relationship took the form of a clanship.
9. The Awami League, the National Awami Party (Muzaffar) and the Communist Party of Bangladesh (Moni Singh).
10. Those who have nothing or who have lost everything—a proletarian party.
11. Siraj Shikder the leader of this Party was arrested on January 1, 1974 and on the next day he was allegedly killed by the government with shots from the back when he was trying to 'escape'.—*Bangladesh Observer*, January 3, 1975.
12. Moulana at one stage led a hunger march and himself went on a hunger strike.
13. The elections were held for the post of 4340 chairmen and 4340 vice-chairmen and 39060 members on the basis of direct adult franchise.—*Ganakantha*, 23.1.1974.
14. The order under Section 144 of the Criminal Procedure Code was challenged in the Supreme Court which delivered an illustrious judgement in August, 1974 declaring the Order under Section 144 illegal. See 26 DLR 1974, p. 376.

15. *Gherao* is a political action of 'encirclement' of a person or office to realise a demand.
16. Persons and offices mentioned were referred to as instrument of corruption, mismanagement and repression by the JSD leaders.—Daily *Ittefaq*, 18.3.1974.
17. An Islam oriented party called Hukumate Rabbania means "Rule of Allah".
18. See Moulana's two major statements in *the Bangladesh Observer* dated 1.1.1974 and 24.4.1974.
19. The Committee for Civil Liberties and Legal Aid Resolution was adopted in the meeting of March 31, 1974. Leaflet circulated on June 21, 1974.—*Samakal*, DIT Avenue, Dhaka-2. The author was elected General Secretary of the Committee with Poet Sikander Abu Zafar and Enayetullah Khan as President and Treasurer respectively.
20. See all the speeches of Mujib in public meetings in 1972. See also *The Bangladesh Observer* 3.1.1973 ; 4.1.1973 ; 5.1.1973 ; 7.1.1973 ; 9.1.1973 ; 16.1.1973 ; 26.2.1973 ; 19.1.1974 ; 6.2.1974, 5.3.1974 and so on upto 26.1.1975.
21. Mujib being the head of the government made scathing remarks about the government of these countries and once he advised President Nixon not to try to solve the Asian problems by sitting in Peking. He said, "nobody gave him the authority to decide the problems of Asia", and that "the American government should know that the Asian nations can decide their own fate and destiny".—Address at a public meeting at Paikgacha, Khulna, Feb. 23, 1972.

    At Calcutta in a public meeting at Brigade Parade Ground on February 6, 1972 Mujib said, "I warn the U.S. government that the days of imperialism are over. No game of the imperialists will be allowed to be played in this sub-continent".

    Mujib and other Awami League leaders constantly attacked China, U.S.A. and Pakistan and their lobbies inside the country in their speeches.
22. *The Bangladesh Observer*, October 10, 1973.
23. Read Khondker Md. Elias, *Mujibbad*, National Publications, Dhaka.
24. He told me in 1972-73 on more than one occasions that he felt like being in a cage. He wanted to be more free and do something productive for the country.
25. *Gona Oykka Jote* meaning Peoples United Alliance.

CHAPTER ELEVEN

THE PROCLAMATION OF EMERGENCY AND SWITCHING TO ONE-PARTY SYSTEM

After the famine and before the year was over, the country reached a crucial stage. What made the situation worse was the gradual realisation that despite all efforts made and all laws enacted to ease the situation, the government had miserably failed to overcome the two basic problems the country faced since independence i.e. the economic crisis and the law and order situation[1]. In both areas the situation continued to worsen and a tremendous socio-political pressure began to be built up both from within and outside the government for taking some drastic measures to overcome the crisis. With the last blow struck by the countless tragic deaths in the famine, a sort of moral recovery became necessary and the primary responsibility for a salvage fell on Sheikh Mujibur Rahman.

As indicated earlier, with the latest development in the country following the famine, opinion was now recirculated that the existing system was not the right kind to achieve the goals Mujib had promised to the people. The two major tasks of improving the law and order situation and the general economic condition could not be accomplished through the existing agencies. By November people close to Sheikh supported by the leaders of the CPB and the NAP(M) started openly discussing how the existing situation could be overcome and wondered what kind of system would be suitable to accomplish a socialist transformation. They revived the earlier argument that "the country was more important than the system". Mujib indirectly used to hint at the need for change but he did not yet openly discuss it with any of his senior colleagues[2].

As a first step towards that direction Mujib resorted to the exercise of power incorporated in Article 141A of the Constitution which was introduced about a year ago through the Second Constitution Amendment Act. At noon on 28th December, 1974 the President by an Ordinance proclaimed a state of emergency in the country suspending the enforcement of fundamental rights during the period of emergency. While justifying such an action, the government eulogised the struggle for achieving independence within a short period of one year. It was further mentioned in the government handout that a free and fair election was held within 3 months thereafter and a government was formed by the duly elected representatives. It also said that a group of people who were opposed to the independence and emergence of Bangladesh as a sovereign state were active in various subversive activities and they were joined by others who failed to attain power through constitutional means. The government spokesman disclosed that some collaborators of the Pakistan Army, extremists and enemy agents in the pay-roll of foreign powers were subverting the state and were engaged in activities which were creating impossible condition in the country for attaining normal political stability and orderly economic progress. It was on these grounds that the President was satisfied that a grave emergency existed in which the security and economic life of Bangladesh was threatened by internal disturbance and the President therefore, issued the Proclamation of Emergency.

The contents of the Emergency were similar to those which the people had earlier experienced in the long history of Pakistan and also during the British colonial rule. The Ordinance authorised the government to make rules which had 3 major aspects. In the first place provision was made for preventive detention in case of prejudicial activities[3]. The second one related to social crimes, such as smuggling, hoarding, black marketeering, illegal possession of arms, counterfeiting, sabotaging, adulteration, corruption, ètc. and the third aspect authorised the government to make rules restricting and regulating the press reports and press freedom etc.

The Ordinance was a comprehensive one embracing all possible areas and authorised the government to exercise power in social, economic and political sphere of life of the citizens. As a result, the Rules made under the Ordinance were very comprehensive and severe in nature. An interesting aspect of the Ordinance was that a huge number of the offences enumerated in it were repetitions of some existing laws dealing with the same crimes. Stringent laws already existed in the Arms Act and Special Powers Act dealing with preventive detention and crimes like holding illegal arms, sabotage, hoarding, smuggling etc. In some cases the provisions made were identical but these were repeated generally to give importance to the gravity of the Proclamation.

But another argument used for proclaiming emergency was equally interesting. Whatever truth there might have been in the suspicion that collaborators were engaged in subversive activities creating impossible conditions for attaining normal political activity, the government in fact was accepting defeat in the sense that even though 3 years had elapsed they were still not able to bring the collaborators under control when the 'entire population' was behind them. On the other hand, the government granted clemency to a large number of people who were imprisoned as collaborators and on the diplomatic front it was trying to normalise its relationship with Pakistan. And yet the government continued to hold the collaborators responsible for the economic collapse in the country.

However, as would be clear from our subsequent discussions, these were not the real reasons why the emergency was proclaimed in the country. It was an attempt to kill two birds at a time. As the situation was really bad, proclamation of an emergency was something which could be applicable for bringing the situation under control. But the main aspect of it was to create conditions which would be congenial for a smooth ushering of a stem which Mujib by that time had already decided to introduce scheme to bring radical changes for not only improving the present situation but to "ensure a socialist transformation for the progress and prosperity" of the country, although the Proclamation of Emergency followed the brutal killing of an Awami League M.P. Golam Kibria[4] and two others at a public prayer on the occasion of Id-ul Azha and there might have been other good reasons prevailing for a long time for an emergency[5].

Accordingly, on 25th January, 1975 only 27 days after the Proclamation was issued for a state of emergency, the country went through the most significant and radical changes in its constitution. As the ultimate design was something different from what the emergency was all about, nothing much happened during these 27 days. The impact of the emergency gradually lost its force as the government did not move to tackle the immediate problems for which the emergency was proclaimed. People expected certain immediate stern action against the hoarders, blackmarketeers, smugglers, armed bandits who were looting banks and bazars and killing people in broad day light. It was expected that the people who were responsible for disrupting the economy of the country would now be brought to book and punished in accordance with law and the government would restore the security of life and property of its citizens. No prominent hoarders, black marketeers, saboteurs or smugglers were however arrested.

The government had neither any plan nor were they serious in actually confronting the criminals for which they claimed to have proclaimed the Emergency. The few actions which were taken were all political in nature. The government prohibited holding of meetings and processions. It also prohibited strikes and lockouts in all undertakings and establishments in Bangladesh. There were of course many speeches by the Home Minister warning that the "final blow will be struck on anti-socials" and "smuggling must be totally stopped"[6] but nothing happened more than that.

So the Proclamation of Emergency seemed to be essentially a political act. As in the past, provisions of emergency have always been invoked to deal with the opposition more than dealing with the social evils. In the case of Bangladesh, the proclamation of emergency was invoked with a political motive because :

(1) the government was duly elected less than two years ago ; (2) it claimed to have massive popular support with nearly 98% seats in the Parlia-

ment ; (3) all the law enforcing agencies including the Army and the Rakkhi Bahini were under its full command ; (4) adequate provisions were already there in the existing laws like the Special Powers Act, Arms Act, Printing Presses and Publication (Declaration and Registration) Ordinance, the Jatiyo Rakkhi Bahini Act and others to deal effectively with the offences which were proposed to be handled under the emergency rules ; (5) provision for preventive detention was already there in the Special Powers Act. If the government with all the public support, laws and powers at its disposal could not bring the social and economic situation under control in the last two years what changes could it expect to bring by merely proclaiming emergency. So they argued that the act of proclaiming emergency had some political ends.

During this intervening period, Mujib devoted more time to formulating a strategy to bring about a further change of a more fundamental nature. When the preparation was complete, beginning on 19th January a meeting of the Awami League Parliamentary Party was held at the Ganabhavan where the members of the Working Committee of the Awami League also attended on a special invitation. While the meeting discussed the national problems, the essential theme was to build up an opinion for a radical change in the system of the government. Although earlier Mujib and some of his close ranks had already started airing their views in private discussions, in this meeting Mujib himself did not come forward with any clear proposal. Mujib however made extremely critical statement analysing the entire state of affairs of the country and narrated the failure of the government in meeting the aspirations of the people. He criticised the behaviour of his own partymen as much as he criticised the opposition[7].

The meeting held deliberations for a total of seven hours spreading over 3 days. There were controversies on different issues but the boat sailed in one direction. None was in a position to controvert what Mujib had said[8]. The vast majority did not take any part as they did not like the trend[9]. In such a situation the members were swayed into accepting the proposition for a change. Mujib's authoritative stature was the single dominating factor in creating an atmosphere for the members of Parliament to bedevil their own status. With the leaders and psychophants around him it was not possible for all of them to muster courage to face the wrath of the leader who was omnipotent. It was under Mujib's single shadow that the members had a place in the Parliament or in the Working Committee of the party. Many claimed that Mujib himself was the Awami League party. Members like M.A.G. Osmani and Moinul Hossain, the two persons who protested and left the party, were too idealistic to be in politics with Mujib. At the end of the meeting in a characteristic manner to show full confidence in the leader, Mujib was empowered "to take any step he considered necessary for resolving the problems the country was facing ".

The Fourth Amendment of the Constitution

Four days later Mujib took the step for "resolving the problems of the country" by causing to introduce an amendment Bill called the Constitution (Fourth Amendment) Bill on Saturday, January 25, 1975. The Parliament passed the Bill into an Act at a speed unprecedented in the history of law-making. Within less than an hour the Bill, although of greatest importance, was passed through without any discussion or debate. In a sweeping change the country entered into a new constitutional arrangement where none but only one political party could exist with a President having supremacy over all executive, legislative and judicial organs of the state. Simultaneously, by the amendment itself, Mujib was made the President of the country. Soon after the Bill was passed through, Mujib took the oath of office in the Parliament administered by the Speaker ousting the quiet and placid Mohammadullah from the office of the President even without giving him an opportunity to resign[10]. As soon as the Amendment was passed Mohammadullah ceased to hold the office of the President and Mujib entered that office[11].

The President becomes the Chief Executive

The management of the executive branch of the state was the most striking feature of the original constitution. It envisaged a parliamentary democratic system making the executive accountable to the people through the Parliament. The Prime Minister was to exercise the executive power of the Republic as long as he enjoyed the confidence of the majority members of the Parliament. The President was a titular head to act in accordance with the advice of the Prime Minister and was to be elected by the members of Parliament. In the Fourth Amendment the entire Chapter I relating to the President and Chapter II relating to the Prime Minister and the cabinet under Part IV were substituted by new provisions. Under the new system, the President was to be elected by the people in a direct election (Article 48) and the executive authority of the Republic was vested in him (Article 56). In the earlier provision no person could hold office of the President for more than 2 terms but in the amendment no such restriction was mentioned meaning that under the new system the President could hold office for an unlimited number of terms.

With regard to the impeachment of the President the procedure was kept the same excepting that (1) the number of members required to sign a notice of motion to initiate impeachment proceeding was raised to a minimum of two-thirds of the total members from one-third and (2) the resolution of impeachment after consideration of charges was to be passed by three-fourths of the total number of members instead of two-thirds provided in the original constitution (Article 53). Similarly, on the question of removal of the President on the ground of physical incapacity the number of votes required in both the cases of initiation of motion and passing the resolution was raised to two-thirds and three-fourths respectively which was previously done by a majority and two-thirds.

The Vice-President

In the amendment in Chapter 1 of Part IV, provision was made to have a Vice-President to be appointed by the President (Article 49) requiring the same qualifications as that of the President (Article 50). The President was to hold office for a term of 5 years (Article 51). The term of the Vice-President was also for 5 years but he could be removed by the President at any time before the expiry of the term (Article 51). Like the President, the Vice-President also enjoyed the immunity from any criminal proceedings (Article 52) but the Vice-President was not given any power to grant pardons etc. (Article 57). The Vice-President was to exercise such powers as were assigned to him by the President (Article 56(2)). The Amendment made provision for the Vice-President to function as the Acting President if any vacancy occured in the office of the President or the President was unable to discharge the function of his office on account of absence or illness or any other cause. In such cases the Vice-President was to act as President until a new President was elected to fill such vacancy or until the President resumed the functions of his office [Article 55(1)]. If, however, vacancy occured in both the offices of the President and Vice-President for the same reasons as mentioned above, the Speaker was to act as the President in such cases [Article 55(2)].

The Council of Ministers

The new Chapter II of Part IV dealt with the new concept of a "Council of Ministers". Unlike the earlier arrangement of a cabinet system with the Prime Minister at its head, the Amendment created a Council of Ministers to "aid and advise the President in the exercise of his functions". Now the ministers, including the Prime Minister, were to be appoitned by the President and would hold office during his pleasure. Unlike the earlier arrangement all or any of the ministers including the Prime Minister could be appointed from outside the Parliament. In other words, ministers were to be responsible to the President and not to the Parliament. The meetings of the Council of Ministers were to be presided over by the President but he could "direct" the Vice-President or the Prime Minister to preside over such meetings (new Article 58). The Prime Minister and all other ministers could be removed from the office at the discretion of the President.

Local Administration

In the original constitution, in Chapter III of Part IV much emphasis was laid on the decentralisation of power and one of its significant features was that it provided for local governments at every administrative unit of the Republic composed of elected persons and such local bodies were to be entrusted with the fuctions relating to the (1) administration and the work of the public officers, (2) maintenance of public order and (3) preparation and implementation of plans relating to public services and economic development. It further provided for making laws to confer special powers on local governing bodies including power to impose taxes for local purposes, to prepare their budgets and to maintain funds. In the Fourth Amendment in order to keep in line with its monolithic structure, the entire Chapter III was deleted[12].

Parliament and Legislation

In the original Constitution the Legislature was considered to be the most vital organ of the State. It was considered supreme and sovereign as a body. It was the source of law and authority and the fountain of power sanctioned by the people. It was to be elected directly under a multi-party system and any party enjoying numerical majority could form the government. It would not only make laws and grant money but would control executive by making it accountable to it. The Prime Minister was to be elected by the Parliament and not by any individual and he and all his ministers would be accountable to it. The President was also to be elected by the Parliament. Its sovereignty was maintained also in the sense that once a bill was passed by the Parliament it became law and none could exercise any veto. No part of the Constitution could be changed or amended without the two-thirds of the members of Parliament.

By the Fourth Amendment all the established ingredients of a parliamentary system were removed from the Constitution. Besides the question of excluding the Parliament's power from making the executive accountable to it, the most important feature of the new arrangement was that the President could now withheld assent to any bill passed by the Parliament[13]. With these amendments the importance of the Parliament was entirely gone and it was turned into a secondary rubber-stamp body in the new political system.

The other important amendment made was related to the sessions of Parliament. It was originally provided that the intervening period between the end of the session and the beginning of the new would not exceed 60 days. In the Fourth Amendment this provision was omitted and provision was made to the effect that there would be "at least two sessions of Parliment every year" reducing the role of the Parliament now to a minimum.

By Article 70 of the original Constitution, a seat of a member of Parliament was to be vacated if he resigned from the party which nominated him as a candidate or if he voted in the Parliament against that party. The amendment made to Article 70 through the Fourth Amendment inserted an explanation to the meaning of voting in Parliament against the party. The explanation provided that even abstaining or absenting oneself or ignoring the direction of the party in such case would be deemed to be voting against the party[14].

Again, Article 76 which originally provided for the Parliament to appoint certain standing committees at the first meeting of each session, was amended omitting such provision and thereby reducing the importance of Parliament even further.

Judiciary

Along with the changes in the executive and legislative fields, some radical changes were also introduced in the organisation of the judiciary contained in Part VI of the Constitution. The judiciary, which traditionally held a special position in every constitution of the sub-continent as a basic organ for the functioning of rule of law was now made completely subservient to the executive. The power, status, functions and authority of the Supreme Court was drastically reduced and the jurisdiction of the Judges in original matters was also curtailed. The amendment changed the entire institutional context of the judiciary which for a long time played an important role in striking a balance between the excesses of the executive and their victims, between the law and its application. But the Awami League leaders agreed that the changes in the judiciary were required in view of the new economic order Mujib was aiming at establishing and so the 'old colonial system' had to go.

In the original Constitution, like in other constitutions of the sub-continent, one of the fundamental state principles was to ensure separation of judiciary from the executive (Article 22). Accordingly, provisions were made to retain as much as possible the status of judiciary in that line. For a long time some tested mechanisms have been employed to secure the organic independence of judiciary as an institution which included ensuring (1) security and permanency of the judges, (2) functioning of the judges without interference from the executive and (3) retaining the service of the officers performing judicial functions as a distinct branch operating according to its own rules, etc.

The entire system including the very basis of the judiciary was changed. On the question of appointing judges other than those in the Supreme Court, the President was given the full authority and he did not now have to make any appointment "after consultation with the Chief Justice" (Article 95). On the question of removal of judges the provision for impeachment was deleted and the same power was assumed by the President who could remove a judge including the Chief Justice simply by an order on ground of misbehaviour or incapacity. So under the arrangement the protection of the tenure of the judges was withdrawn and now it required only notice with an opportunity for showing cause against a proposed action. Similarly with regard to the appointment of additional judges for the Supreme Court, the President could make the appointment now without any consultation with the Chief Justice (Article 98).

In matters of appointment to the subordinate courts the authority of the Supreme Court was wihtdrawn. Article 115 was substituted with the following : "Appointment of persons to offices in the judicial service or as Magistrate exercising judicial functions shall be made by the President in accordance with rules made by him in that behalf". The amendment not only demolished the sanctity of the service but also the institution of the judiciary itself. Thus the authority of the Supreme Court for making appointments to district and subordinate courts was taken away and the mandatory qualifications was not taken into consideration for appointment of district judges and other persons to exercise judicial function.

The power and authority given to the Supreme Court in the original Constitution in Article 116 for the control and discipline of the subordinate courts including the power of posting, promotion and grant of leave including those of the magistrate exercising judicial function, were now vested in the President instead of the Supreme Court. The Amendment however created a new Article 116A to provide that all persons employed in the judicial service and all Magistrates "shall be independent in the exercise of their judicial functions". But in the light of all the changes made in respect of the judiciary as a whole it was seriously doubted how much the judicial officers could be independent in the exercise of their functions.

In the original Constitution, Article 44 guaranteed the right to move the Supreme Court under Article 102(1) for the enforcement of fundamental rights and exercise the original jurisdiction for issue of writs and pass certain orders and directions. The power of the court (Article 102) had been part of a long tradition. The court also had the authority to pass an interim order in all matters and in matters which related to implementing of any 'socialist programme or development work' or being otherwise harmful to the public interest after giving the Attorney General an opportunity of being heard. But the Fourth Amendment envisaged creation of a supreme constitutional court for the enforcement of the fundamental rights (new Article 44). Therefore, the traditional jurisdiction of the High Court for the enforcement of the fundamental rights was withdrawn. Moreover, the new Article 102 also deprived the court from one of its inherent powers of granting interim orders as the relevant provision was amended to exclude the power of the court to make any interim order. The other important amendment was under Article 109 by which the High Court Division's power of superintendence and control over all 'tribunals' subordinate to it was withdrawn keeping such power only over the subordinate courts. With these amendments of far-reaching consequences made in Part VI, the position of judiciary became somewhat secondary in status and subservient in nature. The amendment did not provide any alternative system for the administration of justice.

One National Party

In order to give effect to an one-party political system, provisions were made for the creation of a National Party and they were incorporated in a new Part VIA with a new Article 117A. According to the new arrangement, the creation of the National Party was left with the President. In order to give full effect to any of the fundamental principles of state policy set out in Part II of the Constitution, the President by an order could direct that "there shall be only one political party in the state". Once the President made such an order, all the political parties of the state would stand dissolved and the President would take all necessary steps for the formation of the National Party. The President by an order would also determine all matters relating to the nomenclature, programme, membership, organisation, description, finance and function of the National Party and it was also provided that a government servant would be qualified to be a member of the National Party (Article 117A (4)).

It was further provided that once the National Party was formed each member of the Parliament would have to join the Party within a time fixed by the President, otherwise he would cease to be a member of Parliament and his seat would become vacant. None would be qualified for election as President or as a member of Parliament if such person was not nominated as a candidate by the National party. The Article also provided that none would have any right to form any political party or be a member or otherwise take part in the activities of any political party other than the National Party [Article 117A(5)(c)].

Other Features

The most interesting feature to notice was that the entire scheme of having one National Party in the country was linked with the fundamental principles of state policy. The President was to make a direction to that effect if he was satisfied that formation of such party "was necessary" to give effect to "any of the fundamental principles of state policy". Secondly, provision to make the persons in the service of the Republic, civil or military eligible for membership in the National Party meant that members of bureaucracy could now unlike in the past, take part in politics. Thirdly, members who got directly elected by the people were now liable to lose their membership by operation of law, if they did not join the National Party. Finally, the scheme contemplated that although there would be a one-party political structure, election would take place to the office of the President and members of Parliament on the basis of adult franchise and there would be more than one candidate for each election with the National Party nominating them in each case. It also meant that for each seat in the Parliament, the National Party would nominate one, two or more persons.

Part VII of the Constitution dealt with elections. The most important amendment in this part was made regarding the period required to fill the vacancy, once it occurs, in the office of the President. The original provision was that if such vacancy occured whether due to expiry of the term or by reason of death, resignation or removal, a fresh election to fill the vacancy was to be held within 90 days. The amendment (Article 123) extended the period from 90 days to 180 days in all cases.

Another interesting change, introduced through the Fourth Amendment related to the administration of oath of office. It had been the tradition in the subcontinent that the oath of office of President was administered by the Chief Justice of the country. In the Fourth Amendment this was changed and was substituted to be done by the Speaker. It was alleged that this was done for sheer convenience. Arrangement was made in such a way so that the fundamental change that was brought through the Fourth Amendment could be given effect to almost on the spot and there was no scope for raising any legal dispute over the whole change[15]. Along with this the duty of the Chief Justice to administer oath to Speaker and Deputy Speaker was also withdrawn and the task was now taken over by the President himself[16].

An interesting aspect of the Fourth Amendment was that Parliament now extended its own life for nearly 2 more years. In March 1973, people elected the Parliament for a period of 5 years but by adding a paragraph, the Fourth Amendment introduced a change extending the term of 5 years from the commencement of the new Act and consequently the Parliament gained a further life of another 2 years extending the term of membership to 7 years.

Another most fascinating aspect was that the Fourth Amendment made special provisions relating to the person of the President. A new President was created by the instrument itself without requiring any process of election. The sitting President just ceased to hold his office as soon as the Bill became an Act and he vacated the office without any ceremony or ground specified in the Constitution. On the commencement of the amended Act, Sheikh Mujib became the President of the country. The scheme was such that it was not found necessary even to go through a normal process of resignation by the sitting President or holding the election of the President by any person or body or anything like that.

Although in reality Mujib was supreme, no matter what system was devised or envisaged, the constitution-makers thought that no such process was necessary specially when the matter related to the 'Father of the Nation'. The whole exercise however on the other hand gave the impression that the ruling coterie did not want to take any chance. They were afraid of the scheme being frustrated if not by outsiders than by the members from within. So an element of haste was noticed in this regard also.

In effect what happened was that all the essential institutions required for the healthy growth of a democratic system were dismantled at a stroke and a one-party monolithic system was introduced. The Legislature which was enshrined as sovereign and supreme and considered to be the source of law and authority, was now turned into an important organ of the state. With the President's right to withhold assent to a Bill, it degenerated into a useless forum. The judiciary which was to be a separate and independent organ for ensuring justice and rule of law in the country was now to conduct itself at the mercy of the executive. With the power to remove the judges of the Supreme Court and the administrative and supervisory control of the whole organ gone to the President, the entire branch of the government became an appendage to the executive organ of the State. With the authority of the Supreme Court for the enforcement of the fundamental rights taken away, with creation of a national political party banning all others in the country, the new President emerged as the only source of authority in the newly born country. He was the chief executive and became the fountain of law and justice. He was not subjected to any institution, wholly unaccountable and completely free from any restriction whatsoever, not even from his own National Party of which he now became the chief master.

Justifications for the Change in the System

Why did it all happen that way ? Mujib was known to be a devout democrat, a man who lived and grew with the people, struggled and suffered for nearly 25 years, was jailed on countless occasions and rose to power through the support of the masses. But he now turned bitter about his old values and convictions and transformed the democratic system into an undemocratic monolith. It was as if Mujib was re-born as an architect of a newly conceived system he now proposed without any past. What led him to do this? What was the necessity, the socio-economic needs, political compulsions or contradictions that led him to fly in a diametrically opposite direction ?

As far as Mujib was concerned he was the Bangabandhu, the Father of the Nation and the Prime Minister exercising all the executive power. He was the most powerful man, an omnipotent authority of the country. He was still the most popular and the most dominant personality in the regime. The Government, the Party and the Parliament, all were under his complete command. He had no contender or challenger in the country. His leadership was undisputed and unqestionable. The system through which he chose to rule the country was on his side having 293 out of 300 elected seats under his control. And yet Mujib decided to change the system entirely, re-concentrate the powers he already had in his own hand and dissolve the existing institutions. Is it for mere power that he went for such a change ? Although it is true that the new nation could not make any economic recovery in 3 years under his government, the law and order situation continued to remain out of control and the country was in a state of utter chaos, corruption and mismanagement but were these the only reasons for Mujib to introduce a one-party system ?

Under the Proclamation of Independence drawn up in 1971, Bangladesh was born with a Presidential system having both the legislative and executive powers vested in the office of the President. But Mujib on his return from Pakistan's captivity, abdicated the power on his own free will and turned the system of parliamentary within less than 48 hours of his return. He stepped down from the office of the President and became the Prime Minister in a Westminister type system. In three years time Mujib turned back the system again to a more rigid form and with much more draconian powers in hand, Why did he not then retain the powers under the system introduced through the Proclamation of Independence?

Mujib justified this fundamental change he introduced in the constitution immediately after the Fourth Amendment was passed by the Parliament. In his address on January 25 in the Parliament Mujib narrated the entire situation of the country and asserted that the Constitution was changed in order to establish "the economic freedom of the masses in an exploitation-free society and to establish socialism and democracy of the exploited." Mujib said that the changes were made much to his pain and he was sorry that Constitution had to be amended but he had no other alternative. He could not allow the country to move in the same way as it had been going so far. The system so long pursued had failed to do any good to the ordinary people of the country. Mujib reminded Parliament that he already had a lot of power and as the Prime Minister he enjoyed all the excutive powers of the state but still a fundamental change was neceesary in the constitution "in order to create a healthy administration where people would be able to sleep peacefully and would be free from injustice and repression."

Mujib was highly concerned and critical of (1) the existing bureaucratic system of administration left by the British. He was in favour of a radical change in the structure of the administration; (2) the secret political killings that were going on in the country and particularly the killing of the Awami League workers and leaders including the assassination of 4 Members of Parliament; (3) the alleged role of the 'collaborators, in secret killings and disruption of the economy, sabotage and conspiracy to undo Bangladesh ; (4) the role of the opposition with reference to JSD and underground revolutionary parties and their destructive actions; (5) accumulation of weapons in a clandestine manner in the hands of certain groups opposed to the government ; (6) the bad economic condition culminating in famine—insufficiency of food and dependence on external assistance; (7) the educated class 'the most opportunist class who were the real bad people exploiting the masses'. They derived their education at the cost of the masses but they were not ready to do anything for them ; (8) the corruption in which the poor people were not involved but according to him the 5% educated people were doing all the corruption ; (9) the indiscipline in the administration, education and industry ; (10) the judicial system which was colonial and unworkable required radical structural changes to meet the need of the people ; (11) the exploitation of the common man by a handful of people ; (12) the smuggling, hoarding, black marketeering and profiteering that was going on.

Mujib further argued that these ills of the socio-political life could not be removed without changing the system, as the existing one was not able to cope with the situation. His dream of establishing a 'Sonar Bangla' could not be fulfilled unless people were united and the overall economic system was changed. He wanted to redeem the innocent and illiterate people from their poverty and miseries. He appealed to all to come forward to increase production in the fields and factories and root out the corrupt people from the society and to eliminate the smugglers, black marketeers and hoarders from the soil of Bangladesh. Mujib called it a 'Second Revolution' through which exploitation of people would come to an end. He ended by saying "we have to work sincerely and honestly for the emancipation of the poor people of the country".

Although the speech was unwritten and was a highly emotional one and carried more rhetoric than substance, the intention of Mujib was clear. In 3 years Mujib experienced a diabolically tragic state of affairs, he discovered that the existing system was not working. Although his statement was unsystematic, incoherent and repetitious, Mujib's justification of introducing the Fourth Amendment was not to be seen as being without any purpose. His words were bitter, full of anger and he was extremely critical of the existing socio-economic system.

The scheme envisaged by Mujib through the Fourth Amendment also included establishing the party superiority over the government and as such it would lead to (1) integration of party and the government, (2) integration of party and other organs of the state bureaucracy including the armed forces, judiciary and the Parliment, (3) forging unity of the people through the existence of a single party in the country which would create a "pool of capable people from all walks of life to build the country", but would exclude and eliminate 'collaborators', armed guerillas and political opponents to the new system, (4) democracy of a type where people's representatives would be elected by exercise of vote to elect from amongst 3/4 persons nominated by the party.

Although it appeared that the day the Fourth Amendment was introduced there was no concrete plan in hand, but at a later stage Mujib announced programmes in a more precise form. The objective of his "second revolution" was to establish 'socialist economic order' in the country. Although there was no formal documentation of the programmes he proposed to introduce and the laws to effect the reform were yet to be made but they became known to the public from 4 major statements Mujib made during this period from January to July, 1975[17].

Formation of the Bangladesh Krishak Sramik Awami League (BAKSAL) : Its Philosophy and Programme

In exercise of the powers conferred on him by the Fourth Amendment (Article 117A) Mujib now declared the formation of a new national party for the country under the name and style 'Bangladesh Krishak Sramik Awami League (BAKSAL)" on February 24, 1975. About one month after, on March 26, 1975 Mujib while addressing a public meeting at the Suhrawardy Uddayan[18] for the first time disclosed certain programmes undertaken to make the new system successful. These were :

(1) Compulsory multi-purpose co-operatives in every village. The co-operative would be formed in phases and under a 5-year Plan all the 65000 villages would have such co-operatives[19]. Each co-operative would comprise 500 to 1000 families. These co-operatives would be the economic units of the nation and the union council units would not be there any more. All government aid including the fertilizer, test relief operations and Works Programme would be channelised through these co-operatives. The ownership of the land would not be taken over which meant that ownership of land would continue in the existing form but its produces would be divided in 3 parts; one to the owner, one to the local co-operative and the other to the government. All unemployed and landless people who were able to work would become members of the co-operative and would derive equal benefit from its produce. The youths would take an active role in these co-operatives.

(2) There would be an administrative council for each thana comprising of representatives from the BAKSAL, youths, females, workers, farmers and government officials of different departments. The Council would be headed by the Governor who did not necessarily have to be a member of Parliament or a political worker. He could even be a trusted government official. The process of creating the Thana Councils would however start one year after the District Administrative Councils start functioning.

(3) The existing districts were to be dissolved and each sub-division would now become a district with a new administrative council comprising of representatives from the people, from BAKSAL, from amongst the member of Parliament and government officials. Each Administrative Council would be headed by a Governor who would run the local administration[20]. The entire development outlay of the district would vest in the Administrative Council starting from food, health, education and irrigation to family planning. All the government offices and departments would go under his Control including that of the District Magistrate and Superintendent of Police and the Deputy Commissioner would act as Secretary of the Council. The units of Army, JRB, BDR, Police, etc. posted in the district would be under the control of the Governor. In other words, the entire area of planning, implementation, law and order and day to day administration of the district would now vest in the Governor and the Ad-

ministrative Council. The District Administrative Council would function under the direct control of the Central Government. All these were envisaged as a part of the programme for decentralisation of administration.

(4) The system of dispensation of justice would be drastically changed and its administration would be regulated in such a way that justice become easily available to the common people. For a speedy and cheaper dispensation of justice, tribunals or courts would be established at the thana level[21].

(5) The administrative system at Dhaka would also be changed and the bureaucratic system would be replaced by a 'people oriented' system. The Secretariat would go and the red-tapism would be abolished and more corporations would go directly under the ministers[22].

Besides these 5 major subjects Mujib also threw light on some other aspects reflecting the design of his new system.

(6) The new system would forge national unity at all levels. Under the new system all capable people would be brought together to work for the country. He wanted an integration of all capable people from the Army, Navy, Air Force, civil bureaucrats, BDR, JRB, Police and the politicians. He wanted to create a 'pool' of all experienced and qualified people which would include doctors, engineers, lawyers, government officials, politicians, intellectuals and all others to create unity of thought, expression and belief for the betterment of the people. This unity could be achieved only through a new system of one-party rule and the dedicated cadre to be drawn from people of all walks of life.

(7) The Army envisaged in the new system would be "people's Army". It would not fight against anyone. The Army would be engaged in the nation-building activities and in the defence of the country.

(8) There would be strong political organisation with defined economic objectives, and to achieve these objectives people would be mobilised from the village level.

(9) Productivity would be multiplied and everyone would work harder in the fields and factories. Domestic resources were to be increased.

(10) A completely new education system would be introduced.

(11) Corruption would be weeded out. It was to disappear from the society completely. The existing system was a corrupt one and therefore to stop corruption, the first step required was to change the system itself. The people at the top, the political leaders and workers and the newly appointed Governors would have to set personal examples of honesty, dedication and incorruptibility. Those who took bribes or those who lived beyond their ostensible means would be boycotted from society. The whole people would be mobilised against corruption and 30% of the miseries would be gone if corruption could be stopped.

(12) Although, all the people who were in the Awami League Committees at various levels were made members of BAKSAL automatically and all the people in the Executive, Central, District and other Committees including those

in the frontal organisations were made members of the party without any scrutiny, the party membership would not be easily available. Without being a member of the party none would hold any office in the government.

(13) The 'Second Revolution'[23] was not an end in itself. It was only a step forward for increased production, family planning, fighting against corruption and national unity. The ultimate object was the creation of a society free from exploitation where there would be no torture, repression, injustice or corruption and to retain the honour and dignity of Badgladesh as an independent and sovereign state. The kind of socialism that was to be established in Bangladesh was "not going to be an imported one from outside, from anywhere in the world". It was to be "an ism of our own".

(14) Determination to handle "ruthlessly" those who worked against the independence and were still engaged in sabotaging and conspiring against the independence in connivance with Pakistan. Despite the fact that they were forgiven "some were trying to turn Bangladesh into a province". This group would not be allowed to enjoy any political right.

(15) A national plan for industries with representation from the workers and officials from industries and labour department to run and manage them.

As mentioned carlier, Mujib made these important statements impromptu and thus they lacked cohesion and consistency. It was therefore, difficult to make a correct evaluation of the programmes he had in his mind for the new system. Although the political objective of establishing a society free from exploitation was emphasised again, no comprehensive methodology to achieve such an objective was made known. The statements carried more emotion, angers, frustration, than any concrete philosophy.

Annulment and taking over of Newspapers

On the political front, the first act after the Fourth Amendment Bill was passed was the seizure by the police of the office from where the volatile opposition daily 'Ganakantha' of the JSD was being published[24]. In June, the government promulgated the Newspaper (Annulment of Declaration) Ordinance by which it allowed only 4 daily newspapers to continue publication and banned the rest[25]. All these 4 newspaper were to be owned and managed by the state bringing the news media completely under the control of the government. The most interesting aspect of this operation was the government's taking over of the Daily *Ittefaq* which belonged to a family so close to the Awami League[26]. The banning of newspapers was however done keeping in line with the new system where no political opposition or press freedom was visualised.

National Unity

Under Article 117A(5)(a) of the Fourth Amendment no person could continue to be a member of Parliament beyond a time fixed by the President unless he joined the National Party. Accordingly, 5 out of the total 7 opposition and independent members joined the BAKSAL. Abdullah Sarkar and Moinuddin Manik were the two members from JSD who did not join before the date fixed earlier. Mr. Ataur Rahman Khan joined on the last day on April 25.

In seeking national unity, as indicated earlier, Mujib did not go beyond his own boundary. Nor did he make any effort to bring all the political forces of the country together. Although hundreds and thousands of people at individual or group level, from different walks of life began to join the new party, no national convention or meeting of the representatives of other political parties or groups was convened nor were they taken into confidence. A large number of journalists, trade unionists, associations, government employees and factory workers, lawyers and other groups joined BAKSAL almost every day, 348 Jahangirnagar University employees including its Vice-Chancellor joined the BAKSAL[27]. The Dhaka University Senate expressed its solidarity with the BAKSAL programme and resolved to work relentlessly to materialise the objectives of the 'Second Revolution' in a resolution moved by its Vice-Chancellor Professor Abdul Matin Chowdhury and passed unanimously. Although some individual members of JSD and the NAP also joined the new party their party hierarchies kept aloof from the bandwagon. So the style of forging national unity was somewhat erratic. Mujib did not make any attempt to bring about a formal unity of all the political parties or forces in the country.

However, to summerise what was made known in some sort of concrete form was the reforms in the administrative sector. The districts which were much too large in area and population created by the British, were no longer suitable as administrative units particularly with the phenomenal rise of population compared to what it was 20 or 30 years ago. So the dissolution of the existing district and turning the sub-divisions into districts was not considered undesirable. But the most interesting aspect was that the administration of the district was now vested in a politically appointed Governor as opposed to a bureaucrat like District Magistrate or Deputy Commissioner. All the planning, implementation, maintenance of the law and order and administration of the entire district would now be co-ordinated and supervised by a person holding a political office. Mujib argued that it would (1) take the administration closer to the people and help in replacing the old colonial system ; (2) ensure decentralisation of the administration ; (3) bring all the branches of the government i.e. departments of food, agriculture, family planning, education and all others under one command and the tendency of the government departments working independent of each other or in indifference to each other by shifting responsibilities would go ; (4) ensure participation of people in preparing development plans and their implementation and (5) make the district administration efficient and responsible under a single political leadership.

With a similar system at the thana level which was to come into effect after a year, the overall scheme was in effect to establish a political authority over the administration at all levels. All governors were to be the members of the national political party BAKSAL and to have faith in its objectives—social, economic and political. Although out of the 61 governors 13 were civil servants and one was an army officer of the rank of Colonel, the political overtone in the scheme was predominent. Although in each district there was to be an Administrative Council comprising M. Ps, political leaders and representatives of BAKSAL and district officials of both civil and law enforcing agencies including that of the JRB and the Army, the fact that the District Magistrate would act as Secretary of the Council and the Governor as the Chairman directly appointed by Mujib reflected the policy of retaining complete political control. The Governor being the Chief Executive of the district was made the central figure in the functioning of the Administrative Council.

With regard to the inclusion of as many as 13 bureaucrats as Governors, a section argued that Mujib desired to reduce the tension or conflict that existed between the different professional classes and the politicians and wanted to bring about some kind of oneness between them[28]. It was considered as a part of his endeavour to unite the people of different professions for the welfare of the state and thereby to achieve a greater national unity. The argument of another section was that Mujib could no longer rely on his Awami League members who disappointed him by their poor performance and feared that they would indulge in corrupt practices. So he inducted a good number of bureaucrats to act as his political agents and appointed only 33 Members of Parliament as Governors[29]. Critics would, however, go further to say that Mujib having dismantled a traditional bureaucratic system where civil servants so long had been enjoying the power and privileges of running the district administration, established a political supremacy over the entire state machinery. It was an act to pacify the two most powerful organisations of state management, the bureaucracy and the army. By bringing the politicians under them in some places, he wanted to assure the bureaucrats better treatment under the new system[30].

The next important measure taken was the proposal for a compulsory multi-purpose co-operative in every village without touching the ownership of land. This was to be the basic economic unit of the development strategy. Although excepting what has been stated earlier no further detail was disclosed, the concept was not an absolutely new one and if implemented would have certainly brought a basic change in the productive sector with some hope for the common man, particularly the unemployed and landless farmers of the country. The share of the owners in the crops produced was to be cut into $\frac{1}{3}$ and its distribution among all the working members of the village with government's direct contribution in fertilizer, irrigation, power and other facilities could certainly be termed as a pragmatic reform yielding greater results. As the village co-operatives would be the basic unit, the gradual extinction of the union councils was also considered as a significantly radical reform to be introduced under the new system.

In the judiciary, with the power, status and jurisdiction of the Supreme Court already reduced, the proposal to shift the centre of justice to those levels also drew lot of attention. Although no elaborate mechanism was introduced for the approval of appointing Thana Magistrate (Development) in place of Circle Officer (Development) in the rural areas gave a new dimension on how the judicial administration at the thana level would take place[31].

Apart from what has been stated here, Mujib did not come forward with any other concrete economic or social programme, he did not spell out how the domestic resources were going to be increased, how the standard of living of the people would improve, how discipline would be restored in the nationalised industries, how vices like corruption, blackmarketing and hoarding which were crippling the economy of the country were to be checked, how the organised looting, smuggling, sabotage and secret killing was to come to an end. But even then, the steps he had taken with regard to the district administration and plans he proposed to adopt for compulsory co-operatives, thana magistracy and administration etc. had far-reaching significance.

Summary and Evaluation

Notwithstanding whether the reforms were good or bad or whether they were going to succeed or not in achieving the objectives of a socialist economic order or whether Mujib or his party was capable of implementing such programmes, the fact is that his steps confused the people generally and frightened a large section of the powerful social groups. As a matter of fact his proposed reforms were going to affect almost all the influencial classes of society. The land owners who constitute the rural elite and dominate rural life were in fear of losing their share-interest in compulsory co-operatives, the civil servants were now brought under complete political control, which they never liked. The army was pushed into the background of national activities against their wishes, the judiciary was made subservient to the executive annoying both the Bench and the Bar and lastly his own partymen, the Awami League and the members of Parliament had now become redundant institutions under the proposed new system.

Before answering the questions that may arise in this regard one might try to analyse why the earlier democratic system failed. Was it because of the system's inherent weaknesses or the failure of those people who were responsible for making the system work? It is true that a bourgeois parliamentary system in a poor country like Bangladesh would have lot of failings and might even sometime appear to be a myth but if we examine what actually led to the collapse of the economy, break-down of law and order in the country and rise of organised smuggling and corruption, it will be found that the system had a secondary role to play and the leaders and the party had the primary role in creating such a situation. To make any system work, besides the political will, the most important requirement would be the integrity of those who were engaged in making the system work. If the Awami League with their class character and with the socio-economic background of their individual leaders could not make a bourgeois parliamentary system work, how could they make a socialist system successful ?

It was known to Mujib that his party had failed in meeting the challenge of a newly born country. It was a faction-ridden and indisciplined petty bourgeois political party. It was a multi-class organisation with interregnum groups of people lacking inphilosophical orientation with no lesson on how to manage a socialist economic order. Nor was it unknown to him that his partymen were engaged in organised smuggling and corruption leading to the loss of credibility and public confidence. His partymen were more interested in petty personal gains than in realising the objectives of a 'socialist transformation'[32]. Petty factionalism and personal rivalries led to the killing of a large number of his workers down to the village level. Mujib was disillusioned by all these which led him to convince himself gradually that he had to get rid of his party which he helped to build for nearly 35 years.

So when he finally discarded his own party and went for the creation of a new national party, a fresh hope was raised amongst the people. It was expected that the devils would be put behind the scene and the sane elements in whom people had confidence would be brought into the front line to give a new dimension to the political course of the country. With the backing of his new party; new faces would emerge for the management of the state for realisation of his socialist objectives. Even the groups within the Awami League capable and dedicated to its cause, who were not given much of a recognition since independence, were now expected to have a fair position in the new party. A large number of genuine freedom fighters who were so long neglected and suppressed would now be given an opportunity to participate in building up the new nation.

But notwithstanding the other controversial aspects, the most disappointing feature was that Mujib opted to start his journey with the same people. He discarded his party but could not discard the men. He was disappointed by the performance of his partymen and yet he could not leave them behind. He knew some of them were corrupt and had earned a bad name for him and yet he could not throw them out. As a result, the same people for whom the party lost public confidence and whose guilt and failures led Mujib to the point of going to form a new order were back again in the forefront of the new national party. Excepting a few taken from the NAP(M) the entire body of the new structure was reoccupied by those leaders.

The day Mujib took over the office of the President, a new Council of Ministers was formed under the Fourth Amendment and the new ministers took their oath of office on January 26, 1975. All the ministers of the last cabinet including the State Ministers were retained and except Dr. A.R. Mallick and Dr. M. A. Chowdhury[33] no new entrant was seen in the government. Mr.

A.H.M. Qamaruzzaman recently the President of the Awami League and now out of that post, was taken back as minister again. Syed Nazrul Islam was appointed as the Vice-President and Mr. Mansoor Ali as the Prime Minister.

The next point was to see how Mujib shaped and manned his new organisation BAKSAL which he announced in February. After a long wait of nearly four months Mujib under Article 117(A) clause 3 of the Constitution in June 1975 announced the constitution of the Party and appointed a 15-member Executive Committee, a 115-member Central Committee and Five Fronts of the Party i.e. Jatiyo Krishak League, Jatiyo Sramik Leaue, Jatiyo Mahila League, Jatiyo Jubo League and Jatiyo Chatra League.

Mansoor Ali, a softer personality was made the Secretary-General of the Party and Tajuddin was completely kept out of any of these Committees. The three Secretaries of the Party, Zillur Rahman, Sheikh Moni and Abdur Razzak were included in the Executive Committee and all the members of the Executive Committee were to enjoy the rank and status of a minister. In the Executive Committee none was taken from outside the Awami League and each one held one or other important position in the old set-up.

In the 115-member Central Committee however ten persons were taken from outside the Awami League i.e. 7 from the NAP(M) and CPB,[34] the others were Mr. Ataur Rahman Khan who joined BAKSAL to retain his seat in the Parliament, Mang Prue Syne, Chief of Maniksari, Chittagong Hill Tracts, Haji Mohammed Danesh, an elderly left-wing politician. The Central Committee also included 20 Senior Civil Servants, the Vice Chancellors of Dhaka and Jahangirnagar University, the Editors of *Ittefaq* and *Bangladesh Observer* and the Chiefs of Army, Navy and Air Force. The Committee had individuals from some other walks of life. Many however alleged that they agreed to be in the Committee under pressure and were forced to give their consent. The civil servants holding the post of Secretaries etc. had hardly any alternative but to obey what the political masters decided for them. They were obviously more interested in retaining their jobs than in the political objective of the BAKSAL. However in the overall analysis, the Committees' political content remained predominantly that of the old Awami League.

The 5 frontal organisations Mujib announced on the same day were headed by the old Awami League stalwarts[35] but Moni Singh, head of the Bangladesh Communist Party was made a member of the peasants front—the Jatiyo Krishak League. These committees also mainly comprised people from the Awami League's earlier fronts. So the general impact of the announcement of these committees was frustrating as they failed to generate any new interest about the future political course amongst the people. On the contrary, it created a dark cloud over the future and frightened the people more than ever before. In the absence of fundamental rights and political freedom and with all other political parties banned and newspapers annulled, the situation only aggravated the sense of insecurity amongst the people.

So in the final analysis it appeared that Mujib really could not abandon his Awami League. Although he disliked it and blamed it for all the mistakes it made in the past, he could not leave his old colleagues. Although he discarded the Awami League but in effect he created a new Awami League[36]. Judging the composition of the Council of Ministers, the Executive and Central Committees, the Governors and the five fronts he constituted, the formation of BAKSAL did not make much of difference and for all practical purposes he turned his own Awami League into a new national party. As the men in these bodies were just the same and were dominated by the same individuals, the credibility and confidence his government and the Awami League had earlier lost, could not be regained. The crisis of faith and trust continued to erode the confidence of the people as before.

So Mujib relied on the same people to implement his new programmes. He employed almost the same people in the government and the party to make the new system successful. The question naturally arose that if his people were right, good and honest, the same objectives which he so far proposed could be achieved or implemented under a democratic system. If his people were not able to make a bourgeois parliamentary system work, could they make a socialist system successful ?

This appeared to be the central contradiction in Mujib's thought and deeds. And here the question arose whether Mujib changed the system for really establishing socialism or merely as a cover to hide his personal weaknesses in running the administration of the country. Mujib claimed to have changed the system to enable the society's progress. But was it true in the present case ?

Then again what else could Mujib do or who else could he take ? Since he failed to respond to the demand of Moulana Bhashani made at the very early stage of independence for the formation of a National Government and now having decided not to include the NAP (B), JSD and other democratic forces for a national unity in the true sense, Mujib had no alternative but to fall back on his own partymen. As personal loyalty and trust played the key role in chosing men in politics it was not possible for Mujib to abandon them at this stage. It took years and years to establish political trust and comradeship between him and his political workers. So Mujib did not see things in the way as the Moulana did or Tajuddin or Serajul Alam Khan. When he went in search of personal loyalty and trust he fell back on Sheikh Moni, Gazi Golam Mostafa, Abdur Razzak, Tofael Ahmed and Sheikh Shahidul Islam.

So again the same question arises. What then led Mujib to a one-party system ? Why did Mujib, who struggled and suffered for so many years for a democratic system would now go for something he never preached before ? The reasons why Mujib finally embarked on a monolithic system could be summarised as follows :

Domestic Situation

(1) The economic failure and the deteriorating law and order situation which have been discussed became such that no visible improvement could be made despite the extremely repressive laws and the ruthless employment of the Rakkhi Bahini. The nationalised industries continued to incur heavy losses and the labour unrest brought total indiscipline in that sector. The food production was still menacingly low and the overall mismanagement causing the disastrous famine shook the entire confidence of the people. Almost everyday some Awami League worker was being killed either due to internal fued or political or personal animosity. The political opposition was growing stronger every day and so was the public dissatisfaction and resentment over the performance of the government. Mujib realised that unless he acted in a decisive manner the situation would go completely out of control. His partymen had failed to rise to the occassion and the Awami League could no more be relied upon to remove corruption and improve management within the existing framework. He found that the 'roots of all the evils' were in the 'democratic system' itself and the only way the present state of affairs could be changed was by way of introducing a new system. So Mujib gradually inclined to the view that the economic condition and the existing law and order situation could be improved under a stable system with a more authoritarian rule. The government needed to be strong with more powers in hand so that it could solve the problem without any interference. Hence, the existing domestic situation could have led Mujib to believe that a change in the system could bring the improvement.

Perpetuation of Power

(2) The second consideration could simply be to perpetuate power. In view of the deteriorating situation in all spheres and particularly after the famine Mujib became shaky and insecure. He feared that with the rising opposition and public resentment he could be thrown out of power and as the "Father of the Nation" he could not accept such humiliation. So he went for a one-party rule to remain in power. Another section argued that Mujib had already all the powers he needed in his hand and even if he had gone for election he would have won an overwhelming majority ; his personal popularity with the masses was still at its height and so he was in no danger of losing power. Therefore, he did not change the system just to remain in power. It was his sense of responsibility towards the people that led him to change the system[37].

Socialist Economic Order

(3) The third consideration could be that Mujib genuinely believed that the 'socialist economic order' he was dreaming about could only be achieved through a one-party system. He was led to believe that a bourgeois parliamentary system could never help in establishing an exploitation-free socialist society in any country of the world. It was a luxury which a poor country like Bangladesh

could not afford. Now that he brought independence and was the Father of the Nation, he had to play the role of a "statesman, a nation-builder and philosopher-king". He wanted to be a Castro or a Boummediene if not Lenin or Mao Tse Tung. He wanted to set an example for other countries of the world, particularly the poorer ones. He was led to believe particularly by the NAP(M) and CPB leaders that with Awami League alone he would not be able to materialise his dream. The bad elements of the Awami League were to be discarded and "dedicated cadres like the ones these two parties had" were necessary for implementing socialist programmes. Smuggling, corruption and other social vices could not be eliminated in a bourgeois system and therefore, to remove such ills the established and tested course of a one-party system was essential in Bangladesh. The psychophants around him assumed that the Awami League, NAP(M) and CPB were together capable of making a socialist transformation successful. Finally, Mujib's faith in such arguments grew and after thinking for a long time he changed the system.

If carefully examined, it would be difficult to say which particular consideration led Mujib to change the system. It would be a rash to pinpoint one or the other as the sole cause. Most likely, it was a combination of all the three that convinced him to change the system. One could argue that having failed to manage the affairs of the state he changed the system to rectify it or having feared the loss of authority he opted for perpetuation of power or he perhaps genuinely turned for nation-building through a socialist economy. Whatever might have been the consideration, the irony is that the reasons which were apparently haunting Mujib caused by the poor performance of the government, continued to persist even after the BAKSAL was formed. The attitude, the style of administration, the non-professional approach and above all the inclusion of all those who had created a national crisis of credibility in the new framework, failed to recreate that credibility in the ruling elite. The national unity sought for under the BAKSAL seemed to be only a political bogey and the creation of one-party rule appeared to be mainly a political instrument to sustain the rule of the same elite group.

As mentioned earlier, the introduction of a one-party system with Mujib taking over all the powers raised public expectations once again. It was expected that the security of life and property would be restored and the economic life of the people would improve. The government could no more blame the opposition parties or the 'collaborators' any more for standing in the way of improving the situation. To the common people the high philosophical aspect of a 'one-party rule for a socialist transformation' did not mean anything. They were more concerned about the immediate problems they were confronted with i.e. 'peace and bread' for a normal living. With the change in the ruling system, people expected an immediate improvement. Although the Fourth Amendment was not an army take-over, the essence was the same in the sense that in the prevailing situation such a radical change in the system raised the hope that it would stop the "free style" element in the administration and people would be able to sleep in peace.

But once the one-party was introduced there was hardly any immediate impact felt in the social and economic spheres. Although the new leaders continued to make strong statements and Mujib made appeals to boost production and fight corruption, no immediate alertness was noticed in the fields or factories. Despite Mujib's strong warnings that the extreme action would be taken against those indulging in secret killings and anti-social activities,[38] within less than a month and even before he declared the formation of his national party he lost one of his members of Parliament who was shot dead on February 23[39]. Although Mujib forced the members of Parliament to declare their assets no action was taken to actually find out whether they were involved in acquiring illegal properties or not[40].

The reasons why the immediate socio-political impact was not felt could be summarised as follows : (1) it was a change within the civilian framework; (2) there was no change in the position of people holding offices of power or influence—on the contrary the new system only increased the power and infiuence of the same people who were in the government or the party, and (3) the overall political leadership was inefficient and the change did not bring any significant improvement in administration or socio-economic condition.

Towards Some Improvement : Mujib Seeks Moulana's Support

Another interesting development however was that although Mujib could undermine the strength of the JSD and the NAP as political parties, he could not ignore the political standing of Moulana Bhashani. The two leaders had always maintained a personal relationship and in order to take advantage of it, Mujib called on Moulana on March 8. Despite Moulana's reservation on certain issues, the leader who had earlier "retired" from politics prior to emergency received Mujib with great warmth. In return for a huge sum promised by Mujib for Moulana's proposed Islamic University at Shantosh, Mujib made a political gain in the sense that Moulana did not express his opposition to the new scheme of Mujib. Moulana preferred "to watch the situation" and "allow Mujib some more time" and "a last opportunity"[41]. In a way it was a tacit blessing from Moulana which helped Mujib in creating a better atmosphere as far as the left democratic forces were concerned[42].

Law and Order

On the social front, Mujib was able to tighten the smuggling across the border with the aid of the Army[43]. For recovery of illegal arms 15 days time was granted with the assurance that those who surrendered arms within that period would not be punished and this was to be considered as the last chance given to those who had yet not surrendered unauthorised arms[44]. Steps were also taken to stop the malpractices in rationed goods and unauthorised movement of rationed articles out of any of the 5 rationing districts was prohibited with penal provisions for delay or obstruction in delivery of rice or paddy under the internal procurement scheme[45].

Economic Recovery

By June 1975 however, the economic condition of the country generally improved. It happend not so much because of the change in the system but primarily because of a good *boro* crop and the arrival of the delayed shipments meant to meet the food deficit and the famine earlier suffered by the people. Certain fiscal measures also helped in bringing the economy under some control. The demonetisation of 100 taka notes in April, as a part of the economic squeeze helped in checking inflation and the devaluation of the taka in relation to pound sterling led to increased export earnings. In order to boost the private enterprise in the jute sector, the statutory minimum price of jute was lifted. The budget announced in June aimed at 10% growth rate of national income over the last year. With the Aid to Bangladesh Consortium's much increased support, the development budget was increased by 450 crore over the previous year's Tk.525 crores. The Five-year plan was revised and for the remaining 3 years of the plan, a Three-year Development Programme was presented before the Consortium. The economic measures of demonetisation and devaluation were considered as correct by the aid giving agencies.

As a result, the money supply was reduced from Tk. 9377.6 million in December 1974 to Tk. 8143.3 million in June, 1975 and the foreign exchange reserve increased from Tk. 1114.9 million to Tk. 3508.0 million in June, 1975[46]. With the improved stock position of foodgrains the price of rice started showing a downward trend along with some other essential items. By June the price of rice came down to Tk. 5.50 per seer from Tk. 8/- in January, Long cloth from Tk. 13/- per yard in January to Tk. 11.50 in June, Mustard oil from Tk. 41.68 per seer in January to Tk. 30.37 in June, Potato from Tk. 2.05 to Tk. 1.50, Ruhi fish from Tk. 14.14 to Tk. 10.00 and Kerosene from Tk. 1.40 to Tk. 1.20.

As a consequence the the cost of living index was also showing a considerable improvement. The living index of the middle class people in Dhaka city dropped from a general level of Tk. 458.5 in January to Tk. 416.9 in April and for food from Tk. 546.3 to Tk. 459.0 in April, 1975.

By August, 1975 the situation further improved. With a good monsoon and prospect for a good production of *Aman*, the downward trend of the essential commodities was still continuing, Mujib's new political agents were on their way to completing the one-month training course to assume the role of the Governors from the first of September when the change in the administrative structure of the district was to take effect.

End of the BAKSAL Regime : Brutal Killing of Sheikh Mujib

Mujib did not survive nor did his system. Although there was the prospect of improvement in the economic sector, it had little to do with the change in the system or the economic order he was to introduce, but the fact that certain conditions as described in this chapter improved could not be questioned. And yet Mujib was killed brutally along with his entire family in the early hours of 15th August, 1975. It was a gruesome mass murder, and his youngest son 8 years of age, his two sons with their newly married brides and members of two other near and influential families related to Mujib were not spared. A group of army officers killed Mujib only to hand over the power to his colleagues who in turn buried him and his system and all that he stood for. But in course of time it became clear that the army officers who took lead in the operation had no plan of their own. The question remains why then did they do it and for whom[47]? Did they do it only to relieve people from the tyranny of Mujib or it was an act of vengeance arising out of personal anger or was it a part of a precision-planning to eliminate the prospect of having the country run by a strong political leadership ? Did Mujib pay this price for the mismanagement of the country or for turning it into a one-party state for a socialist transformation? Were his reforms too strong or radical for the vested interest groups to withstand ? If Mujib's colleagues were equal partners in his misdeeds and mismanagement and were equally responsible for his tyranical rule, what was the mystery of handing over power to them and not to others ? Was the killing in jail of 4 Awami League leaders in November a part of the same scheme or it was done only to remove the political rivals ? Each of these questions needs an answer and it will not be easy to find one. The framework of this book does not permit me to go further but it is hoped that one day the truth will be revealed to our future generations.

Anyhow that was the end of Sheikh Mujibur Rahman and the beginning of a new era for Bangladesh. The death of Mujib changed the entire perspective of Bangladesh politics. The new journey began with a general sense of relief in the mind of the people and the countries took lead in according recognition to the new government were i.e. Pakistan, China and Saudi Arabia. Following the change, the dependence on India and the Soviet Union lessened and the relation with China, Pakistan, Saudi Arabia and the West generally improved.

But it did not end there. There was a coup and a counter-coup within the Army in the first week of November, ultimately paving the way for the rise of the Army permanently to power repeating the scenerio in the majority of the countries of the third world. In the process, more killings took place and 4 Awami League top leaders were shot dead inside the Dhaka Central Jail by automatic brushfire. By the second week of November the Army, as young as the country itself, took complete control over the affairs of the State.

Most important of all, besides the change in the economic policies and the tilt in the foreign relation, was the reversal in the social and political trends of the country. The 'collaborators' who were supporting Pakistan and opposing the independence of Bangladesh were restored in society and were allowed to share power. The principles and values achieved through the long struggle by the Bengalis in their nationalist movement where undermined, putting the whole history into controversy. Once again, clique, conspiracy, tricks and treachery became the major instruments for retaining authority in the power game. It would be interesting to see whether these reversals prove lasting or not, whether the history of a people and their achievements can be obliterated so early and within such a short time after they were created at the cost of blood and a war.

FOOTNOTES

1. As far as the law and order situation was concerned people simply lost faith in the law enforcing agencies. There was no security of life or property. From January 1972 to April, 1973, 4925 persons were killed by miscreants and 2035 secret killings of political nature took place. 337 women were kidnapped and 190 women were raped.—*The Bangladesh Observer*, 7.7.1973.
   By the end of 1974 the Awami League claimed to have lost over 4000 workers and leaders. A series of sabotage ruined the economy—fire at jute godowns, and fire at Ghorasal Fertilizer Factory in September, 1974 were the most disastrous ones.
2. Tajuddin Ahmed, Syed Nazrul Islam, Quamaruzzaman, all told the author in November, 1974 that none knew what was Mujib's actual plan.
3. The author was the first person to be arrested after the proclamation of emergency under a preventive detention order, though he had nothing to do with the security of the state or economic disturbance in the country. The author took an active part in the war of independence and at the time of arrest he was not associated with any political party. But the author became an open critic of the government and was one of the very few frequently quoted in foreign press for his dissenting voice. He was the Secretary of the Committee for Civil Liberties and Legal Aid.
4. It was widely suspected that Golam Kibria was killed by his own partymen as it happened in most of the Awami League cases although the government tended to blame the "anti-state" elements or opposition parties.
5. See Enayetullah Khan's article in *Holiday*, September 16, 1973.
6. *The Bangladesh Observer* 13.1.1975 ane 15.1.1975.
7. In January, 1974 Mujib had virtually abandoned the Awami League when he gave up the post of the President of the party although it was claimed to have been done to keep up with the democratic tradition of the party.
8. From the Awami League side, Sheikh Fazlul Huq Moni played the key role in evolving a doctrine for a one-party rule in Bangladesh.
9. A large number of the members of Parliament confided to me later that they did not raise their voice out of fear of being killed by the counter-forces within the party and they would lose the protection and umbrella they were enjoying now. The corrupt MPs supported the move strongly in order to enjoy the shelter for their misdeeds. Mujib allegedly maintained a file for each minister and member of Parliament. There were allegations also that the plan to change the constitution could be processed so easily because tactics of intimidation and blackmail was applied by the key ruling groups over others.
10. Paragraph 35 of the Fourth Amendment read as follows :
    "Special provisions relating to President—Notwithstanding anything contained in the Constitution, on the commencement of this Act—

(a) the person holding office as President of Bangladesh immediately before such commencement shall cease to hold, and vacate, the office of President of Bangladesh :
(b) Bangabandhu Sheikh Mujibur Rahman, Father of the Nation, shall become, and enter upon the office of President of Bangladesh and shall, as from such commencement, hold office as President of Bangladesh as if elected to that office under the Constitution as amended by this Act."

11. As indicated earlier, Mohammadullah was made President only to ease this transition.
12. See paragraph 2 along with Article 11 of the Constitution. The amendment envisaged turning a democnatic system into a one-party monolithic one, omitting or incorporating provisions to suit the new arrangement. In Part II where fundamental principles of state policy were laid down Article 11 contemplated that people would effectively participate through their elected representatives in the administration at all levels in order to ensure a truly democratic system. Article 11 was amended by paragraph 2 of the new Act to omit the democratic aspect of the article.
13. See paragraph 12 of the Fourth Amendment and Article 80 of the Constitution.
14. By making this amendment the provision was made more rigid to debar members from raising any voice against the party.
15. Mujib was advised therefore to introduce the Bill on a Saturday, the day the Supreme Court does not sit. The unusual way of passing the law without any debate or discussion also suggested that Mujib did not want to leave any scope to block the change. The Chief Justice was perhaps not trusted anymore to administer the oath. Otherwise, there could be hardly any reason to change this provision. The Speaker, a party member was readily available to administer the oath of office to the President in the premises of the Parliament soon after the law was passed.
16. See the amendment in the Third Schedule.
17. *Statement in Parliament* on 25.1.1975.
    Addressing a public meeting on 26.3.1975 :
    Addressing the First Central Committee Meeting on 19.6.1975 ;
    Address to the newly appointed Governors on July 21, 1975.
18. This was the last public meeting addressed by Sheikh Mujib.
19. Mujib planned to have about 100 co-operatives first, each supervised by a Central Committee member.
    Initially the landholding ceiling would continue to remain at 100 bighas.
    Mujib also envisaged 61 special co-operatives to be organised and supervised in each new district by the respective governors.
20. In his address on 26.3.1975 Mujib talked about having a 'Chairman' for each Thana Council and in the address to the Governors he mentioned to have 'Administrators' at the Thana level.
21. Mujib spoke at length about the inefficiency of the existing judicial system. He was extremely critical of the lengthy and time-consuming procedure and how people suffered under section 54 of the Criminal Procedure Code where people undergo imprisonment as 'under-trial prisoners'—sometime for years without any trial, just on suspicion and due to misuse of law. Sometimes people live in jails for years together under the aforesaid section which enable a police officer to put a person in jail merely on suspicion. Anyhow no scheme was elaborated further in this regard.
    In a conversation with the author on August 13 prior to his death Mujib said that he had already reduced the jurisdiction of the Supreme Court and would further cut it down and thana headquarters would be made the central place of settling litigations. Accordingly, he would go for major reforms in this field and the civil and criminal procedure codes would be drastically amended. Mujib further said that he would develop each thana as a modern town to be the centre of all economic activities.

22. No elaboration was made on this point either and it is not known what exact plan Mujib had to reorganise the Secretariat and its functional procedures. He talked about the Minister to get the work done by the Joint Secretaries and it was not clear what he actually meant.—See his statement dated 19.6.1975.
23. The Four-Point Programme of Mujib's 'Second Revolution' was said to be (1) building up of a self-reliant economy by boosting production in the field and factory, (2) controlling the population boom, (3) weeding out corruption and (4) unity of Bengali nation. —*Holiday*, March 16, 1975.
24. It happened on January 28, 1975. See *Bangladesh Observer* 29.1.1975.
25. *The Bangladesh Times, The Bangladesh Observer, Dainik Bangla* and *The Daily Ittefaq.*
26. The daily *Ittefaq*, the most popular Bengali daily, was the Awami League mouthpiece for the entire period of the autonomy movement and made great contributions to the emergence of the Awami League as a political party. However, another renowned newspaper '*Sangbad*' was completely banned.
    Sheikh Fazlul Huq Moni, one of the three Secretaries of BAKSAL and a nephew of Mujib however retained his position as the Editor of the *Bangladesh Times* which he owned.
27. *The Bangladesh Observer*, 26.6.1975.
28. See Mujib's statement of 21.7.1975 addressing the Governors.
29. For list of Governors, see the *Bangladesh Times*, 17.7.1975.
30. See how Mujib justified the unification of government officials with the politicians in his statement of 21.7.1975.
31. *The Bangladesh Observer* 23.6.1975.
32. Based on a discussion with Mujib in June, 1974.
33. Dr. A. R. Mallick and Dr. M. A. Chowdhury were already associated with the Awami League since the independence war.
34. Professor Mozaffar Ahmed, Khandaker Md. Ilias, Ataur Rahman of Rajshahi, Pir Habibur Rahman, Syed Altaf Hossain, Mohammed Forhad and Begum Motia Chowdhury.
35. Mr. Phani Bhushan Majumder—Jatiyo Krishak League
    Mr. Yousuf Ali Chowdhury—Jatiyo Sramik League
    Mrs. Sajeda Begum—Jatio Mahila League
    Mr. Tofael Ahmed—Jatiyo Jubo League
    Mr. Sheikh Shahid—Jatiyo Chatra League
36. From the selection of the name of the new party it was clear that Mujib could not leave the Awami League or resist the pressure of his men in the Awami League. So in the new name the words "Awami League" had to be retained.
37. Mujib claimed that he was thinking for a long time to bring a change in the system and he did not change the system for power. See his statement at the first meeting of the Central Committee of BAKSAL.
38. *The Bangladesh Observer*, Dacca, 11.2. 1975.
39. Mr. Abdul Khaleq, M.P. from Netrokona, See also the obituary resolution passed in the Parliament on 23.6.75. During this period of six months commencing from January 25 a good number of BAKSAL leaders and workers were killed. Miss Rousham Ara Bakul, an active BAKSAL female leader was shot dead at Gaibandha, Rangpur in March, 1975. *Bangladesh Observer*, 15.3.1975.
40. Although Mujib dismissed one of his State Ministers, Nurul Islam Manzoor on charge of grave corruption, no formal chage was framed against him and the statements of assets he took earlier from his partymen were used cnly to keep the party stalwarts under control.
    See Enayetullah Khan's articles in *Holiday* on February 2, March 9 and 20, 1975.
41. Weekly *Holiday*, March 16, 1975.

42. In the private meeting between the two, the Moulana however emphasised that Bangladesh should follow a more indepedent foreign policy and improve its relationship with China. Moulana advised Mujib not to give in to India on the question of Farakka and maritime boundary.
Source : From a discussion the author had with Sheikh Fazlul Huq Moni in April, 1975.
43. On Aprial 7, in order to intensify the anti-smuggling measure, movement across the border with India was completely suspended for 3 days.—The *Bangladesh Observer*, 8.4.1975 and 20.4.1975.
44. *The Bangladesh Observer*, 4.4.1975.
Although killing continued and recovery of arms was not satisfactory, the overall situation tended to improve gradually.
45. *The Bangladesh Observer*, 15.2.1975.
46. *Economic Review*, 1974 and Economic Review, 1975-76 published by the Planning Commission, Government of Bangladesh.
47. See for more detail, *Bangladesh : The unfinishedRevolution*, Lawrence Lifschultz, Zed Press, London.

CHAPTER TWELVE

SHEIKH MUJIBUR RAHMAN

Mujib is the greatest phenomenon of our history. His death was not his end. He will continue to remain as a legend in the political life of Bangladesh. Bengalis might have had leaders in their history more intelligent, more capable and more dynamic than Sheikh Mujib but none gave so much to the Bengalis political independence and a national identity. It is Mujib who in the end was able to identify himself not only with the cause of the Bengalis but with their dreams. He became the symbol of Bengali nationalism which gave birth to a movement leading to an independent and sovereign identity. In whatever form Bangladesh exists or whatever reversal it takes in its domestic political content or in its foreign relations, Mujib's position as a leader of the nationalist movement will not alter. Whether or not socialism or capitalism or neo-traditionalism takes its root in the socio-economic structure of the country or whether there is a reactionary or revolutionary government, the fact that there is a country called Bangladesh is a sufficient testimony to Mujib's status as a legend of our age.

But as Mujib was a human being, he had contradictions and weaknesses too. To understand him better it may be worthwhile to divide his role in two parts. The first upto January 10, 1972 and the second from then on till his death. In the first part we find that Mujib was consistent in his commitment for the cause of the Bengalis. He acted like a bourgeois liberal democrat and preached his ideals in consonance with a democratic framework. Gradually through mass-upheavals he was drawn closer to socialist thinking and played the role of a social-democrat. At the height of the nationalist movement he was more led by the young, radical nationalist forces and it became increasingly difficult for him to contain them. His training and habits showed that he was inclined to achieve his goals through negotiation across the table rather than through confrontation. He led a middle-of-the-road party with people mainly drawn from the middle and lower middle class, heterogeneous in character, faction-ridden and indisciplined. When the Pakistan Army cracked down, Mujib surrendered instead of joining his ranks to fight in the war. During the entire period of the independence war, Mujib was absent and the war was won without his direct participation[1].

Anyhow, the first part carried for Mujib a story of great success. Although he faltered on many occasions, sometime vacillated and at the end 'surrendered' to the Pakistan Army leaving everyone plunged into a 'bloody war', he yet proved to be a true hero of the people. The war was fought and won in his name and his return from Pakistan's captivity restored him to a position of a living legend as the Bangabandhu, the Father of the Nation and the President of the new Republic.

But in the second part, as soon as Mujib assumed power he started failing. It was not that he was not a good administrator or that he was not able to manage a government but it was in determining the correct perspective of a new society born out of a war that he faltered. The primary reason for such a lack of understanding was his absence during the entire period of war.

The war produced numerous currents and cross-currents and generated new dynamics in the thought process of the entire population of the country. The people had now had the experience of dealing with arms in hand for the first time in their history and this itself brought a new dimension into the politics of the country. The challenge for Mujib was to understand these new developments which took place during his absence. One can make laws or pass orders to meet a situation like the one in this case but unless one could comprehend the under-currents of an 'armed struggle' of such magnitude, laws and orders or speeches alone were not sufficient to meet such a challenge.

On his return he only heard stories in various versions of an over-zealous group of compatriots, of a faction-ridden ill-disciplined cotery of people who failed to look beyond their own area of self-interest. As most of he Awami League leaders in Calcutta did not take any direct part in the war, for Mujib it became even more difficult to understand the dynamics produced by the war. The result was that, on his return, Mujib engaged himself and his party more for restoration in power than for nation-building ignoring the facts, tragedies, currents and counter-currents, hopes and aspirations, dreams and emotions produced during the 9-month war. This was reflected in the style, approach and behaviour of the new ruling elite of the country. In their recklessness, utter callousness and lack of sense of urgency, it was shown that they came to power through a mere election and not a war. It was like the taking over of the Provincial Government in 1954 through peaceful means by winning an election. Although Mujib blamed the 'collaborators' and the 'armed guerillas' for the "free style"[2] that was prevailing in the country, but it was his own party and the greed of his own men that created the unbearable situation.

Mujib was constrained by the fact that the Awami League was brought to power through the patronage of the Indian Government. Despite an armed struggle it was due to the Indian government's direct support that the Awami League could hold the leadership and attain power. When Mujib arrived, he was confronted by the presence of about 100,000 Indian troops and the understanding the two governments had already reached for Bangladesh to follow a subservient role. For him it was not possible to come out of this situation so easily.

Mujib also failed to manage his relatives, not to speak of his partymen. His feudal tendencies allowed the sychophants to gather round him and his relatives to gain more power than anybody else in the government or the party. This patronisation allowed corruption to creep into the body politic of the nation. As a result, whenever he spoke against corruption or smuggling or other social ills, he did not realise that with these men around him his utterences did not enjoy much credibility. Consequently, none of his measures was able to produce enough success and on the contrary many of them proved to be counter-productive. Mujib wanted to be strict on the question of crime and punishment, but in many cases due to political intervention and sometime by his own, his partymen got away without any punishment. When he called the Army to check smuggling or collect arms he had to withdraw them under the pressure from his own party.

Having failed to improve the situation, when Mujib at last embarked on a one-party system, he was a lone person in the entire exercise. When he gave his 4-point programme as a step to complete his 'second revolution' he was addressing the same men who had earlier failed to rise to the occasion. When he called for a crusade against corruption and nepotism, it went almost unheeded. He was perhaps 3 years too late in mobilising the people for a nation-building action programme. Although thousands of men were joining his BAKSAL and the partymen listened to his emotional and heart-breaking speeches between January 25 and July 21, 1975, it is doubtful how much they themselves believed in his programmes. When he came forward with the grand perception of building a new political and economic order in the country, his old partymen were criticising him in their drawing rooms behind his back.

It is true also that Mujib touched some very basic issues facing the people in his 4 statements made between January 25 and July 21, 1975. He pointed out some chronic ills of the society ranging from the administative set up to the land tenure system. No matter what kind of people rule Bangladesh in future, these fundamental problems will remain as the real challenge to the nation. Ideology apart, it can be argued that unless the agricultural production-relation is reorganised on the basis of organised co-operatives changing the land tenure system and the administration re-structured in order to enable people to take an active part in planning and development within a decentralised framework, the society would continue to lag behind. In a country where the land-man ratio is 4 to 1 acre only and more than 50% of the people have little or no land and the same live below a minimum subsistence level, the primary resposibility of the state is bound to be the amelioration of the sufferings of those people in the quickest possible time.

The problem is, any reform of a fundamental nature would at the initial stage immediately affect 'a class of people' who thrive on he status quo. This class will therefore, be opposed to such reforms and the larger section for whose benefit such reforms are intended do not see it or support it till such benefits actually reach them. There is always a time-gap between the initiation of a reform and the result of such reform reaching the people. A reform therefore has to be given time to prove its worth. But Mujib did not get the time to show the worth of his proposed reforms. In this regard he went ahead of his party and people. As his proposed reforms disturbed the future of the status quo of a powerful class of people including an influential section of his own partymen, they were in their heart opposed to such reforms. The philosophical indoctrination and the strong leadership that it required at every level to confront such classes and to mobilise people for whom such reforms would be introduced, were lacking and as a result Mujib could not succeed.

Although Mujib was often criticised for lacking in intellect and comprehension, but he possessed extremely rich instincts and political perception. Mujib's human qualities, his kindness and generosity were considered at times to be excessive. He would easily pardon someone who committed a grave crime and send food and money to jail for those people he had imprisoned on charges of being 'collaborators'. Mujib's emotional behaviour reflected the life style of the Bengali nation and he combined himself all the characteristics of a Bengali.

Despite Mujib's many failures, the fact that Mujib was sincere and his intentions were genuine and that he loved his people should not be questioned. He was a nationalist and a patriot who secured his principal purpose of leading a people through the creation of a new sovereign state. As an administrator he might have failed, not so much for himself but for the greed and incompetence of his partymen and their class character and the overall unmanageable state of affairs that he inherited following the 9-month war.

As a nationalist he tried his best to bring Bangladesh out of the Indian subjugation. He signed a Friendship Treaty with India but he was able to send out the Indian troops from the soil of Bangladesh within 2 months after his arrival. He flew over the Indian territory to their utter disgust to attend the Islamic Summit at Lahore. By inviting Bhutto to Bangladesh he normalised relationship with Pakistan. By calling on King Khaled and visiting a large number of Arab countries he improved Bangladesh's relationship with the Islamic block. By restoration of trade with a number of middle eastern countries the economic transactions with Arab world generally increased. He took an active part in the non-aligned conference and at the same time improved relationship with the United States. He was able to establish the Aid to Bangladesh Consortium in 1974 and received the Secretary of State, Henry Kissinger at Dhaka. He started to shift his economic policy by providing opportunity for foreign and private investment and accorded a warm reception to McNamara the World Bank President. With McNamara's visit to Bangladesh he also sent emissaries to China for a formal relationship[3]. He removed Tajuddin to reduce the weight of Indo-Soviet influence inside the government. With the membership in the United Nations, he met with the United States President, Gerald Ford. What it all meant was that he was gradually taking a neutral position and continued to play the role of a nationalist to retain and consolidate the independence and sovereignty of Bangladesh.

What kind of people Mujib relied upon and "the affinity of ideology" he sought to have became clear only after his death. The character of these comrades on whom Mujib depended to establish an 'exploitation-free society' remained no longer unknown once Mujib was killed. Due to their "loyalty and allegiance" as Mujib used to boast, he inducted them even after banning the Awami League into his new national party, but once he died the same 'loyalty and allegiance' disappeared overnight to lend support to the beneficiares of the death of the leader. The day Mujib was killed, the government which was formed comprised all his earlier colleagues and workers. Almost all the Executive and Central Committee members switched their allegiance to the new government of the country[4]. It is interesting to note that at a subsequent stage many joined the Bangladesh Nationalist Party formed by Ziaur Rahman which was alleged to be a party of 'collaborators'. Out of the 15 Executive Committee members of the BAKSAL, 2 were killed (Mujib and Sheikh Moni on 15th August), 7 were in jail (3 killed later), 4 were in the new government as President and Ministers, one went to Soviet Union as a Special envoy and the other continued as the Speaker of the Parliament[5].

Finally, notwithstanding Mujib's last endeavour to introduce certain radical reforms addressing some very fundamental issues confronting the country and despite his failures and mistakes, Mujib's return to Bangladesh in itself saved the new country from further and perpetual subjugation. Had Mujib been killed by the Pakistani junta he would have been immortal and he would have perhaps occupied a higher position in the heart and history of the Bengalis. He would have been considered the greatest martyr of our history. But in that case the cost to the people in physical terms would have been much higher. As already discussed, the state of Bangladesh would have been in a flux without him. There would have been a number of governments in the country ; reprisals and battles of attrition would have taken countless lives and 'necessity' would have demanded a permanent position of the Indian Army on the soil of Bangladesh. But Mujib's return saved Bangladesh from a state of subjugation which could continue for an unlimited period. However once Mujib came back and saved the independence of the country there was nothing more he could do to elevate his position further since very few people in the world, particularly in the developing countries can maintain popularity once they assume power and stand face to face with the realities of state management.

It seems that Mujib came back from the pedestal of an immortal being only to die for saving the independence for which he struggled. It is true that Mujib faced a tragic death but he left Bangladesh free and independent. Although that death came from the hands of his own men and in a brutal form, could Mujib not in this particular context be called a martyr?

FOOTNOTES

1. See for more detail on Mujib's role during the period of the first part, Author's book : *Bangladesh : Constitutional Quest for Autonomy.*
2. Mujib used this boxing phrase frequently in his later speeches, meaning absolute lawlessness in all fileds.
3. Bangladesh signed 4 trade agreements with China at Canton in May, 1975 and China was going to accord recognition to Bangladesh soon.—*Bangladesh Observer*, May 20, 1975 and May 5, 1975.
4. All those taken in Khandaker Moshtaque Ahmed's government after the killing were also members of Mujib's government. They were :
   (1) Mr. Justice Abu Sayeed Chowdhury
   (2) Prof. Md. Yusuf Ali
   (3) Sri Phani Majumder
   (4) Mr. Mohammad Sohrab Hossain
   (5) Mr. Abdul Mannan
   (6) Sri. Monoranjan Dhar
   (7) Mr. Abdul Momin
   (8) Mr. Asaduzzaman Khan
   (9) Dr. Azizur Rahman Mallik
   (10) Dr. Muzaffar Ahmed Chowdhury

   Some of them however argued that they were forced to join the new government.
5. BAKSAL 15-Member Executive Commitee :
   (1) Sheikh Mujibur Rahman—killed on August 15, 1975.
   (2) Syed Nazrul Islam—killed on November 3, 1975.
   (3) M. Mansoor Ali—killed on November 3, 1975.
   (4) Khandaker Moshtaque Ahmed—became President
   (5) Mr. A.H.M. Kamaruzzaman—killed on November 3, 1975.
   (6) Abdul Malek Ukil—continued as Speaker
   (7) Prof. Md. Yusuf Ali—Minister
   (8) Sri Monoranjan Dhar—Minister
   (9) Dr. Muzaffar Ahmed Chowdhury—Minister
   (10) Sheikh Abdul Aziz—jailed
   (11) Mohiuddin Ahmed—Envoy to USSR
   (12) Ghazi Golam Mostafa—jailed
   (13) Zillur Rahman—jailed
   (14) Sheikh Fazlul Huq Moni—killed on August 15, 1975.
   (15) Abdur Razzak—jailed

Appendix 'A'

The Proclamation of Independence

Mujibnagar, Bangladesh
Dated 10th day of April. 1971.

Whereas free elections were held in Bangladesh from 7th December, 1970 to 17th January, 1971, to elect representatives for the purpose of framing a Constitution,

AND

Whereas at these elections the people of Bangladesh elected 167 out of 169 representatives belonging to the Awami League,

AND

Whereas General Yahya Khan summoned the elected representatives of the people to meet on the 3rd March, 1971, for the purpose of framing a Constitution,

AND

Whereas the Assembly so summoned was arbitrarily and illegally postponed for an indefinite period,

AND

Whereas instead of fulfilling their promise and while still conferring with the representatives of the people of Bangladesh, Pakistan authorities declared an unjust and treacherous war,

AND

Whereas in the facts and circumstances of such treacherous conduct Bangabandhu Sheikh Mujibur Rahman, the undisputed leader of 75 million of people of Bangladesh, in due fulfilment of the legitimate right of self-determination of the people of Bangladesh, duly made a declaration of independence at Dacca on March 26, 1971, and urged the people of Bangladesh to defend the honour and integrity of Bangladesh,

AND

Whereas in the conduct of a ruthless and savage war the Pakistani authorities committed and are still continuously committing numerous acts of genocide and unprecedented tortures, amongst others on the civilian and unarmed people of Bangladesh,

AND

Whereas the Pakistan Government by levying an unjust war and committing genocide and by other repressive measures made it impossible for the elected representatives of the people of Bangladesh to meet and frame a Constitution, and give to themselves a Government,

AND

Whereas the people of Bangladesh by their heroism, bravery and revolutionary fervour have established effective control over the territories of Bangladesh,

We the elected representatives of the people of Bangladesh, as honour bound by the mandate given to us by the people of Bangladesh whose will is supreme duly constituted ourselves into a Constituent Assembly, and

having held mutual consultations, and

in order to ensure for the people of Bangladesh equality, human dignity and social justice,

declare and constitute Bangladesh to be a sovereign People's Republic and thereby confirm the declaration of independence already made by Bangabandhu Sheikh Mujibur Rahman and do hereby affirm and resolve that till such time as a Constitution is framed, Bangabandhu Sheikh Mujibur Rahman shall be the President of the Republic and that Syed Nazrul Islam shall be the Vice President of the Republic, and

that the President shall be the Supreme Commander of all the Armed Forces of the Republic,

shall exercise all the Executive and Legislative powers of the Republic including the power to grant pardon,

shall have the power to appoint a Prime Minister and such other Ministers as he considers necessary.

shall have the power to levy taxes and expend monies,

shall have the power to summon and adjourn the Constituent Assembly, and

do all other things that may be necessary to give to the people of Bangladesh an orderly and just Government.

We the elected representatives of the people of Bangladesh do further resolve that in the event of there being no President or the President being unable to enter upon his office or being unable to exercise his powers, due to any reason whatsoever, the Vice President shall have and exercise all the powers, duties and responsibilities herein conferred on the President.

We further resolve that we undertake to observe and give effect to all duties and obligations that devolve upon us as a member of the family of nations and to abide by the Charter of the United Nations.

We further resolve that this proclamation of independence shall be deemed to have come into effect from 26th day of March, 1971.

We further resolve that in order to give effect to this instrument we appoint Prof. Yusuf Ali our duly Constituted potentiary and to give to the President and the Vice President oaths of office.

Sd/- PROF. YUSUF ALI
Duly Constituted Potentiary.
By and under the authority
of the Constituent Assembly
of Bangladesh.

Appendix 'B'

Laws Continuance Enforcement Order

Mujibnagar,
Dated 10th day of April, 1971

I, Syed Nazrul Islam, the Vice President and Acting President of Bangladesh, in exercise of the powers conferred on me by the Proclamation of Independence dated tenth day of April, 1971, do hereby order that all laws that were in force in Bangladesh on 25th March, 1971, shall subject to the Proclamation aforesaid continue to be so in force with such consequential changes as may be necessary on account of the creation of the sovereign independent State of Bangladesh formed by the will of the people of Bangladesh and that all government officials—civil, military, judicial and diplomatic who take the oath of allegiance to Bangladesh shall continue in their offices on terms and conditions of service so long enjoyed by them and that all District Judges and District Magistrates, in the territory of Bangladesh and all diplomatic representatives elsewhere shall arrange to administer the oath of allegiance to all government officials within their jurisdiction.

This order shall be deemed to have come into effect from 26th day of March, 1971.

Signed :- SYED NAZRUL ISLAM,
Acting President

Appendix 'C'

PROVISIONAL CONSTITUTION OF BANGLADESH ORDER, 1972

Whereas by the Proclamation of Independence Order, dated the 10th April, 1971 provisional arrangements were made for the governance of the People's Republic of Bangladesh;

And Whereas by the said Proclamation the President is invested with all executive and legislative authority and the power to appoint a Prime Minister;

And Whereas the unjust and treacherous war as referred to in the said Proclamation has now ended;

And Whereas it is the manifest aspiration of the people of Bangladesh that a parliamentary democracy shall function in Bangladesh;

And Whereas in pursuance of the said objective it is necessary immediately to make certain provisions in that behalf.

Now Therefore in pursuance of the Proclamation of Independence Order, dated the 10th April, 1971 and all other powers enabling him in that behalf the President is pleased to make and promulgate the following Order :

(1) This Order may be called the Provisional Constitution of Bangladesh Order, 1972.

(2) It extends to the whole of Bangladesh.

(3) It shall come into force at once.

(4) Definition :

"Constituent Assembly" referred to in this Order means the body comprising of the elected representatives of the people of Bangladesh returned to the N. E. and P. E. seats in the elections held in December, 1970, January, 1971 and March, 1971 not otherwise disqualified by or under any law.

(5) There shall be a Cabinet of Ministers, with the Prime Minister at the head.

(6) The President shall in exercise of all his functions act in accordance with the advice of the Prime Minister.

(7) The President shall commission as Prime Minister a member of the Constituent Assembly, who commands the confidence of the majority of the members of the Constituent Assembly. All other Ministers, Ministers of State and Deputy Ministers shall be appointed by the President on the advice of the Prime Minister.

(8) In the event of a vacancy occurring in the Office of the President at any time prior to the framing of the Constitution by the Constituent Assembly, the Cabinet shall appoint as President a citizen of Bangladesh who will hold the office of President until another President enters upon the office in accordance with the Constitution as framed by the Constituent Assembly.

(9) There shall be a High Court of Bangladesh, consisting of a Chief Justice and so many other Judges as may be appointed from time to time.

(10) The Chief Justice of the High Court of Bangladesh shall administer an oath of office to the President and the President shall administer an oath of office to the Prime Minister, other Ministers, Ministers of State and Deputy Ministers. The form of the oath shall be as prescribed by the Cabinet.

Dated this eleventh day of January, One thousand nine hundred and seventy-two, being the twenty-sixth day of Poush, One thousand three hundred and seventy-eight.

Appendix 'D'

POSITION PAPER PREPARED BY THE RESEARCH CELL, EXTERNAL PUBLICITY DIVISION OF THE BANGLADESH GOVERNMENT IN EXILE, JUNE, 1971

Problems to be faced by the present Government after Independence

The present Bangladesh Government will face the following problems soon after independence or any other kind of settlement that will restore it to power.

I. SOCIAL

(1) (a) Because of the special circumstances communal and racial tension will prevail at the time of achieving independence. Riots will take place and Bengalis now supporting Bangladesh cause will want to take revenge upon the non-Bengalis and Bengali collaborators.

(b) Some people may try to put the blame of such a massacre upon certain group of students and consequently may re-act accordingly.

(c) Students and sections of public may feel very disappointed with Awami League leadership and at the same time being inspired by the left revolutionaries, who by that time will gain some support however disorganised that may be, may even go for a planned assault on the AL Leaders. In order to resist such attacks staunch Awami Leaguers will be joined by other usual opportunists who will again come across to AL, may act in retaliation. This will create another serious situation.

All these, however, irrational though they may appear to be, contain ingrediants of a dangerous and shameful civil war. Charged with emotion and unending enthusiasm at the time of victory our people instigated by miscreants may go for such disastrous ventures.

II. REFUGEES

Nobody exactly knows how many people have crossed the border. The Indian figures of 7 million-plus is based on a vague calculation and, therefore, may not be wholelly correct. Reasonable estimate says that the figure would be around 4 million. If independence comes there will be a rush of the refugees to go back. Considering the economy of West Bengal and Socio-political situation, people originally from Bangladesh who are not very happy here or not settled (figure is estimated to be 7 million including unemployed youths) may find worth trying to go back to Bangladesh. As it would not be possible to check at the initial stage, their return may creates serious socio-economic situation for us.

III. RESTORATION OF PRIVATE PROPERTIES ETC.

Because of the destruction of many offices and complete nonfunctioning of civil administration, papers and documents will be difficult to find for the ownership of land and properties. Moreover, because of loot, distribution and sale of properties by the army destroying the original documents, further complication has been added. Poor and innocent people in the village area will suffer most in this chaotic situation.

IV. ECONOMIC

(1) (a) Total economic ruination has taken place. Capital has been taken away, both by the Government and West Pakistani industrialists. Industries will be difficult to start or restart. Labour mobilisation will have to be re-established and re-organised. When the Pakistan army will finally go they will possibly destroy everything whatever is left now.

(b) Communication is completely dislocated, rail and road system will take long time to re-build. This will affect both the industrial and agricultural sectors and will make the pace of growth even slower.

(c) Banks and Financial Houses would be without resources.

These have rendered our infrastructures of economy completely shattered. Our economy will be so much broken that by the time we achieve independence we will discover ourselves economically at the lowest ebb and perhaps poorest as a Nation in the world.

(2) *FOOD.* There will be a severe shortage of food and famine will continue to starve our people to death. Dislocation on the agricultural sector will be no less serious mainly because of the lack of supply and communication system.

(3) *MILITARY.* Our army would neither be sufficiently disciplined nor adequate to protect our land even if the whole of Mukti Bahini come to the fold of the new Government. It has been found to be difficult in the past of similar conditions, to bring all the liberation forces under one Command particularly when the leadership itself is not a fighting force. There will be a tendency to hold the areas by the respective guerilla leaders once independence is close to being achieved, and those who are some way or other connected to any radical ideology other than AL programmes will not surrender their arms and will continue their war efforts till the goal is achieved. At present, members of the Mukti Bahini irrespective of their political background are overwhelmingly against the present political leadership and it may be that many of them will actively resent their installation as a Government after independence.

The reason they do not come out now to defy the Government is that they are aware without a political leadership like that of AL's they would get little support from outside world and particularly from India. In other words they know that whatever legal and financial backing which they now have is because of the existance of a Government. Therefore, because of the various circumstances that prevail, it is only convenient to let Bangladesh Government continue with its present role.

(4) *POLITICAL.* (a) AL was committed to constitutional politics. It was committed to socialism to the extent which would be achieved only through reforms and legislation, keeping the overall economic system a capitalistic one.

A sober and serious thinking effort is required whether the same politics would suit our people any more in the new circumstances. If not possible then what system is to be advised.

As we have to start from scratch particularly economically, it should be decided right now what system we are going to pursue. What kind of political machinery, we would like to introduce to administer the affairs of the people, what kind of State organs we would like to have and on what philosophical basis ? Where would our emphasis be—development through private or public sector ? Upon this will depend the future of Bangladesh.

(b) Members of the National Assembly were elected for Pakistan as a whole and Members of the Provincial Assembly were elected for legislature whithin the constitutional framework of Pakistan as a whole. Even if the Government plans to hold a fresh election immediately after the independence the respective status of MNAs and MPAs during the interim period will also have to be determined. On the other hand if there is no programme like this or holding election takes time the institutional problem of MNAs and MPAs will have to be solved. Their status, functions and jurisdiction will need to be clearly defined.

(c) Most crucial problem for AL at the time of independence will be to meet the absence of Sheikh (in case we do not get him back). Without Sheikh situation will be terrible and there will be total lack of leadership. This is not a reflection on the present leadership but because of the serious situation that will prevail at the time of independence, we would very much be in need of a leader who could command the people. Sheikh's popularity, stature and personality could be a great asset to counteract factionalism, rivalry within the party members, insurgency and rebellion by section of Mukti Bahini and youths, pressure from the radical left and other factors leading to chaos and instability in the newly born society.

(5) *ADMINISTRATION.* An administrative system through a bureaucracy that we have experienced in the past has already proved to be wrong and a menace. The whole thing would

require thorough and radical change to which AL is already committed through their Election Manifesto. Serious allegations are made both by Mukti Bahini and public that Bangladesh Government instead of having different attitude is completely relying upon the civil servants and its old system and has already established a white-elephant-structure at a huge cost even at this time of liberation struggle. The Government is spending more money on the administration in Calcutta than on the people who are actually fighting inside Bangladesh to liberate the land. The whole approach and set-up has far-reaching repurcussions with potentially serious reactions and consequences.

The Government should face the facts, however, unpleasant they may be. The problems can be solved if a realistic approach is exercised.

Appendix 'E'

TREATY OF FRIENDSHIP, COOPERATION AND PEACE BETWEEN THE PEOPLE'S REPUBLIC OF BANGLADESH AND THE REPUBLIC OF INDIA

Inspired by common ideals of peace, secularism democracy, socialism and nationalism.

Having struggled together for the realisation of these ideals and cemented ties of friendship through blood and sacrifices which led to the triumphant emergence of a free, sovereign and independent Bangladesh,

Determined to maintain fraternal and good neighbourly relations and transform their border into a border of eternal peace and friendship,

Adhering firmly to the basic tenets of non-alignment, peaceful co-existence, mutual cooperation, non-interference in internal affairs and respect for territorial integrity and sovereignty,

Determined to safeguard peace, stability and security and to promote progress of their respective countries through all possible avenues of mutual cooperation,

Determined further to expand and strengthen the existing relations of friendship between them.

Convinced that the further development of friendship and cooperation meets the national interests of both States as well as the interests of lasting peace in Asia and the world,

Resolved to contribute to strengthening world peace and security and to make efforts to bring about a relaxation of international tension and the final elimination of vestiges of colonialism, and imperialism,

Convinced that in the present-day world international problems can be solved only through cooperation and not through conflict or confrontation,

The People's Republic of Bangladesh, on the one hand, and the Republic of India, on the other, have decided to conclude the present Treaty.

ARTICLE 1 : The High Contracting Parties inspired by the ideals for which their respective peoples struggled and made sacrifices together, solemnly declare that there shall be lasting peace and friendship between their two countries and their peoples. Each side shall respect the independence, sovereignty and territorial integrity of the other and refrain from interfering in the internal affairs of the other side.

The High Contracting Parties shall further develop and strengthen the relations of friendship, good-neighbourliness and allround cooperation existing between them, on the basis of the above-mentioned principles as well as the principles of equality and mutual benefit.

ARTICLE 2 : Being guided by their devotion to the principles of equality of all people and states, irrespective of race or creed, the High Contracting Parties condemn colonialism and racialism in all their forms and manifestations and reaffirm their determination to strive for their final and complete elimination.

The High Contracting Parties shall cooperate with other states in achieving these aims and support the just aspirations of peoples in their struggle against colonialism and racial discrimination and for their national liberation.

ARTICLE 3 : The High Contracting Parties reaffirm their faith in the policy of non-alignment and peaceful co-existence, as important factors for easing tension in the world, maintaining international peace and security and strengthening national sovereignty and independence.

ARTICLE 4 : The High Contracting Parties shall maintain regular contacts with each other on major international problems affecting the interests of both States, through meetings and exchanges of views at all levels.

ARTICLE 5 : The High Contracting Parties shall continue to strengthen and widen their mutually advantageous and all-round cooperation in the economic, scientific and technical fields. The two countries shall develop mutual cooperation in the fields of trade, transport and communications between them on the basis of the principles of equality, mutual benefit and the most favoured nation principle.

ARTICLE 6 : The High Contracting Parties further agree to make joint studies and take joint action in the fields of flood control, river basin development and the development of hydro-electric power and irrigation.

ARTICLE 7 : The High Contracting Parties shall promote relations in the fields of art, literature, education, culture, sports and health.

ARTICLE 8 : In accordance with the ties of friendship existing between the two countries each of the High Contracting Parties solemnly declares that it shall not enter into or participate in any military alliance directed against the other Party.

Each of the High Contracting Parties shall refrain from any aggression against the other Party and shall not allow the use of its territory for committing any act that may cause military damage to or constitute a threat to the security of the other High Contracting Party.

ARTICLE 9 : Each of the High Contracting Parties shall refrain from giving any assistance to any third Party taking part in an armed conflict against the other Party. In case either Party is attacked or threatened with attack, the High Contracting Parties shall immediately enter into mutual consulations in order to take appropriate effective measures to eliminate the threat and thus ensure the peace and security of their countries.

ARTICLE 10 : Each of the High Contracting Parties solemnly declares that it shall not undertake any commitment, secret or open, toward one or more states which may be incompatible with the present Treaty.

ARTICLE 11 : The present Treaty is signed for a term of twenty-five years and shall be subject to renewal by mutual agreement on the High Contracting Parties.

The Treaty shall come into force with immediate effect from the date of its signature.

ARTICLE 12 : Any differences ia interpreting any article or articles of the present Treaty that may arise between the High Contracting Parties shall be settled on a bilateral basis by peaceful means in a spirit of mutual respect and understanding.

Done in Dacca on the Nineteenth Day of March, Nineteen Hundred and Seventy-two.

SHEIKH MUJIBUR RAHMAN
Prime Minister
For the Peoples Republic of Bangladesh

INDIRA GANDHI
Prime Minister
For the Republic of India

INDEX

Abandoned property 13, 19, 21, 25
Action Committee 220
Adams, John 6
Administration 75, 115
Administrative and Services Reorganisation
Committee 177-78
Administrative Tribunals 115-16
Adulteration 153
Afgan-Soviet Treaty 188
Agartala Conspiracy 21, 182
Agricultural Revolution 97
Agriculture, socialisation of 162
Ahmed, Moinuddin 148
Aid to Bangladesh Consortium 266
"All Party United Front" 220
Annual Plan, 1973-74 161, 162
Appelate Tribunal 155
Arbitration Courts 32
Arms, politics of 39
Arms with parties 218
Assets and liabilities, sharing of 198
Ataur Rahman Khan 52, 137, 149, 220, 248, 252
Aurora, (Lt. General) Jagjit Singh 1
Austerity measure 72
Awami League :
abandoned properties 25
civil administration 71
election intimidation 142
election manifesto 139
election propaganda 141, 144
failure of law enforcing agencies 67
government 12
government in exile 4
immediate problems 12
impact of famine 223
labour policy 82
majority party 5
on parliamentary system 8, 234
'revolutionary government' 73
sabotage socialism 176
structural change 70
students wing 182

Ayub Khan 21, 94, 102, 150, 215
Azad, Abdus Samad 3, 195

BAKSAL 136, 245, 252, 265
BDR/BSF 191
Bangabandhu 137, 143, 264
Bangalee nationalism 94
Bangla Sramik Federation 147
Bangladesh Army 191
Bangladesh Bank (Nationalization) Order 27
Bangladesh Collaborators Order 119
Bangladesh Cotton Mills Corporation 24
Bangladesh (Freedom Fighters) Welfare Foundation 42
Bangladesh-India relations
see Indo-Bangladesh relations
Bangladesh Jute Mills Corporations 24
Bangladesh Public Servants' (Retirement) Order, 1972 76
Bangladesh Nationalist Party 267
Bangladesh-Pakistan relations 198
Bangladesh, recognition of 195-99, 203
Bangladesh (Restoration of Evacuee Property) Order, 1972 32
Bangladesh Steel Mills Corporation 25
Bangladesh Sugar Mills Corporation 24
Banks 27
Basic democracy 21
Basic issues 265
Bhashani, (Moulana) Abdul Hamid Khan 21, 40, 91, 136, 182, 215, 218, 256
against Awami League 138
fasting to 'death' 229
on food shortage and famine 209
on Friendship Treaty 190
relation with Mujib 222
Bhattacharya, D.C. 17, 58
Bhutto, Zulfiqar Ali 3, 196, 205
Biharis, killing of 1
Biharis, repatriation of 205
Black-marketting 140, 153
Border 191

Boarder Security Force 62
Brahmaputra 190
British Labour Party 212
Bureau of Anti-corruption 67
Bureaucratic machinery 119-20
Burmah 189

Calcutta 91
Capitalist system 162
Central Election Campaign Committee 144
Chief Justice 116
China policy 215
Chowdhury, Abu Sayeed (Justice) 7, 228
Chowdhury, Badrul Haider (Justice) 49, 68
Chowdhury, Mohammad Ali 70, 120
Civil administration 70-76
Civil liberties 222
Civil services 119-21
Civil servants 73, 82
Civil Service of Pakistan 70
Collaborators 39, 42, 49
Committee for Civil Liberties and Legal Aid 222
Communist Party 136
Communist Party of Bangladesh 139, 215, 231, 255
Communist Party of India 216
Constituent Assembly 5, 8, 90, 92
Constitution 7, 9
  amendment of 122-24, 148-9
  basic principles 92
  Bengali text 125
  essential features 94
  Fourth Schedule 125
  Fourth amendment 235
  power of President 102, 105-6
  power of Prime Minister 105
  shortcomings 97
  summary and conclusions 127-30
Constitution-making process 90-135
Consumption 211
Corporations 26
Corruption 140, 213, 265
Cost of living 140
Court decisions 154
Curfew 153

Danesh, (Haji) Mohammad 252
Death punishment 153-54
Defence Services 106-7
Delhi Agreement 202
Democracy 95
Detention 100, 103, 149, 152, 156
District Council 30
District Relief Committee 29
Domestic resources 167
Drugs 153

East Pakistan Public Safety Ordinance, 1958 100, 152
Economic depression 147
Economic development 162-64
Economic policy 160
Economic reorganisation 160-80
Education 81, 97
Education Commission 81-215
Election 118, 138, 141-46, 218
Eleven point programme 21-22
Emergency 100-103, 149, 220, 232-34
Engineering and Shipbuilding Corporation 24
Excise duties exempted on salt 81
Export 26
External resources 167

FIR 154
Famine 212, 222, 223
Farakka Barrage 191
Father of the Nation 137, 143, 264
Fazle Munim (Justice) 70
Fertilizer, Chemical and Pharmaceutical Corporation 24
First Five Year Plan, 1973-78 160, 228
Flood 209
Food 83
Food and Allied Products Corporation 24
Food, flood and famine 207-214
Food Procurement Policy 210
Food Production 208-9
Food shortage 207-208
Food stock 210
Foreign Aid
  dependence on 175-76
Foreign assistance 28, 209
Foreign relations 195-206, 225
Forest Corporation 24
Four State Principles 92
Franklin, Benjamin 6
Freedom Fighters 1, 3, 12, 39
Freedom of association 153

Friendship Treaty 140, 185-88, 220, 266
Fundamental rights 98-100, 124, 129, 150

Gazi Golam Mostafa 253
General election, 1973 136-159
Ghulam Muhammad 70, 102, 120
Gana Oykka Jote 210
Ganakantha 219
Ganges 190
Geneva Convention 196
'Gherao' 219
Gomoti 191
"Gonobahini" 40, 53
Government
  immediate problems 12
  Tajuddin in 2
  Take over 2
  support of Indian Army 2
Gram Karmi Bahini 31
Gross Domestic Product 167
Gruel Kitchen 213

Haksar, P.N. 202
Health 97
Helal Jute Press Ltd. 17
High Court Bench 114, 117-18
High Court Division 154-55
Hijacking 82
'Hindu India' 185
Hoarding 153-54
Hossain, Kamaluddin (Justice) 17, 49, 70, 92, 149
Hossain, S.M. (Justice) 17, 155
Hukumati Rabbania 220-21
Huq, Abdul 220

Income distribution 162-63
Independence movement 216
Independence ; proclamation of 4
Independence War of Bangladesh *see :* war
Indian Army 140
Indian Congress 171, 181
Indian National Independence Movement 216
Indian troops 266
Indian Army in Bangladesh 185
"Indian exploitation" 185
Indira Gandhi 3, 186
Indo-Bangladesh relations 185-92
Indo-Soviet influence 266
Indo-Soviet lobby 225
Indo-Soviet Treaty 188
Industrial productivity 26, 173
Industrial workers 81
Industries 81
Inflation 26, 82
Insurance Companies 27
International Court of Justice on POWs 201
International Crimes (Tribunals) Bill 201
International influence 224
International Law Commission 126
Iskander Mirza 70, 102, 120
Islamic Socialism 22
Islamic Summit Conference 203, 266

'Jamat-i-Islam' 22
Jamuna 191
Jatiyo Krishak League 217
Jatio Rakkhi Bahini *see* Rakkhi Bahini
Jatio Samajtantrik Dal 20, 59, 136, 139, 142, 217, 219
Jatiyo Sramik League 217, 252
Jefferson, Thomas 6
Jinnah, Quaid-e-Azam 119
Joint River Commission 188
Judiciary 97, 113-15, 238
Jute manufactures 26
Jute Marketing Corporation 184
Jute Trading Corporation 184

Kader Siddiqui 1
Kamaruzzaman, A.H.M. 28, 252
Kashmir 196
Khaled, (King) 266
Khan, Liaquat Ali 119
Khan, Serajul Alam 215, 217, 253
Khoai river 191
Khondker, (Group Captain) 1
Kidnapping 82
Killings, Political 138, 140
King Khaled 266
Kissinger, Henry 266
Kremlin 223
Kushiara river 191

Labour policy 81
Lal Bahini 146-48, 170
Land tenure 265
Law and Order situation 39, 139-40, 256
Law-making procedure 110-11

Laws Continuance Enforcement Order 6
Laws, enactment of 148
Legal Framework Order 90
Legal Proceedings Order 1972 81
Legislature 107
Liabilities of the Govt. 126
Livingston, Robert R 6
Legal government 30, 107, 236
Lootings 82, 140

Mallick, A. R. 251
Management Councils 82
Management Boards 82
Mang Prue Syne 252
Manifestos, political parties 138-39
Mannan, Abdul 147
Mansoor Ali 252
Matin Chowdhury 218, 220, 248
McNamara 266
Media control 153
Meghna 190
Mineral, Oil and Gas Corporation 24
Mirza, Iskander *see* Iskander Mirza
Mohammadullah 228, 235
Mohiuddin Ahmed 224
Moinuddin Manik (JSD) 248
Moni, Sheikh Fazlul Huq 2, 224, 252
Moni Singh 136, 252
Moinul Hossain 234
Monoranjan Dhar 149
Moshtaque Ahmed, Khondker 3
Muhuri river 191
Mujib Bahini 2, 39, 183
'Mujibbad' 217
Mujibur Rahman, Sheikh : 263-68
  as an administrator 266
  as a nationalist 266
  assassination of 257
  birthday 219
  declaration of independence 5
  dictator 91
  emotional behaviour 266
  Father of the Nation 4
  human qualities 266
  immediate problems 12
  in captivity 2
  Individual image and popularity 141
  Indo-Soviet lobby 225
  leadership 81
  Martyr 268
  nepotism 265
  on BAKSAL 136, 245, 248, 252, 265
  on Delhi Agreement 202
  on existing system 243
  on fundamental rights 150
  on Friendship Treaty 186
  on nationalization 81
  on opposition 137
  on Pakistani recognition 198
  on Prisoners of War 195
  one party system 227
  primary responsibility 231
  relation with Bhashani 222
  return from captivity 3
  President 4
  Sincerity 266
  situation after death 258
  summit with Bhutto 196
Mukti Bahini 1, 3, 39, 41, 183
  see also Freedom fighters
Mukti Fouz 41
Municipal Committees
  reorganization of 30
Muslim League 21, 216

Nagar Panchayat 31
National Assembly of Pakistan 90
National Awami Party (Bhashani)
  20, 22, 139, 220
  election manifesto 22, 139
National Awami Party (Muzaffar)
  20, 139, 215, 231, 252, 255
National Awami Party of (Wali Khan)
National Defence Committee 210
National Militia 40, 54
National Socialist Party (Jatiyo Samajtantrik Dal) 217
National wage Board 81
Nationalisation 19, 25, 27
Nazrul Islam, Sayed 8, 252
Nepotism 265
Newsprint Control Order 229
Newsprint production 26
Niazi, (Lt. General) Amir Abdullah 1
Non-Aligned Conference 266
Nuclear free zone 187

Ombudsman 110
One party system 226, 231, 240
Opposition parties divided 138
Opposition Unity 220-22

Osmani, M.A.G. 234
Ottis, Jesus 5
Ownership of wealth 96-97

'Package deal' 197
Padma 191
Pakistan Army, surrender of 1
Pakistan Democratic Party 22
Pakistan People's Party 22
Pakistani recognition of Bangladesh 198
"Panchayat system" 31
Parliamentary system 91, 104, 108-12, 231
Party alliance 223-29
Party manifesto 138-39
Per capita income 167
Planning 160-80
Political cadres 163-64
Political consolidation 136-159
Political killings 138, 140
Political parties 215-230
Population 207
Pourashava 30
Prejudicial acts 153
Presidential form of government 8
Press and Publication Ordinance 150-51
Prices 82, 140, 211
Printing Press and Publications
(Declaration and Regulation) Ordinance
151, 229
Prisoners of War 195-206
Private sector 176-77
Provincial Assembly 90
Public administration 119-21
Public Services 119-21
Publication regulation 153
Punishment by death 153-54
Purba Banglar Sharbahara Party 218
Purchasing power 211

Qamaruzzaman, A.H.M., 28, 252

Rab, A.S.M., Abdur 142
Rakkhi Bahini 52-59, 66, 70, 138, 144, 147,
228, 254
Ramna Race Course 1
Razzak, Abdur 217, 252
Recognition of Bangladesh 195-99
Relief aid 29
Relief Committees 27-34, 209
Religious ideologies 96
Repatriation 197, 203
Reza, Masood 25
Rivers of Bangladesh 190-91
Robbery 82
Ruhul Islam (Justice) 49, 50
Rural development 97

Sabotage 153
Salary structure
reorganization of 177
Wages and salaries 177-78
Salt
excise duties abolished 81
Sayem, A.S.M. 8
Scientific socialism 42, 139, 216
Screening Boards 77
"Second Revolution" 244, 247, 265
Secret arrangement 186
Secret killings 82
Section 144, application of 218
Secularism 96
Seven-Party Action Committee 137
Shahar Committee 30
Shaidul Islam, Shiekh 253
'Shapla' 94
Sharbohara Party 218, 220
Shecha Shebak Bahini 147, 170
Simla Agreement 196, 198, 201
Sino-Soviet relations 182
Siraj Sikder 218, 220
Six-point Programme 21, 90
'Sixteenth division' 1, 39, 43
Smuggling 63-67, 140, 153, 209-12
Sobhan, K.M. (Justice) 46
'Socialism' 19, 20, 21, 23, 95
Socialist development 162-64
Socialist economic order 216
"Socialistic economic system" 95
'Socialistic programme' 71-72
"Sonar Bangla" 12, 83
Soviet Union Afghanistan relations
see Afgan-Soviet relations
Soviet Union-India relations
see Indo-Soviet relations
Special Tribunals 153-54
Special Powers Act 152-56, 229
Speedbird Navigation Co. 14
Sramik League 147
State Policy 94
State principles 92
Steel, Paper and Board Corporation, 24
Stranded Bengalis 199

Student League 138, 215-17
Sub-divisional Relief Committee 29
Sugar production 26
Summit meeting
between Mujib and Bhutto 196
Supreme Court 114, 117, 156
Surma river 191
Surrender 1, 183

Taccavi loan 80
Taher, Abu 217
Tajuddin Ahmed 2, 8, 39, 72, 175, 224, 253, 266
Tarakki, Nur Mohammad 189
Taxes and Land ceiling exemption of 80
Teesta Barrage 191
Teesta river 191
Thana Development Committee 30
Thomson, Roger 6
Three-Party Alliance 223, 225
Tipu Biswas 218, 220
Toaha 220
Tofael Ahmed 217, 253
Trade unions 147
Trial of POWs 199, 201
Tripartite Alliance 228
Twenty-point programme 91
Twenty-one-point programme 21
Twenty-two families 23
Two-nation theory 181

United Nations 4, 204, 209, 266
Union Panchayat 30
United Front 21
Universal adult franchise 129

Vietnam 224
Village Relief and Rehabilitation Committee 28
Voting age 119

Wages and salaries 72, 81, 177
Wahidur Rahman 218, 220
Waldheim, Kurt
War
impact of participation and non-participation 1-2
Water disputes 188, 191
'Welfare State' 216
Writ Jurisdiction 115-16

Zamindari 22
Ziaur Rahman 267
Zilla Board 30
Zillur Rahman 252